The Child in American Evangelicalism and the Problem of Affluence

The Child in American Evangelicalism and the Problem of Affluence

A Theological Anthropology
of the Affluent American-Evangelical Child
in Late Modernity

DAVID A. SIMS

PICKWICK *Publications* · Eugene, Oregon

THE CHILD IN AMERICAN EVANGELICALISM AND THE
PROBLEM OF AFFLUENCE
A Theological Anthropology of the Affluent American-Evangelical Child
in Late Modernity

Pickwick Publications
A Division of Wipf and Stock Publishers
199 W. 8th Ave., Suite 3
Eugene, OR 97401

ISBN 13: 978-1-55635-957-6

BR
115
.W4
S58
2009

Cataloging-in-Publication data:

Sims, David A.

The child in American evangelicalism and the problem of affluence : a
theological anthropology of the affluent American-evangelical child in late modernity
/ David A. Sims.

xvi + 330 p. ; 23 cm. Includes bibliographical references and indexes.

ISBN 13: 978-1-55635-957-6

1. Children (Christian theology). 2. Wealth—Religious aspects—
Christianity. I. Title.

BR115.W4 S58 2009

Manufactured in the U.S.A.

For Tamara

Your love is a great teacher

dante Deo, consummatum est, gaudeamus igitur

By the gift of God, it is finished, so let us rejoice!

Contents

Preface

> For the LORD your God is bringing you into a good land, . . . a land where you may eat bread without scarcity, where you will lack nothing . . . Take care that you do not forget the Lord your God . . . (Deut 8:7–11, NRSV).

Humanity's road from scarcity to affluence has been long and arduous. The hope of eating bread (much less meat) without lack has been a common creaturely aspiration since the fall from, among other things, original abundance into scarcity. Until recently, few have believed this hope could be realized short of a new heaven and earth.

But economic realities have changed drastically over the last three hundred years, and new hopes have consequently arisen. Scientific discoveries and advances have led to technological revolutions in the West during these centuries, ushering unprecedented prospects of life without scarcity onto the stage of the human drama. Increasingly, the goal of ending poverty is written, talked about and supported by what appear to be realistic theoretical and empirical models. The exodus from lack to abundance continues, with many thinking they can see the end of the road on the distant horizon of humanity's abiding dream of a world in which their will be no poor.

It seems to me that the vision of a future in which those on affluence's underside are liberated from scarcity to affluence is consistent with God's vision for and blessing of Israel: "there will be no poor in the land" (Deut 15:4, NASB). And although both Moses and Jesus recognized the persistent presence of the poor among them (Deut 15:11; Mark 14:7), as among us, they would no doubt concur that God desires to see poverty eliminated and is pleased with the work of those pursuing this task. After all, the Bible promises it and unequivocally describes the future in such terms.

But what is humanity's report card with affluence? Whether Egypt, Israel, Greece or Rome in antiquity, or Spain, Holland, Britain or America in modernity, human empires seem consistently to fail the affluence test. Abundance tends to rot empires from within.

Does evangelical faith fare any better when faced with affluence? Empires may be found lacking, but what about evangelicals and their churches and children embedded in cultures of affluence? What happens to belief and trust in, not to mention reliance upon, the God of Israel and Jesus when nothing lacks? Does it thrive "with joy and a glad heart for the abundance of all things" (Deut 28:47) or tend to "forget" the Lord God (Deut 8:11)?

This book explores these questions with the American-Evangelical child in view, that is, the child nurtured in the subcultural matrices of an American Evangelicalism thoroughly embedded in and enmeshed with the culture of affluence in the United States. Is it a good thing, evangelically speaking (i.e., from the standpoint of nurturing the gospel in children), to cultivate in our children twin capitalist habits of acquiring and enjoying affluence?

Formation in the socio-cultural context of abundance in the United States is problematic for a number of reasons, which I set out in the Introduction (chapter 1). Remarkably, as demonstrated in chapters 2 and 3, the history of the child nurtured in American Evangelicalism demonstrates little critical awareness among evangelical theologians, educators, pastors and parents of the problems posed by affluence for Christian nurture, or as Paul puts it, raising children "in the discipline and instruction of the Lord" (Eph 6:4, NASB). The model of "interpretive reproductions" adapted from the sociology of children and applied to the child nurtured in American-Evangelical affluence in chapter 4 illumines and illustrates this lack of critical consciousness of the problems posed by affluence for nurturing evangelical affections in children.

The theoretical construct of the Affluent American-Evangelical Child, i.e., "AAEC," provides the lens through which these claims are examined. This neologism is explained and defended in chapter 1. It was the first point defended at the examination of my doctoral thesis in January 2006 at the University of Durham. Traversing the trajectories of research with the AAEC in view since that time has strengthened my convictions regarding the reality and problem of the AAEC and the dubious nature of cultivating in our children twin habits of capitalist acquisition and enjoyment of affluence. Consequently, the heart of this work in chapter 5, "An Evangelical Theology of the AAEC," remains essentially the same as when it was originally defended. Although I have updated the research and tweaked a few things here and there, the theological economics of the child nurtured in American-Evangelical affluence presented here has not changed in substance. I remain convinced that formation in those cultural and subcultural matrices risks evangelical malformation and that unless we cultivate critical-evangelical consciences regarding those matrices and how they interpenetrate and shape our beliefs and practices of the gospel we may very well find ourselves and our children forgetting the Lord God much like the ancient Israelites did when abundance came and scarcity was no more.

Thus, my central argument is that affluence constitutes a significant impediment to evangelical nurture of the AAEC in the "discipline and instruction of the Lord" (Eph 6:4, NASB). Nurture in evangelical affluence is the theological-anthropological problem addressed throughout the work. The issue of "lack" raised by Matthew's rich young man (Matt 19:20) provides the biblical-theological focal point for developing the evangelical theology of the AAEC in chapter 5. The conclusion reached is that nurture in the cultural matrices of the Evangelical affluence generated by technological consumer capitalism in the United States impedes spiritual and moral formation of the AAEC for discipleship in the way of the cross, risks disciplinary formation of the AAEC for capitalist culture, tends to cultivate an unconscious, delusional belief that life consists in an abundance of possessions and hinders the practice of evangelical liberation of the poor on humanity's underside. This represents the AAEC's spiritual-moral "lack" in late modernity.

Following chapter 1's introduction and overview, chapters 2 and 3 provide the diachronic lens for a theological anthropology of the AAEC through critical assessment of the theological anthropologies of the child in Jonathan Edwards, Horace Bushnell and Lawrence Richards. The synchronic perspective of the work is provided by chapter 4's evangelical sociology of the AAEC, drawing upon William Corsaro's theory of "interpretive reproductions", and chapter 5's evangelical theology of the AAEC developed through theological critique of John Schneider's moral evangelical theology of affluence.

Chapter 6 concludes with a recapitulation of the argument and a forecast of possible futures for the AAEC. It is hoped that this book will stimulate evangelical educators, psychologists and sociologists to engage the theological-anthropological, philosophical and theoretical construct of the AAEC presented here with empirical studies that will test my thesis of the AAEC and the arguments made in support. I also hope that pastors, parents and practical theologians will find the work helpful in stimulating critical-evangelical thinking about how formation in affluence may affect and malform nurture of the gospel in our children.

Having spent the last eight years or so looking at these issues intensely, this passion endures: that those who love Jesus and the gospel, who are trying to figure out how to lose their lives through a dispossessing-donating discipleship of true abundance (Mark 8:34–35; 10:19–30) will strive to leverage their benefits and blessings of affluence for the purpose of liberating those billions of poor and marginalized presently suffering on the underside of humanity. There seems to be a growing consensus among evangelicals today that being "eager" for this kind of "faith expressing itself in love" pleases God and shows the world what God is really like (Gal 2:10; 5:6; Heb 11:6; 1 John 3:17–18, NASB). My heart's desire is that this book may in some way spur evangelicals along this path.

Acknowledgments

My debts are many and my gratitude is deep for those who have made this book possible.

I first want to thank you, Tamara, for your partnership in life and particularly in this project. Without your love, encouragement, prodding and well-placed humor (I'm thinking of the T-shirt you gave me somewhere along the way, "Save Endangered Theses"), I simply could not have made it. "Thank you" is not enough, but it's all I have and says all I can at this point. Your love throughout this journey has been a great teacher and source of hope and confidence. Without you the conception, gestation, birth and nurture of the words that have landed on these pages simply would have been impossible. With deepest affection and gratitude, I thank you.

Stephen, thank you for faithfully enduring (and inflicting) the pain of learning as my supervisor at Durham. Neither of us knew, I'm sure, what we were getting into when it all started. I had no idea how terribly far I had to travel on the road to theological-critical thinking at Durham. Surveying the ground covered, I am sincerely grateful for your supervisory patience, gentle wisdom and kindness in making efforts to state much needed critique positively. Thank you also for your writings, hospitality (as well as Helen's, Joseph's and Miriam's) and the time I was blessed to share with you over meals and coffee. These were instruments of evangelical-critical grace in the formative doctoral period of my life. Your practice of "life together" in Christ through these means continues to exercise a profound influence upon the relational practices within the relational matrices of my life. I look forward to reading more of what Dr. Stephen C. Barton (in my view "Professor Barton" is entirely appropriate and well deserved and, hopefully, soon to come) writes and, hopefully, at least a few more times over meals and coffee in Durham before life on this side of the eschaton ends.

I am indebted to Professor Haddon Willmer and Dr. Keith White for their invitation to participate in the Child Theology Movement (CTM). I discovered this movement in 2003 in the course of researching my thesis and was kindly invited by Professor Willmer to his home in Leeds for a lengthy discussion of the thesis as it existed at that time (a theology of liberation for affluent children). This led to an invitation to present a paper on "The Child in American Evangelicalism" at the CTM consultation in Houston, Texas, that year. Without this opportunity I'm not sure my thesis would have come to its final form. Writing that paper set me on a course of critical interaction with American Evangelicalism and the child in view, leading finally to its final form here. Professor Willmer graciously agreed to serve as my external examiner, and although a rigorous examination ensued I am sincerely grateful for the hard questions and testing of the thesis and my arguments. I am convinced they have both enabled and enriched this book. Thank you Professor Willmer.

Dr. Robert Song also played a crucial formative role in this work. Not only did he serve as my internal examiner, but also assisted Dr. Barton in assisting me while on sabbatical. It was during this time that during one of my supervisory meetings Dr. Song suggested I look at the literature on the sociology of children. In due course I discovered Corsaro's model of "interpretive reproductions" that, hopefully, has been employed in a manner that will prove useful to evangelicals as they study affluence in relation to nurture. Thank you, Robert, for that advice and for your encouragement and examination along the way.

The bibliography sets out in some detail the debts I owe to authors who have helped shape this work. I am thankful to God for other minds and the gift of writing that makes learning and transformation possible. Knowledge may puff up and love may edify, but writing illumines both and makes the transforming love of knowledge and the knowledge of love rich and rewarding.

I'm grateful to my seminary professors and other educators along the way, most notably Drs. Roger Nicole, Sinclair Ferguson, John Gerstner, Reggie Kidd, Al Mawhinney, Ronald Nash, Richard Pratt, and R. C. Sproul. Without them I would not have had a biblical-theological foundation upon which to build in postgraduate studies.

Thank you Micah, Rachel, Rebecca, Isaac, Miriam, Elizabeth, Jonathan, and Billy, for your understanding and grace while I was gone in body, mind and spirit researching and writing the thesis and then in bringing it into this final form. I love you all very much. As my children, I desire to help nurture a love for Jesus and the gospel in you as best as

I know how, imperfect as it is. It has been a fun journey thus far, and you have helped me grow immensely in this goal. May you always cultivate your own critical consciousness and, hence, form an evangelical conscience of how affluence affects your relationships to God, others and the world of things.

Finally, I want to thank you, Mom and Dad. Partners in life for over five decades, Dave and Joyce Sims, you have been faithful and loving parents and, in my view, the best grandparents any grandkid could ever have. You have always valued and provided for my education, and you never wavered in that commitment all the way through my time at the University of Durham. Without you this work never would have come into being. As I have said many times, words are inadequate to express my gratitude, but they're the best I have. Once again, thanks, Mom and Dad, from the bottom of my heart.

1

Introduction:
Theological Economics and the Problem of the AAEC

This book is a theological-critical study of the child nurtured in evangelicalism and affluence in the United States. It presents a theological anthropology of the Affluent American-Evangelical Child (AAEC) formed in these subcultural and cultural contexts. As such, the work is properly viewed as a theological economics of the child raised and embedded in those formative contexts.

Research began broadly in the theology of family and then narrowed to the theology of children with a view to how liberation theology might apply to the study of the child in critical-theological perspective. As the scope narrowed to the child in American evangelicalism and the socio-cultural problem of affluence, the pertinence of liberation theology became attenuated. How could it be argued plausibly, much less persuasively, that the child raised in evangelical affluence needed liberation? Research began to focus on the historical, sociological, and theological aspects of the child embedded in evangelical affluence in the United States. Questions relating to nurture in that context were raised in the process of researching and forming the central thesis of the work, which ultimately indicated the need for a theological anthropology of the AAEC in late modernity.

The following six subsections present an overview of the course of research and contours of theological-critical analysis undertaken:

1. The problem of affluence and the AAEC

2. Overview of structure and content

3. Key terms and phrases

4. Theological-critical method

5. Survey of pertinent literature

6. Aim and goals

THE PROBLEM OF AFFLUENCE AND THE AAEC

Mass affluence, or the condition of abundant wealth and material goods for an increasing number of human beings, is a late modern phenomenon unequaled in history. The phenomenon has been so remarkable that economists have resorted to language of mystery and miracle to describe it.[1] As the product of technological consumer capitalism, affluence marks the nations and economies of Western Europe, the United States, Japan, and more recently the East Asian Tigers (also known as Asia's Four Little Dragons): Taiwan, Hong Kong, South Korea, and Singapore.

China and India have learned from the success of economic liberalism in the West and the Asian Tigers and are moving toward free-market economies as well. From 1981 to 2001, China and India made remarkable gains of affluence for their people, along with other Asian countries such as Malaysia. As a result of the rapid economic growth in eastern and southern Asia, it is estimated that 500 million people were liberated from poverty during this twenty-year period. Since 1981 global poverty has decreased by approximately fifty percent primarily as a result of rapid economic growth in Asia. Thus, the march of global affluence is underway.

At the same time, roughly 2.8 billion people, almost half the world's population, currently live on less than $2 a day. Of these poor, approximately 1.3 billion live on the margins of life with less than $1 a day. Most of these poor are in Latin America, sub-Saharan Africa, Eastern Europe, and Central Asia. The most dramatic impact is seen in children. The contrast between affluent and nonaffluent countries demonstrates this clearly. In affluent countries, less than one child in 100 dies before reaching age five, while in the poorest countries the number is five times higher. Fewer than five percent of children under the age of five are malnourished in affluent nations, whereas in poorer countries as many as fifty percent of the children suffer from malnutrition.[2]

---

1. See, e.g., Helpman, *Mystery of Economic Growth*; Baumol, *Free-Market*; de Soto, *Mystery of Capital*.

2. UNICEF, "State of World's Children 2005"; cf. Sachs, *End of Poverty*, 1–25, 51.

The child nurtured within the context of growing global affluence is thus confronted with its blessings and curses. There are goods and poverties of affluence to which the child is subjected in late modernity. Affluence is good insofar as its abundant wealth and attendant cultural, social and economic formations lead to the greater fulfillment of fundamental human needs such as food, clean water, better health care, adequate shelter and meaningful life.

For instance, over the past three hundred years humanity in Western Europe, North America, Japan, and the Asian Tigers has escaped from hunger and premature death in quantum leaps surpassing all preceding human generations.[3] Robert Fogel, 1993 Nobel Prize winner for economics, and Dora Costa, an MIT economist and biodemographer, coined the phrase "technophysio evolution" to describe the synergistic effects of the scientific, industrial, biomedical, and cultural revolutions of the last 300 years that have vastly increased humanity's control over the environment and led to the escape from hunger in the West. The complex interaction between technologies of production and improving human physiology measured in terms of increased life expectancy and stature during this period are offered as proof. These resulted from increased food production made possible by technological advances during the modern period. Thus, the "interaction between technological and physiological improvements has produced a form of evolution that is not only unique to humankind but unique among the 7,000 or so generations of human beings who have inhabited the earth."[4] Fogel contends that this evolutionary process continues presently, will likely accelerate in the twenty-first century, resulting in profound benefits for poor countries as well.[5]

As a result of such advances, many economists maintain that there is a reasonable basis to believe that absolute poverty (i.e., those living on

3. See Fogel, *Escape from Hunger and Premature Death*.

4. Ibid., xvi.

5. This claim is contested by those on the new social, economic and political left who see signs of the inevitable failure and demise of U.S. style technological consumer capitalism and, hence, signs of the end of affluence. See, e.g., Bello, *Dilemmas of Domination*; Johnson, *Sorrows of Empire*; Todd, *After the Empire*; Wallerstein, *Decline of American Power*; Phillips, *American Theocracy*. Their argument certainly is plausible. However, it appears that the wisest course of action at this point would be to maintain a stance of cool criticism on the issue. Previous attempts to declare affluence's end in light of the economic crisis of the 1970s are now seen as quite misguided readings of the times. Ehrlich, *End of Affluence*; Rashcke, *Bursting of New Wineskins*; but cf. Madrick, *End of Affluence*.

less than $1 per day) will be eliminated early in the twenty-first century. Jeffrey Sachs, for example, envisions a world without such extreme poverty by the year 2025. Noting that global economic development is both "real and widespread," Sachs argues convincingly from recent economic history and empirical data that "extreme poverty is shrinking, both in absolute numbers and as a proportion of the world's population."[6]

Cultures and societies enjoying affluence not only have basic needs met in abundance but also experience unprecedented enjoyment of luxuries and leisure previously reserved for elites in the premodern and early modern periods. Although the problems of poverty and affluence continue, it appears that for the first time in human history increasing numbers of humans are experiencing the benefits of affluence while the actual number of the poor is decreasing. Greater opportunities to make the transition from poverty to affluence present themselves to the poor each year.

At the same time, those enjoying affluence are confronted with a problem of overabundance, saturation and waste that seems immoral in the face of 1.3 billion humans presently living in grinding poverty. Fogel notes that in the United States "we have become so rich that we are approaching saturation in the consumption not only of necessities, but also of goods recently thought to be luxuries or that only existed as dreams of the future during the first third of the twentieth century . . . In some items such as radios, we seem to have reached supersaturation, since there is now more than one radio per ear . . . The level of many consumer durables is so high that even the poorest fifth of households are well endowed with them."[7] Fifteen years later, Fogel's observations are a fact of life in the United States. In addition to radios, we now have cell phones, televisions, DVD players, iPods, computers, laptops, and a host of other technological consumables at our disposal.

Thus, the good of affluence is attenuated by two realities. First is the daily existence of hundreds of millions of humans suffering in poverty. The second is found in the supersaturation effect affluence has on the affluent.

This is the problem of affluence identified here and addressed with the AAEC in view. What are the effects of nurture within a subcultural

---

6. Sachs, *End of Poverty*, 51. See also Collier, *Bottom Billion*.

7. Fogel, *Escape from Hunger and Premature Death*, 71, 139 n. 10.

context of evangelical affluence in the United States? Does nurture in that context serve the best interests of the AAEC?

At a fundamental level, evangelical affluence affects nurture of the AAEC in a complex manner at the level of intersecting material and spiritual dimensions of life in late modernity. From an evangelical standpoint, this signals the need for a theological anthropology that explores the divine-human relationship in these dimensions. Understanding of the human dimension is sought through exploration of historical, social and economic aspects of the AAEC's nurture in an evangelicalism embedded in American affluence (chapters 2 through 4). Understanding of the divine-human relational aspect of the AAEC's nurture is sought through critical-theological engagement of the human perspective gained through interaction with history and the social sciences (chapter 5). This process can be seen as an aspect of evangelical faith seeking understanding of *"the sense of the divine presence and living in the light of that presence"*[8] in late modernity. How does the AAEC know God and how is the AAEC known by God in this context? And how does the AAEC respond "with the whole of life . . . under the God who is revealed in Jesus and who graces believers with the Spirit"[9] in the midst of evangelical affluence?

The heart of the problem of the AAEC is found at the intersection of the material and spiritual dimensions of this late modern existence. Evangelicals love Jesus and the gospel. They passionately believe in the historical reality of the death and resurrection of Jesus Christ, love the Bible in which that good news is told, affirm the truths declared in the ecumenical creeds of the Christian faith, and earnestly seek to live those truths out in evangelical faith and practice. It follows that evangelicals also passionately desire for their children to follow in their steps of faith and practice, and therefore they desire to nurture that kind of "discipline and instruction of the Lord" in their children as Paul exhorts in Ephesians 6:4. But the problem is that evangelicals remain critically unaware of the risks inherent to nurture in affluence.

From a developmental standpoint, the problem of the AAEC is located in the first two decades of life nurtured in evangelical affluence. At the heart of the problem lies an unbiblical conception of human freedom

8. Barton, *Spirituality*, 1 (emphasis original).

9. Ibid., 1–2.

in affluence that subverts evangelical nurture to the ends of technological consumer capitalism rather than Jesus and the gospel.

OVERVIEW OF STRUCTURE AND CONTENT

This book is composed of six chapters and two central parts. The introduction and conclusion are set out in chapters 1 and 6, respectively. Part I presents a diachronic perspective of the AAEC in chapters 2 and 3, and part II presents the synchronic perspective of the AAEC in two dimensions: the sociological and theological (chapters 4 and 5, respectively).

Modern social-scientific inquiry and theological anthropology share a concern for understanding human nature in its material, embodied context. Personal and social development is a dynamic, dialectical process involving interaction, adaptation, and change over time (diachronic) in particular spaces and times (synchronic). Evangelicals and their children are embedded in a dynamic cultural-social-economic context of affluence that, to varying degrees, both shapes and is shaped by them. This context did not arise spontaneously in the twentieth century. Like evangelicalism, American affluence can be traced from the eighteenth through the twentieth centuries in discernible, overlapping lines.

One of the primary tasks of chapters 2 and 3 is to trace these lines. An interpretive history of the theological anthropology of the child in American evangelicalism is presented in those chapters through three significant American-evangelical theologians: Jonathan Edwards (eighteenth century) and Horace Bushnell (nineteenth century) in chapter 2 and Lawrence Richards (twentieth century) in chapter 3. Bushnell's seminal theology of nurture is interpreted in light of his theology of affluence to provide the hinge upon which the theological anthropology of the AAEC turns in chapter 3. It will be shown there how those theologies relate to the historical merger of evangelicalism and industrialism in the second half of the nineteenth century. This will demonstrate how nurture of the evangelical child became subordinate and subservient to the interests of capitalist culture in the United States. It was out of this context that the AAEC evolved and eventually emerged in the second half of the twentieth century.

This diachronic perspective of the AAEC provides the foundation for the sociology of the AAEC developed in chapter 4. The sociology of children and childhood emerged in the twentieth century through critical interaction with the history, principles and methods of developmental psychology, which seeks to understand the causes and effects of human motivation and sociality. The sociology of children and childhood builds upon the insights gained from developmental psychology and extends them to the study of children's behavior in group and institutional settings.

William Corsaro has noted that, "As recently as 18 years ago there was a near absence of studies on children in mainstream sociology."[10] Until recently, children and childhood have been marginalized not only in sociology but also in anthropology and theology as well.[11] The reasons in all three disciplines are similar. First, children are subordinate in their societies and cultures by virtue of their relative dependence, powerlessness and inability to represent themselves. Second, children are subordinate in theoretical conceptualizations of childhood. In the sociological, anthropological and theological disciplines, children are generally taken with a view to what they will become rather than who they are, what they are and what roles they play in cultural, social, familial and ecclesial formation. Children generally have not been viewed as active agents in the process of interpreting, constructing, negotiating and defining their relationships, societies, cultures, families and churches. Theologically they have not been viewed as active, formative agents in their relationships with God, others, themselves, society and culture, but rather as passive recipients of formation for such relationships or as young, immature sinners in need of conversion.

As a leading sociologist of children and childhood in the United States, Corsaro offers "interpretive reproduction" as a helpful model to correct the sociological myopia in the study of children. He offers it as an alternative to deterministic and constructivist models of interpreting childhood socialization. Corsaro claims that his model captures the manner in which children not only adapt and internalize culture and society but also how they appropriate, reinvent and reproduce it. This sociological

10. Corsaro, "Sociology's Rediscovery of Childhood," in *Sociology*, 5, citing Ambert, "Sociology," in Adler and Adler, eds., *Sociological Studies*, 11–31. In the United Kingdom, sociologist John Davies has noted that children "tend to be relatively invisible" in the "great mass of social and socio-theological commentary" of the twentieth century. Davies, "Preferential Option," in Barton, ed., *Family*, 220.

11. For this lacuna in anthropology, see Schwartzman, "Children and Anthropology," Schwartzman, ed., *Children and Anthropology*, 15–37. The lacuna in theology is surveyed below.

model takes children seriously as communal participants in the negotiating, sharing and creating processes of socio-cultural interaction with the world of persons and things.

Hence, children are seen as innovative and creative interpreters of their relations to themselves, their peers, adults and the world. They interpret information and then creatively and innovatively appropriate it to their own personal and peer interests. They do not simply internalize society and culture as deterministic and constructivist models assume, but they also actively participate in and contribute to cultural production, reproduction and change. They are both consumers *and* producers of culture. At the same time, as participants in these socio-cultural processes children are caught in its web of relations. That is, they are "*constrained by the existing social structure and by societal reproduction.*"[12] This points to the reality of children's social, cultural and historical embeddedness.

Corsaro's concept of "interpretive reproductions" is applied in chapter 4 to understanding the child in American evangelicalism and affluence in light of the history of the AAEC presented in chapters 2 and 3. This sets the stage for chapter 5's critical-theological engagement of the history and sociology of the AAEC presented in the preceding chapters.

Chapter 5 develops an evangelical theology of the AAEC. The centerpiece of critique is John Schneider's recent evangelical theology of affluence.[13] Schneider is a theological educator at Calvin College, a Reformed-evangelical institution in the United States.

There are several reasons for selecting Schneider. The first is that Schneider's pre-understandings are consistent with contemporary evangelical theology and, therefore, evangelicalism in the United States. He states that his "assumptions in writing theology are classical and orthodox in nature . . . beliefs that modern theologians widely presume to be discredited in our time."[14] His position on Scripture is consistent with evangelical belief in biblical inspiration.[15] Consequently, Schneider uses the "Bible to write theology" in a manner similar to Edwards and his

---

12. Corsaro, *Sociology*, 19 (emphasis in original).

13. First set out in Schneider, *Godly Materialism*, then revised and expanded substantially in *Good of Affluence*.

14. Schneider, *Good of Affluence*, 5.

15. Ibid., 6–7.

evangelical successors in the United States.[16] Thus, he constructs a contemporary moral theology of affluence on explicitly evangelical grounds.

Another reason for selecting Schneider is that he is the first evangelical theologian[17] to argue explicitly for the "good of affluence" on biblical and theological grounds and on that basis to champion a "godly materialism" for Christians "seeking God in a culture of wealth."[18] Schneider unequivocally affirms cultivation of the "twin habits of capitalism—acquisition and enjoyment," believing that these "modern economic habits . . . as they flourish under capitalism"[19] are both pleasing to God and good for evangelicals (and presumably their children). Because Schneider repeatedly refers to the formation of capitalist habits in wealthy Christians, he implicitly raises the issue of how children are formed by such habits in a culture of capitalism. This is taken here as an invitation to engage the formal and practical theological claims made in Schneider's theology of affluence as they bear upon the theological anthropology of the AAEC developed here.

I will argue that the evangelical theology, ethics and practices of affluence Schneider advocates are an obstacle to the nurture of evangelical "discipline and instruction of the Lord" in the AAEC and that they lead to the kind of relationally grounded spiritual-moral "lack" identified in the tradition of the rich young man.[20] Schneider's moral theology inclines evangelical parents and churches to adopt beliefs and practices that engender such lack. As will be shown, evangelical faith and practice in the economic realm of life reflects the culture of affluence in which evangelicals are embedded. This leads to a place where the AAEC is torn between

16. Ibid., 7.

17. Schneider earned his doctorate from Cambridge in 1987 for his work on Philip Melancthon. Schneider, *Melancthon's Rhetorical Construal*. Schneider's brilliant rhetorical skills are evident throughout *Good of Affluence* and are particularly well displayed in the quiet evangelical debate over affluence that work created. See Schneider's rebuttals to the critiques of *Good of Affluence* by Craig Blomberg and Andy Hartropp in "Weighing *The Good of Affluence*: A Symposium," 1–25, sponsored by the Association of Christian Economists. Schneider, "Defense of Delight," 21–21; Hartropp, "Affirmation . . . Ambivalence?" 3–6; Blomberg, "Affluence Good?" 11–14.

18. This latter phrase is the subtitle to *Good of Affluence*.

19. Schneider, *Good of Affluence*, 35, 40.

20. This is demonstrated below in chapter 5 through critical interaction with the interpretations of this narrative by Dietrich Bonhoeffer, Karl Barth, and Pope John Paul II (section 2), as well as by Marion Grau (section 3).

the desire for God and the affluence that technological consumer capitalism produces, and where the AAEC's sociality is deformed because desire has been taken captive to serve the earthly kingdom(s) of capitalism rather than the kingdom of God on earth as it is in heaven. As a result, the AAEC is hindered from entering the path of discipleship with its ethic of dispossession and donation for the sake of Jesus and the gospel.[21]

A third reason for selecting Schneider is that Michael Novak, the foremost neoliberal[22] theologian of capitalism in late modernity, exerts a considerable if not controlling systematic influence upon Schneider's evangelical theology of affluence. Novak was the first scholar in late modernity to write "A Theology of Economics,"[23] setting the course for subsequent neoliberal-theological engagements of economics.[24] He appears regularly in the contemporary theological literature concerned with the economics of democratic capitalism and its underlying anthropology of freedom. Schneider's reliance upon Novak places his theology of affluence in the center of recent theological critiques of that discipline and anthropology. This is seen in his dependence upon Novak as well as the warm intellectual critique of capitalism provided by Dinesh D'Souza.[25] Although Schneider situates his work in the context of the "new" culture of capitalism, his analysis is insufficiently critical of that culture historically, sociologically and theologically.[26] Schneider fails to place his exegesis and theology of affluence in dialogue with the history and sociology of American evangelicalism, resulting in a myopic perspective on whether nurture in the culture of capitalism in the United States serves the best interests of the AAEC. He also fails to account theologically for important contemporary interpretations of the rich young man, which ultimately renders his position hollow when applied to the AAEC.[27] Finally, he fails to engage pertinent works in the theological economics literature.

21. E.g., Mark 4:19; 8:34–35; 10:21–29.

22. "Neoliberal" and "neoliberalism" are defined below.

23. Novak, *Spirit*, 237–360.

24. See, e.g., see Sherman, *Preferential Option* and *Soul of Development*; cf. Nash, "Theological Tests," in *Poverty and Wealth*, 106–13.

25. Schneider, *Good of Affluence*, 2, 20–22, 30, 33, 34, 38–40, 55–56, 219.

26. Schneider's first chapter is titled "The 'New' Culture of Capitalism." Ibid., 13–40.

27. Demonstrated in the last section of chapter 5 through critical interaction with the feminist theological economics in Grau, *Of Divine Economy*, and the Radical Orthodoxy theological economics in Long, *Divine Economy*, and Bell, *Liberation Theology*.

Consequently, he lacks a critical perspective on neoliberal theology's uncritical grounding in an anthropology of liberty.

The conclusion reached in chapter 5 is that nurture in the cultural matrices of evangelical affluence in the U. S. impedes spiritual and moral formation of the AAEC for discipleship in the way of the cross. It risks disciplinary formation of the AAEC for capitalist culture and tends to cultivate delusional belief that life consists in an abundance of possessions. As a result, it hinders the practice of evangelical liberation of the poor on humanity's underside and thus perpetuates formation of the AAEC's spiritual and moral "lack" in late modernity. Thus, chapter 5 sets out my central analysis, argument and conclusions regarding the AAEC.

Chapter 6 concludes in two steps. First, it recapitulates the findings from chapters 2 through 5 and summarizes the contours of the theological anthropology of the AAEC in late modernity. Second, it proposes two potentially promising areas of future research that I hope this project would stimulate. The first is an evangelical ecclesiology of the AAEC, and the second is an evangelical psychology and pedagogy of the AAEC. The need for further research along these lines is indicated by the historical, sociological and theological-anthropological analyses set out here. They could provide additional critical lenses for focusing on how the AAEC is formed, and how best to form the AAEC, in late modern affluence.[28]

KEY TERMS AND PHRASES

Section 1 has delineated the meanings of "affluence," "the problem of affluence," and "the AAEC." It also presented the manner in which those terms coalesce in "the problem of the AAEC." The purpose of this section is to define other key terms and phrases employed in this work.

The first is *technological consumer capitalism*. This phrase connotes the complex of social, economic, governmental and cultural institutions responsible for generating and sustaining mass affluence in the United States. Technological consumer capitalism emerged on the basis of significant scientific discoveries and the technological advances those discoveries made possible over the past several hundred years. The AAEC is nurtured in this context where science and technology are constitutive of social, cultural and human formation. As Michael Polanyi puts it,

28. "How to form human beings [is]," according to Wolfhart Pannenberg, "the central anthropological problem in pedagogy"; Pannenberg, *Anthropology*, 23.

science is generative of technology in the sense that scientific discovery makes "seeing more deeply into the nature of things" possible for everyone, whereas technology entails the ingenious appropriation of scientific discoveries "to surprising advantage" that may not be made available to everyone.[29] In economic terms, this is known as "innovation," a distinctive hallmark of advanced capitalism.[30] The affluence of technological consumer capitalism in the West is a sign of the depth to which science and technology has penetrated human existence in late modernity. This has profound implications for human relationships to others, things, self and God in late modernity.

The term *late modernity* signals three things. First, it distinguishes my project from a "postmodern" theological anthropology that might be developed through engagement with "postmodern theory" of some philosophical or cultural sort. Late modernity points specifically to the social changes that began to take place in the United States after World War II as a result of technological consumer capitalism's growth and eventual "triumph" in 1989. That year appears routinely in the literature since the Berlin Wall fell and Francis Fukuyama wrote his infamous article, "The End of History," and subsequent book, *The End of History and the Last Man*.[31] In this sense, late modernity is essentially equivalent to "postmodernity" insofar as the latter term signals a focus on the social changes arriving with the exhaustion of modernity and a new stage of capitalism after 1950.[32]

Second, late modernity refers to the post-World War II period. This is when both mass affluence and the AAEC began to emerge in the United States. Thus, late modernity is both a diachronic (through, over time) and synchronic (in, with time) descriptor that serves to delineate within the modern diachronic aspects of the work ranging from Jonathan Edwards

29. Polanyi, *Personal Knowledge*, 178.

30. Baumol, "Capitalism's Unique Innovation Machine: Historical Evidence," in *Free-Market*, 245–61.

31. Fukuyama set off a firestorm of intellectual controversy in "The End of History?" 3–18. He attempted to explain himself and develop his thesis in *The End of History and the Last Man*, which he followed with *Trust* and *Great Disruption*. He clarified how his thoughts on the end of history had changed in "Second Thoughts," 16–33, which he developed in *Posthuman Future*. For critical interaction with his original thesis, including an article by Fukuyama, see, e.g., Burns, ed., *After History?*; see also Roberts, "Closed Circle," 15–35; and Lash, "Beyond the End of History?" 252–64.

32. Lyon, *Postmodernity*, 4–7.

in the eighteenth century through Horace Bushnell in the nineteenth to Lawrence Richards in the twentieth.

This leads to the third aspect of late modernity, which has more to do with the synchronic aspects of the culture and society of affluence in which the AAEC is nurtured over the first two decades of life and in which the AAEC becomes embedded once a fully formed (evangelical) human. These are the concerns of chapters 4 and 5.

Agreeing generally with Jürgen Habermas and others who have reflected on late modernity in their writings,[33] the phrase points to an understanding of humans simultaneously as products of their social world and as interpreters-reproducers of that world who stand in differing degrees of criticality to it; that is, from no critical awareness to transformational awareness of their embedded context. The "interpretive reproduction" model of childhood sociology developed by William Corsaro fits well with this understanding of late modernity and serves the purposes of chapter 4's evangelical sociology of the AAEC as an interpreter-reproducer of evangelical affluence. Thus, the third meaning of "late modernity" has more to do with the synchronic aspects of the culture and society of affluence in which the AAEC is nurtured over the first two decades of life and in which American evangelicalism is embedded.

It is important also to understand the terms *evangelicalism* and *evangelical*. An immense body of literature exists on evangelicalism.[34] Although one scholar has argued recently that evangelicalism does not exist and should be discarded in academic study,[35] he admits that evangelicalism is a meaningful term to describe a form of Protestant faith practiced by millions outside liberal mainline Protestant denominations and to identify academic study of this socio-cultural group.[36] He also admits

33. Habermas, *Philosophical Discourse of Modernity*; *Communicative Theory I*; *Communicative Theory II*; Chouliaraki and Fairclough, *Discourse in Late Modernity*; Brown, *States of Injury*.

34. See, e.g., Harris, *Fundamentalism and Evangelicals*; Noll, *American Evangelical Christianity*; Noll, *Rise of Evangelicalism*; Murray, *Revival and Revivalism*.

35. His claim is that after 1950 American evangelicalism no longer serves as a helpful academic term "either for what the neo-evangelicals had in mind or for explaining the kind of religious diversity religion scholars study and interpret." Hart, *Deconstructing Evangelicalism*, 195.

36. "Evangelicalism as a form of Protestantism that is discontent if not at odds with the ecumenical faith developed between 1870 and 1950 among the leaders of the oldest Protestant denominations does indeed exist." Ibid., 194.

that the term is a useful reference to a version of Protestant faith known in Europe as pietism and in the Anglo-American context as revivalism.[37] He describes this kind of evangelicalism as follows:

> Its stress on the subjective character of faith, usually associated with the born again experience, and its skepticism about formal expressions of Christianity, such as creed, ordination, and liturgy, grew wildly in the spiritual greenhouse of the United States' religious free market. To the extent that the neo-evangelical leaders of the 1940s drew upon pietist notions of Christianity and that many Protestants at the beginning of the twenty-first century continue to conceive of the Christian religion in individualistic and experiential ways, evangelicalism does exist, one could say with a vengeance, for the type of Protestantism that scholars and believers most associate with the term *evangelical* is one that is characterized by the classic marks of pietism and revivalism.[38]

Hart's critical, and at times pejorative, description of evangelicalism is balanced well by J. I. Packer and Thomas Oden: "Evangelicalism identifies a core of necessary truth that has remained central through many shifts of the Christian scene over time."[39] Packer and Oden collected, identified and presented extracts of post-1950 evangelical statements of faith drawn from "two related but distinguishable wings of modern evangelical history: the Calvinist, Lutheran and Baptist wing of the Reformation, as distinguished in tone and accent in some ways from the Arminian, Wesleyan, Holiness, Charismatic and Pentecostal wing'"[40] Evangelical Christians are

> those who read the Bible as God's own Word, addressed personally to each of them here and now; and who live out a personal trust in, and love for, Jesus Christ as the world's only Lord and Savior. They are people who see themselves as sinners saved by grace through faith for glory; who practice loyal obedience to God; and who are active both in grateful, hopeful communion with the triune God by prayer, and in neighbor-love, with a lively commitment to disciple-making according to the Great Commission.[41]

---

37. Ibid.

38. Hart, *Deconstructing Evangelicalism*, 195 (emphasis original).

39. Packer and Oden, *One Faith*, 15.

40. Ibid.

41. Ibid., 19.

Packer and Oden continue by describing how historians and theologians variously profile evangelicals and evangelicalism:

> Historians categorize evangelicals as people who emphasize (1) the Bible as the Word of God, (2) the cross as the place where salvation was won, (3) conversion as a universal need and (4) missionary outreach as a universal task. Theologians dissect evangelicalism as a compound of the classic trinitarianism of Nicea, the Cappadocians and Augustine; the classic Christology of Chalcedon; the classic soteriology and ecclesiology of the Reformation; the classic pneumatology of the Puritans and Edwards; and the classic missiology of Carey, Venn and Hudson Taylor.[42]

The Institute for the Study of American Evangelicals (SAE) defines *evangelicalism* as the "religious movements and denominations which sprung forth from a series of revivals that swept the North Atlantic Anglo-American world in the eighteenth and early nineteenth centuries."[43] According to the SAE, the term *evangelical* entails two descriptive dimensions. The first follows British historian David Bebbington's four "hallmarks of evangelical religion: *conversionism*, the belief that lives need to be changed; *activism*, the expression of the gospel in effort; *biblicism*, a particular regard for the Bible; and *crucicentrism*, a stress on the sacrifice of Christ on the cross."[44] The second denotes "the self-ascribed label for a coalition that arose during the Second World War . . . as a reaction against the perceived anti-intellectual separatist, belligerent nature of the fundamentalist movement in the 1920s and 1930s."[45]

Evangelicals and evangelicalism also have particular demographic characteristics. According to a 2004 survey of evangelical religion in America, white evangelicals constitute 23% of the American population. Racially, 74% of evangelicals are white, 15% are African-American, 5% are Hispanic. Politically, 69% are either Republican or independents inclined to vote Republican.[46]

Most evangelicals live in America's middle-to-upper-middle class suburbs,[47] and compared to Americans in general, fewer evangelicals live

---

42. Ibid., 19–20.

43. http://www.wheaton.edu/isae/definingevangelicalism.html.

44. http://www.wheaton.edu/isae/definingevangelicalism.html.

45. Ibid.

46. Greenberg and Berktold, "American Evangelicals," 3, 13.

47. Cf. Shank and Reed, "Challenge to Suburban Evangelical Churches," 119–34.

in large cities (9% evangelicals versus 19% general population) and more evangelicals live in smaller towns (31% versus 22%) or rural areas (25% versus 18%).[48] Most American evangelicals are politically, theologically and economically conservative and enjoy a relatively privileged social and economic status in the United States.[49]

When the term "evangelical" is used throughout this work, it is intended to signify broad theological and historical descriptions of those humans and their institutions which embrace faith in Jesus and the gospel of his death, burial and resurrection. It encompasses what Packer, Oden and the SAE have sought to describe. On the other hand, "evangelical," "American-evangelical," and "American evangelicalism" are used to describe such evangelicals and evangelical institutions in their late modern formative cultural, social and economic contexts; that is, these terms should signal to the reader that I am attempting to emphasize the cultural, social, economic and, at times, political aspects of evangelical formation and embeddedness in affluence, or what has been cultivated and impressed upon and within evangelicals and their institutions over time (historically, diachronically) and in/within time (synchronically) in the culture of affluence in the United States.

The terms *neoliberal* and *neoliberalism* are important for understanding the economic aspects of the AAEC's embeddedness in evangelical affluence and the theological critique of the concept of liberty at the heart of these terms. They are essential to an understanding of the theological economics of the AAEC offered here.

Neoliberalism signifies the genealogy of classic liberal economic thought originating in early modern British moral philosophy with Thomas Hobbes and culminating in Adam Smith. The new science of political economy developed from this philosophical tradition. Political economy evolved finally into classical economic theory, with its emphasis on empirical study and mathematics, in the late eighteenth/early nineteenth century work of David Ricardo.[50] According to Milton Meyers, "The problem giving rise to the birth of the science of political economy was how to resolve the drive of self-interest in terms of the social welfare."[51]

48. Greenberg and Berktold, "American Evangelicals," 2.

49. Ibid., 4–14.

50. Meyers, *Soul of Modern Economic Man*, 5, 127–31.

51. Ibid., 5. Alan Storkey helpfully clarifies two fundamental changes that took place in the evolution from classical to neoclassical economic thought: (1) replacement of

Neoliberal economists and the theologians, philosophers and politicians who embrace their theories, findings and practices are the heirs of this liberal tradition. A neoliberal is, roughly speaking, a political, cultural and economic "conservative" or "neoconservative" in the United States.

Neoliberalism emerged after the Second World War and is generally seen to have reached its late modern social, cultural and political apex in the political administrations of Ronald Reagan in the United States and Margaret Thatcher in the United Kingdom. According to its proponents, neoliberalism has two main tenets:

> The first is that close economic contact between the industrial core [of the capitalist world economy] and the developing periphery is the best way to accelerate the transfer of technology which is the *sine qua non* for making poor economies rich (hence all barriers to international trade should be eliminated as fast as possible). The second is that governments in general lack the capacity to run large industrial and commercial enterprises. Hence, [except] for core missions of income distribution, public-good infrastructure, administration of justice, and a few others [e.g., a small, mobile and lethal military], governments should shrink and privatize.[52]

This leads to a discussion of two other key terms, *theology* and *economics*. Both terms implicate massive bodies of literature and a complex variety of disciplinary approaches, and therefore they must be focused in a manner relevant to the theological anthropology of the AAEC developed here. Interdisciplinary work in these two fields is described as *theological economics*, a relatively new field in contemporary theology.[53]

This work views *economics* as the dominant and definitive social scientific discipline of late modern life. As such, my interest in economics is twofold. The first lies in the historical development of economics from

thinking in terms of production to consumption with thinking in terms of consumption to production; and (2) replacement of the theory of value with consumer utility theory. Storkey, "Postmodernism is Consumption," in Bartholomew and Moritz, eds., *Christ and Consumerism*, 101–9.

52. DeLong, "Neoliberalism."

53. See, e.g., Oslington, "A Theological Economics," 32–44. Novak's 1982 classic neoliberal philosophical theology of democratic capitalism is a seminal work in this field. From the standpoint of Reformed-evangelical theology and tradition, "theological economics" equates roughly with "confessional" or "Christian" economics, though with some nuances and clarifications necessitated by ongoing interdisciplinary work in theology and economics. For further on this, see Smith, *Introducing Radical Orthodoxy*, infra.

British moral philosophy and political economy into classic liberal economic theory during the modern period. In particular, I am interested in the anthropology of human liberty, or freedom, underlying this evolution of modern economic thought.

The second aspect is the manner in which economics evolved as king of the social sciences in late modern American life; that is, how classic liberal economic thought and practice has transformed into neoliberal economic thought and practice in late modernity. Particular attention is paid to the social and cultural aspects of this development, keeping in view the anthropology of liberty assumed by neoliberal economics. Chapter 3 will seek to demonstrate historically how Herbert Hoover helped to engineer the dominance of economics in U.S. domestic and foreign policy in the 1920s and enfolded the child in the process of "diffusing production into consumption," effectively embedding the American child in the age of technological consumer capitalism.

Regarding *theology*, James Smith helpfully distinguishes between two kinds of contemporary theology under the categories "theology[1]" and "theology[2]" and then brings them into interplay with late modern economics.[54] Theology[1] denotes the "Ground-Motive" of the fundamental religious commitments of "Christian confession affirmed by the church, embodied in Scripture, and articulated in the confessions and creeds," whereas theology[2] is the "ongoing work of specifically theoretical, second-order reflection on the church's confession."[55] Smith relies on Herman Dooyeweerd for developing these understandings of theology and applies them critically in his attempt to "introduce" Radical Orthodoxy and correct what he finds to be an incipient Gnosticism in Dooyeweerd's conception of the two kinds of theology that leads him to take "flight to the mystical as the basis for an invisible ecumenism."[56]

Smith claims that theology[2] should "be undertaken in the service of the church, and when it is fruitful, it will inform the church's confession articulated in theology[1] . . . [which] then . . . functions as the root of Christian theoretical reflection across the disciplines."[57] Applying this specifically to Radical Orthodoxy's call for "theological economics,"

---

54. Smith, *Introducing Radical Orthodoxy*, 25, 177–79.

55. Ibid., 177.

56. Ibid., 178.

57. Ibid.

Smith observes that Radical Orthodoxy is "really calling for theological^1 economics, or what in the Reformational tradition would be described as confessional economics or simply Christian economics."[58] Smith argues for a critical "interplay and interaction between theology^1 and theology^2" that draws upon the strengths of Radical Orthodoxy's ecclesiology and at the same time corrects its disavowal of modern philosophy and social theory and practice, including economics.[59]

Smith maintains that Radical Orthodoxy evidences a "robust and substantive" appreciation for the global and historical role played by the church in sustaining theology^1 confession and biblical interpretation, which "should shape Christian theoretical investigation of the world, including theology^2."[60] At the same time, he contends that Radical Orthodoxy should be prepared to acknowledge that modern philosophy, from whence modern social theory and practice arose, "can be Christian insofar as it is undergirded by theology^1."[61] This clarifies the relationship between theology^1 and theology^2 further by establishing that theology^2 must always be grounded in a philosophical framework informed by a theology^1 Christian worldview.

I proceed along these lines by constructing a theological^1 economics of the AAEC in chapter 5. Drawing critically upon the history (chapters 2 and 3) and sociology of the AAEC (chapter 4), the aim is to develop an evangelical theology of the AAEC and stimulate theology^1 and theology^2 engagements with the affluent evangelical child in view. To accomplish this task, the anthropology of liberty that sustains the AAEC's definitive neoliberal economic context in evangelical affluence must be subjected to a focused critique, which is provided in chapter 5.

This leads to the next section's discussion of the eclectic critical-theological method employed in developing and engaging the evangelical history, sociology and theology of the AAEC.

THEOLOGICAL-CRITICAL METHOD

Understanding the divine-human relation with the AAEC in focus requires interdisciplinary dialogue with the social sciences, which illumine

58. Ibid.
59. Ibid.
60. Ibid., 178, 179.
61. Ibid., 179.

the human dimension of that relation. LeRon Shults maintains that this kind of dialogue necessitates "*both* maintaining a commitment to intersubjective, transcommunal theological argumentation for the truth of Christian faith *and* recognizing the provisionality of our historically embedded understandings and culturally conditioned explanations of the Christian tradition and religious experience."[62] The presence of the AAEC in evangelical affluence calls for an evangelical commitment to nurturing the truth about God revealed in Jesus and the gospel, while at the same time acknowledging the provisional nature of such nurture.

Advances in modern science and technology add to the complexity of relating theology and science. The more modern science (e.g., neuroscience) discloses about the human, the more complex understanding the divine-human relation becomes. The finite always struggles to comprehend the infinite.

A tension exists within evangelicalism and evangelical theology in the United States between evangelical commitment to Jesus and the Bible on the one hand and to the reality of evangelical experience of the modern world on the other. Evangelicals have not been known for nuanced theology[1] — theology[2] analyses (Smith) or for their "intersubjective, transcommunal theological argumentation" and ability to recognize the provisional nature of their "historically embedded understandings and culturally conditioned explanations of the Christian tradition and religious experience" (Shults).

Put another way, evangelicals are not known for theological-critical appropriations of modern science. Mark Noll has argued that this tendency within evangelicalism is one aspect of the "the scandal of the evangelical mind."[63] By "intersubjective" and "transcommunal," Shults has in mind the benefits to be gained from theological inquiry into modern psychological insights. The second part of his "postfoundationalist task" of theology signals the importance of sociology ("historically embedded") and anthropology ("culturally conditioned") to late modern theological inquiry.

Generally speaking, evangelicals tend to be suspicious and therefore dismissive of science due to perceived liberal infections of Darwinianism and other modern "liberal" heresies. Noll bemoaned the fact that, tra-

---

62. Shults, *Postfoundationalist Task of Theology*, xii (emphasis original).

63. Noll, *Scandal of Evangelical Mind*; cf. Anderson and Langelett, "Economics and Evangelical Mind," 5–24.

ditionally, evangelicals have relegated the social sciences to the dustbin of extrabiblical irrelevance. He won great popularity with those outside evangelicalism, along with a fair amount of evangelical criticism, for his argument that the scandal of the modern evangelical mind is that it does not exist. By this he meant that evangelicalism's disdain for, withdrawal from, and neglect of modern learning during the twentieth century created a vacuum in evangelical thought, education and theology that has only recently begun to be filled.

Noll makes a good point. Evangelicals should not fear but rather engage the social sciences in a theological-critical manner. There is much to be gained by such work. But this raises an important question: what method should late modern evangelicals use to relate science and theology? Shults writes of the need for a "methodological faith" in light of the late modern quandary in which theology finds itself with science. By this he means the way one relates to disciplinary knowledge or "holds" the relationship between self-understanding and knowledge of the objects under disciplinary study. By using the word "hold" Shults intends to signify a "deeper level of the 'holding structure' that subtends the self and its relation to its worldview" by which one believes something to be true.[64] This is what he means by "fiduciary structure"—an intrapsychic human structure out of which one relates in trusting, believing faith. Shults emphasizes the importance of acknowledging that this kind of "methodological faith" itself is socially situated and constructed, but he emphasizes that this does not negate the validity of truth claims and beliefs that arise from such faith.

Relying on James Loder, Shults suggests that the interdisciplinary dialogue between theology and anthropology should proceed by developing "more complex fiduciary structures for holding on to the relational constructs that have led to challenges to traditional formulations of doctrine in Christian anthropology."[65] Shults relies upon psychologist Robert Kegan for developing the concept of "complex fiduciary structures," by which he means deeper, transformational ways of interdisciplinary work with theology and anthropology.[66] He argues that the "challenges to tradi-

64. Shults, *Reforming Theological Anthropology*, 42.
65. Ibid., 55–60.
66. Ibid., 41–55.

tional formulations of doctrine in Christian anthropology"[67] have arisen because Christians have not engaged the knowledge provided by the human and social sciences through complex fiduciary structures that enable transformational knowing.

Shults applies Loder's theological method of relating theology and science to suggest why North American seminarians may not experience transformational learning. Thus, pedagogy appears in Shults, as it did in Pannenberg, as the telos of theological anthropology.[68] Learning from Loder, Shults is concerned with understanding "human development in theological perspective"[69] and applies his method in this task.

Loder's method of relating theology and science is grounded in the relational logic of the "Chalcedonian formulation of the relationality between the Divine and the human natures in the one person of Jesus Christ."[70] The fundamental problem in bringing practical theology and science together, Loder notes, is that the process requires attempting to bring "*two ontologically distinct realities, the divine and the human . . . together in a unified form of action that preserves the integrity of both and yet gives rise to coherent behavior.*"[71] This can be extended to all aspects of theology, as the works of Loder and Shults indicate.

Loder is dependent upon Barth, Kierkegaard and T. F. Torrance for his christological interdisciplinary method derived from Chalcedon. From Barth and Kierkegaard, he characterizes Chalcedonian divine-human relationality as:

> "indissoluble differentiation," "inseparable unity" and "indestructible (asymmetrical) order." More succinctly, this constellation of factors is designated as asymmetrical, bi-polar, relational unity which is self-involving through faith. This is a faith that understands Jesus Christ as revealing all that is, since all that has been created was created through him and for him (John 1:1–3). He is what God means by God and what God means by what is truly and

---

67. Ibid., 163–242.

68. Shults, "Relationality and Pedagogical Practice" and "Relationality and Spiritual Transformation," ibid., 61–76, 77–93; Pannenberg, *Anthropology*, 22–23.

69. Subtitle to Loder, *Logic of the Spirit*.

70. Loder, "Place of Science in Practical Theology," 23; see also *Logic*, 17–45; *Transforming Moment*, 172; Loder and Neidhardt, *Knight's Move*, 13.

71. Loder, "Place of Science in Practical Theology," 23 (emphasis original).

fully human. In faith one knows, in Kierkegaardian terms, that he
is the One on whom all metaphysics suffers shipwreck.[72]

"Asymmetrical" means that one pole of the bi-polar relation "exercises
marginal control in the relationality."[73] For Loder, this means that the
divine exercises marginal control over the human in the Chalcedonian
formulation in such a way that the two ontological poles are united and
integral while remaining distinct. This relational logic is extended to the
relation between "theology proper and the sciences of creation and human
nature" and thereby brings them into "transformational interaction."[74] If
science negates theology ("the divine reality") or theology negates the "legitimate contributions" of science to understanding human nature, then
the negations "must be negated."[75] Theologically, this means a negation of
science must be negated not by a process of cancellation or rejection but
by incorporation and transformation of the negation into a sub-science of
theological understanding of human nature.

Conversely, where theology negates science the negation "must be
negated and corrected to allow the human sciences to differentiate, specify
and interpret cognate theological themes and phenomena held in common."[76] This is the point at which Loder's dependence upon Torrance's
interdisciplinary method and theological framework is most evident.[77]
Loder illustrates his principle of negating the negation by pointing to
insights gained from the studies of group behavior. He notes that theology must include and transform human scientific understandings of
group behavior as they bear upon Christian life together. Inclusion and
transformation take place in light of theological understanding that life
together is the "communion creating presence of Jesus Christ."[78] Thus, to
the extent the human sciences negate the reality of Jesus Christ they are to

72. Ibid.

73. Ibid., 31.

74. Loder, "Place of Science in Practical Theology," 23.

75. Ibid., 23–24. Loder clarifies what he means by "negation of the negation" and the
legitimate contributions of the human sciences by drawing upon an illustration from
psychological understandings of ego functions in relation to theological understandings
of visions. Ibid., 23–24 n. 1.

76. Ibid., 24.

77. Ibid., citing Torrance, *Theological Science*; and *Ground and Grammar of
Theology*.

78. Loder, "Place of Science in Practical Theology," 24.

be negated and their otherwise valid insights into human nature are to be incorporated and transformed in light of Jesus and the gospel.

Loder's Chalcedonian method resonates the essence of many christological concerns of evangelical theology in the United States. This work introduces Loder's method of relating science and theology to American-evangelical theology and American evangelicalism. In developing a critical-theological history and sociology of the AAEC, I aim to illustrate how American-evangelicals can engage in and perform theological anthropology of children and thus benefit from such interdisciplinary work in doing contemporary theology. More specifically, the goal is to demonstrate how critical-evangelical engagement of history, sociology and economics can assist understanding of the child in American evangelicalism and affluence. Thus, this work presents an eclectic methodology for focusing on the AAEC with a view to advancing knowledge in the fields of American evangelicalism, evangelical theology in the United States, and the theology of children, as well as stimulating further evangelical-critical interdisciplinary studies of the child nurtured in affluence.

SURVEY OF LITERATURE

The first pertinent work warranting mention at the outset is a theological anthropology of children in German. It is germane but not helpful because it does not address either the American-evangelical child or the child nurtured in late modern affluence.[79]

The second is a thesis that "explores the distortion of adolescent vocational imagination caused by the strong alternative vocational formation offered by the cultural-economic system of consumer capitalism."[80] It is concerned with examining the manner in which consumer capitalism captures and distorts adolescent conceptions of work and life. While resonating many of the concerns addressed here, the thesis is written out of a context of a mainline liberal tradition and does not appear to embrace evangelical pre-understandings such as those embraced here. Nor does it focus on the child nurtured in American evangelicalism or the social and cultural aspects of American-evangelical sociology, subculture, economics or history. Targeting primarily pedagogical and psychological con-

79. Fangmeier, *Theologische Anthropologie des Kindes.*

80. Turpin, "Consumer Capitalism and Adolescent Vocational Imagination," quoting from abstract.

cerns, it neither engages the sociology of children nor the child nurtured in evangelical affluence nor the literature on theological economics.[81] As such, although of interest, it does not provide direct, material support for this book.[82]

Third is a work by Ellul scholar Marva Dawn, who has produced a volume in which children are subjected to contemporary theological analysis sensitive to materialism in the United States.[83] Although she does not focus specifically on American evangelicalism and the problem of affluence, Dawn's interest in the adverse effects of late modern American culture upon children resonates with the interest this work has in the AAEC. As an Ellul scholar, Dawn is well aware of contemporary issues pertinent to the culture formed by technological consumer capitalism in the United States.[84]

It is somewhat disappointing, then, to find that her theological-critical analysis of American culture does not engage Ellul significantly or apply his critique of the technological society to the child nurtured in American materialism.[85] Although she addresses issues of materialism, media saturation and contemporary biblical-theological perspectives of idolatry, greed and the human heart, her analysis does not focus specifically on the formative effects of affluence. This is understandable, since critical engagement with wealth and abundance is not her primary concern. Her agenda is much broader and focused more on the ecclesiological concerns of a practical theologian concerned about whether churches have lost touch with children in late modernity. Thus, it is not surprising to find that Dawn eschews interacting with the sociology of children and childhood, the history of American-evangelical affluence, or the tradition of the rich young man in Matthew 19 for what it teaches about how nurture in affluence can result in forming spiritual and moral lack in children.

81. Turpin writes as a practical theologian/religious educator formed as a lifelong member of the United Methodist Church in America. Ibid., 15.

82. I.e., "the development of vocational identity in adolescence." Turpin, "Consumer Capitalism and Adolescent Vocational Imagination," 8.

83. Dawn, *Lost Cause?*

84. See, e.g., Ellul, *Sources and Trajectories*, trans. and comm. by Marva J. Dawn. Dawn completed her doctoral work on Ellul at Notre Dame in 1992, under the supervision of John Howard Yoder. Dawn, "Principalities and Powers."

85. See chapters 8–11 of Dawn, *Lost Cause?* 129–200, where issues of affluence are raised but not critically engaged.

Having addressed these three works touching on the theological anthropology of children in affluence, the following survey focuses (a) on the child in theological perspective and then (b) on the issue of affluence in evangelical theology, with a view to situating the AAEC in relation to these bodies of literature.

Theology

Over the past 150 years, children have received a fair amount of attention from historians, psychologists, religious educators and Christian educators. Their work is an invaluable contribution to understanding children theologically.

However, a review of the literature on religious education, spiritual formation and faith development discloses that nurture in affluence has received scant critical attention in the United States.[86] This is particularly true of work by American-evangelical scholars in these areas.[87]

Systematic theological reflection upon children is sparse, and with regard to the child nurtured in affluence it is non-existent. A review of systematic theologies produced over the past three centuries discloses little serious concern for the theological significance of children. Virtually no attention has been paid to how the theology of children and theology of economics might interface.

Surprisingly, systematic liberationist reflections are no exception. Jon Sobrino, one of the foremost liberation theologians, does not mention children or discuss what significance they may have for understanding the reign of God in his systematic treatment of the subject.[88] Given that Jesus placed the child in the midst of his teachings on the reign of God

---

86. See, e.g., Ratcliff, *Children's Spirituality*; Morgenthaler, "Research Possibilities and Interests," in Morgenthaler ed., *Children's Spiritual Formation*, 265–76; Strommen and Hardel, *Passing on the Faith*; Stonhehouse, *Joining Children*; Spohrer, "Perceived relationship and roles of parents and evangelical churches." In the U.K., at least one educator-theologian has made significant contributions on the issue. Hull, "Christian Education in a Capitalist Society," 241–52, "Spiritual Education, Religion and the Money Culture," 285–301; cf. Sullivan, "Scandalized Child," 550–73.

87. Wilhoit and Dettoni, eds., *Nurture That is Christian*; Gangel and Wilhoit, eds., *Handbook of Spiritual Formation*.

88. Sobrino, "Central Position of the Reign of God in Liberation Theology," in Sobrino and Ellacuría, eds., *Systematic Theology*, 38–74.

and discipleship,[89] it would seem reasonable to find the child in Sobrino's systematic theology of God's reign.

Children have not been overlooked completely in contemporary theology, however. Judith Gundry-Volf has made two recent noteworthy systematic contributions in this regard, both of which focus on the child in relation to the kingdom of God.[90] Bonnie Miller-McLemore has also written a theology of childhood worth noting, although her attempt to "reimagine" childhood suffers, in my view, from a failure to engage the social sciences in a critical manner with regard to affluence.[91]

The earlier theological reflections of Friedrich Schleiermacher,[92] Karl Barth,[93] Karl Rahner,[94] and Hans Urs von Balthasar[95] regarding children should also be noted for their contributions to placing children closer to the theological spotlight. In addition, Spurgeon's nineteenth century pastoral treatise for parents and teachers of children contains rich theological reflection on children.[96]

Nevertheless, children have been given comparatively short shrift in modern theology. Evangelical, liberation, and feminist theologies have been granted a robust hearing in the academy since their advent in the 1960s and 1970s. The academic books, articles and dissertations spawned by these contemporary theologies are legion. The relative neglect of the child in the literature on these theologies is surprising in light of the magnitude of theological work addressing marriage and family issues and in light of the prominence of feminist and liberation theology in the twentieth century. Marriage, family and feminism in theological perspective would seem to implicate the need for focused study of the child in theological-anthropological perspective as well. As was the case with

89. E.g., Mark 9:33–37 and 10:13–16 (and parallels). See Weber, "Child in the Midst," in *Jesus and Children*, 34–51; Best, *Following Jesus*, 75–98, 106–9; Barton, *Discipleship*, 68, 81, 96–104.

90. Gundry-Volf, "Least and Greatest," 29–60; and "To Such as These," 469–80.

91. Miller-McLemore, *Let the Children Come*.

92. See, e.g., Seidel, "Schleiermacher"; DeVries, "Become as Little Children," 329–49.

93. Barth, "Parents and Children," in *CD* III.4, 240–85 (§54.2); Deddo, *Barth's Theology of Relations*, 238–60, 396–402; Werpehowski, "Karl Barth on Children," 386–405.

94. Rahner, "Theology of Childhood," 33–50. Mitchell, "Once and Future Child," 423–37, develops Rahner's ideas regarding the child's "infinite openness to the infinite."

95. Von Balthasar, *Unless You Become*.

96. Spurgeon, *Come Ye Children*.

women before the advent of feminist theology, perhaps children have not had a theological voice in the academy as a result of being embedded in patriarchal cultural and social contexts that marginalized them and hence failed to give them power or a voice.

With regard to evangelical theology, the absence of the child is understandable. For most of the twentieth century, evangelical theology was concerned with surviving the modern onslaught against its orthodox presuppositions. The marginalization of evangelical theology and evangelicals that began in the 1920s with the liberal/modernist-fundamentalist divide, usually signaled in the literature by the Scopes Monkey Trial, resulted in evangelical theology being forced to contend for critical issues such as the historical reality of the person and work of Jesus Christ and the trustworthiness of the Bible. It is not surprising, then, to find that evangelical theologians have neglected the child in their work.

With regard to liberation and feminist theologies, the absence of the child is surprising because children share many of the same characteristics of powerlessness and marginalization that the poor and women share. For instance, Ched Myers asks in his political-theological reading of Mark, "Why should not the child represent an actual class of exploited persons, as does every other subject of Jesus' advocacy in Mark? The impure and the poor and the gentile are representations of real social marginalization; Why not also the child?"[97] This is a good question with relevance to the present work. Why should we not consider children in doing theological economics?

Although a "Child Theology Movement"[98] is underway seeking to make children central to the task of contemporary theology, there has yet to emerge a "child theology" in the academy. The academic consensus seems to be that children remain a marginal theme in contemporary theology.[99]

---

97. Myers, *Binding the Strong Man*, 268.

98. The name of a registered charity in the U.K. headed by Haddon Willmer and Keith White. The movement began several years ago in Penang, Malaysia, as a result of Willmer's and White's theological work with practitioners serving children-at-risk around the world. Willmer and White are currently working on their child theology for SPCK with the working title *Reception Class: An Essay in Child Theology*. See online: http://www.childtheology.org/new/newsletter_3.php

99. Bunge, ed., *Child in Christian Thought*, 3–4, 9; Whitmore with Winwright, "Children," in Ryan and Whitmore, eds., *Challenge of Global Stewardship*, 161–85.

It is not surprising, then, that children do not appear in the emerging literature on theological economics. Research in the evangelical literature on nurture and affluence discloses that this book is the first critical-theological analysis of the child in the subcultural context of American evangelicalism and broader cultural context of affluence in the United States. One wonders whether American evangelicals are aware of the problem of affluence and thus the problem of the AAEC.

By developing a theological anthropology of the AAEC in late modernity, I seek to advance theological reflection upon the child with critical awareness of the problem that affluence poses for Christian nurture. Perhaps new ways of viewing the child in theological perspective will emerge, and perhaps this book will, in a manner similar to liberation theology for the poor, black, Dalits (and so forth) and feminist theology for women, lead to empowerment and representation for the AAEC in contemporary evangelicalism and evangelical theology in the United States.

Affluence in Evangelical Theology

John Schneider, Craig Blomberg[100] and Ronald Sider[101] are three contemporary evangelical theologians who have addressed affluence critically in their writings. The reasons for selecting Schneider as a dialogue partner in this theological economics of the AAEC have already been set out in section 2 above. Although these scholars do not focus specifically on the child nurtured in affluence, their works provide an appropriate literary context for critical-theological study of the AAEC.

Blomberg, a biblical scholar, is much more ambivalent about affluence than Schneider. His thesis on affluence is governed by the plea in Proverbs 30:8–9 (NRSV), "give me neither poverty nor riches; feed me with the food that I need, or I shall be full, and deny you, and say, 'Who is the Lord?', or I shall be poor, and steal, and profane the name of my God." His view represents a mediating position between Schneider and Sider, and in my estimation is a very helpful biblical resource for constructing a theological economics of the AAEC when coupled with the theological and philosophical critiques of liberty set forth here.

100. Blomberg, *Neither Poverty Nor Riches*.

101. E.g., Sider, *Rich Christians*; *Good News and Good Works*; *Just Generosity*; and *Scandal of Evangelical Conscience*.

Sider's works can be described as ethical-prophetic critiques of affluence in the tradition of radical evangelical social theology. Both Blomberg and Schneider critique Sider's evangelical version of liberation theology's preferential option for the poor. As evangelicals, all three theologians ground their arguments biblically. However, they fail to situate their arguments in critical interaction with evangelical history and sociology and, more particularly, fail to critique the anthropology of liberty at the heart of economic life in the United States, which render their biblical arguments somewhat myopic as to the formative effects of affluence.

AIM AND GOALS

The aim here, then, is to focus attention upon the AAEC nurtured in evangelical affluence in the United States by constructing a contemporary theological anthropology and theological economics of the child in late modern American evangelicalism.

Pursuant to this aim, my goals are first to present a critical evangelical history of the AAEC (chapters 2 and 3) and then to construct an evangelical sociology of the AAEC in light of that history (chapter 4). The next goal is to develop an evangelical theology of the AAEC through critical interaction with the diachronic and synchronic perspectives of the AAEC established in the previous chapters.

The theological economics of the AAEC presented in chapter 5 will focus upon the anthropology of human liberty/freedom that underlies the historical, sociological and theological perspectives of the AAEC presented. The purpose of this focus is to provide a theological critique of the AAEC's freedom in evangelical affluence and raise the question whether an unbiblical, neoliberal economic conception of liberty is nurtured during the first two decades of evangelical life in the United States, leading to the formation of a spiritual and moral lack similar to that identified in the story of the rich young man in Matthew 19. In other words, the question raised is whether nurture in late modern evangelical affluence leaves the AAEC free for affluence but unfree to follow Jesus in the way of the cross that may call for its renunciation and donation. This is the problem of the AAEC in late modernity I seek to explore, illumine and redress within evangelical theology.

PART I

The AAEC in Diachronic Perspective

2

Formative Theological Anthropologies of the Child in American Evangelicalism: Jonathan Edwards and Horace Bushnell

> It is significant of every great new birth in the world that it turns
> its face toward childhood, and looks into that image for the pro-
> foundest realization of its hopes and dreams. In the attitude of
> men toward childhood we may discover the near or far realization
> of that supreme hope and confidence with which the great head of
> the human family saw, in the vision of a child, the new heaven and
> the new earth. It was when his disciples were reasoning among
> themselves which of them should be the greatest, that Jesus took a
> child, and set him by him, and said unto them, 'Whosoever shall
> receive this child in my name receiveth me.' The reception of the
> Christ by men, from that day to this, has been marked by succes-
> sive throes of humanity, and in each great movement there has
> been a new apprehension of childhood, a new recognition of the
> meaning involved in the pregnant words of the Saviour.
>
> —Horace E. Scudder[1]

INTRODUCTION

This chapter assesses the theological anthropologies of the evangelical
child found in the thought of Jonathan Edwards and Horace Bushnell. Its
aims are to gain an understanding of the formative theological conceptions of the child in American evangelicalism from Edwards to Bushnell
in light of the American quest for affluence that began in the early 1800s
with the advent of the industrial revolution. Thus, the chapter seeks to
discover the "hopes and dreams" represented by the child in American

---

1. Scudder, *Childhood in Literature and Art*, 102.

evangelicalism during these formative years of the young republic's quest for prosperity.

Jonathan Edwards (1703–1758)

Edwards is commonly viewed as the greatest American theologian of the eighteenth century and perhaps the greatest theologian America has ever produced. One recent life of Edwards describes him as "America's evangelical."[2] Although he never developed a theological anthropology of the child per se, his writings contain reflections on children in theological perspective sufficient to discern a distinct, albeit conflicted, conversionist theological anthropology of the child. The child in Edwards's theological anthropology is located somewhere between nature and grace until converted. The implications for this in the context of American-evangelical affluence are identified and critically assessed through interaction with the subsequent theological reflections of Bushnell in the nineteenth century.

Horace Bushnell (1802–1876)

Bushnell is considered the "greatest figure in American theology in his century"[3] and, with the exception of Edwards, "probably the most creative Protestant theologian that America produced before the twentieth century."[4] He is also regarded as the father of religious education in the United States. His *Christian Nurture* is "now considered to be the basis for the modern development of religious education."[5] That book is the fulcrum upon which the historical aspect of the theological anthropology of the AAEC turns.[6] According to one of Bushnell's early biographers, Bushnell's thoughts on Christian nurture were "ten years in preparation, having had its genesis in an article on 'Revivals of Religion,' published

---

2. Gura, *Edwards: America's Evangelical.*

3. Johnson, *Nature and the Supernatural in Bushnell*, 10.

4. Smith, ed., *Bushnell*, ix.

5. Wyckoff, *Gospel and Christian Education*, 60.

6. Delivered first as lectures and then published in pamphlet form in 1846 as *Discourses on Christian Nurture* and then after controversy over it erupted in 1847 under the title *Views of Christian Nurture and of Subjects Adjacent Thereto.* The final version was published in 1861 simply as *Christian Nurture.*

in 1836 in the 'Christian Spectator.'" Its specific aim was to establish the proposition that

> the child is to grow up a Christian, and never know himself as being otherwise. A very simple statement, but it shook New England theology to its foundations. The phrase, by its very form, challenged the extreme individualism into which the churches had lapsed, and recalled them to those organic relations between parents and children which are recognized in the historic churches, and which also had been recognized to a certain extent by the churches of New England before Edwards.[7]

Bushnell parted company with Edwardsian conversionism in favor of a developmentalist theological anthropology of children and of childhood nurture. Attempting to chart a course between the nineteenth-century Charybdis of Calvinistic-Edwardsian revivalism and Scylla of Unitarianism and Universalism, Bushnell developed a theology of nurture that reflected his theological conception of grace (the supernatural) embedded in nature.[8] Bushnell's developmentalist theology of nurture profoundly shaped the direction of theological and pedagogical thought regarding how children are to be raised in the faith, replacing "revivalism as the dominant influence in religious education."[9]

As this chapter and the next will show, neither conversionist nor developmentalist theological anthropologies of the child have factored affluence critically into their conceptions of nurture. This is due to the fact that both affirm the same neoliberal economic theory and practice, at least tacitly, as evidenced by their embrace of the fruits of affluence that neoliberal economics produces. With Edwards the embrace is by default because the industrial revolution had not taken hold during Edwards's lifetime in the eighteenth-century United States. With Bushnell, on the other hand, the embrace was explicit. As we will see, he wholeheartedly affirmed affluence and developed theologies of the child and affluence that fit hand in glove.

This work raises affluence as a factor in nurture and proposes a theological anthropology of developmental conversionism for the AAEC as a means of critically assessing the formative effects affluence can have on

7. Munger, *Bushnell*, 67.

8. Bushnell, *Nature and the Supernatural*.

9. Krahn, "Nurture vs. Revival," 382. For a helpful survey of the Christian nurture literature, see Downs, "Christian Nurture," 21–23.

evangelical development in the first decades of life. As far as I can tell, this is the first time such a task has been attempted.

The Child in Edwards and Bushnell

My research has uncovered one dissertation that focuses on the child in the thought of Edwards and Bushnell.[10] Completed in 1927, the thesis assesses various theological anthropologies of the child found in eighteenth and nineteenth-century New England Congregationalism. Thus, it critically examines the explicit and implicit theological anthropologies of children found in Edwards and his Calvinistic heirs, the Arminian iteration of New England Congregationalism, and the unorthodox developments of Unitarianism and Universalism. It also provides an insightful examination of the pedagogical application of New England theology to children as found in creeds, catechisms, sermons, parenting literature, educational literature, and Sunday school curricula from the eighteenth century through the 1920s.

The thesis provides a helpful analysis of and window upon the theology of children found in the four primary nineteenth-century controversies in New England theology: Unitarian, Universalist, Arminian, and Bushnellian. The ultimate conclusion of the thesis is that Bushnell's theology of nurture represents the best of nineteenth-century theological reflection on the child. However, the thesis does not examine other aspects of Bushnell's theology, in particular his theology of affluence, nor does it critically address the formative aspects of affluence upon the child.

If modern Protestant religious education in the United States began with Bushnell, it did so with a genuine concern for nurturing evangelical Christian faith in children. However, this concern for evangelical nurture underwent substantive social, cultural and religious transformation in the twentieth century at least partially due to the unprecedented affluence realized after 1950. Bushnell was deeply embedded in the nineteenth century's industrial revolution. His theological labors were both formed by and formative of the evangelical subculture that emerged in the nineteenth century and evolved in the twentieth. As chapter 3 will show, it is difficult to overstate this point. The social, cultural and economic ferment of the industrial revolution deeply penetrated American evangelicalism

10. Wortley, "Status of the Child."

in the nineteenth century. The penetration was so extensive that by the end of that century it had incorporated American evangelicalism's disciplinary methods, principally found in its revivalistic conversionism, and converted them to the interests of industrial capitalism.

According to Bernard Wishy, from 1830 to 1900, the child in American evangelicalism was slowly transformed from being "redeemable" in the new republic to "redeemer" of the new republic.[11] By this he meant that the conception of the child as sinner in need of conversion-redemption-liberation (ala Edwards, et al.) was transformed into a more romantic conception of the child as redeemer or as the one in which future hopes could be fulfilled if only nurture could be made to coincide with grace (the supernatural) embedded in nature (ala Bushnell, et al.). It was a hopeful and heady time for many American evangelicals, it seems, who were full of growing aspirations for affluence inspired by the remarkable economic advances of the industrial revolution after the Civil War.

Wishy divides this seventy-year period roughly into two parts. From 1830 to 1860, due at least in part to a conversionist theological anthropology of the child derived from Edwards, the child was viewed principally as needing transformation or conversion. From 1860 to 1900, however, this view changed. Owing primarily to Bushnell, but also to other evangelical theologians, the child became a sign of hope and an object of formation for the new republic driven by the growth of industrial and consumer capitalism. Thus, the foundations of the AAEC's late modern nurture in evangelical affluence were laid during this time, as evangelicals ceded the child to civil society and religion in the United States. This was the first great compromise of the child in American evangelicalism. In view of the growing prosperity during the second half of the nineteenth century, American evangelicals were prone to see the good of affluence and hope for the liberation it could provide without regard to its potentially gospel-subverting effects. The second compromise would come quite unconsciously in the post-World War II economic boom that began in the 1950s.

Wishy's analysis in *The Child and the Republic* provides evidence for the first evangelical compromise of the child from the writings of

---

11. Wishy, "The Child Redeemable (1830–1860)" and "The Child Redeemer (1860–1900)," in *Child and Republic*, 3–181.

A. D. Mayo, who in 1899 equated the American education system with Christian education,

> the training of the vast majority of American children for an American citizenship that includes the noblest of ideals of a practical, moral and religious manhood and womanhood . . . [It became] the people's university for training young America in that Christian civilization which contemplates the union of all the elements of our cosmopolitan population in the common American life; the great achievement of 100,000,000 people living together to the ideals and methods of human intercourse set forth in the Gospel of Jesus Christ . . . [Finally, after 18 centuries] *the absolute religion of Jesus Christ . . . has won its greatest victory* in the acceptance of the new education by the American people as the last and best organization of the gospel of love for God and man, for the training of American childhood and youth for sovereign American citizenship.[12]

Without Bushnell's *Christian Nurture* and the help of other nineteenth-century evangelicals, such a wholesale accommodation of the American-evangelical child to the American Dream would have been impossible.

The following sections will show how this came about. Bushnell modified Edwards's theology of affections and anthropological conversionism as applied to children. He rejected the conversionist "ostrich nurture" of children and hence rejected the theological anthropology of the child assumed in the American revivalism of the nineteenth century. This set the stage for the equation of Christian nurture with formation for "sovereign American citizenship."

EDWARDS'S CONVERSIONIST THEOLOGICAL ANTHROPOLOGY OF THE CHILD

> The theological substratum of Puritan morality denied to childhood any freedom, and kept the life of man in waiting upon the conscious turning of the soul to God. Hence childhood was a time of probation and suspense. It was wrong, to begin with, and was repressed in its nature until maturity should bring an active and conscious allegiance to God. Hence, also, parental anxiety was forever earnestly seeking to anticipate the maturity of age, and to secure for childhood that reasonable intellectual belief which it

12. Wishy, *Child and Republic*, 167–68 (emphasis added).

held to be essential to salvation; there followed often a replacement of free childhood by an abnormal development. In any event, the tendency of the system was to ignore childhood, to get rid of it as quickly as possible, and to make the State contain only self-conscious, determined citizens of the kingdom of heaven. There was, unwittingly, a reversal of the divine message, and it was said in effect to children, Except ye become as grown men and be converted, ye cannot enter the kingdom of heaven.[13]

At the risk of oversimplifying the Edwardsian and Bushnellian positions as they get worked out today, the conversionist view is held predominantly within more theologically and biblically conservative communities within American evangelicalism that tend to be suspicious of what the human and social sciences might teach or illumine about human nature.

The developmentalist view, on the other hand, is held primarily within more theologically and biblically moderate evangelical communities in the United States and is uniformly embraced within theologically liberal traditions. There seems to be a greater openness in these traditions to theological-critical assessments of the human and social sciences, although these remain largely critically undeveloped in evangelical theology.

It may be true that conversionists often leave "the corpus of empirical research . . . dormant under the church's curse of extra-Biblical irrelevance."[14] At the same time, developmentalists may tend toward less-than-critical biblical and theological appropriations of findings from the human and social sciences. Regardless, I will show that both traditions have failed to consider perhaps the most dominant aspect of the theological anthropology of the child: nurture in affluence.

Edwards, Revivalism, and the Child

It is important to keep in mind the context of American revivalism in which Edwards and Bushnell developed their theological views. Revivals and revivalism played important roles in shaping the theological anthropologies of children found in both theologians.[15] In the nineteenth cen-

13. Scudder, *Childhood in Literature and Art*, 128.

14. Walker, "Psycho-Epistemology of Religious Maturity," 8.

15. Both were also concerned with particular theological errors prevalent in their day. Edwards was concerned with defending orthodoxy against Arminianism, and

tury, these hallmarks of American evangelicalism came to play important roles in directing the currents of the industrial revolution and building a unique alliance between evangelicalism and affluence in the United States. It is fitting, then, to begin with a brief chronology of the works written and published by Edwards in relation to revivals and revivalism in the eighteenth century.[16]

In 1741, Edwards preached a sermon at Yale titled the "Distinguishing Marks of the Work of the Spirit of God," which was published and widely circulated. He developed the sermon into a lengthy treatise regarding the New England revival.[17] In this work, Edwards argued against critics of the revival in favor of religious affections as trustworthy signs of true revival and conversion. He wanted to prove what were "the distinguishing marks of a work of the Spirit of God, including both his common and saving operations," in the course of the revival.[18]

Beginning in late 1742 and concluding in 1743, Edwards preached a series of sermons on religious affections. These were eventually published in 1746 as *A Treatise Concerning Religious Affections, In Three Parts*. As will be shown below, this treatise is where Edwards's theological anthropology is to be found. To my knowledge, this thesis is the first time *Religious Affections* has been read with a view to discerning Edwards's theological anthropology of the child.

In this subsequent, more extensive work, Edwards turned to address the other side of affections in theological-anthropological perspective, "the nature and signs of the gracious operations of God's Spirit, by which they are to be distinguished from all things whatsoever that the minds of men are the subjects of, which are not of a saving nature."[19]

The winds of revival had subsided by the time Edwards finished *Religious Affections*, so he had ample time to weigh the evidence of religious affections in his congregation and throughout New England. Much like Charles Finney in the so-called Second Great Awakening, Edwards seemed to be concerned that perhaps some of the affections arising from

---

Bushnell was concerned with defending his version of orthodoxy against Unitarianism and Universalism.

16. Minkema, "Jonathan Edwards Chronology."

17. Published in March 1743. Edwards, *Thoughts Concerning Present Revival*, 365–430.

18. Edwards, *Affections*, 89.

19. Ibid.

the revivals were not genuine manifestations of a work of the Holy Spirit. In 1750 he lamented that many of those believed to be converted in the revivals had backslidden and the "doctrines of grace" had been discarded to a much greater degree than ever before, adding that Arminian and Pelagian teachings had "made a strange progress within a few years."[20] Edwards thus wished to answer criticism on both sides of the debate over what are true signs of regeneration and conversion. His concerns were grounded deeply in theological anthropology.

Three other works warrant note before moving to consider Edwards's theological anthropology of children in *Religious Affections*. The first is *A Faithful Narrative of the Surprising Work of God* published in London in 1737.[21] This shorter work was written in the form of a letter to a Rev. Dr. Colman, who had written to Edwards's uncle inquiring into and desiring to be "more perfectly acquainted" with the facts of revival conversions.[22] Edwards details various conversions in this letter, including the conversion of many children.

The second work to note is *Freedom of the Will*,[23] which was completed in 1753 and published in December 1754, over four years after Edwards was dismissed from his church in Northampton. This work is important to keep in mind when examining Edwards for his theological anthropology of the child because his conception of the will is the same for children as it is for adults. The freedom of the human will is the mind choosing in accordance with its greatest desire at each moment in time. An unregenerate mind does not choose God revealed in Christ and the gospel because it has no desire for that God in its heart.

The third work is *The Great Christian Doctrine of Original Sin Defended*, completed in May of 1757 and published in 1758.[24] Edwards addresses the issue of depravity in infancy and childhood in this treatise. This view of children, when considered in light of how he sees children in *Religious Affections*, discloses that Edwards was conflicted in this theological anthropology of the child; that is, Edwards never seemed able to get his mind around the God-child relationship, how God relates to children

20. Cited in Smith, *Changing Conceptions*, 11.

21. Edwards, *Faithful Narrative*, 344–64.

22. Ibid., 346.

23. Edwards, *Freedom of the Will*.

24. Edwards, *Original Sin*.

in the first and second decades of life and how children relate to God in those decades.

Children and Human Nature in Religious Affections

Despite the fact he relies heavily in *Religious Affections* upon analogies to the nature of children and to their naturally "gracious" dispositions in order to make his case for evidence of true Christian affections, Edwards never focused his prodigious mind and prolific pen to write a theology of children or theological anthropology of the child. Had his life not been cut short, perhaps he would have turned his attention to such an effort and helped us all think through the mystery of the child and the mysterious nature of how God and children relate.

Catherine Brekus correctly draws attention to Edwards's conflicted views and stance regarding children.[25] According to Brekus, the ministry that Edwards had to children was "one of the most striking results" of what she calls his "new theology of 'religious affections.'"[26] It is surprising, then, to find that Brekus does not present evidence from *Religious Affections* for the theology of children found there. Three of the fourteen arguments (first, eighth, and ninth) in Part III of *Religious Affections* entail significant theological reflections on children. As will be shown below, it is clear that Edwards saw children as naturally possessing and therefore representing those holy and gracious affections he believed were positive proof of genuine conversion in both adults and children.

At the same time, Edwards argued in other works that children are vipers, damnable, unregenerate children of wrath from the time they split the womb. Brekus focuses attention on these works for discerning Edwards's theology of children rather than on *Religious Affections*. This appears to be representative of an unfortunate tendency in some Edwards scholarship to highlight his theology of wrath and other perceived theological-anthropological incongruities, resulting consequently in thin rather than thick construals of his contributions to modern theology.

---

25. Brekus, "Children of Wrath," 300–38.

26. Ibid., 314. Brekus did not have the benefit of Walton's *Jonathan Edwards*. Her claim that Edwards presented a "new theology of 'religious affections'" needs to be revised in light of Walton's work. See also Mathews, "Toward a Holistic Theological Anthropology," 265–79.

Nevertheless, despite the conflicted nature of the positive and negative aspects of his theological anthropology of children, Edwards saw children at all times as needing conversion accomplished by the Holy Spirit and needing diligent discipline and instruction of the Lord. The third part of *Religious Affections* contains considerable references to children from which it is possible to discern the positive aspect of Edwards's theological anthropology of the child. It is composed of fourteen arguments for "distinguishing signs of truly gracious and holy affections" in the converted, three of which (i.e., the first, eighth and ninth) contain important theological reflections upon children: (1) that the spirit of children provides a vibrant analogy of the gracious work of love and adoption by the Spirit in conversion; (2) that children manifest meekness by nature and behavior; and (3) that children are naturally and behaviorally tender in heart. As such, according to Edwards, children constitute paradigmatic examples of the affections that possess and are possessed by true disciples. Edwards comes remarkably close to equating the spirit of children to the Spirit of love and adoption, the affectional presence and grace of the Holy Spirit.

Edwards had much to say about the kinds of affections and relations that prove the presence of saving grace in true disciples, and he spoke of children at times as if they by nature possessed such affections and relations. Nevertheless, what or who children were in relation to God as humans in the time between birth and rebirth apparently remained a mystery in his mind. It remains (or perhaps at least should) a mystery in the minds of those who hold his conversionist theological anthropology of children as well. The same is probably true of developmentalists as well. The child is a mystery. How does God relate to children and how do children relate to God? How do those relationships change over time as human development proceeds? Perhaps this is why Jesus relates children to the kingdom of God, himself and the Father from so many different angles. Jesus tells us that the kingdom or reign of God is a mystery (Mark 4:11) and that it belongs to those "such as" children (Mark 10:14). He further tells us that we must "receive" or "welcome" children and in so doing we "receive" or "welcome" Jesus and the Father (Mark 9:37), while at the same time if we do not "receive the kingdom of God like a child" we will never enter it (Mark 10:15).

In order to see this conundrum in Edwards more clearly, it is necessary to examine in detail his theological anthropology of children found in the first, eighth and ninth arguments of Part III of *Religious Affections*.

However, before proceeding to that task, it will be helpful to introduce those arguments by setting them in their proper context of Edwards's life and thought.

Edwards lived, pastored and wrote in the first half of the eighteenth century. This was during a time when the Scottish philosophy of common-sense realism was helping form American intellectual history.[27] Edwards both stood within and without that philosophy, borrowing its concepts and adapting them to his own unique biblical-theological method and thought. Arguing against the religious rationalists of his day who exalted reason over passion and denounced the emotional emanations of the New England revival, Edwards contended that it was false philosophy to suppose that all exercises of the affections reduce to mere human emotion and that "it is . . . false divinity to suppose that *religious affections* do not appertain to the substance and essence of Christianity. On the contrary, it seems to me that the very life and soul of *all true religion consists in them*."[28]

Edwards developed this both biblically and systematically in *Religious Affections*. Edwards posits in Part I that, "The Holy Scriptures do everywhere place religion very much in the affections; such as fear, hope, love, hatred, desire, joy, sorrow, gratitude, compassion and zeal. . . . The Scriptures place religion very much in the affection of love, in love to God, and the Lord Jesus Christ, and love to the people of God, and to mankind. The texts in which this is manifest, both in the Old Testament, and New, are innumerable."[29] A little later in Part I, Edwards argues that "it is doubtless true, and evident from these Scriptures, that the essence of all true religion lies in holy love; and that in this divine affection, and an

---

27. The iteration of Enlightenment thinking embraced by American intellectuals and leaders that adapted best to American republicanism, independence and primarily Protestant religiosity. See Noll, 'The Evangelical Enlightenment', in *Scandal of Evangelical Mind*, 83–107. This American version of the Enlightenment is known variously as "theistic common sense," "the new moral philosophy" or "commonsense moral reasoning," "evangelical Enlightenment," "*moderate* Enlightenment" (Newton and Locke), and "*didactic* Enlightenment . . . largely a product of Scotland" (Francis Hutcheson, Thomas Reid, Adam Smith, Dugald Stewart); in America, "this form of modern thought provided theologians with an intellectual lingua franca for nearly a century." Noll, *America's God*, 93–95.

28. Edwards, *Thoughts Concerning Present Revival*, 367 (emphasis original).

29. Edwards, *Affections*, 102–3.

habitual disposition to it, and that light which is the foundation of it, and those things which are the fruits of it, consists the whole of religion."[30]

In Part II, Edwards notes that "nothing is more excellent, heavenly and divine than a spirit of true Christian love to God and men; 'tis more excellent than knowledge, or prophecy, or miracles, or speaking with the tongue of men and angels. 'Tis the chief of the graces of God's Spirit, and the life, essence and sum of all true religion."[31]

Finally, in the fourth argument of Part III, Edwards again links affections and love to true religion: "the Scripture often teaches that all true religion summarily consists in the love of divine things. And therefore that kind of understanding or knowledge, which is the proper foundation of true religion, must be the knowledge of the loveliness of divine things. For doubtless, that knowledge which is the proper foundation of love, is the knowledge of loveliness."[32] Edwards's theology of affections was revolutionary in its New England context. His two-pronged theological critique of affections was aimed at two aspects of Calvinistic detractions against revival and conversion. As previously noted, in *Thoughts Concerning the Present Revival*, Edwards argued in favor of religious affections as signs of true conversion. In *Religious Affections*, he turned the case for affections around to argue for the kind of affections that are proof of regeneration and conversion. He wanted to explore theologically what he saw pastorally: signs that many who claimed to be converted in the revivals of religion may in fact not be converted because their affections had not been transformed.

The genealogy of Edwards's thought can be traced back to seventeenth-century Puritan "heart religion," the Reformation and even back to Aquinas, Augustine and Greek philosophy.[33] Edwards was an original thinker and profoundly systemized this tradition in his generation. As Brad Walton concludes, "perhaps for the first time in the history of pietism since Augustine, [*Religious Affections*] offers the kind of systematic

---

30. Ibid., 107.

31. Ibid., 146.

32. Ibid., 271.

33. Walton, *Jonathan Edwards*, 221. Walton's work is the most recent comprehensive critical interpretation of *Religious Affections* in its historical, literary, theological, psychological and philosophical context. It controverts and corrects some of the longstanding misinterpretations of the genealogy and originality of Edwards's theology of affections and the heart.

articulation of heart-psychology which the intellectualist model had received under Thomistic scholasticism."[34] He also notes that it "is arguably the special accomplishment of Edwards that he organized, for the first time since Augustine, Bernard, William of St. Thierry and William Ames, and in a manner perhaps more exhaustive than any of them, a systematization of traditional heart-language into a thorough, clearly defined and fairly coherent analysis of religious interiority."[35]

Walton notes that the theological anthropology of *Religious Affections* entails a version of faculty psychology and substance dualism, both of which have a long lineage in intellectual history.[36] Substance dualism is the view that human nature is composed of two separate substances (body and soul) constituting a human person. Faculty psychology is the view that human nature is composed of interrelating "faculties" or powers of the soul that direct and control the various human bodily functions. Edwards held a bipartite rather than tripartite view of the soul. He included affections within the faculty of the will and distinguished passions from affections. Edwards believed that the "will, and the affections of the soul, are not two faculties; the affections are not essentially distinct from the will, nor do they differ from the mere actings of the will and inclination of the soul, but only in the liveliness and sensibleness of exercise. It must be confessed, that language is here somewhat imperfect."[37]

In Edwards's view, the passions are less rational and thus lower than affections:

> The *affections* and *passions* are frequently spoken of as the same; and yet, in the more common use of speech, there is in some respect a difference; and affection is a word that in its ordinary signification, seems to be something more extensive than passion, being used for all vigorous lively actings of the will or inclination; but passion for those that are more sudden, and whose effects on the animal spirits are more violent, and the mind more overpowered, and less in its own command.[38]

34. Ibid., 223.

35. Ibid., 181.

36. Ibid.; cf. Shults, *Reforming Theological Anthropology*, 165–88.

37. Edwards, *Affections*, 97.

38. Ibid., 98.

Edwards's faculty psychology is most evident in *Religious Affections*: "God has endued the soul with two faculties . . ."[39] One faculty is the under-standing, or the capability of perceiving and speculating by which the soul views, discerns and judges things.[40] The second faculty is that which operates upon, or reacts to the understanding, either with approval or disapproval. It is knowledge that results either in disinterest or neutrality regarding the understanding, or in a disinclination to the understanding, or in an inclination to the understanding. Edwards described this second faculty variously as inclination, will, affections, mind and heart:

> This faculty is . . . sometimes called the *inclination*: and, as it has respect to the actions that are determined and governed by it, is called the *will*: and the *mind*, with regard to the exercises of this faculty, is often called the *heart*.
>
> The exercises of this faculty are of two sorts; either those by which the soul is carried out towards the things that are in view, in approving of them, being pleased with them, and inclined to them; or those in which the soul opposes the things that are in view, in disapproving them, and in being displeased with them, averse from them, and rejecting them.[41]

Edwards's substance dualism entails the belief that God has estab-lished natural laws in the union between body and soul such that the soul has primacy over and dictates bodily functions. The more "vigorous and sensible" exercises of the soul are the affections, according to Edwards, and they emanate from what "perhaps all nations and ages" designate to be the human heart, where we find Edwards's faculty psychology and sub-stance dualism come together:

> through the laws of the union which the Creator has fixed between soul and body . . . the motion of the blood and animal spirits be-gins to be sensibly altered; whence oftentimes arises some bodily sensation, especially about the heart and vitals, that are the foun-tain of the fluids of the body: from whence it comes to pass, that the mind, with regard to the exercises of this faculty, perhaps in all nations and ages, is called the heart. And it is to be noted, that they

39. Ibid., 96.
40. Ibid.
41. Ibid. (emphasis in original).

are these more vigorous and sensible exercises of this faculty that are called the *affections*. [42]

The mind produces the affections on the basis of understanding, and affections are the more vigorous and sensible exercises of the inclination or will of the human soul. The mind, not the body, is seen as the ground or "seat" of the affections. Edwards expresses a radical substance dualism on this point: "it is not the body, but the mind only, that is the proper seat of the affections. The body of man is no more capable of being really the subject of love or hatred, joy or sorrow, fear or hope, than the body of a tree, or than the same body of man is capable of thinking and understanding."[43] Edwards develops this point further:

> As 'tis the soul only that has ideas, so 'tis the soul only that is pleased or displeased with its ideas. As 'tis the soul only that thinks, so 'tis the soul only that loves or hates, rejoices or is grieved at what it thinks of. Nor are these motions of the animal spirits, and fluids of the body, anything properly belonging to the nature of the affections; though they always accompany them, in the present state; but are only effects or concomitants of the affections, that are entirely distinct from the affections themselves, and no way essential to them; so that an unbodied spirit may be as capable of love and hatred, joy or sorrow, hope or fear, or other affections, as one that is united to a body.[44]

The radical dualism of Edwards seems to denigrate bodily existence that might lay the foundations for a sort of "cognitive idolatry" found today in American evangelicalism. It bifurcates human self-understanding and tends to render bodily existence superfluous. Would Edwards say the same thing about the body, including the brain, if he were able to read the neuroscience literature available to us today? His view needs revision in light of scientific, philosophical and theological advances in understanding human nature during the two centuries following Edwards.[45] As LeRon Shults puts it, "What were once called 'faculties' of the soul are now described as registers of behavior of the whole person."[46]

42. Edwards, *Affections*, 96–97.

43. Ibid., 98.

44. Ibid.

45. See, e.g., Damasio, *Feeling of What Happens*; Russell, et al., eds., *Neuroscience and the Person*; Ashbrook and Albright, *Humanizing Brain*.

46. Shults, *Reforming Theological Anthropology*, 180.

Human affections take place in, through and by the central nervous system of the human body, as does Christian nurture of those affections in the child. The process involves a complex chemical-electrical interaction at the cellular level that unites mind and body, the immaterial and material, spirit and cell. Although a certain duality remains in modern anthropology, ontological dualisms such as those found in Edwards and others are no longer tenable. Furthermore, although there may be separate behavioral manifestations of human personality, the view that there are separate faculties of the soul responsible for distinct mental or emotional functions can no longer be sustained in light of advances in scientific understanding. Both substance dualism and faculty psychology have become defunct anthropological concepts in the twenty-first century, necessitating requisite revisions in theological anthropology.[47]

The point to be noted is that Edwards's faculty psychology and substance dualism underlie his conversionist theological anthropology of the child. If the mind *only* exercises affections and not the body (presumably including the brain), then it follows that the most important truth about human nature is its immaterial or spiritual aspect. The material, including how the brain relates to the formation of the person, is practically redundant. An emphasis on conversion proven by the right kinds of religious affections, a profession of faith and praying a sinner's prayer are the logical consequences of a theological anthropology grounded in substance dualism and faculty psychology. It leads to an idolatry of cognition that reduces the child to an immaterial essence stuck somewhere between nature and grace awaiting the soul's awakening. But what role does formation in the gospel play? How are we to understand Paul's admonition to nurture our children in "the discipline and instruction of the Lord"?

This leads now to a close examination of the manner in which Edwards employs children and childhood metaphorically in *Religious Affections* to demonstrate the kinds of religious affections true believers have. Edwards appears to view children as naturally possessing the kinds of gracious, saving affections that mark true Christians. Although he does not develop the implications of his metaphors and in fact denies them in other writings, the question arises as to when children's natural affections turn from gracious and holy to sinful and unholy. This is a question Edwards neither raised explicitly nor answered consistently in his writ-

47. Edwards, *Affections*, 179–88.

ings, and it points us once again to the mystery of the child in the midst of evangelical disciples (Mark 9:33–37; Matt 18:1–14).

Religious Affections *and children*

Children serve Edwards's purpose once in Part I of the treatise to illustrate the ungracious affections that flow from hardness of heart in contrast with the tender hearts of children: "And this is one thing, wherein it is necessary we should *become as little children, in order to our entering into the kingdom of God*, even that we should have our hearts tender, and easily affected and moved in spiritual and divine things, as little children have in other things."[48] According to Edwards, children have tender hearts and are "easily affected and moved" in regard to "other things." They point professing believers to the tender hearts they must have to evidence true religious affections. They must have hearts easily moved and affected by spiritual and divine things.

Part III of *Religious Affections* is composed of fourteen positive arguments "*Shewing What Are Distinguishing Signs of Truly Gracious and Holy Affections*."[49] This is where the best evidence of Edwards's theological anthropology of children is to be found.

As previously noted, children play an important role in the first, eighth and ninth arguments. The following three subsections demonstrate the manner in which Edwards draws upon analogies to children and childhood to argue for "truly gracious and holy affections." Together they set out Edwards's theological anthropology of the child.

The Holy Spirit as Affectional Grace: Children and the *analogia spiritus* (Edwards's First Argument)

Edwards's first argument is that, "Affections that are truly spiritual and gracious, do arise from those influences and operations on the heart, which are *spiritual, supernatural* and *divine*."[50] Toward the end of the argument, Edwards develops a biblical pneumatology from Romans 8 in which he essentially equates "spirit of a child" with "spirit of adoption,"

---

48. Edwards, *Affections*, 117.
49. Ibid., 191 (italics in original).
50. Ibid., 197 (emphasis original).

"spirit of love," "spirit of grace," "spirit of man" and conscience.[51] In doing so, he draws an analogy from the spirit of children to the Holy Spirit, an *analogia spiritus*. His concern is to posit the Holy Spirit's ontological priority as divine grace in the human soul, as affectional grace incarnated in humans by the Spirit through the gospel. Edwards argued that this was the biblical witness of the Holy Spirit over against views that the witness was immediate revelation of facts or impressions to the human soul by the Holy Spirit.

Edwards's practical and pastoral concerns shine through in his argumentation. Evidently, there were those in his day who argued for an immediate witness of the Spirit to the soul similar to that claimed by many modern Pentecostals and charismatics. Edwards took pains to counter this notion with a rather radical argument. For him, the Holy Spirit is the very real, ontological presence of God, the grace of God residing in and affecting the regenerate heart: "Therefore this earnest of the Spirit, and first fruits of the Spirit, which has been shown to be the same with the seal of the Spirit, is the vital, gracious, sanctifying communication and influence of the Spirit, and not any immediate suggestion or revelation of facts by the Spirit."[52]

Edwards drew analogies in this argument from the nature of children in an attempt to demonstrate what he believed to be trustworthy evidence of truly gracious and holy affections in the children of God. At times it is difficult to distinguish between Holy Spirit and the human spirit in the analogies he employs. Hence, commenting on Romans 8:16 and then 8:14–16, Edwards states:

> Here, what the apostle says, if we take it together, plainly shows, that what he has respect to, when he speaks of the Spirit's giving us witness or evidence that we are God's children; is his dwelling in us, and leading us, as a spirit of adoption, or spirit of a child, disposing us to behave toward God as to a Father. This is the witness or evidence the Apostle speaks of, that we are children, that we have the spirit of children, or spirit of adoption. And what is that, but the spirit of love? . . . the spirit of a child, or spirit of adoption . . . is love . . . we have received the more ingenuous noble spirit of children, a spirit of love, which *naturally* disposes us to go to God,

51. Ibid., 237–39.

52. Ibid., 237 (footnote 4 omitted, where Edwards cites Thomas Shepard's *Parable of Ten Virgins*, Pt. I, p. 86).

> as children to a father. . . . This is the plain sense of the Apostle . . .
> So that the witness of the Spirit of which the apostle speaks, is far
> from being any whisper, or immediate suggestion; but is that gra-
> cious, holy effect of the Spirit of God in the hearts of the saints, the
> disposition and temper of children, appearing in sweet childlike
> love to God, which casts out fear.[53]

Thus, Edwards conceives the gift of the Spirit in terms of the spirit of a child, which is the spirit of adoption and love. This spirit "naturally" disposes the recipient to trust God as Father just as the spirit of a child impels the child to trust an earthly father. For Edwards, "it is past doubt . . . that the Apostle has a more special respect to the spirit of grace, or the spirit of love, or spirit of a child, in its more lively actings . . . The strong and lively exercises of a spirit of childlike, evangelical, humble love to God, give clear evidence of the soul's relation to God, as his child."[54]

Although Edwards never indicates the age of the child in his analo-gies, it is apparent from the eighth and ninth arguments, as well as from other writings, that very young children are in view. Edwards apparently did not believe that children maintained the spirit of love and adoption very long after birth. But as previously noted, his theological views of children were ambivalent. He viewed all humans, children included, as having the propensity "to sin immediately, as soon as they are capable of it, and to sin continually and progressively."[55] Thus, Edwards contends that human experience and scriptural evidence disclose that children are "universally committing sin as soon as capable of it; which, I think, is a fact that has been made evident by the Scripture."[56]

Edwards uses 1 John 1:8–10 for his biblical proof of children's uni-versal, immediate manifestation of sin.[57] He never establishes precisely when children become capable of sinning, but it appears to follow closely upon birth. Brekus notes that Edwards maintained that the "time of free-dom from sin" is so small that it is "not worthy of notice."[58]

One wonders, then, in light of the analogies he draws from children in his exposition of Romans 8:14–16, when children might ever exhibit

---

53. Edwards, *Affections*, 237–38 (emphasis added).

54. Ibid., 238.

55. Edwards, *Original Sin*, 135 n. 2.

56. Ibid., 200.

57. Ibid., 135.

58. Brekus, "Children of Wrath," 310; Edwards, *Original Sin*, 136 n. 2.

those gracious affections he identified as essential proof of genuine conversion to Christ and God as Father. Edwards seems to have been of two minds in his views regarding children, as his eighth and ninth arguments in Part III of *Religious Affections* further disclose.

Children Are Naturally and Behaviorally Meek

Edwards's eighth argument is that, "Truly gracious affections differ from those affections that are false and delusive, in that they tend to, and are attended with the lamblike, dovelike spirit and temper of Jesus Christ; or in other words, they *naturally* beget and promote such a spirit of love, meekness, quietness, forgiveness and mercy, as appeared in Christ."[59]

In classic evangelical fashion, Edwards claims that the "evidence of this in the Scripture, is very abundant."[60] He employs extensive biblical citations and exposition in this eighth argument, including references to child texts in Matthew (18:3, 6, 10, 14; and 19:14) and Mark (10:15). In doing so, he relies heavily upon the nature and behavior of children to prove that truly gracious affections in believers "tend to, and are attended with the lamblike, dovelike spirit and temper of Jesus Christ." It is difficult to discern the difference in Edwards's language between this "spirit and temper" of Jesus and children:

> Little children are innocent and harmless: they don't do a great deal of mischief in the world: men need not be afraid of them: they are no dangerous sort of persons: their anger don't last long: they don't lay up injuries in high resentment, entertaining deep and rooted malice. . . . Little children are not guileful and deceitful; but plain and simple: they are not versed in the arts of fiction and deceit; and are strangers to artful disguises. They are yieldable and flexible, and not willful and obstinate; don't trust to their own understanding, but rely on the instructions of parents, and others of superior understanding. Here is therefore a fit and lively emblem of the followers of the Lamb. *Persons being thus like little children*, is not only a thing highly commendable, and what Christians approve of, and aim at, and which some of extraordinary proficiency do attain to; but it is their *universal character*, and *absolutely necessary* in order to enter into the kingdom of heaven; unless Christ was mistaken; "Verily I say unto you, except ye be converted, and

59. Edwards, *Affections*, 344–45.
60. Ibid., 345.

become as little children, ye shall not enter the kingdom of heaven"
(Matt. 18:3). "Verily I say unto you, whoever shall not receive the
kingdom of God as a little child, he shall not enter therein" (Mark
10:15).[61]

It is difficult to reconcile Edwards's belief that children "universally
. . . sin as soon as capable of it" with his belief that disciples of Christ
must aim at being persons "thus like little children" who possess the "universal character" of children as "absolutely necessary in order to enter
the kingdom of heaven." How can children be depraved and at the same
time naturally possess truly gracious affections as emblematic "followers
of the Lamb"? At what point do children cross over to sin from virtue? As
Brekus and others have noted, Edwards was never able to reconcile his
belief that children are totally depraved "vipers" and "children of wrath"
with his belief that children by nature possess truly gracious and holy
affections essential to entering the kingdom of heaven.[62]

Clearly, Edwards was conflicted in his theological anthropology of
children. He believed children are born in original sin and capable of
mischief, bitterness, unforgiveness, deceitfulness and a host of other sins.
At the same time, he believed children (at least up to some point) were
innocent and guileless, exemplary embodied evidence of regeneration.
This ambivalence in Edwards may reflect a general characteristic of contemporary thought in Edwards's day not only toward children but also
toward women as well.[63]

Regardless, it is clear that "Edwards never satisfactorily resolved the
problem of the exact time in a human life when sin declares itself . . . (in
his) persistent wrestlings with the issue of the damnation of infants,"[64] despite the fact that he contended in *The Great Christian Doctrine of Original
Sin Defended* (1758) that children "universally" sin as soon as they have
the capacity for it, "even in families in which the highest moral examples
prevail."[65] If children begin life as innocents, then why, how and when

61. Edwards, *Affections*, 350–51 (emphasis added).

62. See Brekus, "Children of Wrath," 302–4, 316, n. 44.

63. See, e.g., Ruether, "Making of Victorian Family," in *Christianity and Making
Modern Family*, 83–106.

64. Holbrook, "Editor's Introduction," 59, in Edwards, *Original Sin*; see also Gerstner,
Rational Biblical Theology of Edwards II, 330.

65. Smith, *Changing Conceptions*, 29.

do they become guilty? The answer remains a mystery for evangelicals, a conundrum yet to be resolved.

Children Are Tender in Heart

Edwards summarizes his ninth argument in Part III of *Religious Affections* as follows: "Gracious affections soften the heart, and are attended and followed with a Christian tenderness of spirit."[66] Children once again serve Edwards's purposes through a series of comparisons with the true Christian:

> The tenderness of the heart of a true Christian, is elegantly signi-
> fied by our Savior, in his comparing such a one to a little child. The
> flesh of a little child is very tender: so is the heart of one that is new
> born . . . Not only is the flesh of a little child tender, but his mind is
> tender. A little child has his heart easily moved, wrought upon and
> bowed: so is a Christian in spiritual things. A little child is apt to
> be affected with sympathy, to weep with them that weep, and can't
> well bear to see others in distress . . . A little child is easily won by
> kindness . . . A little child is easily affected with grief at temporal
> evils, and his heart is melted, and he falls a weeping . . . A little child
> is easily affrighted at the appearance of outward evils, or anything
> that threatens its hurt . . . A little child, when it meets enemies,
> or fierce beasts, is not apt to trust its own strength, but flies to its
> parents for refuge . . . A little child is apt to be suspicious of evil in
> places of danger, afraid in the dark, afraid when left alone, or far
> from home . . . A little child is apt to be afraid of superiors, and to
> dread their anger, and tremble at their frowns and threatenings . . .
> A little child approaches superiors with awe.[67]

For Edwards, "No other metaphor so perfectly captured his desire to lose himself in God" than the metaphor of a little child.[68] Thus, Edwards expressed his desire "to lie low before God, as in the dust; that I might be nothing, and that God might be ALL, that I might become as a little child," and reflected, "I very often think with sweetness, and longings, and pantings of soul, of being a little child, taking hold of Christ, to be led by him through the wilderness of the world."[69] Edwards apparently believed

66. Edwards, *Affections*, 357.

67. Ibid., 360–61.

68. Brekus, "Children of Wrath," 312.

69. Ibid., 312 n. 31, citing Edwards, *Narrative*.

that little children, both by their nature and their behavior toward others, demonstrate for Christians the nature and behavior of truly gracious and holy affections. Little children are signs of what it means to be saved, to have evidence and assurance that one knows Christ, has the Spirit of Christ and thus calls upon God as Father (Rom 8:1–14).

The argument begins with a discussion of false affections that flow from a hard heart in contrast with true affections that flow from a tender, regenerate heart. Edwards argues that, "An holy love and hope are principles vastly more efficacious upon the heart, to make it tender," and thus produce gracious affections that flow from a contrite, broken heart.[70] Edwards then moves to children as a metaphor to demonstrate the manner in which Jesus "elegantly signified" the tenderness of heart true Christians have.[71] The language employed by Edwards raises questions about whether Edwards believed children actually possess such virtues, whether they were actually tender, meek, humble and innocent by nature and in behavior. If so, to what age do they possess these gracious and holy affections by nature and in their behavior? Edwards seems to make a rather clear distinction between little children and the rest of humanity. There is a radical disjuncture between Edwards's anthropology of adults and his anthropology of children. Consequently, Edwards presents a confusing, unformed, theological anthropology of the child.

As has been shown, at some point the distinction between little children and the rest of humanity dissipates for Edwards. The exact point at which this occurs is unclear. This is a perennial problem in evangelical theology. Debates continue over the age of accountability and the implications of the doctrine of original sin. At the heart of the controversy is repulsion over the thought of a loving but just God punishing children eternally in hell for sins committed as soon as they exit the womb, or before they have developed moral responsibility, or for Adam's sin. There are those within conservative, biblical evangelicalism today who hold to infant damnation on account of Adam's sin alone and on the basis of sins committed before children have developed moral cognitive ability. Most evangelicals in this camp reject an age of accountability. They cite various standard biblical texts, Edwards and rationalistic Calvinists as authority.

70. Edwards, *Affections*, 360.
71. Ibid.

These same evangelicals ignore contrary evidence in Scripture and the evangelical tradition. Reasoning from various biblical texts, for instance, Spurgeon believed in infant salvation and rejoiced in the fact that heaven would be populated with so many millions who died in infancy throughout the centuries. Most evangelical-Reformed theologians have not held to infant damnation, parting company with Edwards who believed that God, because of original sin, would be "exceeding just" if he were to "take the soul of a new-born infant and cast it into eternal torments."[72] In doing so, these theologians have argued that their position extends salvific grace further than Roman Catholic, Anglican, Lutheran or Arminian theological traditions. In the latter, the grace of salvation depends upon rational choice and in the former three it depends on the sacraments. Reformed theology views the vast majority of humanity as saved because so many millions of children have passed away before the age of accountability. Contrary to its caricatures since the Reformation, Reformed theology views God as short on wrath and long on grace, mercy and love, at least in regard to children.[73]

The beginning of the modern debate over issues raised by original sin in children, such as when sin actually manifests itself in children in space and time, can be seen in the about face Horace Bushnell took almost a century after Edwards wrote *Religious Affections*. For Bushnell, children were not to be viewed as vipers or children of wrath. Although not explicit, it is evident that he affirmed the ontology and anthropology of children in *Religious Affections* but rejected Edwards's views that children are born in sin, dead in sin and suffer eternally in hell because of sin unless converted. Bushnell's view of children flourished in the nineteenth century and was an essential ingredient of the religious soup being stirred in the young republic of the United States. As recent scholarship is showing, religious thought of this period was a significant component of the broader ideological and cultural currents shaping the United States, particularly grass roots republicanism and the popular vision of public/private virtue and character formation in dialectical tension with liberal democratic ideology.[74] Bushnell's contribution to the republic was a developmentalist

---

72. Edwards, The "Miscellanies" (entry nos. a-z, aa-zz, 1–500), cited in Brekus, "Children of Wrath," 303 n. 6; see also Gerstner, *Rational Biblical Theology of Edwards I and II*, 530–36, 115–26.

73. Boettner, *Reformed Doctrine of Predestination*, 143–48.

74. On this, see Noll, *America's God*, 53–72 ("Republicanism and Religion"), 73–92

anthropology of the child that helped lay the groundwork for the AAEC's incorporation within the matrices of the American pursuit of happiness in economic progress, growth and affluence.

BUSHNELL'S DEVELOPMENTALIST THEOLOGICAL ANTHROPOLOGY OF THE CHILD: NURTURE IN AFFLUENCE

Bushnell, like Edwards, was a Congregational minister in New England. Unlike Edwards, he entertained doubts about whether Christianity "could ever be demonstrated to the complete logical satisfaction of the understanding."[75] He agreed with Edwards regarding the importance of parental nurture in the spiritual formation of children. He joined Edwards in a strong denial of the liberalizing trend of Unitarianism to view human nature as radically good, rather than radically depraved. He affirmed original sin but modified the doctrine into a less metaphysically refined form than Edwards. This and other theological innovations, including his theology of Christian nurture, embroiled Bushnell in a lifetime of theological controversy.[76]

Regarding his theological anthropology of children, Bushnell conceptualized an "organic nurture" of children through parental-relational formation that would set him apart from Edwards and evangelical revivalistic conversionists of the nineteenth century. The organic laws of the family were the nature-grace pillars upon which he built his theology of nurturing children in the discipline and instruction of the Lord. Bushnell viewed "affections" differently from Edwards as well. His departure from Edwards's theological anthropology of conversion and affections was undoubtedly influenced positively by Samuel Coleridge's *Aids to Reflection* and negatively by the rationalistic Calvinism of Nathaniel Taylor, both of which led him on a life-long path of rethinking and reworking his christology and theological anthropology. He eventually adopted a modified "moral influence" or "suasion" theory of the atonement that included the

---

("Christian Republicanism"), 161–208 ("The Evangelical Surge . . . and Constructing a New Nation"), and 447–52 ("Historiography of Republicanism and Religion"). According to Noll, "The important point for this book is that these more comprehensive accounts of American ideology understand religious thought as fully active in the ideological clearinghouse that was the early United States." Ibid., 450–51.

75. Weigle, "Introduction," in Bushnell, *Christian Nurture*, xxxiv.

76. Mullin, "The Bushnell Controversy," in *Puritan as Yankee*, 6, 151–79.

belief in Christ's literal suffering, but it was a suffering that provided the basis for a progressive renovation of character and awakening of the affections to see, sense, value and choose what is good, lovely and right. He argued that when a soul beholds God in Christ's "beauty, loving and lovely, the good, the glory, the sunshine of the soul . . . the affections, previously dead, wake into life and joyful play," so that what existed in the affections before as "only a self-lifting and slavish effort becomes an exulting spirit of liberty."[77] Thus, Christ impresses his "intense love of God to His law" in the souls of believers with "a most deep and subduing sense" of the sacred value of God's law.[78]

Bushnell's christology informed his theological anthropology of children, particularly in his view of the relational organic nurture of grace in children's lives through parents. God's interaction with children through Christ takes place through parents in the process of character development and renovation. However, Bushnell never could work out a coherent doctrine of the relationship between nature and the supernatural in his christological formulations and theology of nurture.[79]

In the process of developing his organic theology of child nurture, Bushnell substantially reworked Edwards's doctrines of depravity and original sin. If parented properly in the early years of life, Bushnell believed, original sin and depravity in children could be developmentally overcome through the regenerative laws of organic nurture established by God in the parent-child relationship. As Catherine Brekus puts it,

> . . . in a striking innovation, he argued that almost all children, if carefully nurtured, had the capacity to become faithful Christians. As he explained, a child could "grow up a Christian, and never know himself as being otherwise." Rejecting the emphasis on conversion, he condemned Edwards and other Puritans for tormenting impressionable young children with threats of hell—a criticism that other liberals quickly echoed. . . .[80]

This Bushnellian innovation serves as the focal point for the comparison and contrast of Edwards's and Bushnell's respective theological

77. Bushnell, *God in Christ*, 212–13.

78. Ibid., 228.

79. Johnson, *Nature and the Supernatural in Bushnell*; Rece, "Theology in Bushnell"; and Henderlite, "Theological Basis."

80. Brekus, "Children of Wrath," 325.

anthropologies of children. Bushnell called the Edwardsian and related revivalistic views of conversionism a cruel "ostrich nurture," because ostrich mothers bury their eggs in the sand and leave them to hatch on their own.[81] Where Edwards referred to the mother ostrich (Job 39:16) to demonstrate a hard heart devoid of gracious affections,[82] Bushnell turned the metaphor back upon Edwards and his conversionist followers by arguing that those who hold to such a theological anthropology of children are themselves ostrich mothers, devoid of godly affections and responsibility toward their children.

This is probably the juncture at which Bushnell's departure from Edwards's theology of affections began, at least as it applied to children. Edwards cited Job 39:16 early in *Religious Affections*.[83] As was shown above, just before this reference Edwards used an analogy to children in his argument that Christians must "become as little children, in order to our entering into the kingdom of God" by having tender hearts readily affected by "spiritual and divine things, as little children have in other things."[84] Upon reading *Religious Affections* at this point, Bushnell may have been motivated to reflect upon children more deeply in theological-anthropological perspective. Seen in this light, as well as the context of nineteenth-century revivalistic conversionism, Bushnell's *Christian Nurture* may appropriately be seen as a critical interaction with, and application of, *Religious Affections* to children. He advocated a developmental view of nurture dependent upon implanting the holy and righteous souls of Christian parents upon the souls of children. Remarkably, according to Bushnell, virtually all was lost or won during the first three years of life.

Christian Nurture was prescient of developmental views of human nature. It also presaged religious education in profoundly positive and formative ways. Luther Weigle put it this way: "Modern psychology and sociology have confirmed its insights, and the best of modern education is in its spirit."[85] However, its theological anthropology of the child is

81. Bushnell, *Christian Nurture*, 52–73.

82. Thus, Edwards argued that it is "very plain in some places, in the text themselves, that by hardness of heart is meant a heart void of affection. So to signify the ostrich's being without natural affection to her young, it is said, 'She hardeneth her heart against her young ones, as though they were not hers' (Job 39:16)." Edwards, *Affections*, 118.

83. Part I, Sect. II.

84. Ibid., 117.

85. Weigle, "Introduction," in Bushnell, *Christian Nurture*, xxxi.

problematic for several reasons, which will be identified and discussed below.

Bushnell and Family Idolatry

Bushnell would no doubt be surprised to find his theological vision for the organic, grace-imparting unity of the family being critiqued as idolatrous 130 years after the final version of *Christian Nurture* was published.[86] Surprised, no doubt, because he was concerned to protect children and the Christian family from idolatry, not promote it. He took the Bible seriously and reasoned from it extensively in an evangelical manner. This is evidenced by the fact that Bushnell placed Jeremiah 7:18 at the head of the chapter in which he sets forth his theological proof for a semi-sacramental organic unity of the family upon which he constructs his theology of Christian nurture.[87]

Bushnell argued for a law of organic union of nature and divine grace by which the holy, just, non-idolatrous parental nurture of children "will infallibly shape and subordinate" the character of children if "some other spirit, from other families, or the church, or the world, do not reach" them during their early formative years.[88]

Conversely, if children are raised in homes pervaded by an idolatrous spirit, then idolatrous children will be produced: "Who ever expects that an idolatrous religion, in the house, will not uniformly produce idolaters?"[89] For good or ill, for true worship or false, parents form their children for life. Children live and move and have their being in their parents, as Bushnell saw it.[90] The problem is that even the best of parents are fallen creatures embedded in a fallen creation composed of a fallen culture and society. Bushnell never accounted for this reality in his theol-

---

86. Fishburn, *Idolatry of Family*, 41–43. "Bushnell was typical of almost all Victorian social theorists and pastors." Ibid, 43 n. 8, 196, quoted from McDannell, *Christian Home in Victorian America*, 19; see also Dorrien, "Imagination Wording Forth," 111–78; and "Victorian Gospel," 393–411.

87. Bushnell, "The Organic Unity of the Family," in *Christian Nurture*, 76–101. Jeremiah 7:18, as quoted by Bushnell, reads: "The children gather wood, and the fathers kindle the fire, and the women knead dough, to make cakes to the queen of heaven, and to pour out drink offerings to other gods, that they may provoke me to anger." Ibid., 76.

88. Ibid., 88.

89. Ibid., 87.

90. Ibid., 88.

ogy of Christian nurture, nor did he critically engage the formative effect that cultural and social contexts, such as affluence, might have upon parent and child alike.

According to Bushnell, the Christian family is sacramental in the sense that mystery is at work, either the mystery of godliness or the mystery of evil, depending upon the character of the parents. By organic laws admixed with nature and grace, the family shapes and forms desire in children either toward or away from God. He pleads with his readers: "I beseech you, as you love your children . . . Understand that it is the family spirit, the organic life of the house, the silent power of a domestic godliness, working, as it does, *unconsciously and with sovereign effect*—this it is which forms your children to God. And, if this be wanting, all that you may do beside, will be as likely to annoy and harden as to bless."[91] To understand Bushnell fully here, it is important to be mindful that he conceptualized children's development within the familial-parental matrix in two distinct phases or ages: that of "*impressions*" or "existence in the will of the parent" and that of "*tuitional influences*" or "*will and personal choice in the child.*"[92]

The first phase is the most important in Bushnell's theology of nurture. It is the pre-language phase during which, according to Bushnell, more is done for good or ill in children than at any other time in their lives. It is also a phase most Christians overlooked and wasted in Bushnell's day:

> I suspect, and I think it can also be shown by sufficient evidence, that more is done to affect, or fix, the moral and religious character of children, before the age of language than after; that the age of impressions, when parents are commonly waiting, in idle security, or trifling away their time in mischievous indiscretions, or giving up their children to the chance of such keeping as nurses and attendants may exercise, is in fact their golden opportunity; when more is likely to be done for their advantage or damage than in all the instruction and discipline of their minority afterward.[93]

Bushnell went on to claim that "more, as a general fact, is done or lost, by neglect of doing, on a child's immortality, in the first three years of

---

91. Ibid., 98 (emphasis added).

92. Ibid., 199 (emphasis in original).

93. Bushnell, *Christian Nurture*, 201. Bushnell was prescient here. His theological anthropology of human development by the age of 3 is confirmed in many respects by neuroscience and developmental psychology.

life, than in all his years of discipline afterwards. . . . Let every Christian father and mother understand, when their child is three years old, that they have done more than half of all they will ever do for his character."[94] Thus, Bushnell's developmental theology entailed a view of children in two phases, from birth through three years of age and from four years onward.

At this point of his innovative thesis, Bushnell's theological anthropology of children simultaneously exhibits its greatest strengths and weaknesses. One of its revolutionary strengths was that it sensitized Christian parents, educators and theologians to the critical developmental importance of the early years in children's lives. Bushnell appears to have intuited what developmental psychology has been telling us for a century and some of what brain research over the past several decades is showing us. For instance, he was aware how infant children's eyes were "very quick . . . to catch impressions, and receive meaning of looks, voices, and motions."[95]

Brain research tells us that 90 percent of brain development takes place from birth through approximately age three. Research of the infant brain shows an amazing capacity to scan, receive, assess and store images through the eyes, and that infants not only have a preference for high contrast graphics, but that the visual stimulation actually increases brain development. Newborns were once thought to enter the world as blank slates onto which a lifetime of experiences would be inscribed. But neuroscience is helping us discover the universe of the infant brain. They have brains as sophisticated as the most powerful supercomputer. They come wired with approximately 50 trillion connections between their 100 billion cells and have a mind-boggling capacity for growth and knowledge.

Research has also shown that in the first eight months of life the infant brain increases to 1,000 trillion connections. The discovery of infant capacity for memory has startled scientists. But perhaps the most significant discoveries relate to the impact a baby's environment has on brain development. Although Bushnell's organic theory of nurture may trouble theologians, both developmental psychologists and educators alike recognize how truly far ahead of his time Bushnell actually was. Theologians who read Bushnell closely find themselves agreeing with the psychologists

94. Bushnell, *Christian Nurture*, 211–12.
95. Ibid., 204.

and educators as well. Chapter 4 engages Bushnell along these lines in its theological-critical assessment of developmental psychology and neuroscience in the context of the sociology of children, with a view to how those sciences may illumine theological understanding of the AAEC.

The strength in Bushnell's theology of nurture—focus upon parental formation of the child—is also a major weakness for at least two reasons. First, it occludes valuable insights available from other synchronic dimensions pertinent to human development. Thus, Bushnell neglected to give serious consideration to broader sociological and economic aspects of nurture. He failed to consider that the affluent Victorian parents of New England he sought to counsel in Christian nurture were formed and being formed in a complex social-cultural matrix of industrialism and its consequent affluence. This myopia allowed Bushnell to develop a theology of affluence that would facilitate the cultivation of a spirit of prosperity, progress and growth that would, in the twentieth century, evolve into a spirit of democratic capitalism.[96]

The second weakness of Bushnell's exclusive focus on parents relates to the first. Bushnell failed to consider that parents, even the most holy ones, are formed within particular fallen social, cultural and economic matrices of life. Thus, parents bring to their parenting, both consciously and unconsciously, an entire set of culturally formed beliefs, habits and traditions that affect their relationships with their children. Like all humans, parents are products of a fallen world.[97] Pursuant to Bushnell's advice, the fallen souls of parents are to become implanted upon the souls of their children. However, with such formative implantation comes the parents' own fallen social and cultural formation. Bushnell's *Christian Nurture* did not help the Christian parents of his generation see the

96. The definitive neoliberal history of this evolution is found in Novak, "The Ideal of Democratic Capitalism," in *Spirit*, 31–186.

97. This raises the issue of ecclesiology as well. Not only are evangelical parents, children and families formed in a fallen world of neoliberal democratic capitalism, so are evangelical churches. Edwards and Bushnell alike fail to develop the role that the church plays in Christian nurture. Evangelical ecclesiology is routinely critiqued as deficient in modern theology in comparison to its individualism and familism. Evangelical individualism is explored more fully in chapter 4's evangelical sociology of the AAEC and a possible outline for an evangelical ecclesiology of the AAEC is sketched in chapter 6. On individualism, privatization and child-rearing in the U.S., see Wall, "Let the Children Come," 64–87.

diachronic and synchronic dimensions of *their* formation in the young republic of the United States. This is probably due to the fact that Bushnell himself was not self-aware of his own formation within that context. His theological engagement of social and economic issues was insufficiently self-critical and hence uncritical of the nineteenth-century New England and broader American-industrial context in which children and parent alike were formed.

Instead of countering inroads of idolatry into the family, *Christian Nurture* opened the American family to the idolatry of affluence. Like so many good things, the good of affluence can easily transform into an impoverishing idolatry. The human longing for economic security and plenitude is universal. Desires for sufficient food, clean water, good health, long life, meaningful work and even luxurious leisure are fundamental to human nature. These are all good things, or at least they can be. However, when those goods are available in abundance, which is the essence of affluence, the good of affluence can easily lead to a spiritual and moral poverty, or lack.[98] Idolatry always lurks near the spiritual-moral lack (poverty) that affluence can bring, as liberation and other theologians have helped contemporary theology see.[99]

To be fair to Bushnell, however, it must be noted that before the twentieth-century theologians generally were critically unaware of the multiple dimensions affecting formation of the human person. Advances in scientific understanding of the human during the twentieth century forced theology to reconsider many of its orthodox presuppositions and theoretical formulations. Bushnell simply could not have imagined the scientific and technological advances of late modernity. With the help of feminist and liberation theologies during the twentieth century, European and North American theologians began to realize how their theologizing unconsciously reflected the presuppositions inherent to their particular cultural, social and economic formation. Thus, inasmuch as Bushnell was formed as a child and adult within the cultural, social and economic matrices of the industrial revolution in the nineteenth century, care should

---

98. It is interesting to note that Mark uses the same root word to describe the rich man's "lack" (poverty), despite his abundant possessions, and the poor widow's "poverty" (lack) out of which she gave more than the affluent who gave out of their "abundance" (cf. Mark 10:21 and 12:44).

99. See, e.g., Richard, et al., *Idols of Death*, and Goudzwaard, *Idols of Our Time*.

be taken not to censor him too harshly for the Victorian parental myopia that characterizes his theology of nurture.

Nevertheless, Bushnell's theologies of nurture and affluence were grounded in presuppositions of progress and growth that came to dominate American cultural, social and economic thought in the nineteenth and twentieth centuries. This will be demonstrated below in the critical analysis of Bushnell's theology of nurture in light of his theology of prosperity. Bushnell's regenerative "organic laws" of the family were easily subverted to serve the interests of the industrial consumer culture that emerged after the Civil War and was transformed into the technological consumer culture of affluence in the latter half of the twentieth century. Bushnell did not leave room for sufficient critical reflection upon parents and children formed within such a context. Although his insights were profound and were echoed subsequently by developmental psychology, they were insufficient because they did not entail critical assessment of the formative cultural, social and economic dimensions in which the child and the child's family were embedded.

Bushnell's Theologies of Nurture and Prosperity[100]

As we have seen, Bushnell believed the souls of children were formed through organic parental nurture. By "organic" Bushnell meant the nurturing parental matrices of life, particularly the mother. This belief was premised upon the presupposition that God constructed nature with the supernatural embedded within it, which led inevitably either to positive or negative growth and progress, depending upon the parental input. The supernatural provided the germ from which regenerating organic growth would result in a child growing up a Christian and never knowing himself to be otherwise.

Bushnell's conception was distinctly christological and pneumatological. Embedded in the parental soul and in the child as well, Christ by the Spirit (the supernatural) brought progressive regenerating growth through the organic union between parents and child if the parental nurture was good, true and beautiful. If not, then the hope of the child growing up a Christian was probably lost.[101]

100. It should be noted that Bushnell's use of the term "prosperity" is seen as roughly synonymous with "affluence" in the discussion that follows.

101. Bushnell apparently never worked through the issue of nurture for children born

For Bushnell, mothers are the critically important link in the process of forming children's souls for godliness. Mothers can either nurture faith developmentally or follow the ostrich nurture approach of Edwardsian conversionism: "The ostrich . . . is nature's type of all unmotherhood."[102] She simply lays her eggs in the sand and lets the sun incubate them. She heartlessly abandons them and senselessly leaves their nurture to the vicissitudes of nature. This, Bushnell claimed, was the heartlessness and senselessness of the conversionist evangelical anthropology found in the revivalism and ecclesiology of his day.[103] Children were viewed as sinners with bodies housing depraved souls in need of conversion and nothing else. They were told to obey and at the same time they were told that they could not obey unless truly converted. They were encouraged to love God, yet told they could not unless converted. Practically, then, children were excluded from full communion with God's saints and assigned a place in the borderlands between nature and grace.

According to Bushnell's representation, the evangelicals with whom he contended believed that unless God regenerates the hearts of children, there is neither hope nor need of nurture. Bushnell countered this belief and practice by arguing that the family's organic unity "was ordained originally for the nurture of holy virtue in the beginning of each soul's history; and that Christianity, or redemption, must of necessity take possession of the abused vehicle and sanctify it for its own merciful uses."[104] Christians are to "take possession of the organic laws of the family, and wield them as instruments . . . of a regenerative purpose" and to so "live in the Spirit" such that they "have the Spirit for the child as truly for themselves, and the child will be grown, so to speak, in the molds of the Spirit, even from his infancy."[105]

---

to non-Christians or to parents of whom only one was a Christian but its logic could be extended to such situations. Because he believed the feminine pole of the parental equation to be most important, the logic of his theology of nurture seems to be that a child could be nurtured well in a parental matrix composed of a positively Christian mother.

102. Bushnell, *Christian Nurture*, 52–73. Bushnell employed Lamentations 4:3 as the text for this chapter: "The daughter of my people is become cruel, like the ostriches in the wilderness." Ibid., 52.

103. This points to another myopic aspect of conversionist evangelical conceptions of nurture: its neglect of the Old Testament. As will be seen, Bushnell and more explicitly Richards began to recover Old Testament conceptions of nurturing faith in children that do not leave everything to conversion.

104. Bushnell, *Christian Nurture*, 91–92.

105. Ibid., 91, 203.

Bushnell placed a heavy load on mothers. The feminine bent to his theology of nurture reflected the Victorian presupposition of domesticity,[106] which was being formed as a result of the industrial revolution's bifurcation of male and female spheres of work. Men were the breadwinners working outside the home and mothers were the managers and nurturers of faith and life in the home. In fact, according to Bushnell motherhood is a:

> semi-divine. . . . work on the impressional and plastic age of a soul. . . . wrought in by the grace of the Spirit, the minuteness of its care, its gentleness, its patience, its almost divine faithfulness, are prepared for the shaping of a soul's immortality. And to make the work a sure one, the intrusted [sic] soul is allowed to have no will as yet of its own, that this motherhood may more certainly plant the angel in the man, unites him to all heavenly goodness by predispositions from itself, before he is united, as he will be, by choices of his own. Nothing but this explains and measures the wonderful proportions of maternity.[107]

Margaret Bendroth justly notes that placing this much responsibility on mothers for the successful Christian nurture of their children is "almost heartless" and cruel.[108] At the same, however, she fails to note that Bushnell elevated the significance of motherhood and to a very great extent esteemed mothers in a commendable way. He acknowledged the incredible worth and blessing of a godly mother. For Bushnell, the child before three years of age has a plastic soul with no will or volition of its own such that the mother is enabled to "plant the angel in the man."[109] Children's souls, in Bushnell's mind, seemed to be a kind of immaterial putty to be formed through the souls of parents, particularly mothers.

Bushnell's theological anthropology of the child discerned in his theology of nurture was developed in a complex cultural matrix composed of the evangelical-industrial merger, Victorian social ethics, common sense philosophy, liberal democratic individualism and republican civic virtue.[110] The souls of Christian mothers and fathers were formed within

---

106. See Ruether, *Christianity and Making of Modern Family*, 83–106; Bendroth, "Bushnell's *Christian Nurture*," 350–64.

107. Bushnell, *Christian Nurture*, 202.

108. Bendroth, "Bushnell's *Christian Nurture*," 358.

109. Bushnell, *Christian Nurture*, 202.

110. Noll, *America's God*, 53–92, 161–208 and 447–52; Ruether, *Christianity and*

that context, which in turn were impressed upon the souls of their children. Bushnell's primary blind spot was precisely at this point. Although he correctly discerned the formative influence parents can and should have on their children, he was critically unaware of the cultural dimensions that formed and were formed by both parent and child alike.

This is seen most clearly in Bushnell's theology of affluence. Bushnell should not be criticized harshly for unconsciously wedding his theology of nurture with his theology of affluence. He was not alone in his nineteenth-century theology of prosperity/affluence, as chapter 3 will further demonstrate. In fact, both Edwardsian conversionists and Bushnellian developmentalists of the nineteenth and twentieth centuries embraced the same presuppositions about prosperity. Evangelicals embedded in the economic, social and cultural revolutions brought by nineteenth-century industrialization welcomed the economic progress they brought and the hope they presented. It would not be until later in the twentieth century that evangelical theologians such as Ron Sider would begin to question the good of affluence and become ambivalent about its virtues.

How did this come about? Robert Wauzzinski's thesis in *Between God and Gold* documents the historical and theological roots of American evangelicalism's merger with industrialism at the level of ultimate, or religious commitments.[111] It presents a persuasive case that American evangelicalism was "mammonized" in the nineteenth century. Wauzzinski's thesis provides a way to link Bushnell's theologies of nurture and prosperity to this process of evangelical mammonization.

The year 1861 marks two significant events for the child in American evangelicalism. The first was publication of the final version of Bushnell's *Christian Nurture*, and the second was the Civil War. Bushnell's book and the Civil War are the hinges upon which the door of understanding the AAEC's theological anthropology in late modern affluence turns. The Civil War marks an important turning point in American social, economic, religious, political and cultural history. The events leading up to and coalescing after that war would eventually lead to the emergence of the technological consumer culture of the twentieth century. Understanding the

---

Making of Modern Family, 83–106; Bendroth, "Bushnell's *Christian Nurture*," 350–64; and Edwards, "God and Good Mother," 111–37. This latter essay by Mark Edwards provides a critical hinge for analysis of Bushnell's theology of nurture in light of his theology of prosperity/affluence.

111. Wauzzinski, *Between God and Gold*.

correlations between the Civil War and Bushnell's theologies of affluence and nurture is crucial for seeing how the AAEC evolved and emerged in the second half of the twentieth century.

The United States is the global leader in mass "conspicuous consumption"[112] and the technological innovations that sustain it.[113] For the past century, it has been the most zealous advocate and exporter of free market capitalism and the liberal democratic institutions that support it. These economic and political manifestations are grounded in a unique American philosophical anthropology of liberty and equality purportedly designed to guaranty the right to pursue happiness. American evangelicals and their children are embedded within that culture and the society it produces.

The remainder of this chapter will demonstrate the link between Bushnell and this socio-cultural reality. A "thick description"[114] of evangelical enculturation from the industrial revolution to the present will be developed. The goal is to avoid overinterpretation and underinterpretation, a problem inherent in anthropological and theological-anthropological analysis alike.[115] This kind of description is essential if the AAEC's late modern nurture in evangelical affluence is to be properly understood.

The AAEC and Evangelical-Industrial "presupposita"

Wauzzinski's work falls within the "God and Mammon" genre of modern literature,[116] as well as the critical literature on capitalism begun by Max Weber[117] and developed by R. H. Tawney.[118] The primary focus of this lit-

112. Phrase coined by Thorstein Veblen in *Theory of the Leisure Class*.

113. See D'Souza, *Virtue of Prosperity*, 8–10.

114. Geertz, "Thick Description," in *Interpretation of Cultures*, 3–30.

115. The interpretation of cultures entails concern for and attention to "webs of meaning," "thick description," and "deep play," "the confusion of tongues," and "the said of social discourse," and in the last and first analyses is "an attempt to come to terms with the diversity of the ways human beings construct their lives in the act of leading them. . . . the trick is to steer between . . . overinterpretation and underinterpretation, reading more into things than reason permits and less into them than it demands." Geertz, *Local Knowledge*, ix, 16.

116. See, e.g., Hobson, *God and Mammon*; Wuthnow, *God and Mammon in America*; Noll (ed.), *God and Mammon: Protestants, Money, and the Market*; Eskridge and Noll (eds.), *More Money, More Ministry*; Jelen, *To Serve God and Mammon*.

117. Weber, *Protestant Ethic*.

118. Tawney, *Religion and Rise of Capitalism*.

erature is critical assessment of the relationship between economics and religion, most notably the Christian religion.

Wauzzinski's work is unique because it focuses exclusively on American industrialism and evangelicalism from 1814 to 1914. His thesis is that both industrialism and evangelicalism in nineteenth-century America were grounded in, and thus operated from, a shared set of religious "presupposita," which he defines as ultimate commitments or concerns.[119] These concerns shape, guide and direct the culture arising from the prevailing worldview and the synchronic relations generated by those commitments, along with their concomitant formative practices, habits, disciplines, codes, technologies, knowledge, etc. He chooses the term "presupposita" over "presupposition" because in his opinion the Kantian root of the latter word "implies a logical foundation and thus begs the question of origin and mooring. Presuppositions are founded upon more ultimate presupposita."[120]

Wauzzinski claims that the religious commitments of progress and growth were shared by industrial and evangelical worldviews. These merged to create a unique American industrial-capitalist cultural religion. In his view, this religion perverted and therefore misrepresents the evangelical tradition traced from Augustine through Aquinas, Luther and Calvin.

After defining how he uses the term "religion," Wauzzinski proceeds to set out how "The Evangelical-Industrial Worldview" came about. From there, he describes "American Industrialism" in greater detail in a discussion of the three economic essentials of land, labor and capital/money/wealth. This demonstrates how both the merged evangelical-industrial and the industrial-capitalist worldviews clash with his four "Classical Christian Theorists": Augustine, Aquinas, Luther and Calvin. In his next chapter, Wauzzinski seeks to demonstrate the British-American capitalist genealogy in preparation for his sixth chapter's critical nineteenth-century evangelical case studies of Charles Finney (leading revivalist of America's

---

119. Wauzzinski describes "presupposita" variously as "ultimate presuppositions," "fundamental assumptions" and "fundamental presuppositions" that are "religiously rather than logically rooted" and tied to an "ultimate concern [that] is the bedrock of basic commitment and the foundation of various presupposita." Wauzzinski, *Between God and Gold*, 32.

120. Wauzzinski, *Between God and Gold*, 227 n. 22.

Second Great Awakening), Francis Wayland (leading intellectual scholar/ evangelist), and Russell Conwell (leading postbellum pastor).

The second chapter of *Between God and Gold* forms the heart of Wauzzinski's argument. It is most relevant to the present work because it helps corroborate my claim that Bushnell's theology of affluence reflected agreement with other positive evangelical assessments of the "presupposita" of progress and growth that grounded industrial capitalism. Wauzzinski presents a convincing case that nineteenth-century evangelical theology and culture aided, abetted and abided the industrial-capitalist merger of American religion in the nineteenth century.

The final version of *Christian Nurture* appeared around the same time the Civil War got underway. Wauzzinski's analysis of the events leading up to the Civil War from 1820 to 1860 provides a salient cultural perspective of the economic context in which Horace Bushnell's theologies of nurture and prosperity developed from 1847 to 1861.

Bushnell and the Evangelical-Industrial "presuppositum" of Progress

In 1847, the same year the first edition of *Christian Nurture* appeared, Bushnell preached a sermon titled "Prosperity Our Duty," in which his ideals of organic nurture were fused with predominant social ideals of prosperity and progress lying at the heart of the emerging market economy of his day.[121] He took the Protestant work ethic and gave it an ontological basis by fusing public virtue and character in a vision of prosperity. As he saw it, God has interwoven prosperity and virtue into human nature. It simply needs to be nurtured in accordance with Christian truth. God delights in rewarding labor with prosperity on the basis of godly character and public virtue. A man was not a true, responsible man if he did not consider it his duty to pursue prosperity. Consequently, a community was not a true, responsible religious community if it did not esteem and promote economic growth. God blesses creativity, hard work and self-discipline, favoring industry and making ample provision to reward it.

Mark Edwards summarizes the evidence for Bushnell's prosperity theology as follows: "Bushnell wanted capitalist progress to join hands with Christian/republican social morality, but those who daily engaged the competitive marketplace heard him sanctioning their pursuit of

---

121. Bushnell, *Spirit in Man*, 137–45; Cross, *Horace Bushnell*, 44–51.

economic self-interest. He was, to them, the theologian for a producer culture."[122] Thus, Bushnell provided a theological basis for evangelical entry into capitalist consumer culture. The child was embedded within this context. Applying Bushnell's prosperity theology, nineteenth-century evangelicals would help transform American culture into one that democratized equal rights to desire the good life and to be free in the pursuit of happiness in life, liberty and things. To varying degrees, American evangelicals have always embraced that ideal.

William Leach argues that, "American religious institutions [of the nineteenth century], and the spiritual culture transmitted by them, were transformed by the new mass economy and culture and aided in their creation."[123] Bushnell and other nineteenth-century evangelicals such as those critiqued by Wauzzinski laid the groundwork for a theological anthropology of children fit for such an economy and culture. Wauzzinski argues that one of the controlling pre-understandings of the industrial revolution in America was economic and social Darwinism. John Fiske and Edward Youmans applied the evolutionary worldviews of Herbert Spencer, Thomas Malthus and Charles Darwin in Deistic terms to economic theory through "the notion of 'progress,' as it applied to society and economic practice."[124] William Sumner sought to ground economic theory as a social science through natural law and the application of the scientific method to social scientific study.[125]

Theology was simply irrelevant to such an enterprise. The result was that "the goal of economic evolution was an environment of freedom that allowed the sovereign individual to bind and loose as determined. The central virtues of work, temperance, thrift/savings, industry, and self-denial were canonized by this form of capitalism. The good life (or happiness) was believed to come about through economic gain."[126] Thus, Sumner provided a "scientific" economic basis for what America's Declaration of Independence had established several decades earlier. The thought of John Locke and Adam Smith factor heavily into his progres-

---

122. Edwards, "God and Good Mother," 123.

123. Leach, *Land of Desire*, 10.

124. Wauzzinski, *Between God and Gold*, 39.

125. Ibid., 40.

126. Ibid., 40–41.

sive capitalist vision, just as they did for Jefferson and other founding American fathers.[127]

America's version of the "Promethean myth of individualistic self-reliance"[128] arose out of this context. By 1830, industrial and religious virtues of self-discipline and work became fused in a "syncretistic self-understanding of Evangelicalism and Industrialism," as evidenced by Calvin Cotton, "Protestant apologist and Whig advocate" who joined the chorus of preachers supporting the "economic and socially mobile gospel" of success and progress of the day.[129] Cotton believed that the greatest accolade of American society was that it was one in which "men start from humble origin and . . . rise gradually in the world as a reward of merit and industry and . . . can acquire a large amount of wealth . . . Within one's soul lies the capital, the productive power with which to trade."[130] This, according to Wauzzinski, was the extent of evangelical economic critique of industrial culture in antebellum America.

The religious-industrial mood during this period was optimistic. Evangelicals were aglow at this time with the promise of industrial-religious culture and its attendant Victorian domesticity in which Christian nurture was to take place.[131] This is the nineteenth-century economic and social context in which evangelical children were born and nurtured. It has remained unchallenged within American evangelicalism over the past one hundred years. To my knowledge, this thesis is the first work to identify and critique it theologically with the AAEC in view.

Bushnell, Progress, and Forming Children for Affluence

Wauzzinski's analysis is corroborated by Bushnell's *Building Eras in Religion* (1881) and Mayo's article, "The New Education—The Christian Education" (1899).

Bushnell argued during the postbellum era for the Christian use of wealth in the American expansion of the kingdom of God on earth. He

127. Ibid., 41.

128. Wauzzinski, *Between God and Gold*, 43.

129. Ibid., 43. Bushnell also embraced Whig moral and political philosophy. Howe, *Political Culture*, 299–300.

130. Ibid. (endnotes 27 and 28 omitted). Cotton's view of "soul capital" reappears in neoliberal form in Novak and Schneider, as chapter 5 shows.

131. Cf. the critique of this family form and its late modern corollaries as idolatry in Fishburn, *Idolatry of Family*, 39–50.

believed that revival would come once Christians in the United States con-
secrated "the money power of the world" unequivocally to the advance of
the kingdom of God: "One more revival—only one more—is needed, the
revival of Christian stewardship, the consecration of the money power to
God. When the revival comes, the Kingdom of God will come in a day."[132]
Bushnell did not realize that with consecration of the money power to
God came consecration of American-evangelical children to the money
power. This is one of the inevitable results, it seems, of the interface between God and mammon.

Bushnell, however, knew the Scriptures well enough to understand
the dangers of affluence. Nevertheless, he was unsuccessful in avoiding
them. According to Mark Edwards, "The social power of the new wealth
that Bushnell had always feared increased manifold with the unregu-
lated expansion of industrial and finance capitalism after 1865 . . . When
Bushnell tried to confront these socio-economic changes directly, he could
do so only with characteristic ambivalence."[133] He believed that Christian
wealth could advance Christian faith in a great, new era of "building religion" in the United States.[134] This wealth would lead to the expansion of
Christianity in America that would spread to a "world-brotherhood" of
Christian faith.[135] Bushnell did not realize that in the process mammon
could, and very likely would, ultimately trump God.

Bushnell assumed economic progress was essential to the advance
of the gospel. He also assumed that Christian nurture must progress to
advance the gospel as well. Although he never linked the two, it was clear
that economic progress was necessary to fund the "out-populating power
of the Christian stock" through nurture, such that "piety itself shall finally
over-populate the world."[136] Bushnell believed that God had ordained
"laws of population" or "principal modes" by which he establishes his
kingdom on earth: one is conversion and the other is "family propagation."[137] The better way to build God's kingdom was through the law of
propagation rather than the law of conversion, or what he called the law

132. Bushnell, *Building Eras*, 26.

133. Edwards, "God and Good Mother," 130.

134. Bushnell, *Building Eras*, 20–21.

135. Ibid., 26.

136. Bushnell, *Christian Nurture*, xiii, 165.

137. Ibid., 165–66.

of "conquest."[138] The presupposition of growth underlying and uniting his theologies of nurture and affluence can be seen clearly at this point:

> The idea of conquest displaces the idea of growth. Whereas, if it were understood that Christian education or training in the families, is to be itself a process of domestic conversion; that as a child weeps under a frown and smiles at the command of a smile, so spiritual influences may be streaming into his being from the handling of the nursery and the whole manner and temperament of the house, producing what will ever after be fundamental impressions of his being; then the hearth, the table, the society and affections of the house, would all feel the presence of a practical religious motive. The homes would be Christian, the families abodes of piety.[139]

Bushnell argued that revivalism's form of conquest conversion was contrary to true missionary work. To make his point, he drew upon a metaphor from commerce to make his case for the progressive Christian nurture of children. The "true missionary spirit" nurtured in children "would flow as a river," Bushnell contended, "if the church were unfolding the riches of the covenant at her firesides and tables; if the children were identified with religion from the first, and grew up in a Christian love of man."[140] The Christian family as domestic church that embraces the revivalistic "habit of conquest" is like a country that forgets its "own internal resources . . . forsaking the loom and the plow, and all the regular growths of industry," pursuing "prize-money and plunder" across the oceans of the world rather than locally.[141] Christian nurture, then, entails a process of growth and progress essentially the same as nurture of industry in the homeland.

Bushnell, however, was not a base capitalist concerned with profit in disregard of religious ends. He believed in discipline, virtue and character as essential to godly prosperity. He condemned post-Civil War profiteers whom he likened to parasitical plants, men who plundered the misfortune of others and adroitly exploited circumstances to their own greedy

138. Ibid., 187.

139. Ibid.

140. Ibid.

141. Ibid.

ends.[142] This is why the world's money capital must be Christianized. It is essential to advancing the gospel of God's kingdom.

Nevertheless, Bushnell's gospel was, as aptly described by Mark Edwards, "the late Victorian gospel of wealth—a potent symbol of market capitalist triumph."[143] Faith and affluence were compatible in Bushnell's mind, and he hoped that evangelical businessmen would "voluntarily consecrate the rewards of industrial capitalism to the work of the kingdom,"[144] with "trade expanding into commerce, and commerce rising into communion."[145] The child in American evangelicalism was to be formed within this Christianized economic vision.

Bushnell's theological anthropology of children and economics, grounded as they were in spheres of Victorian domesticity and organic laws of nurture, thus developed within the cultural milieu of republican individualism and free market capitalism. Bushnell contributed to the development of a gendered theological anthropology of children in which mothers were the primary nurturers in the home while fathers were economic producers outside the home. Mark Edwards argues that Bushnell locked "efficacious grace in the province of mothers and wives" and "positively encouraged the pursuit of profit as a religious responsibility. His portrait of ideal masculinity after the war was thus less suited to moral progress than imperial acquisition."[146]

Bushnell's theologies of nurture and affluence reflected the post-Civil War mood well. On one hand, there was cautious concern for virtuous character formed from birth for the purpose of advancing the kingdom of God by "Christianizing the money power" to God. On the other, there was an unabashed embrace of a theology of affluence exhorting Christians to pursue prosperity as a religious duty. This theology of nurture in affluence reflected republican and capitalist reasoning that can be found in various transmuted forms in American evangelicalism and theology today.

Technological consumer capitalism and the culture it produces has the mysterious ability to capitalize critique to its own ends, to abstract

142. Edwards, "God and Good Mother," 130, citing Bushnell, "Natural History of the Yaguey Family," 416–17.

143. Edwards, "God and Good Mother," 130.

144. Ibid.

145. Ibid., citing Bushnell, "How to Be a Christian in Trade," in *Sermons on Living Subjects*, 263–67.

146. Edwards, "God and Good Mother," 131.

critical ideas such as those found in Bushnell's conception of the organic Christian nurture of children from their contexts and practice. In the process, it subverts and converts them to the ends of the market.[147] In Bushnell's case, "we begin to recognize the theological and socioeconomic origins of a 'muscular Christianity'"[148] that serves the progressive and competitive interests that technological consumer capitalism stimulates for both good and evil in late modernity.

The warnings Jesus gave about faith and life in such a context come freshly to mind: "You cannot serve God and wealth." Remarkably, however, Bushnell and other nineteenth-century evangelical theologians thought it possible (or perhaps forgot it was impossible) to progress beyond these words. By 1952, the fruits of such evangelical progress would perplex some, as can been seen in the query of Lord Reith, founder of the British Broadcasting Corporation: "What I would like to know is how you Americans can successfully worship God and Mammon at the same time."[149]

Bushnell, Progress, and "The New Education"

Bushnell's theologies of nurture and prosperity legitimized an approach to spiritual and moral formation of children for the republic. This can be seen in an article titled "The New Education—The Christian Education," by A. D. Mayo in 1899, which developed this Bushnellian-evangelical type of synthesis of nurture and economics further.

As was seen above, Mayo equated the American education system with Christian education.[150] According to Wishy, Mayo's sentiments represented prevailing Protestant evangelical thought regarding child nurture at the turn of the nineteenth century. After eighteen centuries of civilization, Mayo believed, "the absolute religion of Jesus Christ . . . has won its greatest victory in the acceptance of *the new education* by the American people *as the last and best organization of the gospel of love for God and man,* for the training of American childhood and youth for sov-

---

147. Cf. Miller, *Consuming Religion*, 17–23; Bell, *Liberation Theology*, 9–41.

148. Edwards, "God and Good Mother," 131.

149. Question put to CBS executives quoted in Twitchell, *ADCULTusa*, viii.

150. Wishy, *Child and Republic*, 167 n. 37.

ereign American citizenship."[151] This evidenced a "Common Christianity of the American People" engaged in nurturing "the Gospel of the New Education" in American children.[152] The problem is that Mayo, like Bushnell, assumed that the economic foundations of this new education for "sovereign" citizenship served children's bests interests.

From Bushnell and Mayo in the nineteenth century to Lawrence Richards in the twentieth, evangelical educators have failed to question the economic presuppositions of their educational theology and practice. They have failed to consider how nurture in affluence affects evangelical pedagogy and practice. The accommodation of the gospel to American civil religion evidenced in Mayo's writings had powerful economic motivations fueled by industrialism and the emergence of a new culture in the United States spun around "fables of abundance" in a land of desire marked by the emerging triumph of materialism.[153]

Since 1950, the culture of affluence in the United States has produced a society of mass affluence that lives on a revolutionary informational-iconic plane with profoundly formative influences upon children. It is a culture fiber-optically connected to human senses in ways Edwards and Bushnell could never have dreamed. James Twitchell argues that we Americans "have not been led into this world of material closeness against our better judgment. For many of us, especially when young, consumerism *is* our better judgment. And this is true regardless of class or culture. We have not just asked to go this way, we have demanded it. Now most of the world is lining up, pushing and shoving, eager to elbow into the mall. Woe to the government or religion that says no."[154]

Versions of child nurture such as those seen in Bushnell and Mayo evolved in uncritical fashion within the cultural embrace of a nascent consumer capitalism emerging from nineteenth-century industrialism. Bushnell's formation within the economic revolution of that century undoubtedly shaped his views of nurture and economics. His theology of nurture played a central role in assuring that evangelical children would be nurtured in affluence. His hopes that successful, prosperous evangelicals would "consecrate the rewards of industrial capitalism to the work of

151. Ibid., 168 (emphasis added).
152. Ibid., citing Mayo, "Education," at 548–49.
153. Lears, *Fables of Abundance*, and "From Salvation to Self-Realization," 1–38.
154. Twitchell, *Lead Us into Temptation*, 268.

the kingdom"[155] may have been realized in late modern "market capitalism and economic individualism,"[156] but the question remains as to whether this has been good for the AAEC. Mark Edwards may understate things when he observes that the attempt Bushnell made "to synthesize past and present—Protestant/republican morality with capitalist socio-economics—would yield ambiguous fruits during and after his lifetime."[157] One of those ambiguous fruits, I suggest, is the ripening of the AAEC in the twenty-first century.

Lying at the intersection of Bushnell's theologies of nurture and prosperity is the anthropological presuppositum of progress and growth. As we will see in chapter 5, this pre-understanding of the goodness of economic growth is embedded in the neoliberal conception of human liberty. With its integration of nurture and prosperity in God's one integrated system of nature within the supernatural, Bushnellian developmentalism served the republic's need for morally disciplined children who could rationally choose to employ affluence for the advance of the kingdom. Through meritorious discipline, the capital that resides in the evangelical child's soul can produce great wealth, which in turn can be used to build God's kingdom.[158] The question remains as to which kingdom this discipline and capital ultimately served. Most evangelicals today decry the liberal theological turn of the late nineteenth and early twentieth centuries. But few, if any, have discerned the link between economic and theological liberalism during this period. In fact, it is surprising how many conservative, fundamentalist and evangelical Christians today simultaneously denounce theological liberalism and yet herald its economic cousin. Evangelicals today should, it seems to me, be careful lest they forget God once again in the midst of their affluence.

Wauzzinski's analysis sheds light on this claim and helps place Bushnell's *Christian Nurture* in its broader cultural context of the nineteenth-century Evangelical-Industrial merger of ultimate commitments to progress and growth. A new theological conception of free will lies at the heart of these presupposita, a view in which humanity is seen no longer as tainted with original sin expressed in theological terms of radical

155. Edwards, "God and Good Mother," 130.

156. Ibid., citing Watts, *Republic Reborn*, 44.

157. Edwards, "God and Good Mother," 112.

158. As will be seen in chapter 5, Schneider's theology of affluence is a late modern variant of Bushnell's theology of prosperity.

depravity.[159] The new view was much milder and therefore better suited to republican ideals of creative, risk-taking industry, republican virtue, and individual initiative and responsibility. Original sin and human depravity were recast as lost desire needing renovation in a manner consonant with these ideals. This new conception of human nature and sin harmonized well with Bushnell's theology of nurture, and it took little effort to adapt it to a theology of affluence suitable to the times.

According to Wauzzinski, nineteenth-century American evangelicalism saw the solution to human problems and social ills in the restoration of desire through resolve, "a quality in abundance in early America."[160] Individualistic free will blended nicely with individualistic free trade. Both industrialism and evangelical revivalism stressed unceasing, productive activity. "Private enterprise and public piety were fused in an era that easily confused enterprising inventors and pragmatically active revivalists. American revivalists, like their British counterparts, were busy attempting to sanctify individuals who would industrialize society."[161] Thus, the Christian and economic visions of the young republic had merged by the end of the nineteenth century.

From the standpoint of theological ethics, Wauzzinski argues that the two pillars of this merger were individualistic progress and voluntary social benevolence. Evangelical revivalism, to be sure, played an important role in the antebellum fights against slavery, poverty, unemployment, child labor and other social ills of the day. Many of these continued into the postbellum period and into the twentieth century as they were transformed into mainstream Protestant social gospel movements. But the perspective of a benevolent private market remained intact. According to Wauzzinski, the religious hope for a benevolent *public* market capitalism was sundered by Lincoln and his Republican party through a political compromise with Democrats that came on the eve of the Civil War, one that assured the marginalization of religion from politics to the private sphere of American domestic life. Both parties thus became aligned in an American vision of *private, voluntary* benevolence and liberal economic individualism.

---

159. For a full account of how views of original sin and human depravity changed in American theology during this period, see Smith, *Changing Conceptions*.

160. Wauzzinski, *Between God and Gold*, 45.

161. Ibid., 47.

This is when the republican vision of economic progress coupled with moral progress (i.e., public, governmentally sanctioned benevolence premised upon a "national Protestant morality"), held by Bushnell and others, vanished from American culture, society and politics.[162] Democrats argued that religion should be private, while Republicans desiring to eradicate slavery argued that legislation should "insure a national Protestant morality."[163] Democrats carried the day. The result for evangelicals and the rest of the American religious was the privatization of faith. Churches were assigned guardianship roles over "private morality and order" and public schools were assigned the task of developing "a public morality, or at least a conscience, that was nonsectarian, rational, and faithful to the dictates of economic progress."[164] It takes little effort to see how political realities have shaped our nation's public-private relationships.

The public forum was left open only to nonsectarian, rational and progressive economic disciplines. Within sixty years of the Civil War, the Scopes Monkey Trial would mark American evangelicalism's complete political, social and cultural displacement. The evangelicalism of the nineteenth century soon became the Fundamentalism of the twentieth, both of which helped bring about the new culture and society governed by the pursuit of happiness in affluence, but its theological voice was no longer welcome in the public sphere. It had been excluded from the boundaries of permissible political debate about human nature and social order. Both evangelical theology and evangelicalism were thus sidelined on such issues. The practical result was that Evangelicalism-Fundamentalism would wage private battles for theological, intellectual and socio-cultural legitimacy while simultaneously embracing the good life with their liberal adversaries and the anthropology of liberty lying at the heart of economic life in the United States.

CONCLUSION

This chapter has traced the theological anthropology of the evangelical child from Jonathan Edwards in the eighteenth century through Horace

162. Wauzzinski, *Between God and Gold*, 49. Both political parties pointed to the 1857 businessmen's revival on Wall Street as support for their respective positions. Wauzzinski, *Between God and Gold*, 48; see also Long, *Revival of 1857–58*, 68–92.

163. Wauzzinski, *Between God and Gold*, 49.

164. Ibid., 61; see also Marsden, *Fundamentalism and American Culture*, 91–93, 206–11.

Bushnell in the nineteenth. It has linked the conversionist anthropology of Edwards to the revivalist anthropology of the nineteenth century and has shown how Bushnell modified that anthropology into a developmentalist vision of Christian nurture. It has also shown how Bushnell's theologies of nurture and prosperity were grounded in an ultimate commitment to progress arising from his view of the supernatural as embedded in nature. Wauzzinski's analysis demonstrated how Bushnell's thought in this regard fitted within the Evangelical-Industrial merger of ultimate concerns in the nineteenth century.

We saw that Edwards held contradictory views regarding the theological anthropology of children. On one hand, *Religious Affections* portrays children as possessing by nature those affections that mark true believers. On the other, Edwards viewed children as damned vipers with whom God is angry every moment of every day and for whom the God's eternal wrath is justly reserved. He resolves this contradiction in a distinctly conversionist fashion, which led in the nineteenth century to an overemphasis on the cognitive aspect of the child's relationship to God. The practical effect of this is to regard the child as suspended somewhere between nature and grace before conversion. The status of the child in relation to God, then, can only be tested by cognitive means, such as a profession of faith and manifestation of truly religious affections. Hence, a conversionist theological anthropology of the child may lead to cognitive idolatry and subjective, indeterminate assessments of the relationship between God and children, leaving the child in a kind of relational spiritual limbo with their parents and churches.

Bushnell called Edwards's conversionist theological anthropology a cruel "ostrich nurture" and modified it to argue for a progressive process of conversion that, if done with the right spirit in the home, would be virtually imperceptible. The child should grow up as a Christian and never know otherwise. Among other things, Bushnell's theology of nurture is deemed deficient by conversionists because of its inadequate doctrine of sin. A child who grows up never knowing himself to be anything other than a Christian may run the risk of never knowing himself to be a sinner. Without such knowledge, conversionists contend, a child may never comprehend what it means to be a Christian, since she will never come to the knowledge of salvation by the forgiveness of her sins (Luke 1:77).

Despite this deficiency, Bushnell's *Christian Nurture* was prescient in many respects and served the interests of children well. Its theology of nurture points to the critical importance of attending to the earlier years of life and also to the importance of the right kind of home in which spiritual and moral nurture should take place. Bushnell thus provided a formative influence upon Protestant religious education and opened a new way for understanding the child's relationship to God and others.

At the same time, Bushnell's theologies of nurture and prosperity/affluence rendered a disservice to the child nurtured in nineteenth-century evangelicalism by laying the groundwork for the child's incorporation into industrial capitalism. Bushnell set the stage for evangelical parents and educators to focus attention upon nurture while at the same neglecting to consider the formative effects of affluence. As the next chapter shows, this set the stage for the AAEC's emergence in the twentieth century.

Thus, Bushnell's theology of nurture contained both good news and bad news for the child in American evangelicalism. The good news is that it helped overcome some of the contradictions of the dominant conversionist theological anthropology of the child inherited from Edwards. But the bad news is that his theology of nurture was co-opted by his theology of affluence. Consequently, both theologies played into the hands of nineteenth-century industrial capitalism and twentieth-century technological consumer capitalism. Rather than being formed for evangelical faith and practice, what we witness in the twentieth century is a simultaneous formation of parent and child alike by and for two kingdoms, God and mammon.

To sum up, the theological anthropologies of the child in Edwards and Bushnell point to an important lesson for evangelical nurture: the AAEC should be called to convert and develop, and to develop and convert, while at all times remaining wary of the perils posed by affluence to formation in the way of the cross, the way of God's reign on earth as it is in heaven.

3

Born in the U.S.A.: Lawrence Richards
and the AAEC in Evangelical Affluence

> . . . not long after 1820, prosperity began flowing in an ever-increasing torrent; with each successive generation, the life of the son became observably more comfortable, informed, and predictable than that of the father.

—WILLIAM J. BERNSTEIN[1]

INTRODUCTION: LAWRENCE RICHARDS AND THE AAEC

Over the past two centuries, evangelical theology has tended to neglect the impact prosperity has had upon human nature. Evangelical anthropology generally has failed to account for the constitutive economic dimension of human being and sociality in the context of affluence. The formative effects of affluence upon human nature are so far-reaching that contemporary theology cannot make sense without critical awareness of that dimension of late modern life.

This chapter examines the theological anthropology of the child found in the writings of evangelical theologian, educator, and author Lawrence Richards (1931–) in the context of twentieth-century evangelical affluence. His writings are critiqued theologically with a view to tracing his Edwardsian and Bushnellian heritage and placing them in the context of American-evangelical affluence. The chapter completes the theological-critical history of the AAEC's evolution and emergence in evangelical affluence in the United States. To my knowledge, it is the first theological-critical interpretation of Richards in relationship to Edwards

---

1. Bernstein, *Birth of Plenty*, 4.

and Bushnell through the lens of affluence and the theological anthropology of the child in American evangelicalism.[2]

Richards is the most prolific evangelical educator in the twentieth-
century and regarded as evangelicalism's most influential theologian,
theorist and practitioner of Christian education.[3] Further, he viewed and
therefore approached Christian education as a biblical-theological discipline. His theological method, pedagogy and philosophy of Christian education are distinctively evangelical, conservative and American. Richards
contended that theological nurture and pedagogy must engage the social
sciences of developmental psychology and sociology, which he then biblically appropriates to develop an evangelical ecclesiology for the nurture
of children. He argues for a socialization model of Christian nurture in
which the family and church are central to formation. He also emphasizes
the importance of considering the relational dimension of nurture. These
aspects of the theology of nurture developed by Richards provide an ideal
theological-critical interface for the contemporary theology of the AAEC
presented in this work.

Richards's theological anthropology of the child can be ascertained
from three of his works: *Youth Ministry: Its Renewal in the Church* (1972),
A Theology of Christian Education (1975),[4] and *A Theology of Children's
Ministry* (1983).[5] Richards believes the Bible is authoritative on the traditional issues addressed in Christian theological anthropology—the
doctrines of human nature, sin and the image of God, among others. He
starts and ends with the Bible, interpreted principally through an evangelical-dispensational hermeneutic, for answering questions concerning
theological anthropology. Thus, he is an appropriate representative of an
evangelical anthropology of the child in late modernity.

2. My research has uncovered one dissertation that critiques Bushnell's and Richards's
respective theories of nurture. Downs, "Christian Nurture." It does not, however, critique
Bushnell and Richards in light of affluence, examine their writings for the theological
anthropology of the child, or evaluate their theologies of nurture in light of the history,
sociology or theology of Evangelicalism in the United States.

3. Benson, "Evangelical Philosophies of Religious Education," in Taylor, ed., *Changing
Patterns*, 64. See also Sell, "Richards," 95–105. Richards has authored "some 200 works,
some of which have been translated into 24 languages"; no other evangelical author has
so voluminously and comprehensively covered "Christian education theory and practice." Ibid., 97, 99.

4. Re-titled as *Christian Education: Seeking to Become Like Jesus Christ.*

5. Re-titled as *Children's Ministry: Nurturing Faith Within the Family of God.*

Richards holds simultaneously to an Edwardsian conversionism and Bushnellian developmentalism, with the Bushnellian component exercising marginal control in the conversion-development polarity. He does not clarify how these twin dimensions of theological anthropology correlate. Richards is more Edwardsian than Bushnellian in his view of the Bible, in the sense that he is much less prone to speculate regarding the God-humanity relation than Bushnell was, and he is much more likely to speak in biblical certainties regarding the divine-human relation, as Edwards was. At the same time, his relational emphasis on family nurture and appropriation of developmental psychology and sociology for Christian education are decidedly Bushnellian.

Although he argues for the importance of understanding processes of socialization in nurture, Richards does not consider how American affluence forms the processes of development and socialization as well as the persons within the social networks of children's lives. Richards, like Bushnell and Edwards before him, fails to consider the enculturating and socializing effects that affluence has upon the formation of children. All this will be shown in due course.

However, in order for these claims to be established, it is necessary to begin where chapter 2 ended and bring the story of evangelical embeddedness within American affluence forward from Bushnell to Richards. That story continues with the role Herbert Hoover (1874–1964) played during the 1920s and 1930s in helping to lay the economic foundations for the political and cultural establishment of technological consumer capitalism in the United States. From there, it proceeds with a critical analysis of Richards's theological anthropology of the child.

HERBERT HOOVER AND THE EVOLUTION OF THE AAEC[6]

> We hold these Truths to be self-evident, that all Men are created equal . . . endowed by their Creator with certain unalienable Rights, that among these are Life, Liberty, and the Pursuit of Happiness —That to secure these Rights, Governments are instituted among Men, deriving their just Powers from the consent of the Governed

---

6. I wish to acknowledge my indebtedness in this section to Leach, "Herbert Hoover's Emerald City and Managerial Government," in *Land of Desire*, 349–78.

... as to them shall seem most likely to effect their Safety and Happiness ...[7]

These words from the Declaration of Independence are grounded in an anthropology of liberty, or conception of human freedom, we Americans take for granted. It casts a vision of life and freedom, safety and happiness inextricably bound to economic concerns.[8] The government's security of rights to "Life, Liberty, and the Pursuit of Happiness" in late modernity helps produce a problematic cultural and social context of affluence that shapes Christian nurture of children in profound ways.

When the American revolutionaries set forth their reasons for dissolving "the Political Bands" that had connected them to England in the seventeenth and eighteenth centuries so they could "assume among the Powers of the Earth, the separate and equal Station to which the Laws of Nature and of Nature's God entitle them,"[9] economic interests predominated the list of accumulated grievances against the British Crown. They grounded their anthropology of freedom in a form of the Christian doctrine of creation harmonious with classical economic theory's conception of human nature. Unbeknownst to them, they set the course for theological economics in the United States that would eventually culminate in neoliberal theologies of economics like those developed by Michael Novak and John Schneider. As chapter 5 will show, what few evangelicals realize is that this conception of liberty is dubiously biblical and increasingly being contested in contemporary theology. What they further fail to realize is that this conception of freedom as essential to human flourishing may be placing the AAEC at risk of malformation for technological consumer capitalism rather than discipleship in the way of Jesus and the cross.

To see this, it is necessary to have a clear picture of the AAEC's historical context. That history in the twentieth century begins with Herbert Hoover's public service as secretary of commerce and thirty-first President of the United States from 1920 to 1933. Over eighty years ago, Hoover began a process of leading the U.S. government into a partnership with American commercial interests that would ensconce economists as

---

7. *Declaration of Independence*, 9.

8. Cf. the economic interpretations of the U. S. Constitution in Beard, *Economic Interpretation of Constitution*, and McGuire, *More Perfect Union*.

9. *Declaration of Independence*, 9.

chief interpreters and arbiters of human well-being in late modernity. To draw upon a religious analogy, economists serve a function today similar to priests in ancient Israel. Just as priests managed God's house (Greek *oikos*, from which we derive "economy") and the collective life of God's people in partnership with the political monarchy, so economists manage the American "house" and the collective life of the American people in partnership with the political triumvirate of executive, legislative and judicial branches.

In a sense, then, economics is the discipline administered by the modern priests of American life, the economists. All other modern priesthoods—law, psychology, the media, and sociology, to mention a few—ultimately serve the economic priesthood. Hoover was the first Secretary of Commerce to enlist economists in the task of setting the American economy on its current course of diffusing production into consumption. As a sincere and energetic advocate for children's rights and welfare, Hoover also set the economic course for nurturing American children in the pursuit of happiness. His work as a public servant tilled the soil and planted the seeds from which the AAEC would eventually sprout after Word War II.

Hoover was raised in a rural Society of Friends (Quaker) home in West Branch, Iowa, a small agricultural town in America's midwestern heartland.[10] His father was a blacksmith, inventor, and local town politician. Although orphaned by the age of ten, Hoover's mother had nurtured a deep respect for the Bible and strong ethical convictions grounded in a Christian worldview. Throughout his life Hoover saw the Bible as the "Book of Books, a postgraduate course in the richest library of human experience."[11] He also sought to apply biblical principles of ethics, stewardship and humanitarian concern in his personal and public lives, which can be seen particularly in his life-long advocacy for children's rights.

At the same time, Hoover was formed by the American tradition of republican individualism and competition so essential to the presupposition of economic progress, growth and prosperity that defines the United States. This can be seen most clearly in his book, *American Individualism*, which was published in 1922. Throughout his life, it seems, he would at-

10. For biographical data on Hoover, see Nash, *Hoover I* and *Hoover II*; and http://www.hoover.archives.gov/ index.html.

11. Hoover, "Message to the National Federation of Men's Bible Classes," on 5 May 1929, in *Public Papers*, 136.

tempt to reconcile, or at least hold in harmonious tension, the Quaker and republican traditions in which he was nurtured. An objective examination of Hoover's public life, however, leads reasonably to the conclusion that the republican tradition of individualism and laissez-faire capitalism came to dominate Hoover's formation both as private citizen and public servant.

By 1930, Hoover developed a partnership between American government, politics, and commerce that continues to this day. He believed that future American prosperity depended upon effective governmental service of large corporations through a variety of means, such as providing critical economic data for domestic production-consumption and representing American business interests internationally. His work in the U.S. Commerce Department helped complete the mammonization of evangelicalism in the United States that began on the eve of the Civil War, as Wauzzinski's work shows. The rest of the twentieth century is, among other things, the history of how mass affluence was diffused throughout the American population. As Leach has demonstrated in *Land of Desire*, Hoover must be credited with a critical role in making this possible. Technique and consumption lie at the heart of the revolution of mass affluence in the United States, and Hoover was one of its principal brokers. Subsequent presidents, from FDR to Clinton and Bush II, would carry his agenda further.

Hoover was appointed as secretary of commerce under President Warren G. Harding, from 1921–1923, and served in that capacity under the presidency of Calvin Coolidge from 1923–1928. During this time, Hoover transformed the U.S. government into a master servant of commerce,[12] and from 1929 to 1933 during his term as thirty-first President of the United States, he solidified this transformation. Every president has inherited the legacy of this transformation, and although presidents may have modified or expanded governmental-commercial relations since, none has sought to dismantle the foundations laid by Hoover.

Two things are intended by the phrase "master servant." First, from 1920 to 1929 the U.S. government took on the role of serving and stimulating rather than controlling domestic and foreign commerce.[13] As

12. The transformation was so dramatic that by 1928 one contemporary biographer of Hoover could write, "The story of Hoover is essentially the story of America." Reeves, *Hoover*, 7.

13. Leach, *Land of Desire*, 351, 479–80 n. 6, citing a study published in 1934 by

western European countries noted at the time, no government had ever undertaken such a role with the breadth and depth that the U.S. government took under Hoover's leadership.[14] Second, by taking on the role of servant, the U.S. government became the master of commerce in the United States. It is to state the obvious that in the United States economic interests dominate American government, politics and life. The good life in America is essentially the economic good life, the ultimate baseline expression of life, liberty and the pursuit of happiness guaranteed by the U.S. constitution. Hoover saw this clearly and helped bring it about. Thus, in Hoover we find the governmental-commercial synthesis of biblical morality, republican individualism, humanitarian concern for freedom from scarcity, and economic engineering of the good life in the interstices of American government and business.

By the time he reached the age of thirty-eight, Hoover was a multimillionaire and had developed a concept of self-worth grounded in financial net worth. He did not believe a man was worth much if his net worth was less than a million dollars by age forty.[15] After graduating from Stanford with a degree in engineering in 1895, Hoover entered the mining business. From the late 1890s through 1916, he earned a reputation of being an honestly industrious and creatively effective manager of programs and people. In 1917, he was appointed director of the Food Administration for the U.S. government by President Woodrow Wilson, and after World War I became director of the American Relief Administration.[16]

Hoover employed his engineering and managerial expertise in first determining and then solving the production-consumption problems that plagued the United States during the 1920s and 1930s. He accomplished this task through a team of economists drawn from leading universities. During this decade, Hoover achieved two primary goals. He laid the governmental-commercial foundations for technological consumer capitalism in the United States. Secondly, he established economics as the

---

President Hoover's Research Committee on Social Trends titled *The Growth of the Federal Government, 1915–1932.*

14. The editor of one European economics journal noted in 1933 that "the Department of Commerce of the United States, largely under the inspiration of President Hoover, has worked in collaboration with businessmen and business organizations to a degree unparalleled by any government in the world." Leach, *Land of Desire*, 372–73, 484 n. 68.

15. Burner, *Hoover*, 54.

16. Leach, *Land of Desire*, 353.

dominant American social science. From this time forward, economists became the leaders of the new American culture of technological consumer capitalism.

The exigencies of the time made accomplishment of these goals possible. These were years of economic recessions that culminated in the Great Depression. Hoover saw consumer capitalism as the solution to the economic woes of the American people. In its ideal form, according to Hoover, capitalism is a system based upon expanding production that is effectively and efficiently diffused into mass consumption. Government's role, as he saw it, was to pave the way for consumption by providing critical economic data and creating a regulatory environment conducive to the harmonious integration of production and consumption. He believed capitalism was the most moral economic mode of organization and believed capitalists were motivated, or at least constrained, to assist others in the pursuit of what he saw as the fulfillment of self-interests resulting in socially harmonious ends. Thus, Hoover sincerely believed that consumer capitalism, if organized and managed wisely by government, would lead to human flourishing through the elimination of scarcity and poverty. This would require effective governmental calibration of production with consumption.[17] Grounding such management was an economic anthropology of human desire for happiness and freedom.

Hoover embraced the prevailing economic consensus of his time that the United States was destined for accomplishing a full-growth economy that would eliminate the problems of scarcity and poverty. Hoover was correct in this assessment, at least insofar as scarcity and poverty were measured in the 1920s. It is clear that after 1950 technological consumer capitalism can be credited with virtually eliminating scarcity in food, water, health care and housing for the first time in U.S. history.[18] True, there are certainly many poor in the United States who go to bed hungry and who do not have adequate access to basic human necessities. But the reality is that the U.S. economy produces sufficient food and resources to meet the basic needs of its population. When basic needs are unmet, more often than not it is due to systemic or distributive problems rather

17. Hoover, *American Individualism*, 1–33.

18. One recent Wesleyan theological critique of poverty in America bearing upon children identifies two kinds of poverty, material and relational, but it does not argue that scarcity in the sense of absolute material poverty is a problem in the U.S. Couture, *Seeing Children*; cf. Sen, "Poor, Relatively Speaking," 153–69.

than scarcity. It is not that resources are scare. It is that resources do not arrive. This is true of all advanced liberal democracies with capitalist economies.

Hoover can be credited with being one of the principal architects and engineers of the transformation of affluence in the United States. This may be a surprising claim in light of the facts that while serving in the U.S. Department of Commerce from 1920 to 1929 America was experiencing its worst recession in thirty years and, worse, he took office as president on the eve of the 1929 stock market crash and consequent commencement of the Great Depression. He is often remembered as a heartless Republican politician of big business who cared little for the suffering poor.

Nevertheless, Hoover maintained a steady course from 1920 to 1933 as secretary of commerce and president, despite the fact that he was actually blamed for causing the Great Depression.[19] Hoover saw his task clearly: establish the government-commerce partnership through liaisons with American business interests and manage the damaging fluctuations in business through such liaisons by technical means with the help of a cadre of leading economists.[20] This, he believed, was government's role. Managed wisely, government could assist consumer capitalism in eliminating the misery caused by economic recessions and depressions, while simultaneously creating a society marked by expanding prosperity. As Hoover and his economic advisers saw it, the key was government-assisted stimulation and management of human needs and wants by American business.

Leach demonstrates this convincingly from what he describes as the "most famous report, *Recent Economic Changes*, written by academic economists" that Hoover had arranged to be published while serving as

19. "Once upon a time my political opponents honored me as possessing the fabulous intellectual and economic power by which I created a world-wide depression all by myself." Hoover, http://www.geocities.com/americanpresidencynet/31st.htm.

20. Hoover's heritage in this regard can be seen in the power of money capital in the United States managed by economists through the Federal Reserve Board. Since the recessions in 1970 and 1980, the primary technical means of controlling damaging economic fluctuations has been through monetary policy, as is seen in the profound influence interest rate pronouncements have upon the American economy. Alan Greenspan served under four U.S. presidents as Chairman of the Reserve, the single most important and powerful banking institution in the United States. Greenspan earned degrees in economics from New York University (BS, 1948; MA, 1950; PhD, 1977). See http://www.federalreserve.gov/bios/greenspan.htm.

secretary of commerce.[21] That report shows the dominance exercised by the discipline of economics during the 1920s in American government and business, a dominance that continues to this day. It therefore warrants close scrutiny. According to Leach, *Recent Economic Changes* and other writings by Hoover, particularly his *American Individualism*, reveal Hoover as the most "consumption-minded person up to this time ever to hold the highest position in the U.S. government."[22] Significantly, Leach also shows that Hoover was the most proactive governmental advocate for children's welfare and that his advocacy included a platform for children in the emerging consumer paradise he envisioned and was in the process of creating while serving in the government.

Hoover wanted to eliminate all barriers between the flow of goods and the consumer, including the child as consumer. He and his team of economic advisers, drawn from elite institutions like Harvard and the University of Chicago, saw that both production and consumption needed systems of creation and management. They did not assume that consumption automatically followed production or that production created demand. As public servants, they saw that demand needed to be stimulated. Human desire must be stoked and, as best as possible, production must be planned accordingly.

Hoover and his economic team believed that a primary flaw of economic thought prior to 1920 was that it failed seriously to consider consumption. It was a flaw that led to the condition of overproduction after World War I and the resultant recessions that culminated in the Great Depression. Thus, in *Recent Economic Changes*, Hoover reported that economic progress in the United States

> proved conclusively what had long been held theoretically true, that wants are almost insatiable: that one want satisfied makes way for another. The conclusion is that economically we have a boundless field before us, that there are new wants which will make endlessly for newer wants, as fast as they can be satisfied. . . . Economists have long declared that consumption, the satisfaction of wants, would continue with little evidence of satiation if we could *so adjust* our economic processes as to make dormant demands effective.[23]

21. Leach, *Land of Desire*, 355.
22. Ibid. 355–56.
23. Ibid., 355 (emphasis original).

The function and aim of government, then, was to assist businesses in accomplishing the task of fitting production with consumption to the end of stimulating a cycle of endless desire. This was the key to fulfilling the constitutional right to life and liberty in the pursuit of happiness in the twentieth century. Making mass affluence possible was the partnership in which the U.S. government joined with American commerce in a manner unprecedented in the history of modern governments. Hoover was proud of America's standard of living and its ability to make goods and services considered previously luxuries reserved only for elites into commodities for the masses. This translated into an unequaled standard of living for Americans, one that proved in Hoover's mind the wisdom of his policies. Thus, according to Leach, Hoover could report in *Recent Economic Changes* that:

> America's high standard of living' was the nation's most precious gift to 'civilization.' 'Our ancestors . . . came to these shores with few tools and little organization to fight nature for a livelihood. Their descendants have developed a new and peculiarly American type of civilization,' one in which mass services and mass consumption 'have come to rank with other forms of production as a major economic factor.'[24]

Of course, in the twenty-first century and throughout the past several decades, many nations in the world contest whether the "standard of living" in America is "standard" and question whether it is a "gift," but few shun the affluence it brings for their populations. Evangelicals should question whether the standard is a gift and question whether nurture in affluence is good for their children. The tendency among most evangelicals in the United States today, it seems, is to seek uncritically to improve their stake in the standard as they enjoy the good of affluence.

In light of Hoover's governmental alliance with commercial interests in the United States, an alliance united by the discipline of economics and guided by economic elites, it should not surprise critics in the twenty-first century that in the United States children are "born to buy"[25] or that childhood has been subjected to a "hostile takeover" by consumer interests that produces "consuming kids"[26] in late modernity. Although

24. Leach, *Land of Desire*, 356.
25. Schor, *Born to Buy*.
26. Linn, *Consuming Kids*.

the works of such critics may contain captivating titles and some helpful synchronic insights into children embedded in the socio-cultural matrices of affluence, there really is nothing "new" about "consumer culture" or "consuming kids" in the United States, and there never has been a "hostile takeover of childhood." Americans, evangelicals included, have willingly gone along with the revolution of technological consumer capitalism and happily formed their children within the culture of affluence it has afforded. As chapter 2 has shown, the roots of consumer culture and consuming kids born in the U.S.A. were sunk deep in the nineteenth century. It simply remained for the fruit of consumerism to grow and ripen in the second half of the twentieth century, fruit that has become the subject of an immense and growing literature on consumption.[27]

The concern here is not to critique that literature but to develop a perspective of the AAEC nurtured in affluence. This requires a perspective of where evangelicals and their children in the United States have come in late modernity and how they have traveled through Hoover's America. Such a perspective will assist evangelicals in discerning the formative dimensions of affluence so they can help their children see them critically in their lives together.

The diachronic perspective of the AAEC can be enriched by examining Hoover's "managerial statism,"[28] with a view to how children fell within its ambit and were incorporated into its network of production diffused into consumption. Hoover was deeply interested in protecting the welfare of children. In the process of developing the governmental-commercial partnership during the 1920s, Hoover held numerous conferences to cement the relations between consumption and children's best interests. Leach documents that some of the conferences bore directly upon children's interests and that most had indirect impacts upon children's lives. For instance, as president, Hoover continued his work on behalf of children that he had begun with the American Child Health Association in 1920.[29] The work of this association was eminently commendable, inasmuch as it sought to alleviate many of the malingering

---

27. See, e.g., Princen, Maniates and Conca, eds., *Confronting Consumption*; Mason, *Economics of Conspicuous Consumption*; Slater, *Consumer Culture*; Miles, *Consumerism*.

28. Leach, *Land of Desire*, 354.

29. Hoover recorded in his memoirs that the work of the Association was "carried . . . forward during my whole term as Secretary of Commerce, during my term in the White House, and on to the year 1935—a total of thirteen years." Hoover, *Memoirs*, 97.

hangovers of the industrial revolution that adversely affected children's best interests.

Beginning several months after taking office in 1929, Hoover began organizing the White House Conference on Child Health and Protection.[30] The conference was held in 1930, and in addition to reaffirming the principal goals of the child welfare movement that began in the mid-nineteenth century and took root in America's Progressive Era (1900–1920), Hoover added his own vision for improving life for children: nurture in single family homes away from industrial districts and brothels, and near schools, churches and shopping centers. Hoover helped government redefine the world of American children and began the process of seeking to establish children's rights to desire and consume equal to those possessed by adults.

The report of the 1930 White House Conference on Child Health and Protection was titled *The Home and the Child: Housing, Furnishing, Management, Income and Clothing.* Remarkably, the report concluded that children develop their personalities by having the freedom to shop for their own "things," because they learn to express their personalities "through things."[31] The report elaborates upon other ideal ways to insure children's well-being and to protect them from harm as they develop:

1. Children should have their own rooms in single-family residences, if at all possible.

2. They should have furniture and eating utensils designed for their ages and sizes.

3. They should live in homes "within relatively easy access of churches and schools, and civic, cultural and shopping centers."

4. They should have homes with playrooms stocked with "toys, velocipedes, sawhorses, wagons, wheelbarrows, slides, and places to keep pets."

5. Children should be consulted when the family intends to make a purchase for common purposes, such as furniture and musical instruments.[32]

30. Ibid., 259.

31. Leach, *Land of Desire,* 371–72, quoting from *The Home and the Child.* Leach dates the conference in 1929, but it was actually held in 1930. Hoover, *Memoirs,* 97.

32. Leach, *Land of Desire,* 371, quoting from *The Home and the Child.*

Hoover believed that mass diffusion of consumption was in the best interests of children, something that cultural and theological critics alike question today. There is truth and error in this belief. The truth is found in the good affluence can bring, such as food, housing, health care, etc. The error is located in the poverty, or lack, affluence can bring in the affluent. As a general rule, this tension inherent in affluence remains uncritically assessed in American evangelicalism today. The tendency is to accept the blessings of affluence without regard to deleterious effects it can have on evangelical nurture.

Evangelical ambivalence in the midst of affluence is understandable. Few critics of affluence are able to offer any realistic solution for overhauling the culture and society produced by technological consumer capitalism. Evangelicals know that true life is found only in God as revealed in Jesus Christ and the Bible, and therefore they know that life does not consist in an abundance of possessions. At the same time, they have experienced the good of affluence and are ambivalent about what giving it up means or practically how renunciation or donation of it should work. Absent from evangelicalism is a robust ecclesiology that sustains a tradition of prophetic critique of affluence and witness as to how evangelicals should live or nurture their children in light of the late modern problem of affluence.

This ambivalence can be seen in Herbert Hoover as well. On one hand, he was a child welfare reformer who, as commerce secretary and president, genuinely had the best interests of children in mind. On the other, he was a consumerist who believed human desire and flourishing could be met ultimately through affluence and should be constantly stimulated so as to unearth latent desires. He genuinely believed nurturing affluence and stimulating the desires that fueled it would be good for children. Thus, Hoover's vision for nurturing and protecting children's health:

> incorporated . . . his entire concept of the "standard of living"—an emphasis on the consumption of goods and children's special role in that consumption. And, in the end, the commercial side was the predominant side of his vision. In the White House conference as in all the other conferences he had convened as secretary of commerce and as president, his intent was to "raise" the standard of living and to advance and "equilibrate" the levels of production and consumption. Whatever he did—whatever most of the

government did—was compatible with the goals of the mass consumer order and of the "new day."[33]

Hoover thus linked children's welfare to affluence and envisioned a crucial role for children within its cultural and social matrices. Children were to be regarded as individuals with the same needs and rights to desire and consume as adults. Remarkably, Hoover and his advisers believed that failure to regard children in this way could jeopardize their "physical, mental and social development."[34] Central to Hoover's vision of the child's world and nurture, therefore, was a cornucopia of goods made possible by parents. Since 1930, then, the U.S. government has been intent on forming children who are born to buy and destined to become consuming kids. With little critical awareness, evangelicalism since 1930 has embraced this vision and approach to nurture with little, if any, critical reflection. Evangelical rhetoric about social ills and professed loyalty to the Bible notwithstanding, evangelicals seem to have found life in Hoover's America acceptable. At the same time, they have overlooked the obstacle affluence presents to finding an answer to the question about what is lacking in late modern life.

One additional aspect of Hoover's days in the U.S. commerce department warrants attention. It is Hoover's vision for single-family home ownership as an ideal for child health and protection. Vincent Miller, a contemporary theologian in the United States, has argued recently that single-family home ownership is profoundly formative of American identity.[35] Miller's critical-theological analysis of the single-family home is worth noting in light of Hoover's dream of single-family home ownership for every American. It further illumines the socio-cultural reality of being born in the U.S.A. Generally speaking, the AAEC is nurtured in suburban single-family homes grounded in a consumerist vision of the good life, a vision with foundations in the Declaration of Independence that began to be realized in the Hooverian joint venture between American government and commerce.

While secretary of commerce, Hoover created the Division of Building and Housing in 1922 and partnered with the Better Homes Movement,

33. Leach, *Land of Desire*, 372.

34. Ibid., 371.

35. Miller, *Consuming Religion*, 46. Miller's critique of the single-family home is engaged more fully below in the sociology of AAEC in chapter 4.

a private organization composed of more than "eighteen hundred Better Homes local committees," to provide the public with new ideas to improve, furnish and finance homes for the good of families and children.[36] The Division of Building and Housing published pamphlets, such as *Own Your Own Home*, and arranged for their distribution through the Better Homes network along with other Better Homes publications, advertisements and a film, *Home, Sweet Home*, made possible by a $250,000 grant brokered by Hoover.[37] The Division also served "as a liaison to builders, real estate developers, social workers, and homemakers [and] . . . did economic research and published materials on zoning laws and on methods of home purchase and financing."[38]

Hoover saw the right to build a home at least once in life as a primary American right. His rights-oriented vision linked consumerism and home ownership to children's health and protection.[39] He cleared a space for children within consumerism and within the home, while simultaneously clearing a space within the home for consumerism. Thus, he wrote in his memoirs:

> A primary right of every American family is the right to build a new house of its heart's desire at least once. Moreover, there is the instinct to own one's own home with one's own arrangement of gadgets, rooms, and surroundings. It is also an instinct to have a spot to which the youngsters can always come back.[40]

In order to insure the health and protection of children, Hoover reasoned, American families and governments should protect consumerism in the home. Hoover argued that the best interests of children would be served by protecting the right of children to their own spaces in suburban homes with their own gadgets freely shopped for, chosen, possessed and arranged. As the report from Hoover's 1931 Conference on Home Building and Home Ownership stated, Hoover and his administration wanted homes near shopping centers "within a radius of a quarter to a

---

36. Leach, *Land of Desire*, 369.

37. Ibid.

38. Ibid.

39. For a critique of the rights-orientation of American political discourse, see Glendon, *Rights Talk*.

40. Hoover, *Memoirs*, 5.

half mile and concentrated on the boundary streets of a residential area."[41] Hoover would, no doubt, be pleased to see this aspect of his vision almost universally fulfilled in twenty-first-century America. The vast majority of American evangelicals experience the fulfillment of that vision each day.

Hoover formed this vision into a bill of rights for children and "secured its adoption" by the conferees at the 1930 White House Conference on Child Health and Protection.[42] Hoover summarized his view of childhood and children as follows:

> We approach all problems of childhood with affection. Theirs is the province of joy and good humor. They are the most wholesome part of the race, the sweetest, for they are fresher from the hands of God. Whimsical, ingenious, mischievous, we live a life of apprehension as to what their opinion may be of us; a life of defense against their terrifying energy; we put them to bed with a sense of relief and a lingering of devotion. We envy them the freshness of adventure and discovery of life; we mourn over the disappointments they will meet. [43]

On this basis Hoover conceived nineteen rights for children. Although access to shopping centers was not one of those rights, the right to an American standard of living certainly was. Thus, Hoover and the conferees agreed that children were entitled, among other rights, to:

- "grow up in a family with an adequate standard of living and the security of a stable income as the surest safeguard against social handicaps";

- "every child protection against labor that stunts growth either physical or mental, that limits education, that deprives children of the right to comradeship, of play, and of joy";

- "a home and that love and security which a home provides";

---

41. Leach, *Land of Desire*, 370, 484 n. 64, quoting from Gries and Ford, eds., *Housing Objectives*, 150–201.

42. Hoover, "Development of Child Welfare," in *Memoirs*, 261. The children's bill of rights was initially called a "Children's Charter" and was revised for the 1930 conference. It set forth nineteen distinct rights for children and concluded with this declaration, "For every child these rights, regardless of race, or color, or situation, wherever he may live under the protection of the American flag." Ibid., 261–64.

43. Hoover, *Memoirs*, 260.

- "a dwelling place safe, sanitary, and wholesome, with reasonable provisions for privacy, free from conditions which tend to thwart his development, and a home environment harmonious and enriching"; and

- "an education which, through the discovery and development of his individual abilities, prepares him for life; and through training and vocational guidance prepares him for a living which will yield him the maximum of satisfaction."[44]

Of course there is much good expressed in such rights and it would be difficult to argue against them. The question is how to secure those rights for children. What compromises arise for children and childhood as a result of privileging economics and the governmental-commercial partnership necessary to secure the consumerist rights of the child? The decision to diffuse the vision for an American standard of living and consumption into childhood had far reaching implications for American children in general and the AAEC in particular.

If, as the evangelical believes, life does not consist in an abundance of possessions and if nurture in the context of affluence may present stumbling blocks to entering God's kingdom, then Hoover's programs for children presented a dilemma from the outset. They entailed an uncritical subordination of evangelical pedagogy and praxis to the economics of diffused consumption as the means to the presumed good of prosperity. The AAEC born in the U.S.A. would be nurtured in a suburban home, for "a living which will yield him the maximum of satisfaction" and "for an adequate standard of living and the security of a stable income as the surest safeguard against social handicaps." Of course evangelicals both in Hoover's day and now would object that they know the Bible precludes the reduction of evangelical life to this kind of economic depiction. But knowing and doing are two different things, as the evangelical well knows.

Lawrence Richards was born into Hoover's America in 1932 after his parents had been formed in it during the first decades of their lives. As will be shown below, it would appear that Richards may not have questioned his own nurture in this context. It is clear from his writings that affluence was not a factor accounted for in his theology of nurture.

44. Ibid., 262–64.

BORN IN THE U.S.A.: RICHARDS AND THE AAEC

> In the United States as elsewhere, the bourgeois ethos [of the nine-
> teenth century] had enjoined perpetual work, compulsive saving,
> civic responsibility, and a rigid morality of self-denial. By the early
> twentieth century that outlook had begun to give way to a new set
> of values sanctioning periodic leisure, compulsive spending, apo-
> litical passivity, and an apparently permissive (but subtly coercive)
> morality of individual fulfillment. The older culture was suited to
> a production-oriented society of small entrepreneurs; the newer
> culture epitomized a consumption-oriented society dominated by
> bureaucratic corporations.[45]

The society produced by technological consumer capitalism in the twentieth century, with its four pillars of property rights, scientific rationalism,
capital markets and explosively efficient communications and transporta-
tion, has resulted in the formation and socialization of three generations
of American evangelicals in levels of affluence unprecedented in human
history.[46] Richards, who grounded his theology of Christian education in
socialization theory, failed to account for the multi-dimensionally formative effects that affluence undoubtedly had upon him and his generation
of evangelicals. Consequently, his theology of nurture failed to account
for affluence.

As the examination of Hoover has shown, the path for the evolution
and emergence of the AAEC was set by 1930. Richards has lived along
that path and been a vital participant and leader on it. By the time he
was born, his parents had been formed for a decade in Herbert Hoover's
transformation of the U.S. Department of Commerce into what would
become within fifty years the most potent governmental-commercial
partnership in human history.

Richards attended the University of Michigan, where he earned a degree in philosophy in 1958. From there, he enrolled in Dallas Theological
Seminary (DTS) intent on majoring in Greek. His first introductory course
in Christian education caught his interest, so he changed his major to that
field.[47] During his time at DTS, Richards embarked on "another quest
of personal Bible study that by his testimony was carried on five hours

---

45. Lears, "Salvation to Self-Realization," 3.

46. On these factors, see Bernstein, *Birth of Plenty*, 4–5, 15–17, 51–188.

47. Downs, "Christian Nurture," 116, quoting Richards from a personal interview.

per night, seven nights a week, for three years" and provided the biblical foundation for his early theological writings on Christian education.[48]

Richards graduated from DTS and was ordained in Independent Grace Bible Church of Dallas in 1962. He took a job as an editor in the nursery department of Scripture Press Publications in Wheaton, Illinois, where he focused his attention on helping children learn to worship by developing materials for children's church. In 1965, Richards joined the Christian Education Department in the Graduate School of Theology at Wheaton College, a leading evangelical college in the United States. He served as an associate pastor of the Wheaton Evangelical Free Church, where he was responsible for Christian education during his time in Wheaton.

By 1962, after the third decade of life, Richards the evangelical pedagogue was fully formed. He had witnessed Hoover's United States emerge victorious from World War II and negotiate a military peace in Korea (1950–1953). He was in the midst of America's final transition from the industrial to information-postindustrial revolutions, from the anxieties of scarcity to the anxieties of affluence.[49] By his educational choice of DTS and church memberships, Richards placed himself squarely within evangelical fundamentalism in the United States. Thus, Richards was formed within the culture and society of technological consumer capitalism in which the evangelical subculture was embedded.

Richards's doctoral work provided the basis for what would become his *Sunday School Plus* curriculum, published in 1975 three years after receiving his PhD. His thesis entailed developing a theoretical socialization model of nurture, in which he sought to unite evangelical church and home in a joint venture of Christian formation of the gospel in children.[50] Both his model and ministry have contributed significantly to advancing evangelical nurture of children in the twentieth century. His writings reflect an original and helpful critique of American evangelicalism in relation to its ecclesiology, pedagogy and practice of evangelical nurture.

However, Richards appears to have been critically unaware of how his theology and pedagogy of Christian nurture reflected the dominant economic presuppositions of American culture and society. As a result,

---

48. Ibid.

49. See Horowitz, *Anxieties of Affluence.*

50. Richards, "Pre-Evaluative Research."

his theological critique of the foundations and practice of Christian education fell short of its intended goals, because it failed to account for the broader formative social and cultural aspects of affluence in the United States. In other words, Richards's critique of evangelical nurture missed an important dimension because it failed to start with a theological critique of American evangelicalism embedded in affluence. There is no evidence in his writings of a critical awareness of the problem of affluence, the economic context within which Christian education evolved in the United States or how economic interests contribute to the formation of children within the socio-cultural matrices of late modern American life.

By 1967, Richards had become doubtful of the educational models employed in evangelical churches in the United States. He saw a radical disjuncture between what he interpreted the Bible to teach about Christian nurture and what he saw practiced in evangelical churches. Between 1967 and 1970, he would formulate the theological position for his critique of evangelical nurture that remains essentially the same today.

As Richards saw things, American evangelicalism had uncritically incorporated secular educational models of nurture into their Christian education programs.[51] Richards wanted to see evangelical churches ground their theories of nurture biblically in what can be described as an ecclesiology of socialization. He advocated a familial-ecclesial partnership in the nurture of children grounded in biblical theology. Richards became so concerned about the evangelical shortcomings in Christian education during the 1960s that he "actually removed his own children from the local church program . . . he was directing because he felt . . . the process was . . . 'destructive to their own faith!' Needless to say, this created certain tensions in his [pastoral] relationship with the church."[52]

This evolution of discontent led Richards in 1970 to relocate his family and ministry to Phoenix, Arizona, where he began Renewal Research Associates. This allowed him a wider berth and freedom in ministry within American evangelicalism and would lead to diverse teaching opportunities at colleges and seminaries such as Wheaton College, Princeton Theological Seminary and Talbot Theological Seminary. His primary

51. Richards's critique of the cognitive emphasis in evangelical nurture is similar to Freire's critique of the "banking model" of education: children's heads are empty accounts that need to be filled with educational credits of knowledge. Cf. Freire, *Pedagogy of the Oppressed*; and Richards, *New Face for the Church*.

52. Downs, "Christian Nurture," 117.

work throughout has been as a writer and evangelical spokesperson for child nurture, church renewal and church leadership. Richards became the twentieth century's most prolific and influential evangelical author writing on the nurture of children.

Through Renewal Research Associates, Richards sought to renew the evangelical churches' approaches to child nurture. He wrote and spoke extensively on nurture during this period (1970–1982), producing twenty-eight books, including *A New Face for the Church* (1970), *Youth Ministry: Its Renewal in the Church* (1972), *A Theology of Christian Education* (1975), and *Sunday School Plus* (1975). He would apply his theology of Christian education specifically to child nurture in 1983, initially under the title *A Theology of Children's Ministry* and subsequently as *Children's Ministry: Nurturing Faith Within the Family of God*. Before examining this latter work for its theological anthropology of the child, it will be helpful to place it in context with *Sunday School Plus*, *Creative Bible Teaching*, *Youth Ministry* and *A Theology of Christian Education*.

Foundations of Richards's Theology of Nurture: Sunday School Plus = *the Church* + *the Family*

Richards titled *Sunday School Plus* to communicate a biblical philosophy of education that envisions the unification of the church and family in the nurture of children. Currently published and utilized, the curriculum incorporates an essentially Piagetian familial-ecclesial socialization model of nurture, in which Richards advocates a developmentally aware partnership between evangelical church and home in the process of Christian nurture. His emphasis is on both relationships and cognition. By relying on Jean Piaget, it appears that he wanted to challenge evangelicals to be aware of the developmental nature of cognition in children.

The interest in this curriculum here is with its biblical-theological foundation rather than its reliance upon developmental psychology as applied in the sociology of children. The focus is upon Richards's use of Deuteronomy 6:1–9 as the foundational text for his model of nurture.[53] The central task of the *Sunday School Plus* curriculum was to equip parents to train their children in the Bible at home so that they would not

---

53. Richards, *Theology*, 24, 35, 68, 193, 203, 217; *Children's Ministry*, 23, 46, 79, 81, 225, 250, 405, 407.

need Sunday School curricular help. Two years after it was published, Richards wrote that it is a "divine imperative" that:

> the family is the place where Christian faith and life must be com-
> municated . . . : 'You shall teach . . . your children.' (Deut. 6:7).
> Deuteronomy 6 is a key Old Testament passage that focuses our
> attention on how to teach the Scriptures in such a way that the re-
> ality of God is communicated together with the biblical content.[54]

Richards maintained "that as a family learns to live together and to share faith in the Deuteronomy 6 way that the great promise [sic] of Proverbs 22:6 will be fulfilled for us all: 'Train up a child in the way he should go, and when he is old he will not depart from it.'"[55] Despite the problem of viewing Proverbs 22:6 as a promise, a common evangelical error, Richards brought a fresh focus on Deuteronomy 6:1–9 for evangelicals that may be considered one of his most significant and lasting contributions to American-evangelical child nurture. This biblical text is a standard for Christian nurture in American evangelicalism. It is cited by evangelicals with Ephesians 6:4 more than any other biblical text for buttressing their theology of nurture and can be found in scores of evangelical resources ranging from sermons to books.

However, it is rare to find in such resources critical concern for the problem of affluence posed in Deuteronomy 6:10–12 and developed more fully in 8:7–20. The danger affluence presents to nurture of evangelical faith and practice in children is that it tempts parent, church and child to forget God in the presumption, pride, independence and simple theological amnesia that affluence can bring (6:12; 8:11–14). The peril of forgetting God and the constant calls to remember God's redeeming activity as the theological imperative for ethical conduct and the nurture of children are themes running throughout Deuteronomy.[56]

In chapters 6 and 8 of Deuteronomy, for instance, affluence is presented as a major risk factor for cultivating faith in the Lord God in both child and adult, and yet evangelicals routinely fail to identify and account for it in the cultural and social processes of Christian nurture. Without a critical consciousness of affluence, the evangelical nurture of children will, as Bushnell's theology of nurture proved, ultimately serve the dominant

54. Richards, "Why Sunday School Plus?" 21.

55. Ibid.

56. E.g., Deuteronomy 4:9, 23; 6:12; 8:11, 14, 19; 9:7; 28:47; 32:18.

cultural, social and political ends of the United States: affluence grounded in an economic vision of life defined by progress and conceived as the diffusion of production into consumption. In the end, the means to such ends can radically subvert the nurture of evangelical faith in the AAEC.

Richards's *Sunday School Plus* represents a twentieth-century Bushnellian vision of Christian nurture recast in palatable American Evangelicalese. Richards knew the biblical language and rhetoric of American evangelicalism. He was formed within it and has not deviated from its biblicism. Because he theologized and theorized on nurture with ample quotes from the Bible, Richards appears to have been able to develop a modified form of Bushnellian developmentalism acceptable to the biblical sensitivities of American evangelicals.

At the same time, Richards's theology of nurture represents a modern version of Edwardsian conversionism. However, it seems clear from his writings that the developmental predominated the conversionist aspects of his theology of nurture. It is also clear that Richards, like Edwards and Bushnell, never adequately worked out the theological-anthropological correlation between conversion and development. These aspects of his theory of nurture can be seen in his first and most enduring pedagogical work, *Creative Bible Teaching* (1970), as well as his foundational theology of nurture in *A Theology of Christian Education* (1975).

Richards sees the principal aim of Christian nurture as "personal knowledge of God" that begins in "salvation, then more and more deeply in maturing experiences."[57] Bible teaching is the means to this end. It is the means of nurturing life and, upon conversion, eternal life in the "human personality, toward likeness to the God who gives it."[58] While the dependence appears to be unconscious, here we see an incipient form of the Bushnellian view of the supernatural in nature. God gives life and eternal life in the human personality. According to Bushnell, the ideal place to cultivate such life is in the family, and according to Richards it is in the family plus the church (i.e., Sunday School). Whereas Bushnell focuses on the family in his *Christian Nurture*, Richards focuses on the church *and* the family in partnership. In this sense, Richards's theology of nurture is an improvement upon Bushnell's because of its ecclesiological dimensions. Because he interspersed biblical quotations with Hebrew

57. Richards, *Creative Bible Teaching*, 62. Perhaps Richards's most enduring work.
58. Richards, *Theology*, 22.

and Greek word studies, Richards's Bushnellianism apparently entered American evangelicalism undetected.

Richards sought to maintain an orthodox conception of the supernatural in his theology of nurture. Although not explicit, his dependence upon Bushnell seems clear. He argues that in Christian education "God works *through natural means in a supernatural way*."[59] By this he means two things. First, that God used human persons to write the Bible. This is the evangelical conception of organic inspiration, the view that the special revelation God gives to humanity in the Bible was "enscripturated" through ordinary human beings who, when they wrote, expressed themselves organically—that is, the biblical authors reflected "their personalities and experiences and culture, and yet at the same time express[ed] perfectly in words the Spirit chose, the thoughts and words of God."[60]

The second way God works through natural means in a supernatural way is in the ministry of the gospel. God decided to work through "men like Peter . . . and like you and me" to proclaim and practice the gospel through which the supernatural work of God is accomplished.[61] This choice entailed the decision to utilize the natural means of human language, speech and sociality to accomplish the ends of the gospel. Like Bushnell, Richards conceived of God's creating, redeeming and transforming work as accomplished primarily through "the unspectacular . . . natural means which God has built into the human personality to transmit any belief or culture," rather than "spectacular interventions . . . in history."[62]

Unlike Bushnell, however, who was striving to counter the ostrich nurture of nineteenth-century conversionist revivalism, Richards is quick to assure his evangelical readers that conversionism is well and good, provided proper respect for developmentalism is retained. He also is concerned to preserve a strong Edwardsian emphasis on God's sovereignty in Christian nurture. Richards believes that maintaining due regard for God's ordinary means of accomplishing supernatural ends does not fail to "attribute to God His direct, supernatural intervention in conversion

59. Ibid., 323 (emphasis original).

60. Ibid.

61. Ibid.

62. Ibid., 324.

or in growth."[63] Without the person and work of Jesus and the Holy Spirit nothing is accomplished. God's sovereign grace in Christ and the Spirit are the ultimate ground of nurture. It all depends upon "the determination of God to touch us, to bring us to Himself as His children, and, as children, to superintend our growth."[64] Thus, like Edwards, Richards reads the Bible as describing supernatural means of grace sovereignly ordained and administered by God. And like Bushnell, he reads the Bible as describing natural means of grace in the processes of nurturing and transforming human nature.

Nevertheless, Richards appears finally to revert back to a form of Bushnellian developmentalism in his attempt to reconcile Edwardsian conversionism with nurture. Thus, "we still find ourselves bound to bend our every effort to shape those means God's power infuses with effectiveness."[65] As I interpret it, this is Bushnell's organic nurture decoded into twentieth-century Evangelicalese. Biblically we can affirm that God "has chosen to work within rather than outside the natural processes of growth and transformation," and therefore these "*must* be processes we are committed to encourage in our local situations."[66] The goal is transformation, "a progressive reshaping of the believer toward Christlikeness . . . that pattern of life revealed in Scripture as God's ideal for man, His special creation."[67]

Like Bushnell, Richards does not believe that transformation takes place in a singular event such as conversion or a post-conversion second blessing event of the Spirit. Progress, growth, transformation. These are the terms Richards uses to describe the essence of Christian nurture. Conversion begins new life, which is then nurtured in the processes of transformation. It is a "process of socialization" that gradually replaces previously dominant worldly "values and motives and behavior" with Christ-like "values and behavior which find their source and validity in the nature of God, and which have been revealed by Him in Scripture."[68]

63. Ibid.
64. Ibid.
65. Ibid.
66. Ibid. (emphasis original).
67. Ibid., 296.
68. Richards, *New Face for the Church*, 47.

This is well and good for Christian nurture as far as it goes. Children no doubt benefit from evangelicals holding to these insights, developing them and applying them wisely in ministry to children. But at least two flaws are embedded in Richards's theological anthropology of nurture. The first concerns children as sinners. Richards simply passes over the question whether children are sinners dominated by worldly values, motives and behavior or at what point in time such may occur. As we saw in chapter 2, Edwards resolved the question in an ambivalent manner by arguing that children sin as soon as capable of it even though by nature they represent truly gracious and saving religious affections. Furthermore, chapter 2 demonstrated that Bushnell never addressed the cultural and social aspects of nurture in industrial capitalism. He simply assumed that the pursuit of prosperity was a good thing that, with the right kind of Christian nurture, would lead to the Christianization of the world. Richards seems to land on the side of Bushnell and against Edwards, impliedly claiming biblical agnosticism on such issues. This is problematic because Richards, like Bushnell, fails to consider the formative effects affluence can have on Christian nurture.

This relates directly to the second flaw in Richards's theological anthropology of nurture. The fundamental problem is that the familial-ecclesial organicism of Richards remains critically unaware of the socio-cultural context of evangelical affluence. It is true that children are formed within parental-ecclesial matrices of evangelical life in the United States, as Richards both correctly and helpfully contends. But evangelical families and churches are formed within the broader culture of affluence and are constituent parts of the society that culture produces. This defect, it appears, is latent in every theology and theory of child nurture presented in the United States since Bushnell first published *Christian Nurture*. They share this myopia to affluence because they have ignored the economic foundations of American life and the affluence those foundations have produced.[69]

---

69. The sociocultural view of human development in Soviet psychologist Lev Vygotsky (1896–1934) may provide a psychological theory needed for development of a Marxist sociology of children and family, but my research has not uncovered such a sociology in the American context. See Corsaro's discussion of Vygotsky's relationship to the sociology of childhood in *Sociology*, 13–15. One recent dissertation was found that applies Vygotsky's constructivist framework of child development to "interrogate the manner in which television constructs and deploys detailed scripts about human relationality and intersubjectivity, volition, self-regulatory capability, and attitudes of commitment

This has significant implications for the theology of nurture offered by Richards. For him, "the essence of our [evangelical] faith is life!"[70] If evangelical life in the United States is interpenetrated and essentially determined by economic interests, then a critical assessment of the socialization process for children embedded in such "life" is missing if economics is ignored. Yet, not only biblically but also social scientifically, Richards has failed to account for the economics of affluence in his familial-ecclesial socialization theory. For him, "Christian education seeks to communicate and to nurture faith-as-life" and "is concerned with progressive transformation of the believer toward the character, values, motives, attitudes, and understandings of God Himself."[71]

If so, it seems appropriate to expect critical treatment of God's economic warnings in the socialization processes of nurture. Economics is a profoundly formative dimension of life for the child born in the U.S.A. Until recently the discipline of economics has been overlooked in theological anthropology and has yet to be engaged in a thorough, theological-critical manner within evangelical theology in the United States. Critical interaction with Richards demonstrates that American-evangelical theology and evangelicalism have neglected the economic dimension of Christian nurture and, as a result, retarded its full theological-critical development.

Richards's Theology of Nurturing Faith and the AAEC

This section examines Richards's theology of nurture in *A Theology of Children's Ministry*, subsequently re-titled as *Children's Ministry: Nurturing Faith Within the Family of God*, with a view to discerning its theological anthropology of the child.

When he wrote *Children's Ministry*, Richards hoped the book would "provide those who minister with children a theological framework within which to think about their ministry, and . . . to better love and nurture the next generation of Jesus' people."[72] He structures his theology

---

and trust." Gugino, "Television's Impact," quoting from the abstract. Gugino's thesis is a philosophical-psychological focus on a specific technological aspect of affluence, i.e., television.

70. Richards, *New Face for the Church*, 23.

71. Ibid., 15, 22.

72. Richards, *Children's Ministry*, 12.

of nurture in three parts. The first addresses the theological and developmental frameworks for nurturing Christian faith in children. The second discusses these frameworks in the context of Christian home, church and school. And the third focuses on how to use the Bible in nurturing faith in children.

Richards addresses the doctrines of human nature and sin together. It is both surprising and disappointing to find in his theologies of Christian education, children's ministry and youth ministry a form of biblical agnosticism on these doctrines. On both, Richards maintains that "the Scripture seems to simply assume certain things about all human beings, and then to go on to show us how to love children, to live with them, and to help them grow."[73] He justifies this on the ground that the Bible does not provide specifics as to how these doctrines apply to children. "However important these issues may seem to the theologian, they are not the issues with which the Scriptures seem primarily concerned."[74]

This move allows Richards to maneuver past theological issues that present a thicket of philosophical and psychological thorns. As an evangelical theologian doing "biblical theology," it allows him to proceed with more "practical" concerns. Thus, Richards sets out the "assumptions that are particularly important to us about persons" as they are presented in the Bible, and notes that these are not "the usual theological ones."[75] By taking a simple Bible approach, Richards navigates past the thorny theological issues raised by the problem of affluence in late modernity, particularly those related to human nature and sin in the context of a culture formed by technological consumer capitalism. The navigation proceeds with no awareness of the knotty anthropology of liberty lying at the heart of the problem of affluence and thus at the heart of nurturing children in that context.

In a relatively short space, then, Richards is able to summarize what he understands conservative evangelical theology to be on the doctrines of human nature and sin. He sidesteps these important issues that bear upon the theology of nurturing children in evangelical affluence. Consequently, he proceeds to develop his theological conception of the child as a learner

73. Ibid., 73.
74. Ibid.
75. Ibid.

in formative relationships with family and church without the benefit of engaging these crucial doctrines.

The Child as Relational Learner

Richards's theological anthropology of the child flows from a simple, moderately critical reading of the Bible from evangelical-dispensational presuppositions. Humans are "learners" in relative states of educational freedom to grow and be transformed. According to Richards, "the Bible teaches us to view persons (including children!) as *free*, responsible individuals, whose growth can be influenced but never determined, and whose progress in faith is linked with personal relationship to God."[76] Children "are free . . . [and] can be influenced" by nurture through the natural processes that "the God who works within them . . . has shown us [in the Bible and] . . . by which openness to Him and growth in faith are stimulated."[77]

Because humans are made in God's image, they "share with God all the attributes of personality. Mind, emotion, will, individuality. . ."[78] Even though sin may be a problem, the child still has the capacity to learn. This is the essence of the child's freedom, regardless of whether the child is converted. Regeneration does not change the processes by which humans learn and develop: "New life will not necessarily change a person's intellectual powers, make him a better scientist, or a better carpenter. *Neither will the gift of God's life change the essential way that human beings learn and grow.* The commonness of our humanity is vital to grasp."[79] Use of the word "free" in Richards's theology of nurture warrants closer scrutiny, since as we have seen freedom or liberty lies at the heart of the problem of the AAEC. As Richards sees things, children are free to learn. This is a relational freedom to grow and be influenced by their parents and churches. And of course it follows, as in Bushnell, we only experience this freedom to flourish in contexts of positive parental and ecclesial influence.

But this brings us back to the problem identified in Bushnell's *Christian Nurture*. Parent and child and church alike are formed in af-

76. Richards, *Children's Ministry*, 74 (emphasis added).

77. Ibid., 76.

78. Richards, *Theology*, 14.

79. Ibid., 15 (emphasis original).

fluence, formed as consumers for a culture and society produced and sustained by technological consumer capitalism. As will be developed more fully in chapter 5, it is doubtful that the anthropology of freedom sustaining this culture and its economy equates to a truly evangelical anthropology of freedom. As is true with the doctrine of sin, Richards does not engage the doctrine of freedom with any depth in his theology of nurture. Although Richards may be correct in locating human liberty in the *imago Dei*, failing to critique freedom biblically and theologically subjects his theology of nurture and its conception of educational-pedagogical-anthropological freedom to a fatal flaw. In the end, as was true of Bushnell and Mayo, Richards may be incapable in his theology of nurture and education of escaping the process of delivering evangelical children to the clutches of consumer culture. As chapter 5's interaction with the tradition of the rich young man in Matthew 19 will demonstrate, the failure to account for the anthropology of liberty that sustains late modern affluence risks disciplinary formation of the AAEC for capitalist culture.

According to Richards, there are five biblically revealed processes of human freedom "that influence the growth of faith."[80] These processes must (1) "communicate *belonging* to a vital faith community"; (2) "involve *participation* in the life of a vital faith community"; (3) "facilitate *modeling* in members of the faith community"; (4) "provide biblical *instruction as interpretation-of-life*"; and (5) "encourage growing *exercise of personal choice*."[81] The manner in which Richards explicates these processes in his theological framework for nurture indicates that his theological anthropology of the child is premised upon a conception of the human as a "free" being-in-relation encouraged to cultivate "personal choice", as opposed to a conception grounded in substance ontology and faculty psychology.[82] But, again, one searches in vain for any evidence that Richards is aware of the broader social and cultural processes at work and interwoven with these processes.

---

80. Richards, *Children's Ministry*, 76. Richards discerns these biblical processes from the previous three chapters of *Children's Ministry*: "Nurture in the Old Testament," 17–36; 'Nurture in the New Testament," 37–54; "The Role of Scripture in Nurture," 55–72.

81. Richards, *Children's Ministry*, 76 (emphasis original).

82. Richards, "Processes Influencing Spiritual Growth," in *Children's Ministry*, 76–81; cf. Shults, "Substance Dualism and Faculty Psychology," in *Reforming Theological Anthropology*, 165–74.

This is unfortunate because in focusing on the relational aspects of nurture Richards was on the right path. He simply did not take his relational analysis and critique, presumably arising from his interaction with the social sciences, quite far enough. Although he does not explicitly identify the philosophical and psychological foundations of his theology of nurture, Richards can be seen as standing at the cusp of the twentieth-century anthropological "turn to relationality" in philosophy, psychology and theology.[83] It appears that Richards may have entered the turn to relational anthropology directly through the works of Jean Piaget and Lawrence Kohlberg in developmental psychology[84] and perhaps indirectly through his undergraduate exposure to philosophy.[85] Although Richards affirms the individual personhood of each child, his emphasis is on the child as relationally and socially constituted in the family and church. Thus, he sees the child as a dynamically embedded self in formative communal relations with others in family, church and school. Consistently evangelical in his reasoning, Richards finds a strong biblical basis for his emphasis on human relationality and sociality, concluding that the New Testament describes "a relational climate that is normative for the Christian community."[86] This biblical grounding of nurture in familial and ecclesial relations can be traced throughout his theology of nurture and represents a positive advancement of evangelical child nurture.[87]

Nevertheless, Richards did not turn quite far enough in his embrace of relational anthropology. Although he correctly focused upon children's

---

83. See, e.g., Shults, "Relationality from Hegel to Levinas" and "The Responsibility of Theology," in *Reforming Theological Anthropology*, 22–36. Richards's church-home relational anthropology of nurture resonates themes in the twentieth-century resurgence of trinitarian relational theology. Cf. Grenz, *Social God and Relational Self*, 5 nn. 16–20.

84. In *Theology*, Richards relies upon Piaget at 168, 170, 177–78, 180–82, 185–87, 191; and Kohlberg at 169–70, 177–78, 180, 182–87, 191.

85. By the time Richards earned his undergraduate degree in philosophy, British philosopher Alfred North Whitehead was perhaps the most influential philosopher who began questioning the traditional Aristotelian substance metaphysics. See, e.g., Whitehead, *Process and Reality*, *Modes of Thought*, and *Essays in Science and Philosophy*. Sartre was also questioning substance anthropology by this time. Sartre, *Being and Nothingness*.

86. Richards, *Children's Ministry*, 43.

87. See, e.g., Richards, "Life's Dynamic: The Church's 'Family' Relationship," 40–47, "An Interpersonal Dimension," 106–14, and "The Role of Relationships," 314–15, in *Children's Ministry*, and "Nurture in the New Testament," 45–47, "Social Relationships of Children," 132–44, "The Impact of Family," 181–200, "Patterns in the Home," 265–74, and "Nurture in Faith Community," 371–72, in *Theology*.

relationships in the home, church and school, he failed to focus on the child's relationship to the world of things, images, money and commerce in the United States. Richards overlooked perhaps the most formative aspect of nurture. The AAEC's parents, peers, teachers and church leaders are all formed within the matrices of advanced technological consumer capitalism. Foundational to those matrices is an anthropology grounded in economic interests.[88] Without critical awareness of this aspect of American life and history, processes of socialization and nurture remain subservient to economic concerns, thus retarding formation of evangelical faith.[89]

Sociological studies like Wuthnow's *God and Mammon in America* and Penning and Smidt's *Evangelicalism: The Next Generation* make perfect sense in light of this evangelical blind spot.[90] Americans in general and American-evangelicals in particular fail to realize how religious their economic vision of life in the United States actually is. They do not realize that the socialization processes of the evangelical subculture and broader culture of the United States are intricately intertwined, interdependent, and interrelated in the economic realm. Forming a child for one forms a child for the other, and vice versa, yet with little if any substantive distinction. The economic interests of both are essentially one and the same.

88. For a dense, critical perspective of the intellectual history of this grounding from the standpoint of theology, philosophy and social theory, see Milbank, "Political Economy as Theodicy and Agonistics," in *Theology and Social Theory*, 27–48.

89. Cf. Beard, *Economic Interpretation of Constitution*, 324: "The Constitution was essentially an economic document based upon the concept that the fundamental rights of property are anterior to government and morally beyond the reach of popular majorities." See also McGuire, *More Perfect Union*, for a new economic interpretation of the Constitution.

90. See, e.g., Wuthnow, *God and Mammon in America*; Penning and Smidt, *Evangelicalism: The Next Generation*. Penning and Smidt are evangelical political science educators and researchers at Calvin College. Their empirical study updates and expands James Hunter's seminal 1987 study of students attending nine evangelical colleges, Hunter, *Evangelicalism: The Coming Generation*, providing a recent social scientific window into the theological, moral, social and political views of evangelical college students and thus a perspective on what the first two decades of evangelical formation in the United States is producing in its children.

The Child as Relational Learner in the Matrices of Sin

Economics aside, Richards is satisfied in his theology of nurture with simply accepting the biblical representation of humanity as simultaneously "dead in sin" and "bearing the mark of the eternal!"[91] Spiritual death with the image of God in humanity was transmitted to every human from the original garden. Thus, he does not concern himself with the complexities of original sin in relation to children as Edwards did.

Hence, Richards is unconcerned with whether children are sinners and if so when and how they become such. He assumes they are and that they are free to learn and be formed in familial, ecclesial and educational contexts. Because the Bible does not address such issues, the important point is to determine how to help children grow in accordance with their developmental capacities and simultaneously grow in the knowledge and experience of God.

But this raises some difficulties for Richards's theology of nurture, as it did for Bushnell. If biblical agnosticism is claimed on the doctrine of sin as applied to children, a host of biblical and theological problems arise for the theology of nurture. The most obvious is the theological-anthropological problem of the "noetic effect of sin" seminarians first learn about in systematic theology. Sin affects the mind, so shouldn't we attend carefully to how sin affects the learning process and, at a deeper level, how it may distort and capture human freedom?

Second, if children are born as "damned vipers" until regenerate, as Edwards and his modern descendants claim, then it would seem that the most important aspect of nurture will be conversion. This tends to orient nurture toward a theological-anthropological understanding that views sin as an impediment to nurture, something to be overcome through discipline and instruction in the gospel of Jesus Christ. Just as there is a noetic effect of sin, there is also a noetic effect of regeneration-conversion. The ultimate goal in education, then, would be conversion which can then bring about sanctified development in the child. This may be viewed as the conversionist reading of the evangelical mandate in Ephesians 6:4 to nurture children in the "discipline and instruction of the Lord." On the other hand, if a Bushnellian approach is taken, the tendency is to focus on the word translated "bring them up" and thus to emphasize the developmental side of the equation in nurture. This usually entails the

---

91. Richards, "An Understanding of Man," in *Theology*, 14.

subordination of the conversionist dimension to developmental understandings of the child and can lead to a denial of sin (liberal Christianity), a de-emphasis or mysticization of sin (Bushnell) or a decision to embrace biblical agnosticism in regard to sin (Richards) as it relates to children.

Perhaps it is best in a theology of nurture to hold both noetic doctrines in interactive tension as a conversionist developmentalism or developmental conversionism. Such an approach would deal realistically and hopefully with the noetic effects of sin and salvation. It would entail keeping the gospel central to nurture and education as the one thing that must be of "first importance" (1 Cor 15:1–4, NASB).

In either case, whether a theology of nurture tends toward the Bushnellian or Edwardsian sides of the spectrum, the impoverishing characteristics of nurture in affluence are overlooked. Both fail to take into consideration the economic context in which the AAEC is formed, because both are supported by a theological economics receptive to and uncritical of the liberal democratic institutions that form them. As such, both remain unaware of the anthropology of individual freedom upon which those institutions are built.

Comfortable with claiming biblical ignorance and embracing basic "assumptions" about human nature and sin, Richards assures that his theology of nurture will continue critically unaware of this context. This is reflected in a series of biblically revealed dialectics about evangelical faith and experience, in which Richards claims Bible-believing Christians

> struggle to balance Scripture's exalted picture of human beings created in the image of God with its brutal honesty about human debasement and sin. We know what it means to be members of a lost humanity but remain objects of God's love. We have experienced the inner grip of death, traced it back to Adam, and felt the tug toward sin that warps society into a jumble of injustice and pain. We balance in our own experience an awareness of our freedom and powerlessness, and the touch of a sovereign yet gentle grace. We know the delicacy of God's touch, as He comes to us with invitation, yet never crushes us with that sense of His power that would rob us of personal responsibility. All these things we know, for they are the great realities our faith affirms and our experience echoes. These are the givens: the convictions about the shape of reality unveiled in Scripture, held by the church through the ages.[92]

92. Richards, *Children's Ministry*, 73–74.

According to Richards, these biblical "givens" are not "the assumptions we need to state as we look for a theological framework for ministry with children."[93] Instead, the assumptions with which a theology of nurture must be concerned are those that "help us understand humans as learners."[94]

It would seem, however, that understandings of human nature, human sin and humans as created in the image of God might bear heavily upon understanding "humans as learners." But Richards does not think so. He sums up the "important testimony of Scripture about persons as learners (including children!)" by asserting, presuppositionally, that children are "*free*, responsible individuals, whose *growth* can be influenced but never determined, and whose *progress* in faith is linked with personal relationship to God."[95] Echoes of the presuppositions of progress and growth in Bushnell's theology of nurture resound here, as does the anthropology of liberty that lies at the heart of neoliberal economic conceptions of human nature in late modernity.

But does not the "inner grip of death, traced . . . back to Adam" affect learning? And what about "human debasement and sin"? Does not the "tug toward sin that warps society into a jumble of injustice and pain" shape children as learners as well? And how is learning affected by nurture in the matrices of technological consumer capitalism? Such questions point to the reality that the problem of nurture in an American evangelicalism embedded in affluence intersects every dimension of human existence and experience in late modernity. Yet, this reality is overlooked in evangelical nurture of the gospel.

The Bushnellian manner in which Richards bypasses such questions is problematic. The assumption that children are free, responsible individuals subject to influence by others does not overcome the realities that nurture takes place within the matrices of a warped, jumbled society "of injustice and pain." Richards is both enigmatic and Bushnellian here. Like Bushnell, he fails to see that the very theology of nurture he espouses incorporates the germs that retard its development.

The failure to assess critically the anthropological assumptions inherent in a perspective of children as "free" to learn, grow, and progress

93. Ibid., 74.
94. Ibid.
95. Ibid. (emphasis added).

in evangelical faith infects Richards's entire theology of nurture from the start. Thus, just as Bushnell's *Christian Nurture* served rather than transformed his Victorian and republican cultural context, Richards's theology of nurture serves rather than transforms nurture within an American evangelicalism embedded in affluence. Richards, like Bushnell, granted a central role to God's supernatural working through the natural processes of human learning. He hoped to overcome sin's reach into child nurture, just as Bushnell did.

Unlike Bushnell, however, Richards was not so bold as to say that a child properly nurtured in an evangelical home will grow up never knowing himself not to be a Christian. This implies that a child can grow up in such a home knowing God but not knowing sin. But this is wishful thinking at best, and theological nonsense at worst. An evangelical theology of nurture must contend with the doctrine of sin intelligently, not enigmatically. This is the task of the synchronic focus in part II of the thesis, in which attention is given to how sin manifests itself in nurture within the context of American evangelicalism and affluence. The sociological and theological perspectives developed there should help evangelicals nurture their children with critical awareness of the formative affects of affluence in late modernity.

CONCLUSION

From 1880 to 1930, driven by technological innovation and managerial expertise, America's capitalist consumer culture emerged, ushering in a societal and political apparatus characterized by mass "diffusion of comfort and prosperity . . . not merely as part of the American experience . . . but instead as its centerpiece."[96] The American Dream became infused with the hope of affluence and freedom from scarcity for every American. This involved the promise of equal social, political and economic rights to desire and pursue the good things in life for children.

By 1880, the process of "democratizing . . . desire" that began politically on the eve of the Civil War was firmly in place.[97] As the political career of Herbert Hoover and every American president since proves, American leaders sought to insure their constituents with not only the

---

96. Leach, *Land of Desire*, 6.

97. Ibid.

opportunity to hope for but also to realize liberation in the emerging consumer culture of the United States. Thus, "American culture . . . became more democratic after 1880 in the sense that everybody—children as well as adults, men and women, black and white—would have the same right as individuals to desire, long for, and wish for whatever they pleased."[98]

The history of American evangelicalism and evangelical theology regarding children, from Horace Bushnell to Lawrence Richards, discloses the formative nature of this social and economic matrix. The American-evangelical child entered the twentieth century embedded in the emerging culture of affluence and the society constructed by technological consumer capitalism. From 1880 through the 1920s, most American children were nurtured in a system of education grounded in nineteenth-century Protestantism fused with and subordinated to the industrial-capitalist presupposition of consumer capitalist progress. The evangelical Protestantism of this period would fragment into liberal and fundamentalist camps in the 1920s about the same time Herbert Hoover was engineering a monumental governmental-commercial partnership in the United States.

The advance of affluence in the United States, particularly since 1950, has been so dramatic and extensive that the economic dimension of human formation has been assumed rather than critically assessed. The anthropology of liberty that sustains modern economics has profound implications for understanding human nature and sociality. Technological advances made possible by affluence give rise not only to advances in anthropological understanding but also to fundamental changes in human nature. For most of the twentieth century, evangelical conservatives were preoccupied with fighting for intellectual, political, cultural and social legitimacy in their battles with theological liberals. In the process, both camps disregarded the formative effects of economics in American life.

Although they may have disagreed over the social and political implications of the gospel in modern American life, theological liberals and conservatives alike were in essential agreement that capitalist consumer culture was proving to be the best economic option for all Americans, children included. As a result, evangelicals overlooked an important aspect of nurture and thus were complicit in the evolution and emergence of the AAEC in the second half of the twentieth century. The aim of chap-

98. Ibid.

ters 4 and 5 is to demonstrate the sociological effects of this oversight and how those effects are perpetuated in John Schneider's moral theology of affluence, in which he encourages cultivation of the twin capitalist habits of acquisition and enjoyment.

PART II

The AAEC in Synchronic Perspective

4

An Evangelical Sociology of the AAEC

It appears, then, that the consumer capitalism of pre-1930 America
has achieved a new level of strength and influence. It seems to be
making advances everywhere, especially in the wake of the col-
lapse of communism. It also appears to have a nearly unchallenged
hold over every aspect of American life from politics to culture,
so much so that the United States looks like a fabulous bazaar to
much of the rest of the world. . . . Just as cities in the United States
once operated as generators of consumer desire for internal markets, today America functions similarly on a global scale.

—WILLIAM LEACH[1]

INTRODUCTION: THE SOCIOLOGY OF CHILDHOOD AND THE AAEC

Born in the U.S.A., the AAEC is nurtured in a "fabulous bazaar" of consumer culture. Chapters 2 and 3 (part I) have demonstrated the evolution
of the AAEC within that culture and the role that Evangelicalism played
in bringing it about. This chapter brings a sociological lens to bear upon
this historical representation of the AAEC.

The diachronic perspective of Part I will be interpreted synchronically in this chapter through the development of an Evangelical sociology
of the AAEC by applying William Corsaro's sociological model of childhood "interpretive reproductions" to the child nurtured in Evangelical
affluence in the United States.[2] This will be accomplished in three sections
below.

1. Leach, *Land of Desire*, 388.
2. Corsaro, *Sociology* 2nd, 18–26, 107–32.

Section 1 introduces Corsaro's theory and "orb web" model that depicts the peer cultures of children as "spun on the framework of the knowledge and institutions of adult society."[3] Human development is conceived in his theory as *embedded in the collective production of a series of peer cultures that in turn contribute to reproduction and change in the wider adult society or culture.*[4] This model will prove helpful in looking at the AAEC's embeddedness.

Section 2 proceeds from there by applying Corsaro's theory of "interpretive reproduction" to the AAEC, and in the process discerns the sociological contours of the AAEC's nurture in affluence. Section 3 concludes the chapter and sets the stage for the evangelical theology of the AAEC presented in chapter 5.

"INTERPRETIVE REPRODUCTION" AND THE AAEC

Corsaro is a leading sociologist of children and childhood in the United States. His theory of children's interpretive reproductions builds upon traditional sociological theories that have been applied to the sociological study of children: deterministic and constructivist models.

There are two kinds of deterministic models of the sociology of childhood: functionalist and reproductive. Corsaro identifies Talcott Parsons as the seminal functionalist thinker in the United States. Functionalists view socialization of children as the internalization of the functional requirements of society. Reproductive theorists extend functionalist analysis to seek an account for how internalization of society's functional requirements leads to systemic reproductions of societal and class inequalities in children during childhood.

While providing helpful insights, according to Corsaro, such deterministic approaches to the sociological study of children and childhood oversimplify complex social and cultural factors, overemphasize the outcomes of socialization in children, and underestimate the dynamic nature of the socialization process. Furthermore, most early studies in the socialization of children were influenced by leading theories in developmental psychology, particularly behaviorism, which led to viewing children as reflexive participants in the socialization process. They conceived chil-

3. Corsaro, *Sociology*, 25.
4. Ibid. (emphasis in original).

dren in this process as passively formed and disciplined through adult rewards and punishments.[5]

The constructivist model of socialization, on the other hand, developed out of new perspectives arising from developmental psychology that viewed children as active rather than passive in the process of human development. Children are seen as actively appropriating and internalizing formative information and experiences from their relationships to others and the world of things. This is the psycho-social process through which children interpret life, develop their personalities and construct their understandings of the world of persons and things. Corsaro interprets Jean Piaget's theory of cognitive development and Lev Vygotsky's sociocultural theories of psychological internalization and the zone of proximal development as providing the foundations for the constructivist model of childhood socialization.[6]

But according to Corsaro, the constructivist model suffers from two primary weaknesses. First, like deterministic models, they overemphasize individual development. "Constructivism offers an active but lonely view of children . . . There is little, if any, consideration of how interpersonal relations reflect cultural systems, or how children, through their participation in communicative events, become part of these interpersonal relations and cultural patterns and reproduce them collectively."[7] The second weakness is an inordinate concern for the goal, or end, of the child's development. In other words, the overemphasis upon the child's maturation from childhood to adulthood limits the sociological study of children. It results in missing the sociological significance of children's relationships with peers as well as adults and the broader culture. It also results in a sociological blinder arising from employing Vygotsky's internalization principle such that "many now view the appropriation of culture as the movement from the external to the internal. This misconception pushes children's collective actions with others to the background and implies that an individual actor's participation in society occurs only after such individual internalization."[8] The sociology of children has learned that the process is much more dialectic and dynamic.

5. Corsaro, *Sociology*, 7–18.

6. Ibid., 10–17.

7. Ibid., 16.

8. Ibid., 17.

More recent sociologists of children have extended Piagetian and Vygotskyian constructivist theory to focus on agency and peer interaction as important factors in childhood sociology.[9] This has led to a variety of sociological studies of children's agency, including the study of children as economic agents.[10] Corsaro incorporates these extensions of Piaget and Vygotsky in his interpretive reproduction theory. Following and appropriating cultural psychologist Barbara Rogoff's thought, Corsaro sees the individual, interpersonal and communal dimensions of human development as "a process of *people's changing participation in sociocultural activities of their communities.*"[11] The developmental processes at work in these dimensions must be analyzed together. The goal is to discern how an individual's participation in collective actions involves developmental appropriations of shared meanings and events, such that "the individual's previous participation contributes to and primes the event at hand by having prepared it."[12]

This perspective is central to Corsaro's theory of interpretive reproductions. With it he seeks to build upon and at the same time remedy the problems he sees as inherent in deterministic and constructivist models of childhood socialization. He claims that his approach captures the manner in which children not only adopt and internalize culture and society but also how they appropriate, reinvent and reproduce it. This sociological model considers children as communal participants in the process of negotiating, sharing and creating culture and society. Children are viewed as innovative, creative interpreters of adults and the world. They interpret sociocultural information and experiences in creative ways that lead to innovative appropriations that meet their own personal and peer interests. They do not simply internalize society and culture, but they also actively participate in and contribute to cultural production and change. Children are both consumers *and* producers of culture. As we saw with Hoover, this has been the commercial-governmental goal in the United States since the 1920s.

At the same time, as participants in these socio-cultural processes children are enmeshed in a web of relations that give rise to these processes.

9. Ibid.

10. See, e.g., Levison, "Children as Economic Agents," 125–34.

11. Corsaro, *Sociology* 2nd, 17 (emphasis original), citing Rogoff, *Cultural Nature of Human Development*, 32 [sic; correct page is 42].

12. Corsaro, *Sociology*, 18.

That is, they are "*constrained by the existing social structure and by societal reproduction*."[13] In other words, although children interpret and creatively reproduce their cultures, they are simultaneously bound by the societies from which those cultures emerge. Their societies and cultures have been formed and affected over time, which for the AAEC is the history of industrial and technological consumer capitalism. Corsaro's theory of interpretive reproduction points to the importance of understanding the AAEC as nurtured in an American Evangelicalism both formed within and formative of the industrial, technological and informational-iconic revolutions of the nineteenth and twentieth centuries. In other words, Evangelicals have been crucial players in producing and sustaining the culture and society of late modern technological consumer capitalism in the United States.

Corsaro emphasizes two aspects of children's sociological development: (1) "the importance of language and cultural routines" and (2) "the reproductive nature of children's evolving membership in their culture."[14] Language is a "symbolic system" that enables children to encode, or program, their "local, social and cultural structure" and also to establish, maintain and create "social and psychological realities."[15] The function and use of language by children is a "deeply embedded" psycho-social reality, which is "instrumental in the accomplishment of the concrete routines of social life."[16] These routines cultivate the security and consciousness of group belonging in children. Language and cultural routines are therefore seen as an evolving relational dialectic in children that impels them to interpret and participate in their cultures, and as a result they collectively create their own peer worlds through creative adaptations and modifications of their broader cultures.[17] Echoes of Bushnell can be heard here in Corsaro's conceptualization of language and cultural routines.

Corsaro analogizes his interpretive reproduction model to the orb web spun by the common garden spider. This heuristic device is used graphically to illustrate his model of sociological interpretive reproduc-

13. Ibid., 19 (emphasis original).
14. Ibid.
15. Ibid.
16. Ibid.
17. Ibid., 24.

tion in childhood.[18] This model is helpful to this work in several ways. It provides a mechanism for viewing the AAEC's development in social, cultural and historical light. Not only is the AAEC formed as a result of being nurtured within affluence, the AAEC also contributes to the reproduction of the culture of affluence through active and passive participation, interacting with the world of others and things embedded in that culture, learning through language and cultural routines how others interact with that world and at the same time developing their particular preferences, interests and desires in affluence. As a result, the AAEC is not only a consumer but also a producer and reproducer of that culture. This can be seen in the manner in which commerce in the United States expands its social, cultural and developmental analyses for marketing, advertising and branding purposes.[19]

This sociological understanding of the AAEC opens another window into theological understanding of the Evangelical child born and nurtured in the U.S.A. As chapter 3 demonstrated, the Hooverian dream of production diffused into consumption was realized in the twentieth century. It catapulted the U.S. into the twenty-first century with a Gross Domestic Product (GDP) of $16 trillion, a GDP dwarfing other advanced liberal democratic economies. Evangelicals, like all citizens of the United States, are born into the production-consumption web of relationships that constitute American culture and society grounded in such a dominant economic formation. From birth they are relationally connected and neurologically formed through their senses to a world of others and things formed by and for affluence in the socio-cultural and socio-economic context of the United States. An essential component of their individual, cultural and social development consists in an abundance of goods, images and experiences that late modern American prosperity affords.

As the AAEC develops, interpretive reproductions are made that simultaneously consume and produce the culture of affluence in which they are embedded. Evangelical parents and churches participate with their children in the socio-cultural processes of affluence with little critical awareness. They and their children delight in the material prosperity made possible by mass affluence, as John Schneider commends in *The Good of Affluence* (see chapter 5). They seek to nurture evangelical faith

18. Ibid., 26.

19. See, e.g., Quart, *Branded*; Klein, *No Logo*; Miller, "The Commodification of Culture," in *Consuming Religion*, 32–72.

and practice with scant critical awareness of the spiritual and moral problems affluence presents. In the process, Evangelicals interpret and reproduce the culture of affluence in which they are embedded without developing a critical stance toward it. In addition to consuming, interpreting and reproducing the "good" that late modern abundance makes possible, they produce their own "Christian" versions of affluence for diffusion into consumption.[20] This is the result of the social and cultural interaction of Evangelicals embedded in a virulent culture of affluence such as the United States. But without critical awareness of the historical, social and cultural context of American affluence, evangelicals will miss the impoverishing aspects of affluence that the Bible they love warns against.

THE AAEC'S INTERPRETIVE REPRODUCTIONS OF AMERICAN-EVANGELICAL AFFLUENCE

One of the beneficial insights of Corsaro's childhood socialization theory is that children produce their own peer cultures through an interactive process of interpreting and reproducing the society in which they are embedded. It is a "collective, productive-reproductive view" of children spontaneously participating "as active members of both childhood and adult cultures."[21] When applied to childhood in a culture of Evangelical affluence, this perspective yields valuable insights into the AAEC's formation.

The AAEC's interpretive reproduction begins in an Evangelical family and extended in an Evangelical church. It projects forward into the developmental horizon through a process of collective interactions with family members, peers and churches. The AAEC creatively appropriates the language, symbols, knowledge and relations experienced through these interactions, all of which are embedded in a world of Evangelical affluence.

---

20. A visit to the Christian Booksellers Convention, any number of Christian bookstores (e.g., Mardel's which is owned by the Christian billionaire founder of Hobby Lobby), churches with bookstores and coffee shops, etc., should provide sufficient anecdotal evidence of this claim. Hopefully, this chapter will stimulate empirical studies by Evangelical sociologists, economists, educators, and anthropologists that will test and corroborate it.

21. Corsaro, *Sociology*, 27.

As the AAEC encounters peers through play, church relations, school and other activities, the creative appropriations from the adult world of affluence begin to take on a life of their own and emerge as a series of peer cultures of affluence "based on the institutional structure of the adult culture."[22] This structure is neoliberal democratic capitalism grounded in a technological consumerism generated by scientific advances and managed by economic disciplines. As the peer cultures of the AAEC engage, form and transform this culture to their interests and needs, the interaction contributes to the production and extension of the broader culture of affluence. It also helps ensure the continued subversion of evangelical theology and practice to the economic interests of American society and culture.

To my knowledge, this is the first attempt to apply the sociological theory of interpretive reproductions to the child in American Evangelicalism and affluence. The AAEC has neither been identified nor studied in the sociology of childhood. Thus, evidence of the AAEC's interpretive reproductions in Evangelical affluence must be adduced through a theoretical application of Corsaro's model to the AAEC. This will be accomplished by interacting with appropriate selections from the relevant bodies of literature on Evangelicalism and affluence. The aim is to identify some of the salient language and cultural routines of Evangelical affluence and the interpretive-reproductive nature of the AAEC's evolving membership in the culture of Evangelical affluence.

Consistent with Corsaro's theory, this will involve a search for the "symbolic system" that enables the AAEC to encode his "local, social and cultural structure" in Evangelical affluence and also to establish, maintain and create "social and psychological realities" within that culture.[23] It is a search for the AAEC's "deeply embedded" social instrumentalities utilized by the AAEC in the process of accomplishing "the concrete routines of social life" in affluence.[24] According to Corsaro's theory, these routines cultivate the security and consciousness of the AAEC's group belonging in affluence and lead to the AAEC's collective construction of

---

22. Corsaro, *Sociology*, 44.
23. Ibid.
24. Ibid.

Evangelical peer worlds through creative adaptations and modifications of the broader culture of affluence in the United States.[25]

Sociological studies of Americans and Evangelicals point to a recurring conclusion in the sociology of religion in the United States: a strong majority of Americans, Evangelicals included, consistently embrace religious, social and economic individualism, charitable voluntarism, and the individual's responsibility for personal conversion and change.[26] Corsaro's theory provides a means of seeing these sociological factors in relation to the AAEC. The AAEC interpretively reproduces and extends these aspects of American Evangelicalism, including the problem of affluence.

The following subsections develop these sociological findings. Together, they will provide a synchronic perspective of the AAEC's cultural and social embeddedness in the subculture of Evangelical affluence in the United States.

The AAEC's Interpretive Reproductions of American Individualism

Chapters 2 and 3 demonstrated that Richards's hybrid developmental conversionism shares a fundamental oversight with the theological anthropologies of the child in Edwards and Bushnell. Although he factored sociological and psychological aspects into his biblical theology of human development, Richards failed to consider the manner in which economic concerns penetrate and perhaps even dominate the social, cultural and psychological dimensions of human development in the United States. Thus, he perpetuates in his theology of nurture an Evangelical myopia to economics that was in Edwards and, to a much greater extent, Bushnell before him.

One aspect of the economic penetration of life in the United States can be seen in American individualism. This was demonstrated in the interaction with Hoover and his *American Individualism* in chapter 3. This subsection adduces further evidence of this socio-cultural reality within which the AAEC is formed.

Dennis Hollinger has made a convincing case that during the two decades from 1956 to 1976 individualism profoundly shaped Evangelical leaders as a metaphysical system of belief, a system of values and a philoso-

---

25. Ibid., 24.

26. See, e.g., Wuthnow, *God and Mammon in America*; Penning and Smidt, *Evangelicalism: The Next Generation*; Hunter, *Evangelicalism: The Coming Generation*.

phy of social life.[27] These were decades of growth for both Evangelicalism and affluence in the United States. Hollinger critically assessed the literature produced by Evangelical leaders during this time period to demonstrate his claims.

His first point is that these leaders consistently demonstrated individualist conceptions of social ethics. Secondly, they held to an atomistic view of sin and society that negated the need for structural social change. Third, they embraced the conservative side of liberal economic theory (i.e., free market capitalism with minimal governmental intervention) as the best solution to economic issues. And fourth, their political theory and public policy positions emphasized personal freedom, minimal governmental intervention in the individual's life, and conservative resolutions of the dominant socio-political issues of the era (i.e., communism, race and foreign policy). Hollinger summarizes the profoundly individualistic thought of these leaders during this formative period as follows:

> a metaphysic with an atomistic worldview; a value system heralding freedom, privacy, autonomy, and self-sufficiency; and a social philosophy with a particular view of the relationship of individuals to society . . . [which] stresses personal morality over social ethics, individual transformation as the key to social change, laissez-faire economics, and a politics extolling freedom of the individual and a limited state.[28]

Christian Smith's subsequent, detailed sociological study of American Evangelicalism confirms these characteristics of Evangelical leaders as well.[29] It provides another illuminative lens for seeing the AAEC's interpretive reproductions of Evangelical affluence in the United States. Consistent with other sociological studies of religion and Evangelicals in the United States,[30] Smith finds that Evangelicals in the United States approach social and economic issues in essentially the same way as other Americans of similar socioeconomic status. However, according to Smith, Evangelicals approach such issues with "an exaggerated and spiritualized version of the broader culture's individualism."[31]

---

27. Hollinger, *Individualism and Social Ethics*.

28. Ibid., 44.

29. Smith, *American Evangelicalism*.

30. See, e.g., Wuthnow, *God and Mammon*; Penning and Smidt, *Evangelicalism*.

31. Smith, *American Evangelicalism*, 192 n. 3.

These findings are consistent with those of chapters 2 and 3. Nineteenth and twentieth century Evangelicalism in the United States was both formative of and formed by a republican individualism grounded in liberal economic theory. As Wauzzinski has shown, this enculturation process involved the mammonization of Evangelicalism as it engaged in a Faustian bargain with American industrialism. Evangelicals such as Bushnell, with others like those critiqued by Wauzzinski and Leach,[32] contributed to constructing a religious, social and cultural milieu in which a political-commercial engineer like Hoover could build a great American consumer paradise in which both God and mammon could be served together with little conflict of conscience.

Hoover's *American Individualism* and studies like Hollinger's and Smith's demonstrate that this Hooverian sociocultural construction was made possible, and continues to be sustained, in large part by American Evangelicals. It is not difficult to see why Evangelicals, as Smith demonstrates, have a difficult time seeing the contradictions in their beliefs and practices in affluence. With potent social, cultural and political influence during the nineteenth century, which was only temporarily displaced in the early twentieth century (as the recent Evangelical resurgence in politics and culture shows), it seems that Evangelicals have a difficult time assessing themselves self-critically on such issues.

This is particularly true in regard to economic issues. After all, there is no real difference between American Evangelicals and other similarly situated Americans when it comes to affluence. Most enjoy the good of affluence with little critical reflection upon the spiritual and moral lack (poverty) it tends to cultivate. And those who seriously consider such issues eventually short circuit in "an increasingly uncomfortable cognitive dissonance," as Smith puts it.[33] The result is that Evangelicals enjoy the blessings of affluence along with most other Americans, while solutions to social problems remain within the individualistic domain of private conscience, voluntary charity and the "personal influence strategy" of Evangelicals.[34]

32. Wauzzinski focused on Charles Finney, Francis Wayland and Russell Conwell. Wauzzinski, *Between God and Gold*, 126–58; Leach focused on the sad evangelical legacy of affluence found in John Wannamaker, his son and grandson. Leach, *Land of Desire*, 32–35, 221–24, 263–64.

33. Smith, *American Evangelicalism*, 212.

34. Ibid.

Smith develops a "subcultural identity" theory of religious persistence and strength within pluralistic, modern societies to study American Evangelicalism.[35] He utilizes this theory to discern a relational "personal influence strategy" employed by American evangelicals in regard to religious, moral, social and economic issues, which provides another window into the AAEC's formation in affluence.[36] Before looking at how Smith utilizes his theory to study one of the ironies of Evangelicalism's subcultural distinctiveness, i.e., "how evangelicals think the Christian Gospel should affect the world of work, business, and the economy,"[37] it will be helpful first to look more closely at his subcultural identity theories of religious "*persistence*"[38] and "*strength*"[39] as applied to American Evangelicalism.

Smith constructs the theory from "a variety of elementary sociological principles into a single theoretical interpretation of the fate of religion in modern society."[40] Analyzing the massive amounts of data gathered in his study through the lens of his subcultural identity theories, Smith discovered that American Evangelicalism has been able to thrive in the pluralistic, late modern United States because it combined clear subcultural distinctives with intense social engagement during its twentieth century embattlement. Compared with mainline, liberal and fundamentalist Protestantism in the twentieth century, Evangelicalism demonstrated remarkable growth, persistence and strength. Smith focused on the relative vitality of Evangelicalism compared to other forms of American Protestantism. He found that its strength lies in two dimensions: (1) it "capitalizes" on the pluralistic culture of the United States in which it is embedded by socially constructing "subcultural distinction, engagement

---

35. Ibid., 89–119.

36. Ibid., 187–203.

37. Ibid., 203–10.

38. The theory of persistence is that, "*Religion survives and can thrive in pluralistic, modern society by embedding itself in subcultures that offer satisfying morally orienting collective identities which provide adherents meaning and belonging.*" Ibid., 118 (emphasis original).

39. The theory of strength is that, "*In a pluralistic society, those religious groups will be relatively stronger which better possess and employ the cultural tools needed to create both clear distinction from and significant engagement and tension with other relevant outgroups, short of becoming genuinely countercultural.*" Smith, *American Evangelicalism*, 118–19 (emphasis original).

40. Ibid., 90.

and tension between itself and relevant outgroups," and (2) it "flourishes on difference, engagement, tension, conflict, and threat."[41]

Decoding this academic jargon of the sociology of religion into evangelicalese, the American Evangelical will recognize what Smith is saying. The language, rhetoric and subcultural routines of Evangelical life in the United States are laden with warfare metaphors drawn from the Bible and applied to modern life. Children raised in Evangelical homes and churches readily identify with issues of competition and warfare, and they are able to understand the concepts of winning and losing very well. Liberal hostility to Evangelical or "Fundamentalist" (the two are often confused and pejoratively conjoined in the media) doctrinal and moral beliefs engenders deployment of such metaphors by both believers and leaders alike within these social groups. Evangelicals see and experience the antipathy expressed toward them and their beliefs by the secular and religious liberal culture, political institutions and society in the United States not only as attacks upon them personally and upon their religious freedoms, but also as attacks upon their God and Christ. The AAEC interprets this social and cultural warfare through his parents and church, along with his peers, and rests in the fact that he is on the right side because it is, at the end of the day, his parents (and God's) side.

But this warfare and the attacks have worked for good, if Smith is right. Evangelicalism has benefited from the persecution, if it can be called that, and has learned to capitalize on the liberal society's assaults through subcultural routines of engagement, tension and distinction that have produced a vibrant Evangelical subculture. Furthermore, it seems that the hallmark of Evangelical flourishing within the secular liberal culture is that it incorporates the distinction, engagement, tensions and conflicts that liberal culture in the United States brings to it. The threats posed by the broader cultural attempt to wipe God from the American landscape actually served to identify, mobilize and strengthen Evangelicalism during the twentieth century. The result is that the AAEC is now embedded in a vibrant, growing and powerful cultural force in the United States.

What should not be overlooked, however, is that the resources for Evangelicalism's strength flow from the same font of affluence as the resources for other social, cultural and religious groups in the United States. The affluence that began in the 1950s and triumphed in the 1980s was

---

41. Ibid., 153.

made possible by neoliberal economic theory and practice in the United States, and all cultural groups (whether secular or religious, liberal or conservative) have embraced the blessings and benefits affluence brings. Affluence made the culture wars possible and sustains them to this day.[42] Evangelicalism seems to have been able selectively to appropriate certain beneficial aspects of modernity in its struggle against liberalism. In particular, it seems to have been able to harness the good of affluence in the liberal warfare by marshalling billions of dollars in capital to fund its efforts since the 1950s.[43]

Conservative and liberal rhetoric aside, there is remarkable agreement that neoliberal economic theory and practice expressed in technological consumer capitalism works very well to spread affluence to large masses of the population. Despite the ongoing debates over "the growing gap between rich and poor" in late modernity, both liberals and conservatives along all social, political, cultural and religious spectrums in the United States wholeheartedly embrace the benefits of affluence. The evidence for this claim is the fact that none of the intellectuals, scholars or theologians I have read or know of who decry this growing gap can be found moving to the slums of the world to join in solidarity with the poor to help alleviate their suffering on humanity's underside. There are few followers of Mother Theresa and the Latin American liberation theologians in late modernity. Indeed, affluence is very hard to leave. Moreover, though thankful for the care and concern of those who actually do join them in their suffering, the poor are incredulous that someone would move from affluence to poverty when their greatest hope is to move from poverty to affluence. Thus, since 1989 virtually every government on the planet now looks at the successes of consumer capitalism in the West (Europe and the United States) and in Japan, Australia, Singapore and other successful liberal democracies to combat poverty and lift the masses into middle class happiness.

Smith's sociological theory misses this foundational and formative economic aspect of American life grounded in neoliberal economics. He reads the agreement between Evangelical and secular conceptions of economics as evidence of contradiction embedded within Evangelicalism,

42. See, e.g., Hunter, *Culture Wars*; Green, Guth, Smidt and Kellstedt (eds.), *Religion and the Culture Wars*, 174–92; Browning, et al., *Culture Wars to Common Ground*.

43. See, e.g., Hamilton, "Financing of American Evangelicalism Since 1945," in Eskridge and Noll (eds.), *More Money, More Ministry*, 81–103.

which leads to Evangelical ineffectiveness in bringing about "distinctively Christian social change."[44] One of the ironies Smith sees in Evangelicalism's strength of subcultural distinction is its inability to effect economic change in the United States. But apparently he fails to realize the role Evangelicalism played in bringing the economic substructure of American culture and society about. This can be seen in the way he interprets Evangelical perspectives on the way the "Christian Gospel should affect the world of work, business, and the economy."[45]

The value in Smith's interpretation is that it illumines the social world in which the AAEC is nurtured. The AAEC's social world is one constructed by Evangelicals with a narrow focus on "interpersonal relationships and individual morality" that, in regard to economic and other social issues, prevents them from moving "beyond the limits of the personal influence strategy or beyond merely improving the morality of individual business people through the influence of personal associations."[46] In other words, the persons who constitute the AAEC's primary formative relationships are generally incapable of sustaining a sociocultural critique of technological consumer capitalism because they are delimited by the horizon of their interpersonal relationalism.

This is true insofar as it goes. But it is also true of most Americans, as the results of Smith's study show, and it seems that most Americans like things that way (Evangelicals included). It is hard to argue against affluence. Whether Evangelical or liberal Protestant, secular or religious, very few renounce affluence and embrace poverty. This is true of even the most trenchant critics of affluence, whose literary efforts at denouncing affluence have often been rewarded well.[47] Smith simply shows sociologically that Evangelicals, and by implication the AAEC, are formed by and for affluence. They end up loving it and living for it because their parents and churches do. From a biblical standpoint, this is problematic. Affluence brings with it "the cares of the world, and the lure of wealth, and the desire for other things" in the world that can "come in and choke the word" of the gospel (Mark 4:19).

---

44. Smith, *American Evangelicalism*, 178.

45. Ibid., 203.

46. Ibid.

47. See the examples in Horowitz, *Anxieties of Affluence*, 129–61.

Thus, although Smith points out that Evangelicals "leave the existing larger structures of business and the economy largely unquestioned,"[48] he is stating the obvious about Evangelicals and the vast majority of Americans. His subject-specific economic critique of American Evangelicals from the data of his study arises from his reading of the Bible, Christian tradition and literature that fails to account sufficiently for the many goods affluence affords.[49] He fails to note that there are few examples of successful Christian resistance against the hegemony of technological consumer capitalism. Evangelicals and most Americans, whether secular or Christian, leave the structures and institutions largely unquestioned. The ones who seek to challenge them have proven ineffective in changing the way of the capitalist world in the United States and, arguably, the other nations that seem to be on the path of embracing technological consumer capitalism as the engine for political, social and economic solutions in late modernity.[50]

But this assumes that Evangelicals might be prone to mount the "radical social critiques of mainstream American society and culture" for which Smith apparently longs from religious communities in the United States.[51] The reality is that they are not. The AAEC inherits this tendency to eschew critical assessment and renunciation of affluence not only because affluent Evangelical families and churches lack resources for critical resistance but also because affluence so easily incorporates, disciplines, commodifies or simply obviates critique.[52]

---

48. Smith, *American Evangelicalism*, 207.

49. Ibid., 196, n. 5. Spanning three pages, this footnote surveys the literature and presents Smith's perspective of the "cultural tools" available in the Christian tradition for challenging the normative systems of injustice he perceives to be embedded in the social and cultural structures of the United States. He concludes by stating that, "It is against these potential alternative practices and critiques that contemporary American evangelicalism's actual individualism and personal influence strategy stand in such stark contrast." Ibid., 198.

50. See, e.g., Miller, *Consuming Religion*, 77–83.

51. Smith, *American Evangelicalism*, 196–98 n. 5.

52. Cf. Miller, *Consuming Religion*, 17–23, where Miller seeks to demonstrate how consumer culture commodifies dissent. See also Bell, *Liberation Theology*, 9–41, 40 n. 98, 144, where Bell understands capitalism as "an ensemble of technologies of desire that exercises dominion over humanity and disciplines desire" via the state-form of technologically advanced governments, seeing its ability to captivate, discipline and form human desire as serpentine "infinite undulations."

The AAEC sees the social effects of affluence and interpretively reproduces them in his own generation. Parents are most formative, as Corsaro's orb web model shows, but as the AAEC interacts with peers and the broader culture and society, the world of affluence opens before him. The result, as the next section shows, is that formation of the AAEC can tend to be dominated or overly influenced by economic concerns. The brute facts of economics tend to eclipse any value theology can offer.[53] This, I submit, can lead to the AAEC's interpretive reproduction of a "lack" or poverty of affluence capable of subverting the evangelical tradition's passionate pursuit of bringing children up "in the discipline and instruction of the Lord" (Eph 6:4).

Interpretive Reproductions of Affluence by the "Bridger Generation" AAEC (1977–94)

The second source of evidence for the interpretive reproductions of the AAEC is found in the generation of seventy-two million American children born between 1977 and 1994, the second largest generation of Americans.[54]

One study found that seventy-five percent (75%) of the entering freshman class of this "Bridger" generation considered economic success essential to well-being, and over seventy-five percent (75%) expressed a desire to attend college so they could enhance their earning capacity.[55] Assuming Evangelical demographics pertain to the Bridger generation, this means that approximately twelve million Bridger Evangelicals have interpretively reproduced the broader Evangelical subculture's prioritization of economics, which is expressed in education for the sake of earning a good income.[56]

53. As chapter 5 will examine further, Long critiques this "fact-value" distinction between economics and theology, seeing it as derived from Max Weber and responsible for marginalizing theological discourse on economic matters in modernity. Long, *Divine Economy*, 3–6, 177–79.

54. The first largest was the boomer generation (1946–1964). Rainer delineates America's twentieth century generations as the "Builders" (1910–1946), "Boomers" (1946–1964), "Busters" (1965–1976) and "Bridgers" (1977–1994). Rainer, *Bridger Generation*, 2–10.

55. Ibid., 86.

56. Ibid.

Focus group data gathered by one researcher from Bridgers raised in Evangelical homes suggest a strong interest in the accoutrements of affluence, particularly money. One member of the focus group, who seemed "obsessed with money and material success," represented the group's perspectives on affluence well:

> My parents have been talking about money and what they do and don't have ever since I can remember. They have drilled it into my head that making it financially is really important in this uncertain world.
>
> You know . . . I really do want a lot of things in this world . . . my own home, . . . a nice car, . . . nice clothes. There's nothing wrong with that, is there?
>
> . . . in this world of downsizing and layoffs, you really need to cover your rear. If the economy means that there will be "haves" and "have nots," I want to be in the "have" group.[57]

This would appear to be an example of Corsaro's interpretive reproduction of the child in American evangelicalism and affluence. Bridgers were born into and nurtured within familial, ecclesial and broader social networks formed during the most rapid advance of technological consumer capitalism in American history. Bridgers and their parents witnessed the triumph of technological consumer capitalism and perhaps believe it was engineered by Ronald Reagan's conservative social and political version of neoliberal economic policies. They unwittingly embrace a kind of social Darwinism to the extent they uncritically accept the late modern blessings of neoliberal economic theory and practice in the United States. Hard work, including diligence in education lead to meritorious rewards on the playing field of free market competition in capitalist society, resulting in a just survival of the economic fittest.

The result is a Bridger generation intensely interested in making money, Evangelicals included. Thom Rainer lists four reasons for this psycho-social condition. These can be interpreted through Corsaro's model.[58] First, the Boomer generation of Bridger parents bought into American materialism and practically demonstrated the central importance of making and having money. The interpretive reproductions of their children reflect the same concerns and motivations.

57. Ibid.
58. Ibid., 27–28.

Second and third, familial breakdown and corporate downsizing resulted in financial hardship for many Bridger families and parents. The divorce revolution that began in the early 1970s caused many Bridgers to experience the emotional and financial loss attendant to family breakdown. As studies have shown, this usually resulted in income losses for women and their children, because mothers were typically awarded primary residential responsibility for the divorcing parents' children. Child support and alimony rarely equates to what was enjoyed while the marriage was intact. Further, corporate downsizing caused many Bridgers to experience the uncertainty, stress and depression associated with parental loss of a career and income. The interpretive reproduction of these formative factors is reflected in the desire to have financial security, and if securing an education will further that goal then it follows that educational attainment in a technologically advanced and determined world is an essential interpretive reproduction in affluence.

Fourth, Rainer notes that the Bridgers themselves evidence extremely materialistic values. Bridgers have been born into and nurtured within the relational matrices of the affluence generated by technological consumer capitalism. As of 1994, Bridgers eight to ten years old were spending approximately $6 billion a year of their own discretionary funds, and ten year olds were each making an average of over 250 shopping visits each year.[59] Assuming Evangelical demographics apply to the Bridger generation, at least twenty-three percent of "shop and spend" eight-to-ten year old Bridgers would be children nurtured in Evangelical homes and churches. Such behavior is an example of the AAEC's interpretive reproductions in affluence.

Rainer's findings are corroborated in Juliet Schor's study of the commercialized child and new consumer culture in the United States.[60] She claims that the available evidence indicates that contemporary "tweens [8 to 12 year olds] and teens [13 to 19 year olds]" in the United States "have emerged as the most brand-oriented, consumer-involved, and materialistic generations in history. And they top the list globally."[61] The affluence

59. Miller and Porter, *Shadows of the Baby Boom*, 19, cited in Rainer, *Bridger Generation*, 28, 129 n. 27.

60. "Kids and teens are now the epicenter of American consumer culture," and "Plenty of evidence now confirms how far-reaching this process of commercialization has come." Schor, *Born to Buy*, 9, 13.

61. Ibid., 13.

of American children is both staggering and growing. In 1989, children four to twelve years old spent $6.1 billion; in 1997, $23.4 billion; in 2002, $30 billion (a 400% increase); they also are estimated to have "directly influenced $330 billion of adult purchasing in 2004 and "evoked" another $340 billion.[62] Twelve to nineteen year olds spent $101 per week on average (a total of $170 billion) in 2002, and it is estimated that globally "tweens" influenced over $1 trillion of spending in 2002.[63]

How do we know? Because American companies know. They tailor marketing and advertising to children according to detailed demographics of age, gender, ethnicity, zip codes and product segments, studying their data with rigorous social scientific discipline. Twelve to nineteen year olds are particularly crucial for marketers, because they set the consumer stage for the four to eleven year olds. They are the peer culture that helps form and forecast younger tween and child consumer behaviors.[64] The younger peer culture interprets and reproduces the older adolescent peer culture along the path of the human spirit's inexorable ego development during the first decades of affluent life in the United States. Both of these cultures are the result of the interpretive reproductions made by young and middle adulthood consumer cultures.

Corporations employ psychologists and rely upon insights from developmental psychology to gain a better understanding of children at various developmental stages so as to enhance marketing strategies to promote and secure consumption by children.[65] The attempt to reach into the consumer's brain has resulted in "neuromarketing," which utilizes insights from neuroscience for the purpose of exploring the consumer's consciousness and, at least theoretically, even subconscious in the hope of exploring the deepest dimensions of consumer desires and motivations to consume.[66] Technological advances in neuroscience thus assist consumer

---

62. Ibid., 23.

63. Ibid.

64. Massive amounts of raw economic data are supplied by the U. S. Department of Commerce to corporations on a regular basis. This was one of the core aspects of the partnership between government and business Hoover started. Leach, *Land of Desire*, 349–78.

65. Linn, *Consuming Kids*, 23–26; see also Acuff with Reiher, *What Kids Buy and Why*.

66. Schor, "Inside the Child Brain," in *Born to Buy*, 109–12; see also "Dissecting the Child Consumer: The New Intrusive Research," ibid., 99–118.

capitalism's quest for market share of the consumer's brain, the AAEC included. Economic colonization of human neurology is well under way.

A deeper look into neuromarketing will help illumine the dialectical relation between affluence and the brain of the AAEC. Neuromarketing is a new field of marketing research that employs medical technologies, such as functional Magnetic Resonance Imaging (fMRI) and Zaltman Metaphor Elicitation Technique (ZMET). fMRI measures brain activity of how a consumer evaluates a product, object or advertisement. ZMET supposedly is able to help researchers explore the unconscious, underlying beliefs and feelings that influence the behavior of consumers. It is claimed to be a technology capable of "transporting thoughts and feelings from the unconscious to the conscious mind."[67] The patent owners of ZMET also claim to use

> patented priming and implicit association techniques and brain imaging techniques that reveal unconscious reactions to various marketing stimuli. These techniques generally are more reliable indicators of consumer thought and behavior than are explicit methods such as questionnaires, standard interviews, and focus groups. Implicit measures can be adapted to measure responses to visual, written, and sound stimuli. They are particularly well-suited for evaluating advertising concepts, competitive brand positionings, brand names, and in selecting deep metaphors surfaced by ZMET research.[68]

The information gained from fMRI and ZMET is used to measure consumer preferences and then to apply this knowledge in product design and marketing campaign development. Neuroscience and its technological progeny are now employed in partnerships between higher education, private research firms and Fortune 500 businesses in the United States. Hoover's dream of diffusing production into consumption through governmental-commercial means in the 1920s has now been realized at the neurological level.

---

67. For instance, "ZMET research revealed a connection between a mother's feelings about her child's first day of school and her purchase and use of cereal," and thus facilitated a company's marketing efforts at brand positioning. See "Interviewing the Brain" at http://www.olsonzaltman.com/oza/zmet.html.

68. http://www.olsonzaltman.com/oza/zmet.html.

BrightHouse™ is the world's leading neuromarketing firm. It has a "Neurostrategies™ Group" that assists its clients in asking and answering the following strategic business questions:

> How can we build strong, long-lasting preference among consumers?
>
> How can we better plan communication efforts so as to increase message effectiveness?
>
> How can we increase the relevance of our product and/or category among consumers?
>
> How can we better engage consumers with our brand?[69]

> These are some of the most common questions asked by strategic planners in business today. They are also questions that can be informed through neuroscience, the study of how the brain thinks, feels and motivates behavior. BrightHouse Neurostrategies Group was created in 2001 to bridge the gap between the rapidly growing base of knowledge in the human behavior sciences and the increasing need for consumer understanding in the business arena. We offer a variety of consultative projects designed to deliver insights and ideas that articulate and dimensionalize a scientific understanding of human behavior in ways that are relevant for companies and their brands in today's marketplace.[70]

BrightHouse's creative innovation and application of neuroscience to business would probably amaze Hoover. He could not have foreseen this future application of his vision for diffusing production into childhood consumption.

The implications of the neurological penetration of commerce are profound. Affluence follows the diffusion of production into consumption through the steady progress of technological advances in consumer capitalism. Invention, innovation, improvement, economies of scale, licensing and a host of other capitalist technologies (e.g., patenting, trad-

---

69. http://www.thoughtsciences.com.

70. http://www.thoughtsciences.com. According to the owners of ZMET, "ZMET is a patented process (#5,436,830)" and "'Interviewing the Brain' is a registered trademark (#2,488,773). Some of the activities encompassed involve three patented techniques: Metaphor Elicitation Method and Apparatus (#5,436,830); Neuroimaging as a Marketing Tool (#6,099,319); Metaphor Elicitation Technique with Physiological Function Monitoring (#6,315,569)." These registered trademarks and patents indicate the depth of commercial and technological penetration into the human brain.

marking, servicemarking, etc.) all coalesce in the economic discipline of late modern life. These have dramatic impacts upon human nature and human life, much of which benefits humanity in significant ways. But what does commercial colonization of the brain forebode for children, the AAEC included?

Perhaps the AAEC and Evangelicals will experience the dystopia forecast in Aldous Huxley's *Brave New World*. Whether an Alpha, Beta, Epsilon or Gamma, the AAEC may become homogenized with other children in a neurologically determined future. Like the citizens of *Brave New World*, the AAEC may inhabit a world in which pain and misery has been eliminated. Disease, social conflict, depression, insanity, and all physical or psychological maladies have been eliminated through biotechnological advance. Everyone is happy and healthy because government ministry superintends the gap between desire and its fulfillment such that the realization of wants and needs is virtually instantaneous. Such a world would necessarily entail designing children with the ideal genetic makeup, which would be followed by the best technologically prescribed nurture available.[71]

Such a world is problematic for an evangelical reading of the Bible by Evangelicals, or at least it should be. Overcoming all human maladies occasioned by sin and evil and death, as well as the ultimate fulfillment of human desire, can be realized only through the death and resurrection Christ appropriated through repentance and faith until his parousia. But if affluence penetrates human nature to such an extent as it encircles the globe, what hope can there be for nurturing evangelical faith and practice in the AAEC? Cultivating the habits of resisting and renouncing the encroachments of affluence becomes problematic in a context where science, technology and economics combine to colonize all human spaces, including the neurological.

Hoover's dream of diffusing consumption-production into childhood seems to have been realized in the United States. Just eighty years after he engineered the governmental-commercial partnership necessary to bring it about, the child's practical right to consumption advocated by Hoover has been secured. The child has become a powerful constituent of American consumer culture. Schor summarizes it this way:

---

71. Cf. Peters, "Designer Children," and *For the Love of Children*.

Kids and teens are now the epicenter of American consumer culture. They command the attention, creativity, and dollars of advertisers. Their tastes drive market trends. Their opinions shape strategies. Yet few adults recognize the magnitude of this shift and its consequences for the futures of our children and of our culture.[72]

Schor can be read as describing the fulfillment of what Hoover hoped for in 1930. As will be recalled from chapter 3, that year witnessed the report on the White House Conference on Child Health and Protection, *The Home and the Child: Housing, Furnishing, Management, Income and Clothing*. Its consumerist developmental conclusions were certain. Children develop their personalities by shopping and being free to make their own purchases and build their personalities through their relationships to "things."[73] Children's best interests are served by giving them their own rooms in single-family dwellings furnished with age-appropriate items. These homes must be "within relatively easy access of churches and schools, and civic, cultural and shopping centers."[74] They are to be stocked with "toys . . . and places to keep pets."[75] Schor describes the fulfillment of Hoover's dreams for American children, the AAEC included. Children now influence parental consumption in the billions of dollars each year. In addition, they annually spend billions of their own money as well. Seeing the degree to which children both form and are formed by the consumer culture of the United States, would Hoover be concerned?

Vincent Miller's theological critique of the American single-family home in consumer culture provides one final means of discerning the AAEC's interpretive reproductions within this Hooverian context. Although Miller tends to reduce Christian faith and practice to tradition, his critique is illuminating. This will bring to a close the application of Corsaro's theory to the AAEC's interpretive reproductions within American-Evangelical affluence.

72. Schor, *Born to Buy*, 9.

73. Leach, *Land of Desire*, 371–72, quoting from *The Home and the Child*; see also Hoover, *Memoirs*, 97.

74. Ibid., 371.

75. Ibid.

The AAEC's Interpretive Reproductions
in the Evangelical Single-family Residence

Miller's interest in the single-family residence is a central motivation for his exploration of "how consumer culture transforms religious belief and practice by transforming the way that people avow, interpret, and employ the beliefs, symbols, values, and practices of their religious traditions."[76] He sees the "suburban single-family home" as "fundamental to our culture" and as a structure that has come to dominate "the American landscape."[77] He claims that it is so "ubiquitous" and "deeply ingrained in the fabric of our lives" that its "profound significance (and contingency) is overlooked"; this manner of American living "forms our lives profoundly" because it is "the fundamental structure of our dwelling."[78] At the heart of this structure are relational matrices of consumption that, as Miller sees it, both form and transform Christian faith and practice in the United States.

Evangelicals can benefit from Miller's analysis of religion in the context of consumer culture. The single-family home is the domestic and suburban space in which the AAEC is nurtured and from which the AAEC's interpretive reproductions of Evangelical affluence take place. Two particularly helpful insights derive from the manner in which he utilizes the insights of anthropologist Talal Asad and theologian Kathryn Tanner to enrich Clifford Geertz's conception of "thick" description in the interpretation of cultures. Asad and Tanner assist Miller in developing a contemporary theological method of thinking about consumer culture.[79]

Miller notes Asad's criticism of Geertz for his tendency to "theologize" in his anthropological studies by holding uncritically to the assumption that human behavior can be traced directly to religious meanings or beliefs, and vice versa. Asad demonstrated that human behavior often contradicts religious belief.[80] Asad's critique is consistent with biblical testimony, because Jesus and the prophets can be read as making the same point. The contradictions between faith and practice in regard to the re-

---

76. Miller, *Consuming Religion*, 31.

77. Ibid., 39, 46.

78. Ibid., 46.

79. Ibid., 15–31.

80. See Asad, "Anthropological Conceptions," 242, 245; cited in Miller, *Consuming Religion*, 20–21, 230 nn. 12–15.

lationship between poverty-affluence are well known in premodern life as reflected in the writings of the Old Testament prophets and the New Testament authors.[81] Thus, Asad's correction of Geertz can assist evangelical theology by raising awareness of the contradictions in evangelical faith and practice that arise as a result of the God-mammon conundrum confronting the AAEC during the first decades of life.

In addition, Kathryn Tanner's work in theological anthropology further illumines the complexities of thinking clearly about consumer culture and, hence, understanding the AAEC's embeddedness in that culture. She notes that contemporary anthropology is keenly aware of the dynamic nature of culture and the difficulties attendant to interpreting cultures. Those doing anthropology, theologians included, must be careful not to oversimplify the relationships between beliefs and practices or to project onto culture their need to find a coherent, static order.[82] Furthermore, as they search for coherence and meaning, theologians must be careful to nuance interpretations of their excavations into the untidiness of Christian practice, so as to avoid producing their own idealized version of the way they think things should be.[83] Of course, if they are sufficiently embedded or have been nurtured within the particular tradition they are seeking to assess, theologians doing theological anthropology operate as insiders, not outsiders as anthropologists do. The theologian's task is not only to interpret but also to identify, challenge and correct contradictions between belief and practice.

Applying these insights here, Tanner helpfully cautions against either an Evangelical nostalgia for the halcyon days of "traditional values" when America was purportedly a "Christian nation" or for an idealized Evangelical utopia of perfect harmony between faith and practice in the goods and poverties of affluence. Written by an American-Evangelical insider seeking to present an evangelical-theological economics of the AAEC in late modernity, this book charts such a course.

---

81. E.g., Amos 2:6–7; 4:1; 5:11 ("Therefore because you trample on the poor and take from them levies of grain, you have built houses of hewn stone, but you shall not live in them; you have planted pleasant vineyards, but you shall not drink their wine."), 8:4–6; and Luke 16:19–31("There was a rich man who was dressed in purple and fine linen and who feasted sumptuously every day. And at his gate lay a poor man named Lazarus, covered with sores, who longed to satisfy his hunger with what fell from the rich man's table . . ." vv. 19–21).

82. Tanner, *Theories of Culture*, 47.

83. Ibid., 76.

Tanner and Asad assist Miller in thinking about the commodification of American culture as reflected in the Hooverian dream of single-family home ownership for every citizen of the United States. Miller sees the American single-family home as resulting in "social isolation, narrowed political and social concern, and the fragmentation of culture."[84] The engine of such isolation, narrowing and fragmentation is the transformation of the home from an agricultural center of production to a "cash-intensive" suburban center of consumption.[85] He argues that "the rise of the single-family home is a milestone in the shunting of the need for social standing into consumption in a way that ensures the endless perpetuation of consumer desire."[86] He makes some valid points about suburban living in the single-family home that may be applied to understanding the AAEC's interpretive reproductions in that context.

Miller claims that the "most significant effect of the rise of the single-family home . . . is its impact on the mediation of culture from generation to generation."[87] Practically, the economic costs associated with such living inculcate social isolation, the narrowing of personal, moral, political and cultural fragmentation of the extended family into the nuclear family. This fragmentation accelerates cultural change because each generation is atomized further and further from the previous generation, with the distinguishing marks becoming more pronounced as a result of intergenerational interpretive reproductions. Marketing techniques identify the generational trends and capitalize upon them, thus perpetuating the reproductive-productive dialectic found in children's peer cultures. Miller partially confirms Corsaro's theory of interpretive reproduction, stating that, "Culture is thus constructed as something one learns from peers' appropriations of commercial popular culture, not wisdom handed down from elders."[88] Although it appears Miller gives greater weight to elders in the interpretive reproduction process, his point is well taken. The atomizing, individualizing and acquiring social processes of American

---

84. Miller, *Consuming Religion*, 48.

85. Ibid., 48.

86. Ibid., 50. Miller cites Schor, *Overspent American*, 43–63, for this claim. Miller, *Consuming Religion*, 233 n. 49. Cf., however, S. Lebergott, *Pursuing Happiness*, particularly "Consumers and Their Critics," 3–11, which points out fallacies found in critiques of consumers and so-called "consumerism" like those found in Schor and Miller.

87. Miller, *Consuming Religion*, 52.

88. Ibid., 53.

culture are centrally located in the single-family residence. This is where the AAEC obtains his vision and expectations for life in the processes of nurture and interpretive reproduction that take place in the home. The incubator for the AAEC's enculturation in the problem of affluence is the single-family residence.

Most often the AAEC grows up in a suburban context of material prosperity and delight, where the pain and horrors of late modern poverties are carefully sheltered from Evangelical consciences through selective media channeling and choices. This is where, as Schneider puts it, the "modern economic habits of acquisition and enjoyment as they flourish under capitalism"[89] are nurtured in the AAEC, something, as we will see in chapter 5, Schneider wholeheartedly affirms. The language and cultural routines of this American existence center around a consumption-oriented lifestyle. It is the common, uncritically received economic vision of the American pursuit of happiness. Suburban peace, security, acquisition and enjoyment are its hallmarks. This is the society and culture the AAEC interprets and plays a central role in reproducing.

CONCLUSION

Since 1950, the AAEC has emerged with his American peers as a creative interpreter-reproducer of American society and culture. Hoover's dreams for children have been largely realized in single-family home ownership and the diffusion of production into consumption. The AAEC is embedded in a land of desire, interpreting and reproducing it with peers and adults alike.

Corsaro's model of interpretive reproduction in childhood has proven to be a useful sociological model for understanding the language and cultural routines of the AAEC and the reproductive nature of the AAEC's evolving membership in her subculture of Evangelical affluence. The AAEC is both formed by and formative of that subculture. They learn the language and cultural routines of individualistic American Evangelicalism and reproduce, modify, expand and adapt them to their interests within their own peer cultures.

By the time of adolescence, the AAEC is socially formed in the problematic tensions of affluence with little critical self-understanding within

89. Schneider, *Good of Affluence*, 40.

that context. Few, if any, resources are available to the AAEC during the first decades of life sufficient to resist the encroachments of consumer culture. Affluence remains immune to penetrating, transformational critique. Hence, it would appear that development of an evangelical-critical consciousness of affluence in the AAEC has been stunted. This indicates the need for an evangelical faith seeking transformational understanding and practice in the socio-cultural context of the affluence generated by technological consumer capitalism.

The evangelical sociology of the AAEC's interpretive reproductions of affluence presented in this chapter has served to shed further anthropological light upon formation of the AAEC in affluence. Examining the AAEC's interpretive reproductions in Evangelical affluence in this chapter has served several purposes.

First, it has helped link the history of the AAEC previously traced in chapters 2 and 3 to a sociological perspective of the AAEC. It thus fills a gap in evangelical understanding of affluence as it bears upon the AAEC. Evangelicals, it seems, indicate scant historical self-understanding of the unique role Evangelicalism played in bringing about mass affluence in the United States. Without such awareness, transformational understanding of the formative affects of affluence is retarded.[90]

Second, the interpretive reproductions of the AAEC in affluence have illumined the affluentizing processes—the language and cultural routines of Evangelical affluence—at work in the AAEC's first decades of life. This facilitates a fuller critical understanding of the modified Bushnellian socialization theory that Richards incorporated into his theology of Christian nurture. This should lead to a deeper awareness of affluence as a significant factor in the AAEC's formation. Critical awareness of the formative effects of affluence is needed during the first decades of life if Evangelical parents and churches hope to cultivate counter-disciplines of resistance in the AAEC. By the age of legal majority and the time for college or career arrives, the AAEC is fully formed by, formed for, and enmeshed in American affluence. Critical self-understanding

90. Chapter 5 will demonstrate this in relation to Schneider's theology of affluence. In the second chapter of *Godly Materialism*, for instance, titled "Christians & Money Through the Centuries," Schneider cites liberation theologian Justo Gonzalez with approval: "Without understanding the past, we are unable to understand ourselves." Schneider, *Godly Materialism*, 18. It is surprising, then, that neither in *Godly Materialism* nor *Good of Affluence* does Schneider demonstrate a sociological or historical awareness of American Evangelicalism's problematic symbiosis with affluence in the United States.

of Evangelical embeddedness in affluence is needed much earlier in life. Perhaps Evangelicals will come to see that the AAEC's development in affluence, "playing innocently and safely in a [suburban] landscape that has become to them a wonder-filled world of projects and endless fantasies,"[91] may dull rather than sharpen the nurture of a truly evangelical "discipline and instruction of the Lord" (Eph 6:4).

Third, the evangelical sociology of the AAEC provides a bridge to the evangelical theology of the AAEC in chapter 5. Economics lie at the heart of social history and formation in the United States and also at the heart of Schneider's theology of affluence. The economic determination of modern life in the United States entails a unique anthropology, which American-Evangelical theology has uncritically incorporated in its theological economics. Schneider's embrace of the dominant neoliberal economic tradition as represented by Michael Novak entails a problematic theological anthropology, one I contend should concern Evangelical parents and churches. Schneider ignores recent theological critique of this dominant tradition and the anthropology upon which it is premised. As a result, his theology of affluence is deficient and, if embraced by Evangelicals, may very well help perpetuate the AAEC's developmental enmeshment within the malformative matrices of Evangelical affluence in the United States.

Thus, the goal of chapter 5 is to present the second synchronic lens for the theological anthropology of the AAEC constructed here. As the centerpiece of my project, the critical focus is on Schneider's theology of servant dominion and delight in late modern affluence, with a view to how that theology might lead to the nurture of a spiritual-moral evangelical "lack" (poverty) of affluence in the AAEC.

91. Schneider, *Godly Materialism*, 15.

5

An Evangelical Theology of the AAEC

. . . what do I still lack?

—MATTHEW 19:20

Any theology that denies it exists within a structure of economic exchange simply has no awareness of the conditions for its own possibility.

—STEPHEN LONG[1]

. . . it is not possible to understand man on the basis of economics alone, nor to define him simply on the basis of class membership. Man is understood in a more complete way when he is situated within the sphere of culture through his language, history, and the position he takes towards the fundamental events of life, such as birth, love, work and death.

—JOHN PAUL II[2]

INTRODUCTION: MODERN ECONOMICS, CONTEMPORARY THEOLOGY AND THE AAEC

A contemporary theological anthropology of the child can neither eschew economics nor allow it to dominate its concerns. Economics alone is insufficient for anthropology and, thus, for theological anthropology. But neither can economics be ignored, and contemporary theology has

---

1. Long, *Divine Economy*, 261.
2. John Paul II, *Centesimus Annus*, par. 24.

begun to engage this social science and its underlying philosophical pre-understandings with serious theological-critical discipline.

The global spread of the market made possible by monumental scientific and technological advances in modernity has forced this on contemporary theology in unprecedented ways. The technologies spawned by modern science are raising the specter of a "posthuman" future,[3] and economics is the discipline that manages both the fruits and futures those technologies bring. Early in the twentieth century, Nicholas Berdyaev saw the economic foundations of modern society clearly: "The power of economics was never so strong as in our time. Now nothing can escape its influence . . . The life of the whole world moves beneath the sign of economism, and economic interests have put all things under their feet."[4] And at least one cultural critic can now claim that American-style economics has gone hegemonically global in the twenty-first century as "the first universally valid science of human behavior."[5] The power and discipline of modern economics are grounded in an anthropology of modern economic man which assumes the phenomenon of lack, or scarcity, as the root motivation for human self-interest. At the heart of this anthropology is a view of freedom contemporary theology only recently has begun to contest.

This chapter completes the theological-critical focus on the AAEC by attending to the economic realities in which the AAEC is nurtured. The historical and sociological analyses of chapters 2 through 4 are honed into an evangelical theology of the AAEC in three steps. The first section assesses John Schneider's theology of affluence. The second brings that theology into critical interaction with contemporary interpretations of Matthew's story of the rich young man found in Karl Barth's *Church Dogmatics*, Dietrich Bonhoeffer's *The Cost of Discipleship*, Pope John Paul II's *Veritatis Splendor* and feminist theologian Marion Grau's *Of Divine Economy*.[6] The theological-anthropological focus is upon the issue of "lack" as it is raised in the narrative.[7]

3. See, e.g., Fukuyama, *Our Posthuman Future*.

4. Berdyaev, *Fate of Man in the Modern World*, 77–78.

5. Purdy, "Universal Nation," 107.

6. Barth, *CD* II.2, 613–30; Bonhoeffer, *Cost of Discipleship*, 77–86; John Paul II, *Veritatis Splendor*; Grau, *Of Divine Economy*, 41–89.

7. Matthew's rich young man raises the issue with Jesus (Matt 19:20), whereas Jesus raises it with Mark's rich man (Mark 10:21) and Luke's rich ruler (Luke 18:22).

The third section engages the theological economics of Grau, Stephen Long and Daniel M. Bell, Jr., with a particular focus on the anthropology of liberty at work in the neoliberal theological economics of John Schneider and Michael Novak. In my view, Schneider overlooked the works by Long and Bell to the substantial detriment of his contemporary theology of affluence. Grau's feminist theological economics, on the other hand, was published two years after Schneider's *The Good of Affluence*. It provides a means of critique for what is lacking in Schneider's theology of affluence as well as a means of critically assessing Long's theological economics.

Together, the interpretations of the rich young man by these contemporary theologians help clarify the spiritual and moral "lack" lying at the heart both of Schneider's theology of affluence and evangelical (i.e., gospel) nurture in the United States. They corroborate my claim that leaving Schneider's moral theology of affluence uncontested would not be in the AAEC's best interests.

The aim of the chapter, then, is to raise critical-evangelical awareness to this issue of lack in relation to nurture in Evangelical affluence. While the psychological and theological experience of "lack" in Matthew's rich young man is not identical to the fundamental principle of "scarcity" in classical economics, there is a significant correlation between the two concepts.[8] At the most fundamental correlative level, spiritual-moral lack and economic scarcity intersect in the motivational dimension of human nature: desire and self-interest, worship and service. As Douglas Meeks notes, "The insatiability of human nature is said to be the ground of [the modern economic definition of] scarcity."[9] Desire bears directly on the God-neighbor relationality, the two biblical dimensions of being in the world that cannot be sundered without doing damage to both. Love of God and love of neighbor go together. They are inseparable.

The narrative of the rich young man concretely illustrates "the impossibility of serving God and mammon" (Matt 6:24)[10] and thus opens theological inquiry into what relation his lack may have to his "many possessions" (i.e., affluence). It highlights the internal conflict "between the desire for God and the desire for security that comes with capital,"

8. Cf. Meeks, "A Trinitarian Understanding of the Holy Spirit: God and Scarcity," in *God the Economist*, 170–77; Grau, *Of Divine Economy*, 44 n. 8.

9. Meeks, *God the Economist*, 172.

10. Davies and Allison, *Matthew III*, 39.

a sort of "paradoxical scarcity."[11] These desires are paradoxical because the young man claims to have kept the commands, which Jesus does not contest, and yet knows he lacks something in relation to eternal life that he cannot name. He comes to Jesus because somehow he knows, or at least suspects, that only Jesus can name it for him and call him to the path where it can be found.

Thus, the AAEC serves as a complex metaphorical system that can help structure evangelical discernment of the kingdom of God by Evangelicals embedded in late modernity.[12] At the same time, the AAEC signals the need for change, humility and a reorientation of evangelical conceptions of what it means to enter and to be great in the kingdom of God that is present in the twenty-first century yet confronted with mass affluence in the West, growing affluence in Asia (i.e., India and China) and the still grinding poverty in the two-thirds world of the global South and East. The AAEC placed "in the midst" of Schneider's theology of affluence, so to speak, both hides and reveals the meaning of the kingdom as sign and gift, "for it is to such as these that the kingdom of heaven belongs" (Matt 19:14).

Ched Myers writes persuasively that, "The child is not a mere symbol in [the Gospel of] Mark, but a *person*. To deal with this person is to deal with our own repressed past, the roots of violence, and the possibility of a transformed future, our own and our children's."[13] Myers's political reading of the child texts in Mark and the symbolic function of the child's personhood is helpful to reading the AAEC in late modernity. As one of those who possesses God's reign because it has been given to those like them, the AAEC can serve as a sign-gift of the kingdom's presence and a call for American Evangelicalism to examine itself in view of its affluence.

Particular attention will be given in the first section of the chapter to Schneider's treatment of Luke's stories of Jesus and the rich ruler, Jesus and Zacchaeus, and the Parable of the Pounds. The theology Schneider derives from these stories exercises a controlling influence in his overall project. Schneider agrees with Walter Pilgrim and "many other scholars"

---

11. Grau, *Of Divine Economy*, 44.

12. Cf. Scott, "Rules of the Game," 117–24, 123, on the idea of "*The Kingdom is a Child* as a structural metaphor."

13. Myers, *Binding the Strong Man*, 271. See also Weber, "Unless You Become Like a Child," and "A Child in the Midst of Them," in *Jesus and Children*, 22–51.

that Luke addresses the problem of affluence primarily with the rich in view.[14] Thus, Schneider sees the Gospel of Luke as "the only work in the New Testament with this particular focus" and therefore as "the most promising source available to modern affluent Christians for finding answers to their particular questions."[15] Schneider concludes that the Parable of the Pounds, "which moral theologians have almost completely ignored . . . [is] a kind of paradigm for Christians living and working in today's economic culture."[16] This paradigm and the ethics it entails are contested below insofar as the child nurtured in Evangelical affluence is concerned.

SCHNEIDER'S THEOLOGY OF AFFLUENCE

Pure liberty is pure power—whose other name is evil.[17]

These people, it's no mystery where they come from . . . You sharpen the human appetite to the point where it can split atoms with its desire, you build egos the size of cathedrals, fiber-optically connect the world to every eager impulse, grease even the dullest dreams with these dollar-green gold-plated fantasies, until every human becomes an aspiring emperor, becomes his own god, and where can you go from there?[18]

Schneider presented his first theology of affluence in the 1994 publication of *Godly Materialism*. That book begins with the story of an Evangelical college student who happened to appear in his academic office one day. The young, presumably affluent Evangelical had just returned from spending a summer at an urban mission in San Francisco. The student was distressed. He was suffering an identity crisis, "an almost paralyzing crisis of guilt over who he was—a Christian with money and privilege in an age of suffering."[19] The intentional resonance of the subtitle to Ron

14. Schneider, *Good of Affluence*, 143.

15. Ibid.

16. Ibid., 143.

17. Milbank, "Sovereignty, Empire, Capital, and Terror," 161.

18. The character John Milton (the devil), played by Al Pacino, in the film *The Devil's Advocate*.

19. Schneider, "The Identity Crisis of Rich Christians," in *Godly Materialism*, 10. The phrase "age of suffering" echoes Sider's phrase "age of hunger" in the title to his 1977 classic, *Rich Christians*.

Sider's Evangelical classic, *Rich Christians in an Age of Hunger*, cannot be missed here.

Schneider does not appear to have entertained the thought that the student may have been living out an episode similar to Matthew's rich young man. Nor does Schneider appear cognizant that the student seeking his practical-theological counsel may in fact have had an encounter with the risen Jesus while in San Francisco similar to that experienced by Luke's rich ruler or Matthew's rich young man. Perhaps both this twentieth century student and his first century brother were formed in economic systems that had captured and distorted evangelical desire, turning it away from the source of its ultimate satisfaction in Jesus and the gospel into a path where the "one thing" was still lacking.[20]

Like many of Schneider's students, this young man was no doubt nurtured in Evangelical affluence. For Evangelical parents and churches in the United States, undergraduate education is a serious matter. Many Evangelicals desire their children to attend a conservative Evangelical college if their affluence will allow it, and therefore they plan and save accordingly. Schneider's student attended a college that sought to continue the process of nurture in the contemporary American-Evangelical faith that his parents and, presumably, their church sought to inculcate.

Schneider admits that the Jesus this student discovered among the urban poor of San Francisco "was a very different Jesus from the gentle figure who inhabited the temples of his evangelical upbringing."[21] He had seen similar crises of Christian faith and identity before. Schneider's depressed student was a fully formed AAEC. *Godly Materialism* sets forth Schneider's counsel for such students, and *The Good of Affluence* was written eight years later to help them seek God in the Evangelical affluence their work, family and church relations had by then embedded them.

20. Schneider notes that the student was the son of a middle-class marketing executive who went to work for his father's corporation "in a state of surrender, resignation and guilt, because he felt that what he was doing was sinful at bottom." Schneider, *Godly Materialism*, 13. Yet, instead of seeing any parallels with Matthew's rich young man, who "went away grieving" (19:22), Schneider chose instead to develop an affluence-affirmative theology for the "many Christian professionals [who] suffer from unresolved moral conflict and guilt over their economic identities." Ibid., 14; cf. "The Life and Demands of 'the Radical Jesus,'" 125–30, where Schneider addresses Luke's story of "the rich young [sic, 125] ruler" but does not entertain the possibility that a contemporary illustration of it might be found in the student's sad story.

21. Ibid., 10.

This later work, published in 2002, began as a revision of *Godly Materialism* but "grew into what really amounts to a new work on Christian faith and wealth."[22] Schneider claims that its "argumentation stands more solidly and conspicuously upon well-established scholarship" and also has been "brought up to date by the inclusion and engagement of important works that have been published since 1995."[23] As previously noted, however, he overlooked Stephen Long's *Divine Economy* and the work by Daniel M. Bell, Jr.[24] This is a considerable oversight because Long extensively critiques Novak's theological economics upon which Schneider relies heavily,[25] and Bell critiques capitalism and liberation theology, both of which are concerns taken up by Schneider.[26] Not only this, Long demonstrates Novak's dependence upon Max Weber for the social science of economics and also for "the fact-value distinction" by which Novak limits the role of theology to giving economic "*facts* a meaningful critique through the *value* that theology offers."[27] Schneider interacts briefly with Weber, apparently ignorant of Long's critique of both Novak and Weber.

Long notes that a "foundational theological theme" employed by contemporary theologians engaging economics "is an anthropology which assumes the human person is free to choose" and through the exercise of such freedom "gives value to things in the world."[28] This is, according to Long, theology's reduced contemporary role in relation to economics.

22. Schneider, *Good of Affluence*, ix.

23. Ibid.

24. Schneider also fails to address significant works that bear upon his thesis of the "cosmic good of affluence." See, e.g., Gorringe, *Capital and the Kingdom*; Meeks, *God the Economist*; Duchrow, *Alternatives to Global Capitalism*; Atherton, *Christianity and the Market*; Goudzwaard, *Capitalism and Progress*; Duchrow and Hinkelammert, *Property for People, Not Profit*. Due to space limitations, these works cannot be addressed in any detail but would certainly prove fruitful in further work on the late modern theological anthropology and economics of the AAEC developed here. Although I perceive a fundamental flaw in these works arising from overinterpretation regarding capitalism and neo-Marxist or socialist readings of economics, and hence believe Schneider and I would probably land roughly on the same side of the argument in relation to them, nevertheless they are important works to read and to answer in doing evangelical-theological economics in the twenty-first century.

25. "With the help of others (particularly Michael Novak). . . ." Schneider, *Good of Affluence*, 2.

26. Bell, "Men of Stone" and *Liberation Theology*.

27. Long, *Divine Economy*, 11.

28. Ibid., 10, 11–12.

Theology gives value to economic facts. In other words, theology functions only to affirm the value of the anthropology of liberty upon which economics is premised. Schneider and Novak put this in terms of human freedom to co-create with God through the creative power of capitalism rooted in and generated from the human mind. Thus, echoing Novak, Schneider can exclaim that capitalism is "the greatest liberating power in human history" and produces a culture that provides Evangelicals with "unusually good" opportunities for the free expression of genuine faith, virtue and practice.[29] Schneider is certainly correct to note the liberating effects of capitalism. Millions have been lifted out of poverty through it, and many millions more no doubt will be liberated in the twenty-first century. And as Francis Fukuyama has noted, it is certainly true that since World War II no liberal democracies enjoying affluence have engaged in wars with each other.

Nevertheless, despite all the very good things Schneider says and accomplishes in his theology of the "good" of affluence, his embrace of the "new culture of capitalism" at the beginning of his book is where his argument gets off track. It leads, in my view, simultaneously to over-interpretation of the goods and underinterpretation of the poverties of affluence in late modernity. Theologies like Schneider's uncritically validate the anthropology that sustains the liberating power of capitalism, and accordingly give spiritual and moral value to the economic facts of the system it produces. Instead of forming spiritual and moral values in the AAEC, however, such an anthropology leads to a spiritual-moral lack because it sees freedom as an end in itself rather than as a means to the end of Jesus and the gospel. Theology gives value to such a conception of liberty but cannot critique or transform it evangelically. As Long argues, the end result of this *analogia libertatis* is the subordination of Christology and ecclesiology to a doctrine of creation, because the highest good is not "Christologically determined" but instead is determined by what is "*useful*" in practice.[30] In other words, economics functions on an individual-social calculus of good grounded not in Christ but in an atheological conception of what serves the end of maximized individual-social freedom.

29. Schneider, *Good of Affluence*, 2–3.

30. Long, *Divine Economy*, 12 (emphasis in original).

As I read it, Schneider's doctrine of creation dominates the theology of affluence he constructs, resulting in subordination of the doctrines of Christ, the church and nurture to cosmology in a realized eschatology of neoliberal capitalism. His doctrines of human nature and sin are made to fit his doctrine of the "cosmic good" of affluence he finds throughout the Bible. The result for the AAEC, I contend, is nurture in a cosmic good of affluence that eclipses or at least dulls critical awareness of the spiritual-moral poverties (i.e., relational lack with regard to God and others) that affluence can cultivate in parent, church and child alike in late modernity.

In the following two subsections I will summarize (a) the primary aim and conclusions of Schneider's most recent theology of affluence as I understand them and (b) the arrangement and arguments of that work. The purpose is to set forth clearly Schneider's position so that it may be subjected to theological critique below in sections 2 and 3.

Primary aim and conclusions of The Good of Affluence

Schneider intended to write "a book of Christian theology . . . to help people seeking God in the culture that has grown from modern capitalism."[31] Desiring to "forge a theology of affluence for Christians seeking to live with integrity within this culture of capitalism,"[32] he intends it to be an "integrated Christian spiritual and moral theology on what being affluent means in our time," and as such it is primarily "a theological interpretation of sacred Scripture on the place of material affluence."[33] In pursuing this task, Schneider follows a narrative theological method of interpreting Scripture which allows the reader to compare a narrative interpretation with the text "and then make an informed judgment regarding its truth."[34]

Schneider situates his method of theological interpretation-integration within the culture of affluence in the United States, which he notes is unlike ancient cultures where few were rich and most were poor.[35]

31. Schneider, *Good of Affluence*, 1.

32. Ibid., 40.

33. Ibid., 2, 3.

34. Ibid., 7.

35. Cf. Kidd, "The Social Provenance of the Pastoral Epistles: A Christian Middle Class?" in *Wealth and Beneficence in the Pastoral Epistles*, 35–109.

Instead, it is a culture in which most are rich, relatively few are poor and even "the poor people are fat."[36] Hence, the "economic circumstances" then and now "could not be more different."[37] Schneider concludes from this that the "spiritual and moral traditions of the church in its teachings on wealth and poverty (going back to the New Testament)" are inapplicable because they are outdated.[38]

Although dubious, the distinction is determinative for Schneider. He argues that Christian tradition going back to the New Testament is inapposite because the "old" culture of mass poverty and the "new" culture of capitalism are eons apart. Schneider claims that the distinction justifies

> a strong assumption of my book—that the majority of [modern] writers interpret capitalism and the unique culture to which it gives rise in terms that are quite antiquated. These are largely the terms received from social theorists Karl Marx and Max Weber. . . . And furthermore, Christian tradition going back to very ancient times has been mainly negative in its judgments on the morality of affluence. . . . . it . . . only disposes Christian theorists to accept the negative social analysis of capitalism and its manner of life. The *underlying thesis of this book* is that both these common perspectives—the cultural and the biblical—on faith and wealth have to be renovated in the light of fresh evidence and theory.[39]

Schneider's primary aim thus appears to be renovation of both ancient Christian tradition and modern Christian critique of capitalism. Schneider's personal experience with many wealthy Christians conflicted over their good fortune is what motivated Schneider to write.[40] Such Christians both want and need answers.[41] He seeks to accomplish this task in light of "fresh evidence" for the good of affluence made possible by technological consumer capitalism and in light of "fresh theory" sup-

36. Schneider, *Good of Affluence*, 21, quoting D'Souza, *Virtue of Prosperity*, 75, who is quoting a friend from Bombay.

37. Schneider, *Good of Affluence*, 2.

38. Ibid.

39. Schneider, *Good of Affluence*, 2 (emphasis added). Schneider develops his argument upon "new evidence" of capitalism's liberating power. Ibid., 13–40.

40. Ibid., 4.

41. Schneider claims, "they look to the intellectual leadership in the church for direction. My primary aim in this book is to do my best as a Christian theologian to give it to them." Ibid. Cf. Novak, *Spirit*, 237: "Corporate executives and workers, white-collar workers and teachers, doctors and lawyers—all have need of spiritual guidance."

plied particularly by Michael Novak, convinced that "historic Christian teaching on wealth and poverty is as much a product of ancient economic times as it is of the full biblical narrative" and therefore "our scriptures on the whole" do not support that teaching.[42]

This new evidence and theory led Schneider to believe that it is "grievously" mistaken "to interpret the workings of capitalism in terms of exploitation, class warfare, and oppression (as Marx does), and its human vision and habits of economic life as incompatible with true Christianity (as Weber does)."[43] He strongly believes that "capitalism (for all its problems) is not just *the greatest liberating power in human history*, but also that its cultural workings provide an unusually good opportunity for the expression of true Christian faith and virtue."[44] Schneider genuinely believes that the "creative destruction" of capitalism, to use Joseph Schumpeter's well-known term,[45] currently provides the best hope for liberating millions of the world's poor from poverty. Because of this, Christians are confronted with the opportunity to do great good through their affluence—i.e., help the poor with their abundance and also help the poor become affluent through participating in the "new" culture of capitalism. It follows that Christians should nurture their children in the disciplines, language and routines of this culture.

Schneider seeks to establish in his moral theology that there is a good way of being affluent. It is the way of "delight" which, if correctly understood, "reflects the good created order of God . . . in the same way that conditions in Eden, the Promised Land, and the Messianic Banquet are said to be good."[46] This is necessary because of the predominance of the mistaken "wealth-negative assumption" of Christian theology.[47] This assumption must be overcome because, although the Bible is clear that there is an evil way to be rich, there is plain scriptural proof "from be-

42. Schneider, *Good of Affluence*, 3.

43. Ibid., 2. This is a thin reading of Marx and Weber. I think Schneider would have benefited from Long's critique of these "social theorists."

44. Schneider, *Good of Affluence*, 2–3 (emphasis added). For a Reformed evangelical, this is a remarkably imprudent claim to make without equivocation or explanation. Has the power of capitalism supplanted the power of the cross?

45. Schumpeter, *Capitalism, Socialism and Democracy*, 83. For a concise summary of how Schumpeter's phrase has developed into the economic concept of "innovative externalities," see Baumol, *Free-Market...Growth Miracle*, 136–38.

46. Schneider, *Good of Affluence*, 3.

47. Ibid.

ginning to end" that there is a way to be rich that is good and pleasing to God.[48] Thus, "the good of affluence" is delighting in the goodness in God's creation in the same way that Adam and Eve, the Patriarchs and Prophets, and Israel and Jesus all delighted in it. Their examples of delight are "good in the potential they have for human flourishing and, through it, the flourishing of the cosmos as God wills it to be."[49] The cosmological, eschatological and social conflate here for Schneider. God wills affluence "rightly understood . . . for all human beings"—it is what God desired for humans at creation, desires for them eternally and "(circumstances being right) desires for human beings now."[50]

Schneider wants his theology of affluence to be seen as inhabiting a safe, biblical space between radical Christianity's "wealth-negative prem- ise" and prosperity theology's "wealth-affirmative premise."[51] He hopes to position it in a third space that navigates the errors found in these two ex- tremes. At least in practice, however, it is difficult to discern much differ- ence between Schneider's theology of affluence and the prosperity gospel. Schneider affirms with the prosperity theologians that "God's primary will is that his human creatures should flourish materially."[52] He tries to distinguish his theology of affluence from both camps on a simple prem- ise. The error of both is that they assume God never wills a person to be poor. Schneider believes, against both radical and prosperity theologians, that there are times when God in fact wills some humans to be poor. As he sees it, "both greatly oversimplify the teachings of Scripture and underestimate the role of culture in making wealth possible."[53] Radicals inappropriately generalize that affluence is evil in light of poverty, a warn- ing of God's judgment. Prosperity theologians incorrectly believe that affluence is always good, a sign of God's blessing.

---

48. Ibid.

49. Ibid., 3. Schneider frequently uses phrases such as "rightly understood" and "circumstances being right" in *The Good of Affluence* but unfortunately fails either to explain or develop them. These phrases call for interpretation and leave many questions unanswered.

50. Ibid.

51. Ibid., 4.

52. Ibid.

53. Ibid., 5.

Schneider concludes with an epilogue titled "Being Affluent in a World of Poverty."[54] His attempt to address the issue of poverty in that chapter is insufficient and, in light of human suffering today, arguably insouciant. After quoting Novak from a debate with Ron Sider on "The Ethical Challenges of Capitalism" in 2001,[55] Schneider briefly summarizes the terrain he has covered in the preceding chapters. He claims to have demonstrated in his first chapter that "the culture of modern capitalism (distinct from older versions) is unusually well suited to the expression of Christian virtues."[56] The subsequent chapters, he contends, demonstrated that the Bible both affirms and challenges rich people. It affirms them in their affluence through the doctrine of creation because "God designed human beings for conditions of material delight."[57] It challenges them through the doctrine of redemption because the affluent live in a fallen world and are therefore "to embody the character of God as revealed in the exodus, exile, Incarnation and Pentecost."[58] That is, they are to delight in the blessings of creation and act like God in his beneficent bestowal of those blessings on humans as shown in the biblical record of human liberation from Adam to Christ.

But a close reading of Schneider at this point discloses the metaphysics of Evangelical individualism and a neoliberal conception of freedom at work. Affluent Christians are called to co-create wealth through the power of capitalism and to use that wealth for liberating other humans. The culture of wealth created by capitalism provides great opportunities for Evangelicals to choose whether to use their wealth for the good of others. Whatever norms exist are individualistically determined. This is what lies at the heart of the problem of affluence for American Evangelicals. The freedom to choose is an end in itself. By embracing a neoliberal anthropology of liberty, Schneider subjects his doctrines of creation and redemption to Long's withering critique of this anthropology of liberty

---

54. Ibid., 211–20.

55. According to Schneider, Sider argues that Christians have a moral responsibility to care for the "2.8 billion people whose average income is 2$ [sic] or less" and how they discharge this duty will be indicative of their moral quality. Schneider rejects Sider's claim. Ibid., 211.

56. Ibid.

57. Ibid., 212.

58. Ibid.

found in the "dominant tradition" of theological economics.[59] That critique raises a serious question as to the theological insufficiency of Schneider's anthropology and cosmology.

What needs to be noted here is the manner in which Schneider brings his principle of "moral proximity" to bear upon the issue of poverty. This principle is developed in previous chapters of *The Good of Affluence* and states that the obligations of affluent Christians to help the poor "are confined to their relevant defining communities — in terms of both society and unique vocation."[60] What this means is that no strong theological case can be made for the claim that affluent Christians have an obligation to care for the poor outside their zone of moral proximity. It also means that Christians are free to delight in their affluence as God's good gift of creation. And it is at this precise juncture that the spiritual-moral problem of the AAEC coalesces, because simultaneous to the exercise of this principle of moral theology Evangelicals are to cultivate twin capitalist habits of acquisition and enjoyment of affluence. Built into the moral theology is an ethical conundrum, acquire and enjoy or liquidate and donate within the zone of moral proximity? Evangelicals and their children are free to choose.

Schneider fails to note a major fallacy in the principle of moral proximity. The problem is with the term "defining communities," which he never definitively defines. But it would appear that a good case could be made for the fact that the defining communities of the affluent would be composed of the affluent. And of course the affluent are not the poor who need help. Thus, the affluent are free to help the affluent, not the poor. The affluent live in communities with those like them, and on Schneider's principle the affluent are free to delight in their material prosperity and free to forget the poor because the poor are not part of their defining communities.

The best Schneider can do, it seems, is suggest that there may be some obligation of the rich to the poor outside their communities. But it is "something quite personal . . . [a]nd most often it may be a matter of special divine communication and calling, the work of the Holy Spirit

---

59. This phrase means "that human selection which 'seizes the ruling definition of the social.'" Long, *Divine Economy*, 10 (footnote 4 omitted), citing Williams, *Marxism and Literature*, 125. According to Long, theologians in this tradition "do not find . . . democratic capitalism . . . a threat to Christian theology." Long, *Divine Economy*, 10.

60. Schneider, *Good of Affluence*, 212.

'laying a burden' on the heart for some cause or other in a distant place."[61] Thus, once again, we see American Evangelicalism's individualistic metaphysic and practice at work. Social responsibility is reduced to individual self-interest and God's mysterious prompting. It remains safely outside the scope of any prophetic, transformational critique.

Schneider buttresses his personal ethic of moral proximity with the work of Peruvian economist Hernando de Soto. He presents De Soto's work in a straightforward, uncritical manner. Schneider is enthralled with the Peruvian economist's discovery of the "mystery of capital."[62] Thus, Schneider can claim that this "rising" star is ascending to heights that might allow him eventually "to tower above everyone else" like Marx and Weber did, for he has discovered "new things of modernity [that] have not only burst the wine skins of Christian tradition. . . . [but] have also 'scattered the proud' in things economic, . . . [such that] theorists are groping madly to find fresh unifying accounts of what is happening in economic life."[63]

Reformed Evangelicals in the United States, it seems to me, should have a deep sense of chagrin over Schneider's incautious economic overstatement that leads him to such an unequivocal theological approbation of De Soto. Although De Soto provides helpful insights into how capitalism has proven to be good for the poor while at the same time expanding affluence for millions during the twentieth century, and although his work is essential reading for understanding the problem of affluence in late modernity[64] and neither should be derided nor dismissed, neglected

---

61. Ibid.

62. De Soto, *Mystery of Capital*; Schneider, *Good of Affluence*, 213.

63. Ibid.

64. De Soto's thesis is that the poor in developing countries own billions of assets in "dead capital" outside the formal property system because of corrupt or inefficient governments. This precludes the poor from access to the economic system and thus from unlocking the true potential of their assets. It also excludes billions of dollars of assets governments could have as a tax base. The enlarged base of taxation would help fund infrastructure development so that utilities such as gas, water and electricity can be expanded to reach undeveloped areas. De Soto concludes *Mystery of Capital* with a very clear statement that he does not embrace unbridled neoliberal capitalism and that he is an advocate for the poor, genuinely believing that capitalism has been proven to benefit the poor much better than communist and socialist options have. Thus, he writes: "I am not a die-hard capitalist. I do not vie capitalism as a credo. Much more important to me are freedom, compassion for the poor, respect for the social contract, and equal opportunity. But for the moment, to achieve those goals, capitalism is the only game in

or ignored as those on the theological left are prone to do,[65] he should not be permitted to provide the final word on capitalism or how to solve the problem of global poverty as Schneider seems to think. Furthermore, he should not be allowed to provide the final theological word on capitalism as Schneider allows him to do.[66] Schneider employs De Soto theologically as "scattering" proud anticapitalist thoughts in relation to economic matters, but it is doubtful De Soto would feel comfortable in such a role.[67] He is an economist who has conducted extensive theoretical and empirical research for several decades now and advises many heads of state around the globe, but thus far he has not ventured into theology. Anyone familiar with De Soto's *The Other Path* recognizes that the Peruvian economist cares deeply for the poor and is motivated by a desire to help lighten their burden. That work is a modern example that the pen is mightier than the sword. The Peruvian communists who followed the "Shining Path" failed to kill De Soto and failed to win the hearts of the Peruvian people because their economic policies did not work. De Soto's did.

But this is hardly a license for appropriation of De Soto's economics to an evangelical moral theology in the United States. Schneider's theology of affluence ultimately fails as an evangelical theology because it neglects to bring critical-theological attention to the manner in which the cultural system produced by the "mystery" of capital denies and even subverts the "mystery" of God's kingdom, Christ and the gospel. Nurture of the AAEC in the principle of moral proximity and the theological doctrines from which Schneider derives that principle would be, I contend, mal-formative for the AAEC. Should Schneider's theology of affluence come to dominate the faith and practice of affluent Evangelicals, the consequences could be

---

town. It is the only system we know that provides us with the tools required to create massive surplus value." De Soto, *Mystery of Capital*, 228. His earlier work, *The Other Path*, argues against the Peruvian terror group, Shining Path, in favor of a capitalism properly understood and applied, which he claims would provide the economic answer to poverty that lies at the heart of terrorism. This work resulted in at least one attempt on De Soto's life. De Soto, *Other Path*, xi–xvi.

65. For example, Duchrow, Hinkelammert, and the Radical Orthodoxy theologians have this tendency.

66. See the insufficiently brief, dismissive critique of De Soto in Duchrow and Hinkelammert, *Property for People, Not Profit*, 170–71, 202–3 n. 7.

67. Schneider claims that De Soto's work "encourages thoughtfulness on the part of affluent Christians, guiding us lest our compassion be misplaced." Schneider, *Good of Affluence*, 220

grave. They would be grave for the AAEC because nurture would result inexorably in the formation of a spiritual-moral "lack" of affluence. And it would be grave for the poor of the world, including millions of children, because the inevitable practice of affluent Christians would be to justify their delight in prosperity in good conscience while the poor are left to languish in their poverty. Since the poor are not a part of the "defining communities" of the affluent, they are excluded from the zone of moral proximity within which wealthy Christians can be called prophetically to social responsibility for them.

Thus, I argue that instead of liberating the AAEC and the poor on the underside of humanity's growing affluence, Schneider's moral theology would help continue to enslave them under the delusive claims of capitalist liberation. It would continue to facilitate for the AAEC an ongoing spiritual and moral impoverishment in the "lack" of late modern affluence and blunt evangelical practice of renunciation and donation for the sake of Jesus, the gospel and the poor. At the same time, it would facilitate the ongoing impoverishment of millions who suffer in the face of a global affluence presently sufficient to meet their needs yet always just out of their reach. Schneider leads Evangelical parents and churches with their children down the wrong path. This can be seen further in the arrangement and substance of Schneider's theological argument for the good of affluence.

Summary of chapters 1 through 8 in The Good of Affluence

Schneider sees his theological task as involving two levels of interpretation: Scripture and late modern economic culture. It is a Niebuhrian problem of interpreting "Christ and culture."[68] Thus, Schneider proceeds in chapter 1 to set forth his interpretation of present day capitalist culture. It is a glowing report derived principally from Novak and *The Virtue of Prosperity* by neoliberal intellectual Dinesh D'Souza. It leads him to a "provisional conclusion" that has particular relevance for the theological anthropology of the AAEC developed here:

> modern economic habits of acquisition and enjoyment as they
> flourish under capitalism are not necessarily immoral. Nor is it
> obvious that they are always destructive to the human psyche and

68. Niebuhr, *Christ and Culture*; Schneider, *Good of Affluence*, 9, 13–14, 129.

thus to the inner spiritual strength of society. They can be shaped into habits that are immoral and destructive, to be sure. . . . But that is not a necessity, and the evidence is the affluent people in whom it is not present. It remains to see whether sacred Scripture supports this judgment.[69]

Schneider builds his case upon dubious premises and questionable evidence in favor of affluence, arguing that Christians should affirm modern capitalism and seek to form themselves within it for good ends. He is convinced that the culture of modern capitalism is suited well to the evangelical formation of Christians and, presumably, to the "discipline and instruction of the Lord" (Eph 6:4b). It is precisely at this point that the historical and sociological perspectives of the AAEC presented in chapters 2 through 4 illuminate the tenuous nature of Schneider's claims. Had Schneider critically engaged the history and sociology of capitalism and Evangelicalism in the United States, perhaps he would have developed a sufficiently critical-theological position regarding the culture of American-Evangelical affluence in the United States. However, close scrutiny of the first chapter discloses a questionable reading of the literary evidence on the culture of capitalism. And as a result, the entire argument of *The Good of Affluence* gets off on the wrong foot from the start.

Schneider proceeds in chapters 2 through 8 upon this foundation to present an extended cosmological and christological interpretation of the "new" culture of capitalism. He begins with the narrative of creation in chapter 2 and continues with the narratives of exodus in chapter 3 and exile in chapter 4 (where he addresses the prophetic and wisdom literature). He then turns to examine the social and economic world of Jesus in chapter 5 and the manner in which Jesus lived in that world in chapter 6 (where he addresses Luke's narrative of the rich ruler). These chapters set the stage for chapter 7's exegetical and theological treatment of four key "parables of affluence" in Luke (the Rich Fool, the Rich Man and Lazarus, the Dishonest Manager, and the Pounds). Instead of teaching Christians to embrace poverty, Schneider contends, these parables teach them to embrace affluence in a proper way. Chapter 8 engages key economic passages in Acts, Paul and James in a manner consistent with his thesis of the "cosmic" good of affluence found in the Bible and proven by the "evidence" adduced from late modern capitalism.

69. Ibid., 40.

Schneider finds the theme of delight in affluence running from Genesis through James. As he puts it, "the narratives of creation establish a cosmic vision that . . . at its core is God's deliberate institution of material prosperity and flourishing as the proper condition for human beings in the world and before God. . . . this condition of 'delight' . . . endures throughout the biblical story as the vision God has for all human beings."[70] Consequently, even the narratives of exodus and exile contain "pervasive spiritual and moral directives" that flow not from the negation but the affirmation of affluence.[71]

THE AAEC AND THE RICH YOUNG MAN

> The young man said to him, "I have kept all these; what do I still lack?" Jesus said to him, "If you wish to be perfect, go, sell your possessions, and give the money to the poor, and you will have treasure in heaven; then come, follow me" (Mt 19:20–21).

Having set out the contours of Schneider's theology of affluence, the stage is now set for a focused critique of Schneider's interpretation of Luke's narratives of the rich ruler and Zacchaeus.[72] In this section, I will first present Schneider's arguments from these narratives and how he links them to the Parable of the Pounds. These arguments will then be examined in light of the interpretations of Matthew's story of the rich young man by Bonhoeffer, Barth and Pope John Paul II.

In this tradition, the presence of "lack" in the young man signifies the presence of some form of evil that prevents him from doing the "good deed . . . to have eternal life" (Mt 19:16). Truth, faith, hope and love are in some sense "lacking."[73] It is falling short of that which is good, true and beautiful in the encounter with Jesus and his call to discipleship. In Paul's theology it is to lack God's glory (Rom 3:23), and in Matthew's it is to lack God's perfection ("If you would be perfect . . .", Mt 18:21; cf. 5:48).

Schneider fails to address the issue of lack in his interpretation of Luke's rich ruler. He lays the groundwork for interpreting Luke's story of the rich ruler in chapter 5 of *The Good of Affluence*, where he presents the

70. Schneider, *Good of Affluence*, 10.

71. Ibid., 10.

72. Found in the sixth chapter of *Good of Affluence*.

73. Cf. Milbank, *Being Reconciled*, 21–22.

"life and economic identity" of Jesus through the lens of the Incarnation.[74] This is a move indicating dependence on Novak's consistent incarnational approach to capitalism. Schneider concludes that Jesus' first-century economic life and identity are "normative as a model for Christians."[75] Thus, Jesus

> led relatively privileged people into new lives of economic redemption and redemptiveness. As he pulled them out of their safe worlds of social and economic stability, he placed them in contact with the very soul of the suffering world—the poor in economic, social, and spiritual senses. By bringing them together, the rich (in all relevant senses) and the poor (likewise in all relevant senses), he created a new community that was electrified by grace and liberation for everyone in different ways. In a strange way the rich became poor and the poor became rich. At bottom, this was the expression of poverty or lowering of spirit by one group in order to free and empower the spirits of the other one. And the economic expression of this was not some form of leveling or egalitarianism but something very like the order of the exodus people of Israel under the laws of Moses. The rich did not so much enter into economic poverty for the sake of the poor as they did into a new life of economic dynamism, of *power born of renewed compassion*, and they went on a way that they could never have imagined before Jesus called them to follow him.[76]

Economic "redemption and redemptiveness" apparently mean that following Christ entails liberation of the economic dimension of life, which in turn leads to practicing economic compassion with others. But compassion is obligatory only in the zone of personally determined moral proximity.[77] There is little hope, then, that the "economic dynamism[, the] . . . power born of renewed compassion" of which Schneider speaks will lead to the formation of a life of liberating economic practice in the AAEC, unless of course it can be shown how cultivation of twin capitalist habits of acquisition and enjoyment are turned to liquidation and donation. Put another way, how does delighting in Disneyworld and other American

74. Schneider, *Good of Affluence*, 138.

75. Ibid., 118.

76. Schneider, *Good of Affluence*, 138 (emphasis added).

77. Schneider's use of the word "compassion" is further complicated if by it he means the prevailing cultural and political 'compassionate conservatism' of the United States. Cf., e.g., Olasky, *Compassionate Conservatism*.

consumer paradises get converted to self-denial, saving and donation on behalf of the poor?

Schneider's treatment of Luke's narrative of the rich ruler succeeds in sheltering the AAEC from prophetic critique of the formative effects of affluence. Not only does Schneider overlook lack, he also errs by focusing exclusively on the question whether Jesus' call to dispossession and donation is normative for all Christians in all times and cultures. This causes him to miss the theological significance of the rich ruler's refusal to obey Jesus' call to discipleship in the way of the cross and thus the implications that refusal might have for an evangelical ethic in the context of late modern affluence.

The rich ruler in The Good of Affluence

It should be recalled that Schneider decided to focus exclusively on the Gospel of Luke because it is the Gospel with the greatest interest in issues of wealth and poverty. Schneider claims this indicates that Luke specifically developed a narrative theology for the affluent.[78] Thus, according to Schneider, "Luke is the most promising source available to modern affluent Christians for finding answers to their particular questions."[79]

Schneider's primary sources for interpreting Luke's story of the rich ruler (as well as Zacchaeus and the Parable of the Pounds) are Luke Timothy Johnson, Walter Pilgrim and David Moessner.[80] Schneider correctly notes that these scholars have provided "groundbreaking works of Lukan scholarship" for reading the prophets as the framework for interpreting Luke and for seeing the Moses of Deuteronomy as "a typological model for Luke's presentation of Jesus."[81] His interaction with these scholars is helpful and enlightening at many points, showing how they serve to deepen "our understanding of what leaving everything and following can mean in economic terms."[82]

Schneider reaches one conclusion that bears on an important point here: the literary function of possessions in Luke points to the fact that

78. Schneider, *Good of Affluence*, 142–43.

79. Ibid., 143.

80. Johnson, *Sharing Possessions*, and *Literary Function of Possessions*; Pilgrim, *Good News to the Poor*; Moessner, *Lord of the Banquet*.

81. Schneider, *Good of Affluence*, 144.

82. Ibid.

dispossession and discipleship "can mean very different things for different people in different circumstances."[83] While this may be true insofar as it goes, ultimately it provides little effective guidance for the rich Christians Schneider seeks to help. Practically it means that the affluent are free to decide what "leaving everything" and following Jesus means. They are immune from prophetic critique. It also blunts the prophetic force of the encounter between Jesus and the rich ruler. Schneider misses the theological depths of "lack" the story brings to the surface. At least as far as the AAEC is concerned, this error is fatal to a critical-evangelical anthropology.

Schneider's concern to demonstrate that it is possible for Christians both to retain and to remain in their wealth while following Jesus in the path of dispossession and discipleship leads him down the wrong path. Instead of exploring what Jesus meant by the "one thing lacking" (Luke 18:22), Schneider attempts to reconcile problematic texts in Luke[84] in order to prove that no contradiction exists between the radical Jesus he sees in the story of the rich ruler and the Lord of delight he sees in the story of Zacchaeus. He appeals to "several instances of disciples who satisfied the requirement [of dispossession and discipleship] by remaining where they were and retaining wealth."[85] This is because in Luke the semantics of poverty, wealth, dispossession and discipleship clearly extend beyond the literal into "the realm of potent metaphor."[86] Thus, Schneider concludes that Zacchaeus is the best model for affluent Christians to emulate. His story provides the key for understanding that model in what he sees as the paradigmatic "parable of affluence," the Parable of the Pounds.[87]

In order to arrive at this conclusion, Schneider must first overcome Luke's radical narrative of the rich ruler. The details of his interpretation are as follows. Following Johnson, Schneider reads the encounter between Jesus and the rich ruler as the climactic story in a series of affluence-negative narratives that began in Luke 6. The adversarial, prophetic

83. Ibid., 144.

84. E.g., "So therefore, none of you can become my disciple if you do not give up all your possessions" (Luke 14:33).

85. Schneider, *Good of Affluence*, 144.

86. Ibid.

87. Schneider presents four "parables of affluence" in chapter 7 of *Good of Affluence*: the rich fool (Luke 12:13–21), the rich man and Lazarus (Luke 16:19–31), the dishonest manager (Luke 16:1–9) and the pounds (19:11–27).

encounter Jesus has with the rich ruler is a concrete illustration of the curses he pronounced in Luke 6 against the system of oppression, wealth and rule in first century Israel. Jesus plays an "elementary, cruel trick" [sic] in the encounter by omitting the command against coveting, such that the ruler "exposes himself as a very model of that unreflective self-righteousness that Jesus has been condemning among the religious and political authorities all through the Gospel."[88] Schneider claims that Jesus is explicit with the rich ruler and condemns him without hope of entering the kingdom of God if he does not liquidate his affluence, give to the poor and follow him. Not only this, the same severe judgment falls on every affluent person who follows in the rich ruler's footsteps.

Upon arriving at these conclusions Schneider admits incredulity: "it seems that Jesus wants to liberate the rich from their prosperity. How can this be?"[89] Schneider answers himself in the following steps. First, he presents Luke's wealth-negative theology. Next, he summarizes traditional interpretations of the radical demand Jesus placed on the rich ruler. In a relatively short space, Schneider rejects traditional ascetic, Catholic, liberationist and Protestant options as insufficient because they do not resolve the problem presented by the "outer circle of disciples who did not literally leave everything and follow Jesus but rather retained their working lives and assets."[90]

In light of this dilemma, Schneider sees two options. We must either admit with Barry Gordon that Luke failed to reconcile the wealth-negative demands with the wealth-affirmative teachings that Luke and other biblical writers have given us,[91] or we must accept Schneider's picture of Jesus as the Lord of delight. As an evangelical, Schneider rejects "the widely held assumption that the differences between the narratives [of other Gospels] entail theologies, or complete moral views, that are in logical

88. Schneider, *Good of Affluence*, 145. Although it might be explainable as incautious hyperbole, Schneider's suggestion that Jesus engaged in an act of cruelty is surprising. Most evangelical theologians are loath to suggest anything that might cast aspersions upon the character of Jesus and thus contradict the doctrine of his sinlessness.

89. Schneider, *Good of Affluence*, 146. Unfortunately, Schneider rhetorically dismisses this possibility as an impossibility.

90. Ibid., 150.

91. Ibid., 141, 150. At page 141, Schneider cites Gordon for his claim that Luke, who concerned himself with issues of wealth and morality more than any other New Testament writer, "failed to resolve the tensions he experienced concerning discipleship and the economic problem." Gordon, *Economic Problem*, 70.

conflict with each other."[92] Gordon's option is unacceptable because Luke neither contradicts other Gospel writers nor fails to reconcile the radical and delighting Jesus in the theology of wealth set out in his Gospel.

Two things are necessary to see this. First is the inclusion of Zacchaeus in the circle of salvation and discipleship, as well as other disciples who did not (and do not) sell *everything* and give to the poor in the literal economic sense, and then follow Jesus with their treasures invested in heaven. It may be hard but it is not impossible for an affluent person to enter the kingdom of God. Second, we must understand Luke's negative assessment of affluence in terms of Jesus as a type of the prophet Moses (Acts 3:22). Appropriating Johnson and Moessner to his thesis, Schneider argues that a narrative theological reading of Luke with this typology in view renders an understanding of Jesus as the Lord of delight. Such understanding harmonizes his radical demands for renouncing wealth with his permission to enjoy wealth in a proper way. It is important to see how Schneider arrives at this conclusion.

Luke presents Jesus as a Moses-type figure leading his people on a journey of redemption. When he begins to proclaim the gospel to his inner circle of disciples and turns to Jerusalem for the final confrontation with the elders, chief priests and scribes (Luke 9:22), the prophetic element of his teaching and ministry begins to spring forth. The message and ministry of Jesus divides people into two groups, those who listen and those who do not. The ones who reject his message are represented principally in "the rich rulers, scribes, and Pharisees who love their affluent lives more than they love God."[93] Those who accede to their values and system share in their condemnation: "these religious leaders become a living typology of the rich whom the prophets condemned centuries earlier for similar arrogance and hardness of heart toward the poor and powerless."[94] Schneider never clarifies what "a living typology" is, but the implication is plain enough. The story of the rich ruler (and those who choose to be like him) applies only to those who uphold corrupt systems like those of the corrupt religious leaders in Jesus' day.

Those leaders and all who follow them stand in sharp contrast to Jesus and his disciples. The disciples represent the kingdom and its judg-

---

92. Schneider, *Good of Affluence*, 141.

93. Ibid., 152.

94. Ibid.

ment of the corrupt system represented by the "typology of the rich." They are called to "stand conspicuously apart from a cultural system ruled by people of great corruption" while embracing "the cosmic good of affluence, which is delight."[95] In other words, "Jesus directs them not to be rich in a manner that affirms the corrupt and corrupting system and the ways of the people who rule and profit from it most."[96] This is a helpful point in Schneider's theology of affluence only if we accept his cultural analysis of the "new" culture of capitalism. If he is correct about capitalism, then the AAEC and all Evangelicals are free to participate in that system under the individualistic ethical rubric of moral proximity. But if he is wrong, if in fact there are significant, essential parallels between the "corrupt and corrupting" systems of the first and twenty-first centuries, then Schneider's entire theology of affluence implodes.

Again, Schneider went astray by failing to address the theological-anthropological issue of lack. While he correctly notes that the story of the rich ruler cannot mean that the demand is normative for all Christians in all times, he misses the deeper point Jesus prophetically identified when he said, "There is still one thing lacking." The ethical aspects of the story are comprehensible only when its theological anthropology is resolved; that is, only when the God-neighbor problem is worked through. Schneider overlooks this in his attempt to overcome the "otherwise baffling addendum to the wealth-negative demand" placed on the rich ruler with his picture of Jesus as the Lord who delights in the cosmic good of affluence.[97]

What did Jesus mean when he said that those who leave houses, wives, siblings, parents and children for the kingdom of God will "get back very much more in this age, and in the age to come eternal life" (Luke 18:29–30)? As Schneider sees it, Jesus calls disciples through this verse into "an existence of intense material delight. . . . typical of the prophetic narratives, in which the men of God come eating and drinking in a right and sacred way—over and against the rich who do so in a wrong and godless manner."[98] This supposed manner of proper consumption "is part of the prophet's display of God's condemnation of the present generation.

95. Ibid., 153.
96. Ibid.
97. Ibid., 153–54.
98. Ibid., 154.

It is to set true delight in opposition to the revelry and evil of the ruling rich."[99] These are valid and helpful insights. But the problem remains, a problem Schneider never addresses: the "right and sacred way" of consumption he brings into the twenty-first century from this text is, in the end, determined by an anthropology of liberty immune to social critique. The individual is sovereign in exercising the redeemed dominion of affluence that Christ has restored to him through the gospel. As a result, the ethical practice of sharing affluence by the affluent is individualistically determined as well.

This becomes clear from the manner in which Schneider develops the theme of celebration and feasting in the Gospel of Luke. He reads much into the few texts bearing upon this point, particularly Luke 7:34 where Jesus quotes the accusation of his adversaries, "a friend of tax collectors and sinners!" Unlike John the Baptist, Jesus came "eating and drinking." From this Schneider concludes that "Jesus and his followers lived a celebrative life, one which expressed the reality of the kingdom of God."[100] This means they were to embrace material prosperity in the "right and sacred" manner. It follows that twenty-first century Christians should do the same. For although the economic worlds of those centuries "could not be more different,"[101] they share this in common: intense delight in material blessings. What the first disciples enjoyed briefly with Jesus all affluent believers can now enjoy because of the new culture of capitalism. This culture has brought unparalleled opportunities for millions to enjoy "cosmic" material delight.

In other words, affluence is a cosmic good to be pursued, acquired and enjoyed in a way pleasing to God and shared with the poor on a subjective basis determined by each beneficiary of affluence according to the dictates of individual conscience. According to Schneider, Luke's story of Zacchaeus and the Parable of the Pounds provide the perfect templates for understanding how this should work today through participation in the material joy made possible by "The Radical Jesus as the Lord of Delight."[102] These are things contemporary moral theologians simply have failed to see.

99. Ibid.

100. Ibid., 155.

101. Ibid., 2.

102. Ibid., 139, title to chapter 6 of *Good of Affluence*.

Zacchaeus and the Pounds in The Good of Affluence

Schneider claims that Zacchaeus "forever embodies, in cultural form, the ancient truths of the creation, the exodus, the prophets, the books of wisdom, and the Incarnation."[103] He juxtaposes the stories of the rich ruler and Zacchaeus in chapter 6 to establish two identities of Jesus. One is a radical Jesus who confronts the rich ruler (and those like him), and the other is a delighting Jesus who confronts Zacchaeus (and those like him). Schneider wants to harmonize these identities into a coherent vision because on his reading of the Gospels the "poor of the kingdom came . . . from different groups [of the affluent as well as the literal poor], and so we might suppose that they can also come from the more affluent classes of our day."[104]

Jesus is the Lord of delight because he feasted with Levi and other sinners at a great banquet, rather than fasting like John the Baptist and his disciples (Luke 5:27–39); because he turned water into wine at a wedding "simply to preserve a precious moment of celebration and delight for his friends" (John 2); and he accepted the disreputable woman's extravagant gesture of anointing him with expensive nard (Mark 14:3, John 12:3).[105] These are the key reasons Schneider cites for his claim that Jesus is Lord of "the cosmic good of affluence, which is delight."[106]

Jesus' condemnations of the rich in Luke are condemnations of the wrong kind of enjoyment, not the condemnation of affluence per se. It is clear to Schneider that this flows from the fact that Jesus' mission was to fulfill God's promise of material delight made to Abraham.[107] Jesus called the inner and outer circle of disciples to participate in the fulfillment of this promise. The same is true for Christians today. It takes place in many different ways, but all are called to enjoy the right kind of material delight. Some will have it hard and must pay "the price" of rejection and sacrifice, while others will have it good and must pay "the price . . . [of] radical

---

103. Ibid., 166.

104. Ibid., 140.

105. Schneider makes much of the fact that Jesus said his disciples could not fast while he was with them, but he neglects to mention he indicated they would fast after he left (Luke 5:33–35). Schneider sees the "traditional" view that Jesus was poor as being in the class of "old wineskins." Ibid., 156.

106. Ibid., 153.

107. Ibid., 160.

redirection of religious and moral life toward the goals of the kingdom as envisioned by Jesus."[108] Schneider reads the story of Zacchaeus as providing the paradigmatic example of the "radical reorientation of economic life" required by religious-moral redirection effected by Jesus.[109] His repentance, proven by his fifty percent divestiture to the poor and payment of damages for taking fraudulent taxes, is an example of leaving everything and following Jesus without really leaving everything. There are many other examples as well from the "second circle of disciples": for example, the women who provided for Jesus and the disciples (Luke 8:3), Joseph of Arimathea, Lazarus and his sisters, etc.[110] These "left everything and followed" Jesus in different ways "in the sense that they directed considerable portions of what they had to Jesus and his mission," and thus "it follows . . . that they . . . met the demand to leave everything."[111]

According to Schneider, Zacchaeus serves a particularly important function in Luke's rhetorical strategy to answer the problem posed by the story of the rich ruler: how a rich person "might be saved without ceasing to be rich."[112] Noting that the story of Zacchaeus follows shortly after the story of the rich ruler, Schneider believes, on "narrative rhetorical suppositions," that it answers Peter's vexing question: "Then who can be saved?" (Luke 18:26).[113] The "ironic," "improbable" and "remarkable" story of Zacchaeus provides a vivid example of how the affluent can be saved without divesting themselves of their affluence.[114] Citing Pilgrim, Schneider believes that the story of the diminutive chief tax collector is "the most important Lukan text on the subject of the right use of possessions. . . . [and] that Luke intends this text as the paradigm par excellence for wealthy Christians in his community."[115]

The fact that Luke placed the Parable of the Pounds right after the story of Zacchaeus supports these judgments. This is because the story of Zacchaeus is the last confrontation Jesus has with someone who is wealthy and because the Parable of the Pounds is the last teaching Jesus gives on

108. Ibid.
109. Ibid.
110. Ibid., 161.
111. Ibid.
112. Ibid., 163.
113. Ibid.
114. Ibid.
115. Ibid., citing Pilgrim, *Good News*, 129.

affluence. Thus, Schneider views these placements as making the "parable a great deal more important to our moral theology than is commonly known."[116] This leads Schneider to come back to the story of Zacchaeus in his engagement of the "key parables of Jesus on being rich . . . and [to] treat it together with the Parable of the Pounds as a unified narrative."[117]

Schneider sees the Parable of the Pounds as portraying "God as a warrior-king" and bemoans the fact that "Christian theology today" fails to honor that God or "the courage of godly people in the marketplace."[118] In a burst of rhetorical-theological flourish, Schneider claims it is

> a parable of power and the enlargement of dominion through wealth. . . . that honors the courage and strength of a warrior and king, who will not stop until his realm is enlarged over all the earth . . . that honors the strength and courage of his servants who are fruitful in the worldly realms of power . . . that honors the *en-largement* of people who would become stronger, and would make their master stronger, through the creation of wealth.[119]

Not only this, "it is a parable of dire warning against a spirit of timidity and fruitlessness in our response to the world."[120] Thus, the failure to be bold, courageous and fruitful in free market capitalism becomes the basis for condemnation. Schneider resonates a powerful, muscular Christianity much like Bushnell's.

It is difficult to see how Zacchaeus can serve as a paradigm for such claims, however. And it is even more difficult to see how they square with the story of the rich ruler. Jesus did not commend Zacchaeus for his conduct as chief tax collector, and we know very little about his life after conversion. We have no idea whether he pursued the path Schneider commends, but in light of both Luke and the New Testament as a whole it is doubtful that he did. Instead of pursuing delight in material affluence, Zacchaeus probably pursued a lifestyle of almsgiving and a passionate pursuit of justice in his taxing relations. Unlike the rich ruler, he proved by his repentance that he was a son of Abraham. Jesus condemned the rich ruler for refusing to divest himself of the fruits of his affluence and

116. Schneider, *Good of Affluence*, 164.

117. Ibid.

118. Ibid., 189.

119. Ibid. (emphasis in original).

120. Ibid.

failing to renounce his attachments so he would be free to follow on the path of discipleship. Hence, the manner of life Schneider commends appears similar to what the rich ruler refused to leave. It smacks more of American-Evangelical muscular Christianity of the nineteenth-century Busnhellian variety or of twenty-first century Evangelical right-wing warrior theology.

Despite relying upon Johnson for interpreting Luke, Schneider departed from him in regard to the Parable of the Pounds. For instance, he fails to note Johnson's position that the theme of possessions is "subsidiary to a political one."[121] Johnson views the parable within the larger literary framework of Luke-Acts. The parable interprets Luke's larger story that Jesus was about to enact upon his entry into Jerusalem and subsequent suffering, death, resurrection and ascension. Those in the parable who faithfully administered the possessions entrusted to them would receive authority to rule in the kingdom inaugurated by Jesus. They are the "Twelve, whom we shall see in the narrative of Acts exercising just such authority over the restored people of God."[122] Thus, contrary to Schneider, Johnson does not view the parable as emphasizing the character traits of the "two praiseworthy servants" who succeeded in their profit-making for their warrior-king as opposed to the "servant who has failed."[123] Instead, the parable serves the political-ecclesial purpose of establishing the Twelve in their position of authority in the kingdom and administrative trust in the Church of the risen Christ.

Nevertheless, Schneider persists in his claims that the parable serves the interests of technological consumer capitalism. It is so profoundly theological that it "takes us back, through Christ, into something more profound even than the social ethics of the prophet. . . . to the very foundations of their [sic] message, which is the creation itself, and the existence of dominion and delight that God envisioned for human beings."[124] Thus, Jesus is warning us "against being so conscious of our master's severity that we retreat, withdraw from the world, and thus render our economic lives fruitless. . . . The true servant of a warrior-king cannot be a cow-

---

121. Johnson, *Gospel of Luke*, 292.

122. Ibid., 294.

123. Ibid., 189–90.

124. Ibid., 189.

ard."[125] He continues: "The economic world is a battlefield, and it takes wit, bravery, and a strong will that is loath to retreat, much less surrender. . . . the parable . . . is a strong warning against those who would erode the strong, aggressive, competitive spirit of behavior (particularly economic behavior) among Christians who believe that their king has given them pounds to trade until he comes."[126] The American-Evangelical penchant to draw on warfare metaphors and apocalyptic futures is well-known, and Schneider is no exception.[127]

The theology Schneider derives from the Parable of the Pounds is far-reaching. The poor are not in the picture, or at least the virtue of the praiseworthy servants is unrelated to caring for the poor. The master in the parable, a figure of Christ, is "a powerful figure, a man of fierce enlargement. . . . [which] is the right metaphor for understanding and applying the whole story."[128] Rather than finding their virtue in connection with "an obligation to the poor," it is found rather in "their obligation to enter the world and, by means of trade and investment, to enlarge the master's power and dominion within it while he is away."[129] Thus we see Hoover's political, commercial and social vision in the 1920s come full circle in symbiosis with Schneider's moral theology of affluence in the 2000s. American individualism and the pursuit of happiness in production diffused into consumption have secured their Evangelical endorsement in Schneider.

Schneider succeeds in helping the AAEC's parents and churches find the "right and sacred" way to produce and consume within the "new" culture of technological consumer capitalism in the United States. If the AAEC hopes to represent the character of God in late modernity, this parable is the key to knowing what needs to be nurtured because it shows "the sorts of people that a warrior-king can identify with, be proud of,

125. Ibid., 190.

126. Ibid. At this point, Schneider sounds like he is advocating a theology of economic warfare which could call for the formation of the AAEC as an "economic hit man" serving U. S. commercial-governmetnal interests. Cf. Perkins, *Confessions of an Economic Hit Man.*

127. See, e.g., Northcott, "The Warrior Ethos and the Politics of Jesus," in *Angel Directs the Storm,* 134–76.

128. Schneider, *Good of Affluence,* 189.

129. Ibid.

and approve at the end."[130] Although he does not appear to have children and their formation in view, Schneider is aware that his interpretation of the Parable of the Pounds may lead some to conclude that Luke's Jesus actually pronounced "an unqualified blessing upon economic gain," so he attempts to qualify his advocacy for courageous economic warfare in the free market of late modern life.[131] What he offers is less than clear, however. Supposedly, Jesus' manner of life and his teachings "all demonstrate the conditions for godliness that must exist before our gains become true enlargement of his kingdom, before they become fruitfulness."[132] But Schneider never describes what those "conditions" are, how to identify them when they "exist" or when they have been "recreated," such that "then the creative, productive economic life becomes something that is absolutely *true to our humanity* and to the identity of God."[133] The implication for the AAEC is that this is the kind of "discipline and instruction of the Lord" his parents and church should nurture in him. New culture, new cultivation indeed.

This is seen in the manner Schneider treated the story of Zacchaeus "with the Parable of the Pounds as a unified narrative text."[134] The deeper meaning of Zacchaeus' story is that it discloses "the redemption of the world, the world of culture, including its morally questionable economic forms."[135] Schneider sees great hope for affluent people in this story. Surely if a chief tax collector working for the corrupt social system of Herod and Caesar could be saved, then there is hope that the rich in our day can be saved. But will it lead to the salvation of the AAEC? Put another way, will it lead to the AAEC following Jesus in the way of the cross?

Schneider is correct to agree with Johnson and others that the story is offered by Luke as an answer to the soteriological question raised by Peter in view of the rich ruler incident (Luke 18:26). However, he goes beyond Johnson when he claims that the story teaches "not that a man *is* saved *from* the economics of the world, but that the world is redeemed

---

130. Ibid., 190.
131. Ibid.
132. Ibid., 190–91.
133. Ibid., 191 (emphasis added).
134. Ibid., 164, 186–92.
135. Ibid., 165.

in and through the salvation and new economics of the man."[136] This is a highly suspect claim and further evidence that he may be overinterpreting the new culture of capitalism. Schneider imagines that Zacchaeus became an instrument of great good in the region he ruled as chief tax collector after his encounter with Jesus. Thus, it is reasonable to conclude that this model of the conversion of a wealthy ruler who proves his repentance by deeds of divestiture and restitution "is exactly the model Luke puts forth for all wealthy Christians."[137] This is because most affluent believers do not engage in anything as corrupt as the tax system of Zacchaeus' day. Thus, it is appropriate to take the chief tax collector as a model for rich Christians "to follow in terms of the disposition and principles he displayed."[138]

Schneider's reasoning raises some troubling questions. Why would Zacchaeus be a paradigm of virtue and practice in the twenty-first century when comparatively few wealthy Christians are rulers or tax collectors and the well documented tax-collecting abuses in which Zacchaeus engaged are foreign to the twenty-first century? In an age of mass affluence, does Zacchaeus serve the purpose Schneider seeks? Furthermore, for the wealthy who profess to be Christians and also happen to be rulers (e.g., President G. W. Bush, Vice President Cheney, et al.) or who work for the Internal Revenue Service, is Schneider calling them to repent like Zacchaeus did? Clearly he is not. He does not call upon wealthy, ruling Christians to liquidate half their wealth and donate it to the poor. In fact, he argues against the possibility of such a prophetic claim. Schneider fails to draw out the significance of Zacchaeus' statement to Jesus, "*I am giving half of my possessions to the poor*,"[139] which indicates that he is describing not only "his willingness to share . . . [but a] regular practice of sharing . . . his possessions with the poor, not as a single gesture but as a steady commitment."[140]

Nor does Schneider call affluent Evangelicals to search their hearts and financial records to see where they may have "defrauded anyone of anything"[141] (Lk 19:8). Upon conversion, the chief tax collector was far

136. Ibid. (emphasis in original).

137. Ibid.

138. Ibid.

139. Johnson, *Gospel of Luke*, 285 (emphasis and translation are Johnson's).

140. Ibid., 287.

141. I.e., cheated anyone of anything or taken money from anyone by false charges for anything. The verb Luke uses in 19:8 is the same as 3:14, from which we derive our

from an avaricious disposition but instead was diligent to find any profits made "on the basis of shady practice" and to pay them back "at the maximum demanded by Torah."[142] In the twenty-first century, this kind of accounting for profits would require some deep searching of American-Evangelical hearts and records. If the theological critics of contemporary capitalist culture are correct to any degree, the system that has produced such great affluence for so many Evangelicals has roots that sink deep into "shady" practices. Schneider overlooks such obvious ethical implications derived from the story of Zacchaeus.

Schneider also fails to note why salvation "happens" for Zacchaeus. He welcomed the prophet into his home and disposed of his possessions. These are the reasons salvation happened to Zacchaeus. He believed and obeyed the call of the gospel. Johnson points out that he committed to the practice of giving alms and immediately gave half of his estate to the poor, "which for Luke is the true sign of righteousness (6:30–31, 38; 11:41; 12:33; 16:9; 18:22, 29)."[143] Schneider fails to call affluent Christians to such commitment or practice. This would be imitating Zacchaeus "in a literal, slavish way."[144] Calling affluent Christians to practice repentance like Zacchaeus would be going beyond what the text allows. Instead, modeling Zacchaeus means "we can find creative ways to shape our institutions — families, churches, schools, banks, corporations, businesses, and also our larger political system — into instruments of redemptive power. At least we can become agents of such power for good within them."[145] Consistent with Evangelicalism's history, private social benevolence and individualistic Evangelical social ethics are outcomes of Schneider's theology of affluence.

Perhaps sensing the contradictions inherent in his call to "find creative ways to shape our institutions," Schneider falls back to the tra-

---

English nouns "sycophancy" and "sycophant." Zacchaeus may have, therefore, been confessing to Jesus that if he has been a self-seeking, servile flatterer or fawning parasite as chief tax collector he will prove his repentance in the manner described. It is more likely, however, that Zacchaeus was saying "if I discover" extortion/defrauding then fourfold will be repaid. Ibid., 286.

142. Ibid., 287. As Johnson notes, this was going beyond the Mishnah's tendency to limit the fourfold restitution requirement to twofold. Ibid., 286.

143. Ibid., 286.

144. Schneider, *Good of Affluence*, 165.

145. Ibid., 166.

ditional American-Evngelical hope of changing society and culture one individual exercising liberty at a time. This shelters his theology of affluence from prophetic social and cultural critique as well. It mutes the prophet's calls to repentance that flow from the model of Zacchaeus. Such would be inappropriate because they would be slavishly literal, causing us to miss the crucial point, according to Schneider, that "the improbable example of Zacchaeus forever embodies, in cultural form, the ancient truths of creation, the exodus, the prophets, the books of wisdom, and the Incarnation."[146] This is a remarkably extensive theological and biblical claim. It assures joyful formation of acquisitional habits in Evangelicals and their children rather than habits of dispossession, donation and scrupulous accounting for unjust profits modeled by Zacchaeus.

The foregoing survey of the role Luke's Gospel plays in Schneider's theology of affluence demonstrates that nurture in Schneider's theology of affluence would assure the AAEC's formation in a muscular, competitive Evangelical faith not unlike the kind of Christianity Bushnell advocated in the nineteenth century. In such a view, the AAEC's parents and churches remain immune to prophetic critique that the stories of the rich ruler and Zacchaeus provide. Schneider's interpretation of the Parable of the Pounds would supply the formative theological ethics for the relational matrices in which the AAEC develops. By the age of twenty, habits of acquisition and enjoyment of Evangelical affluence would be (and in fact are) formed in the AAEC as a result of such theological economics. This would result, I suggest, in the cultivation of a capitalist "warrior" spirit that boldly and courageously seeks to enlarge the dominion of the warrior-king Jesus contrary to genuine evangelical nurture.

THE AAEC AND THE AFFLUENT EVANGELICAL MAN

Schneider thus unwittingly joins Bushnell in the vision of a coming revival once wealthy Christians consecrate the power of capitalism to the advance of the kingdom: "One more revival—only one more—is needed, the revival of Christian stewardship, the consecration of the money power to God. When the revival comes, the Kingdom of God will come in a day."[147] Schneider, like Bushnell, has failed to grasp that with consecration

146. Ibid.

147. Cf. Bushnell, *Building Eras*, 26, with Schneider's affirmation of Novak's point about rich people leading the next revival. D'Souza, *Virtue of Prosperity*, 144, quoting

of the money power of capitalism to God, among other things, comes the consecration of Evangelical children to the same socio-cultural means that system employs in reaching the ends it values.

Nurture in such a context leads to formation of the AAEC between God and Mammon upon a neoliberal anthropology of freedom. The interpretations of the rich young man in Matthew 19 by Bonhoeffer, Barth and Pope John Paul II help illumine how Schneider's theology of affluence risks forming this kind of freedom in Evangelicals and thus risks cultivating a spiritual-moral lack in the AAEC.

Bonhoeffer and Barth on the rich young man

According to Walter Moberly, the "story of the rich young man . . . has . . . been powerfully interpreted by such eminent Protestant theologians as Barth and Bonhoeffer, and . . . comparative reflection on the interpretations could be illuminating."[148] At the time, Moberly was suggesting that Pope John Paul II would have benefited from reading Bonhoeffer's and Barth's respective interpretations of Matthew's story of the rich young man in the course of developing the moral theology of *Veritatis Splendor*. Similarly, Schneider would have benefited from comparative reflection on their interpretations as well.

Bonhoeffer on obedience, faith and affluence

Bonhoeffer's theological reflections on the story of the rich young man begin in chapter 2 of *The Cost of Discipleship* ("The Call to Discipleship"), continue throughout chapter 3 ("Single-Minded Obedience"), and run into chapter 4 ("The Cross and Discipleship").[149] Bonhoeffer addresses broader issues of affluence in chapter 17, "The Simplicity of the Carefree Life," through an engagement with Matthew 6:19–24.[150]

Bonhoeffer arrives at the story of the rich young man after setting out what he understands the call to discipleship means. Simply put, disci-

---

Novak; Schneider, *Good of Affluence*, 4.

148. Moberly, "Use of Scripture," 11 (endnote 1, omitted).

149. Bonhoeffer, "The Call to Discipleship," in *Cost of Discipleship*, 77–99. The rich young man reappears in chapter 8, "The Righteousness of Christ," and in the conclusion. Ibid., 137, 219.

150. Ibid., 192–201.

pleship is following Jesus. It requires decisive action, which demonstrates faithful obedience to the call of Christ. It entails both a commitment to follow and concrete steps of following. The first step "cuts the disciple off from his previous existence."[151]

Throughout this discussion, Bonhoeffer is concerned with the recurring problem within the Protestant (particularly German Lutheran) tradition to use faith as an excuse for disobedience. He arrives at an important principle that bears directly upon how he interprets the story of the rich young man: "The idea of a situation in which faith is possible is only a way of stating the facts of a case in which the following two propositions hold good and are equally true: *only he who believes is obedient, and only he who is obedient believes.*"[152] Thus, the human "who disobeys cannot believe, for only he who obeys can believe."[153]

This is Bonhoeffer's notion of true human freedom. It is a significant contrast with the neoliberal theological conception of liberty. In particular, Bonhoeffer's perspective is that biblical freedom is the actual choice of obedience immediately upon hearing the call of Christ. Bonhoeffer wants to contest the conception of freedom simply as the freedom of choice determined by individual conscience. Bonhoeffer sees this as cheap grace and as the absence of biblical faith. The affluent young man is free to choose only that which Jesus calls him to choose. Thus, "the first step of obedience . . . calls upon the young man to leave his riches. Only this new existence, created through obedience, can make faith possible."[154] The first step commences with an "external work, which effects the change from one existence to another. It is a step within everybody's capacity, for it lies within the limits of human freedom. It is an act within the sphere of the natural law (*justitia civilis*) and in that sphere man is free."[155] In contrast with the neoliberal anthropology of liberty, Bonhoeffer's conception of human freedom is evangelically and christologically grounded. True liberty is the freedom to obey the call of Christ to discipleship rather than simply a neoliberal freedom to choose whether to obey. When Christ calls there is only once choice to make.

151. Ibid., 65–66.
152. Ibid., 69.
153. Ibid., 73.
154. Ibid., 70.
155. Ibid.

The rich young man is called to take the first step of obedience, which is determined by the gospel. This is what Jesus calls him to do. He is called to "perform the external work" of renouncing all attachments that hinder him from performing the will of God.[156] Bonhoeffer is after true faith, seeking to navigate safely between cheap grace and legalism. The rich young man can say neither "I don't have faith" nor "I have faith" without obeying. Bonhoeffer says that either option is "trifling with the subject. If you believe, take the first step, it leads to Jesus Christ. If you don't believe, take the first step all the same, for you are bidden to take it. No one wants to know about your faith or unbelief, your orders are to perform the act of obedience on the spot. Then you will find yourself in the situation where faith becomes possible and where faith exists in the true sense of the word."[157]

This is the dilemma in which the AAEC has been placed by Evangelical parents, churches and theologians who embrace a theology of affluence like Schneider's. By moralizing upon whether Jesus could have possibly meant for the rich young man (and all those like him) to sell *everything*, give to the poor and *then* come follow him, Evangelicals miss the possibility of true faith. The issue is not whether Jesus is telling all rich people for all time in all circumstances to liquidate and donate all their possessions to the poor as the precondition of discipleship. The issue is obedience of this particular young man. Whatever Jesus says to you, rich young man or AAEC or whoever you are, obey it. This is precisely Bonhoeffer's point, and Evangelicals who wish to address the practice before the substance of the faith that Christian moral theology presumes miss the essential point Jesus is making to the rich young man. As Bonhoeffer puts it, "The truth is that so long as we hold both sides of the proposition together they contain nothing inconsistent with right belief, but as soon as one is divorced from the other, it is bound to prove a stumbling-block."[158]

Thus, we must say to the obedient part of a believer's soul, "Only those who believe obey," and we must say to the believing part of the obedient soul, "Only those who obey believe."[159] Schneider's theology of affluence misses this. In his desire to help wealthy Christians by developing a

156. Ibid.
157. Ibid., 72–73.
158. Ibid., 74.
159. Ibid.

theology that frees them to acquire and enjoy the fruits of the new culture of capitalism, he has obfuscated Jesus' call to discipleship, which is the call to obey. Instead of liberating wealthy Christians to evangelical freedom, Schneider's theology of affluence frees them for a neoliberal liberty that leads either to cheap grace or legalism. Following Schneider, the AAEC would be formed to question whether to obey the radical call to follow Christ through dispossession and donation like the rich young man or through almsgiving and restitution like Zacchaeus. The AAEC would be trained to trifle over whether the call to discipleship could possibly mean a call to sever all attachments that hinder obedience to discipleship in the way of the cross. According to Bonhoeffer, this is not an option: "If the first half of the proposition stands alone, the believer is exposed to the danger of cheap grace, which is another word for damnation. If the second half stands alone, the believer is exposed to the danger of salvation through works, which is also another word for damnation."[160] This is the point at which the affluent are found lacking, at the point of obedience. Failure to obey is the lack of faith. The rich young man's failure to obey in the concrete terms Jesus commands constitutes the lack about which he inquires. It is a lack arising from the "attachments" to things that hinder obedience.

Thus, when Bonhoeffer turns to a pastoral application of the call to discipleship, he counsels pastors to advise recalcitrant modern believers to take the first step of obedient faith, which is to tear themselves "away from all other attachments" and follow Jesus because "the first step is what matters most. The strong point which the refractory sinner had occupied must be stormed, for in it Christ cannot be heard. The truant must be dragged from the hiding place which he has built for himself. Only then can he recover the freedom to see, hear, and believe."[161] This sheds a new light upon the AAEC who has been formed within Evangelical affluence, the possibility that the AAEC is formed to become like Bonhoeffer's "sinner [who] has drugged himself with cheap and easy grace by accepting the proposition that only those who believe can obey."[162] Schneider's theology does not lead Evangelical parents and churches to "storm" the

160. Ibid.
161. Ibid., 76.
162. Ibid., 77.

citadel of affluence formed within the AAEC. Instead, it encourages them both to esteem and to guard it.

Instead of detaching for kingdom-oriented obedience, the AAEC is counseled in Schneider's theology toward capitalist-oriented attachments. The AAEC is advised to cultivate twin capitalist habits of acquisition and enjoyment with the spirit of a capitalist warrior befitting a warrior-king. Bonhoeffer's interpretation of the rich young man could have helped Schneider see how "the very devil lurks" beneath questions of moral theology separated from the call to obedient faith: "Only the devil has an answer for our moral difficulties, and he says: 'Keep on posing problems, and you will escape the necessity of obedience.'"[163] The temptation to ask moral questions before obedience is a replay, Bonhoeffer says, of the script written in the Garden of Eden. Succumbing to it "means disobedience from the start. Doubt and reflection take the place of spontaneous obedience. The grown-up man with his freedom of conscience vaunts his superiority over the child of obedience."[164] Bonhoeffer could have pointed also to the fact that this Edenic drama was re-enacted in the wilderness temptation of Jesus where the second Adam successfully re-wrote the script.

Bonhoeffer's display of what the call to discipleship means is a trenchant critique of neoliberal theological conceptions of liberty. As he notes, modern neoliberal man "must decide for himself what is good by using his conscience and his knowledge of good and evil. The commandment may be variously interpreted, and *it is God's will* that it should be interpreted and explained: *for God has given man a free will to decide what he will do.*"[165] This is the argument Schneider, Novak and other neoliberal theologians make from the doctrines of creation and human freedom in support of the good of affluence that flows from the spirit of democratic capitalism. But is it the way of Christ and the cross? And will it form the AAEC in the way that remedies evangelical lack? Bonhoeffer answers, "There is one thing only which Jesus takes seriously, and that is, that it is high time the young man began to hear the commandment and obey it."[166]

---

163. Ibid., 79, 80.
164. Ibid., 80.
165. Ibid. (emphasis added).
166. Ibid.

Bonhoeffer sees the young man's question, "what do I still lack?", as the height of disobedience. The young man lacks in his relationships with God and others because of his ultimate attachment to the world from which he has derived his possessions and hence his identity, purpose and meaning in life.[167] He cannot see how his claim to have kept all the commands Jesus listed is contradicted by what his affluence discloses about his life. But Jesus "sees how hopelessly the young man has closed his mind to the living Word of God, how serious he is about it, and how heartily he rages against the living commandment and the spontaneous obedience it demands."[168] According to Mark, Jesus looked at the young man and loved him, so he wanted to help him find the answer to the lack that was gnawing at him. Jesus says that the answer is found in immediate liquidation, donation and discipleship, which in his case was unquestioning obedience that made true faith possible.

Bonhoeffer notes three things from the answer Jesus gives, two of which are particularly pertinent to the critique of Schneider with the AAEC in view.[169] First, Jesus confronts the young man with a very specific delineation of a commandment that, if he keeps it, will remedy his lack. Jesus wants to eliminate all doubt for the young man whom he loves. He calls him voluntarily to embrace poverty because it is the means to the end of discipleship and the answer to his original question about eternal life. It is the answer for his lack and also for his desire. Jesus must be specific because the danger is always lurking for the young man to "fall back into his original mistake, and take the commandment as an opportunity for moral adventure, a thrilling way of life, but one which might easily be abandoned for another if occasion arose."[170] Because Jesus loves the

---

167. Cf. Johnson's helpful theological reflection on embodiment in the modern world. Johnson, *Sharing Possessions*, 31–78.

168. Bonhoeffer, *Cost of Discipleship*, 80–81.

169. The first point is that Jesus is now clearly confronting the young man as God, delineating in unmistakable terms what God requires of him in light of his lack. Bonhoeffer's presentation of Matthew 19:16–22 imports Mark's answer to the original question, "what good deed must I do to have eternal life?", into Matthew's version (ibid., 77), which raises a redactional question as to why Matthew might have wanted to change Mark at this point. Davies and Allison probably put it best: "Because in Matthew Jesus is untainted by even the most indirect touch of sin, the evangelist has sought to avoid a possible inference from Mark's text, namely, that God is good but Jesus is not." Davies and Allison, *Matthew III*, 42 (footnote 22 omitted).

170. Bonhoeffer, *Cost of Discipleship*, 81.

young man he wants to eliminate all doubt. It is an "irrevocable situation," one that makes it impossible for the young man to conclude that he has reached "the logical conclusion of his search for truth in which he had hitherto been engaged, as an addition, a clarification or a completion of his old life."[171]

Second, Jesus' conditional answer, "If you wish to be perfect," to the question of lack indicates that he is closing the circle of the young man's attachments to himself as the perfect one who fulfills the law and the prophets. It is a call to abandon all attachments in favor of one and only one attachment, the person of Christ. Hence, the young man now

> stands face to face with Jesus, the Son of God: it is the ultimate encounter. It is now only a question of yes or no, of obedience or disobedience. The answer is no. He went away sorrowful, disappointed and deceived of his hopes, unable to wrench himself from his past. *He had great possessions.* The call to follow means here what it had meant before—adherence to the person of Jesus Christ and fellowship with him. The life of discipleship is not the hero-worship we would pay to a good master, but obedience to the Son of God.[172]

All of this is missed in Schneider's theological ethics of the good of affluence which encourages acquisition and enjoyment rather than dispossession and donation, whether like that of the kind demonstrated by the rich ruler or Zacchaeus. Those ethics encourage the formation of the AAEC for worship of a warrior-king who is proud of aggressive, competitive warriors in the marketplace rather than a king who calls the affluent to voluntary poverty or commends those like Zacchaeus for repentance from affluence proven by the practice of almsgiving to the poor and restitution for taking more than what is just.

Evangelical parents and churches, it seems, should benefit more from reading Bonhoeffer than Schneider on affluence. Bonhoeffer gives evangelicals across the decades of modernity access to a particular doctrine of grace premised upon "simple obedience."[173] Schneider, on the other hand, gives evangelicals a general doctrine of grace premised upon an anthropology of individualistic liberty that leaves them free to choose

---

171. Ibid., 81–82.

172. Ibid., 82 (emphasis added).

173. Bonhoeffer, *Cost of Discipleship*, 91.

whether or not to obey as the rich ruler or Zacchaeus did. As Bonhoeffer argues:

> By eliminating simple obedience on principle, we drift into an un-evangelical interpretation of the Bible. We take it for granted as we open the Bible that we have a key to its interpretation. But then the key we use would not be the living Christ, who is both Judge and Saviour, and our use of this key no longer depends on the will of the living Holy Spirit alone. The key we use is a general doctrine of grace which we can apply as we will. The problem of discipleship then becomes a problem of exegesis as well.[174]

Evangelicals are passionate about the Bible and believe it holds the key to living in faithful obedience to Christ. But in general they remain critically unaware of the contradictions posed by the problem of affluence in late modernity. Bonhoeffer's exposition of the narrative of the rich young man helps evangelicals see that it is possible to put the key in the wrong hole. Barth's does as well.

Barth and the rich young man's lack

Barth's interpretation of the rich young man is more extensive than Bonhoeffer's and involves a deeper exploration of the issue of lack. Barth, like Bonhoeffer, reads the story of Matthew's rich young man systematically as if it is essentially the same as Mark's.[175] His purpose in using the story is "to stress the final and decisive christological determination of the form of the divine command."[176]

Barth's interpretation of the story effusively resonates the themes of simple obedience and absolute devotion to the person of Christ that

174. Ibid.

175. Thus, he refers to it as "the story of the rich young man in Mk. 10:17–31 and par." Barth, *CD* II.2, 613.

176. Barth, *CD* II.2, 613. By finally exploring "the christological determination of the form of the divine command" through the story, Barth intends to show how "the narrative describes very fully the form of the divine claim." Ibid. The "form of the divine claim [is] . . . the form and manner in which the command of God meets man, in which it imparts to him, in which it becomes . . . a claim on him. . . . how man—corresponding to the basis and content of the command of God—becomes its addressee and recipient. We ask concerning the distinctive mode of its revelation or, in relation to man as its addressee and recipient, concerning the particular hearing which it demands and creates for itself in him as it claims his obedience." Ibid., 583.

Bonhoeffer found in the narrative. It comes as the concluding section of his theological ethics in relation to the command of God.[177] He argues that the story "shows that the demand of the living divine command made in the person of Jesus aims at the genuine, joyous and sustained decision of man for this person and therefore at the fulfillment of the one entire will of God. It shows this negatively in the figure of the rich man who was unequal to this demand, and positively in the disciples of Jesus who have become obedient to it."[178] Importing Mark into Matthew, Barth notes that the man's lack is identified in connection with the love Jesus had for him precisely at the point of his affluence.[179]

These aspects of the story lead Barth to explore two interrelated dimensions of lack, the christological and the ethical. In the christological dimension, the rich man lacks the fullness of "what Jesus has, and has for him," that is, the fullness "with which Jesus loves him and is therefore willing to be responsible for him."[180] He needs only to invite Jesus to "remedy this lack" by simply being willing and ready to allow Jesus' fullness, and therefore God's fullness, "which is ready even for him, [to] stream over him and benefit him. His sin is that he is not ready for that which is ready for him in Jesus."[181] Because he is not ready for this grace and does not invite it into his life, he "is not the covenant-partner of God. He does not love his neighbour. He does not belong to Jesus. This is what he lacks."[182]

The three ethical commands that follow identification of the man's lack at the point of his affluence and the personal love of Jesus are found in the command to sell, give and follow. Because Jesus loves the man, he tells him the truth. As we saw in Bonhoeffer, the fundamental issue is obedience which gives rise to the possibility of true faith. Jesus tells the rich man that the practical remedy for his lack is to sell all his possessions, give the proceeds to the poor, and then come follow him. "This is what the man lacks for the life of an heir of eternal life."[183] It is the ethical sum and

---

177. To be precise, his interpretation is found in subsection 3 ("The Form of the Divine Claim") of § 37 ("The Command as the Claim of God") of Chapter VIII ("The Command of God") of volume II.2 ("The Doctrine of God") in *Church Dogmatics*.

178. Ibid., 613.

179. Ibid., 617–19.

180. Ibid., 618.

181. Ibid.

182. Ibid.

183. Ibid., 619.

substance of the command of God, of all the commandments he claims to have obeyed. It is a call, an opportunity to have eternal life, and it remains so even after the rich man departs.

Barth then proceeds to explore in greater depth what the "essential content of this Word of Jesus" (i.e., to sell, give and follow) means.[184] Understanding that these three imperatives constitute "a characterization of that one thing, that whole, which Jesus has said to the man in answer" to the question about lack, the three aspects of the one command must be held together and seen as of equal importance.[185] One cannot dominate the others.

In regard to the first, Barth argues that the rich man's inability to liquidate his many possessions is proof that he lacks freedom as God's covenant-partner. His possessions are his lord, master, god. He cannot live out the requirements of the second tablet of the law, as he claims, because in the first instance he cannot live out the requirements of the first. He is not free to live as God's covenant-partner if he is bound to his possessions (i.e., cannot sell them) because as such he is obligated to look upon his neighbor as a fellow covenant-partner of God. But in order to be "genuinely free" in his neighbor relations he must be "freed by his absolute obligation to God; freed from all other divine or quasi-divine masters; and therefore freed for an action which will really do justice to his neighbour."[186] The fact that he is unable, because unwilling, to obey the command to sell all he has and give it the poor proves that he is a transgressor of both tablets of the law. He is captive to another god. He is possessed by his possessions in the manner which God alone in Christ would possess him were he willing.

God simply will not endure the man's refusal to detach from his affluence. Even though other gods or lords "might tolerate man's subjection to the commands of mammon or similar lords as well as to themselves, the command of the gracious and compassionate God who has chosen and called man to covenant with Himself does not tolerate a division of this kind."[187] Jesus loved the rich man and leaves the door open for him to

---

184. Ibid.
185. Ibid.
186. Ibid.
187. Ibid., 620.

repent, but it is clear that as "long as he has great possessions, they have him, and as long as they have him, God cannot and will not have him."[188]

Barth argues that the second command to donate the proceeds of liquidated abundance to the poor discloses that the rich man lacks the love of neighbor he has claimed for himself. The refusal of the rich man to choose relations with his neighbor in this specific manner is a precise demonstration that he refuses to act as God's covenant-partner. God is the richest of the rich and demonstrates his gracious richness by giving at all times without expecting anything in return. "God is rich in the sense that He gives away what belongs to Him without return, without making man subservient, but free. And it is in this way that man may and should become His imitator in relation to his neighbour."[189] By contrast, mammon distributes its "dazzling gifts . . . only to make man more and more subservient to himself."[190] This is the lack about which Jesus speaks to the rich man and therefore commands him to give all to the poor. By giving to the poor he would prove that he is not possessed by his possessions but by God. This is the proof of true freedom. Practically, it is the freedom to invest treasure in heaven through donation to the poor and following Christ. The invitation Jesus gives is an invitation to "see the substance and the aim of all the commandments."[191] It is the freedom of the children of God that fills what is lacking.

Finally, the rich man is called to follow. This is "the third form of the one demand" to allow the love of Jesus to fill the one thing that is lacking.[192] This third form clarifies the two previous imperatives. The first obligates the rich man to "sell what he has and therefore become free for God", and the second obligates him to donate those proceeds "to the poor and therefore become free for his neighbour."[193] According to Barth, both of these derive their meaning and force from this "final demand . . . [to] come and follow Jesus."[194] This is because precisely at this point the inability of the rich man to follow Jesus in the oath of discipleship is

188. Ibid.
189. Ibid.
190. Ibid.
191. Ibid., 621.
192. Ibid.
193. Ibid., 622.
194. Ibid.

made manifest. He is not truly free. He may think he is free, but he is not according to God's definition of freedom, which is the freedom God has made possible in following Jesus. When Jesus offers treasure in heaven in exchange for obedience to the three forms of the one demand, he is offering that freedom he has incarnated, fulfilled and realized through the gospel. This is why the rich man's rejection of the offer warrants such great condemnation, because it is a rejection of the person and work of Christ, which is to reject God the gracious covenant-partner. Jesus is the "final and decisive . . . form of the divine command."[195] Thus, rejecting him is rejecting God. Disobeying his command is disobeying the command of God.

Jesus is the glory of God offered as the answer to the man's lack. The young man must only make the right choice. But he chooses to remain lacking God's glory. As a result,

> he could only go away sorrowful: sorrowful at the unattainable remoteness and strangeness of the glory of God which he had encountered, and sorrowful at his own incompetence and insufficiency in relation to it; sorrowful in face of the contrast between God's will and his own. . . . What opened up at his feet was the abyss of the absolute impossibility of the relationship between God and the man who has committed sin and who as sinner sets himself in opposition to God.[196]

The story of the affluent college student told by Schneider at the beginning of *Godly Materialism* comes to mind at this point. Barth's theological plumbing of the rich man's lack could have illumined the counsel Schneider gave to the student. On Barth's interpretation, the lack identified in the rich young man is christological. The inability to detach from the relations of affluence indicates the lack of freedom to be with and for God in Christ, and the inability to give to the poor indicates a lack of freedom to be with and for the neighbor in a manner consistent with the way God is free as the covenant-partner of humanity in Jesus Christ. Ultimate sorrow and sadness inevitably follows living in this kind of lack.

Both Barth's and Bonhoeffer's interpretations of the rich young man provide critical lenses for assessing Schneider's theology of affluence with the AAEC in view. Both clarify the essential aspect of human freedom

---

195. Ibid., 613, 630.
196. Ibid., 622–23.

in the context of affluence. The young man is not truly free to the extent his affluence hinders him from following Jesus in the way of the cross. Evidence of his lack of freedom is found in the inability to liquidate his possessions, give to the poor and follow Christ.

The theological-ethical reflections of Pope John Paul II on the rich young man in *Veritatis Splendor* further demonstrate that a faulty conception of human liberty lies at the heart of the problem of affluence in late modernity, and thus lies also at the heart of the problem of the AAEC. Just as he would have benefited from reading Bonhoeffer and Barth, Schneider's moral theology of affluence can benefit reading the Pope as well along with these two great modern Protestant theologians.

John Paul II on Matthew's rich young man

The purpose of the Pope's encyclical on "the splendor of truth" is to reflect on the entirety of the Catholic Church's moral teaching over the past two centuries.[197] This was deemed necessary in light of the growing prevalence *"within the Christian community itself. . . . of an overall and systematic calling into question of traditional moral doctrine, on the basis of certain anthropological and ethical presuppositions. At the root of these presuppositions is the more or less obvious influence of currents of thought which end by detaching human freedom* from its essential and constitutive relationship to truth."[198]

Thus, the entire encyclical is an extended theological reflection upon liberty and truth. The focus here is on the Pope's use of Matthew's story of the rich young man for contemporary moral theology. Particular attention will be paid to what he says about the issue of lack in the story and how it might illumine further theological-anthropological understanding of the AAEC. From there, the encyclical's practical applications to contemporary family and economic life are examined with the AAEC and Schneider's theology of affluence in view. The evangelical theology of the AAEC presented here benefits from the Pope's moral-theological "meditation" on the story of the rich young man, in which the Pope discerns "the essential elements of revelation in the Old and New Testament with regard to moral action. . . . : the subordination of man and his activity to

---

197. John Paul II, *Veritatis Splendor*, para. 4, p. 13 (emphasis added).
198. Ibid., para. 5, p. 15.

God, the One who 'alone is good'; the relationship between the moral good of human acts and eternal life; [and] Christian discipleship, which opens up before man the perspective of perfect love. . ."[199]

The Pope interprets the narrative as setting out a universal description of "every person who, consciously or not, *approaches Christ the Redeemer of man and questions him about morality.*"[200] It demonstrates the universal truth that in the "heart of every Christian, in the inmost depths of each person, there is always an echo of the question which the young man in the Gospel once asked Jesus: "Teacher, what good must I do to have eternal life?' (Mt 19:16)."[201] It is a question about what life really means, the fundamental impetus which lies "at the heart of every human decision, the quiet searching and interior prompting which sets freedom in motion."[202] It is the resonance of God's call for everyone to seek "the absolute Good which attracts us and beckons us."[203] The young man's question signals that there is an inseparable connection between morality and eternal life. It is an unavoidable question because it flows from the heart, which has its genesis and fulfillment in God.

For evangelicals, the "absolute Good which attracts and beckons" is found in following Jesus and the gospel. Consequently, they are passionate about the moral teaching that lies at the heart of that Good. However, as has been demonstrated, evangelicals since Edwards have overlooked affluence in their theological anthropology and thus have overlooked how it affects evangelical nurture of their children. They have failed to recognize what Johnson describes about human nature: "The values attached by a society, or a subgroup of shared perception within a society, to bodily expression and the disposition of possessions emerge in turn from an overarching theological anthropology."[204] The incoherence of Evangelical social thought and the individualistic metaphysics upon which it is grounded demonstrates that the overarching theological anthropology of

199. Ibid., para. 28, p. 43.

200. Ibid., para. 7, p. 17 (emphasis in original).

201. John Paul II, *Veritatis Splendor*, para. 116, p. 140.

202. Ibid., para. 7, p. 17.

203. Ibid., para. 7, p. 17

204. Johnson continues: "This is an understanding, frequently incoherent and implicit, to be sure, of what it means to be a worthwhile human being in the world and where the ultimate source of that worth is to be found." Johnson, *Sharing Possessions*, 42.

American Evangelicalism rests on an anthropology of liberty determined not by evangelical interests but by the interests of technological consumer capitalism.

John Paul II can help Evangelicals see this. He states that, "If we . . . wish to go to the heart of the Gospel's moral teaching and grasp its profound and unchanging content, we must carefully inquire into the meaning of the question asked by the rich young man in the Gospel and, even more, the meaning of Jesus' reply, allowing ourselves to be guided by him."[205] The question indicates something foundational for theological anthropology. It points to the crucial issue of human freedom in late modernity.

According to the Pope, Jesus puts the matter simply. Keeping the commandments, those having to do with neighbor love, is true liberty. The answer Jesus gives to the young man's original question shows that he affirms the law as embodying the ethical substance of eternal life to which every human is called. This is a call to true freedom to live in accordance with the commands God has given. Neighbor love simultaneously embodies the dignity and the fundamental rights inherent in human nature. It encompasses the specific commands quoted by Jesus from the second tablet of the law. These "negative precepts" are designed to "safeguard *the good* of the person, the image of God, by protecting his *goods* . . . [and thus] express with particular force the ever urgent need to protect human life, the community of persons in marriage, private property, truthfulness and people's good name."[206] Obeying these commands are the starting point of true human liberty, "the *first necessary step on the journey towards freedom*" because they are the indispensable condition and evidence of neighbor love.[207]

As has been noted, the young man claims to have kept the neighbor love commands yet knows he still lacks something. Unlike Bonhoeffer and Barth, the Pope does not contest this claim but proceeds directly to address the issue of lack in the young man's life.[208] What he lacks is

---

205. John Paul II, *Veritatis Splendor*, para. 8, pp. 18–19.

206. John Paul II, *Veritatis Splendor*, para. 13, p. 25 (emphasis in original).

207. Ibid., para. 13, p. 25.

208. The Pope acknowledges the difficulty of making such a claim "with a clear conscience . . . if one has any understanding of the real meaning of the demands contained in God's Law," but his point is to emphasize the young man's lack in the presence of Jesus: "And yet, even though he is able to make this reply, even though he has followed the

the perfection that Christ alone incarnates. The Pope turns back from Matthew 19:21 to the Beatitudes in order to make his point about perfection. There we find a basis for understanding the proper relation between the commandments and freedom.

Both the commands and Beatitudes refer to the ultimate Good, or eternal life, because they have their ground and fulfillment in Jesus. Jesus fulfills and incarnates both the Law and the Prophets, both of which are held together and beautifully displayed in the Beatitudes.[209] Thus, the Beatitudes are "above all *promises*, from which there also indirectly flow *normative indications* for the moral life. In their originality and profundity they are a sort of *self-portrait of Christ*, and for this very reason are *invitations to discipleship and communion of life with Christ*."[210] Thus, the answer to the young man's lack is Christ himself. He lacks because he has not entered into the transforming relational dimensions of "discipleship" and "communion of life" with Christ. He lacks because he cannot truly meet the moral demands of neighbor love until he enters into those dimensions in accordance with Christ's prescription. This is the perfection he lacks and which his heart desires.

Similar to Bonhoeffer and Barth, the Pope believes that the answer to the young man's lack is the person of Christ. He does not share, however, their emphasis on obedience to Jesus' commands to sell, give and follow. In fact, the Pope does not look at them as commands but as invitations, focusing on the conditional aspect of the language Jesus uses, "*If you wish to be perfect*" (Mt 19:21). Perhaps this is where Moberly thinks the Pope may have benefited from consulting Bonhoeffer and Barth. Instead of immediate obedience as the key to freedom, the Pope believes "that the young man's *commitment* to respect all the moral demands of the commandments *represents* the absolutely essential ground in which the desire for perfection can take root and mature, the desire, that is, for the meaning of the commandments to be completely fulfilled in follow-

---

moral ideal seriously and generously from childhood, the rich young man knows that he is still far from the goal: before the person of Jesus he realizes that he is still lacking something." Ibid., para. 16, p. 28 (emphasis in original).

209. The Pope writes beautifully here: "*Jesus brings God's commandments to fulfillment*, particularly the commandment of love of neighbor, *by interiorizing their demands and bringing out their fullest meaning*. Love of neighbor *springs from a loving heart* which, precisely because it loves, is ready to live out *the loftiest challenges*." Ibid., para. 15, p. 27 (emphasis in original).

210. Ibid., para. 16, p. 29 (emphasis in original).

ing Christ."[211] But the Pope makes it clear that the desire for perfection through liquidation and donation is optional because Jesus issues it as an invitation, not a command. Keeping the commandments, however, is not optional. They are "the first and indispensable condition for having eternal life."[212]

The Pope wants to accomplish two things by taking this position. First, he wants to establish a sure foundation for the biblical basis of the moral truth claims he is asserting in the encyclical. Second, he wants to establish *"the fundamental relationship between freedom and divine law."*[213] This is why the Pope reads Jesus as unequivocal about the commandments but only invitational regarding liquidating possessions, giving to the poor and following in the path of discipleship. For the Pope, the latter is a call to transcend the law and find its personal fulfillment in Christ alone. Human liberty is the freedom to respond to the call to perfection which *"demands that maturity in self-giving to which human freedom is called."*[214] This kind of maturity arises from a commitment to respect the ethical demands of the commandments and leads to the perfection that is lacking in every human apart from Christ.

Thus, the Pope is able to establish in the commandments a sure biblical foundation for moral theology because Jesus has set them out as ground zero for all moral demands. From there humans are called to the perfection of freedom by choosing the path of maturation through self-giving. The choice to pursue that path is the choice and work of perfect love to which all are called. The possibility of perfecting maturity is open to the rich young man if he accepts the invitation to invest his treasure in heaven by liquidating his affluence, donating the proceeds to the poor and following Jesus. For the Pope, this demonstrates the fundamental relationship between human freedom and divine law.[215]

---

211. John Paul II, *Veritatis Splendor*, para. 17, p. 29 (emphasis added).

212. Ibid., para. 17, p. 30.

213. Ibid., para. 17, p. 30 (emphasis in original).

214. Ibid., para. 17, p. 30 (emphasis in original).

215. Of course this highlights one of the fundamental Protestant-Catholic divides, with Protestants rejecting the Catholic belief in a grace-infused human nature capable of evangelical obedience. However, reading Bonhoeffer and Barth on obedience in this context, with their respective emphases on the call to obey, illustrates just how problematic this traditional representation of the divide can be.

The invitation Jesus gives to exercise human freedom toward the pursuit of perfection is unrestricted. The promise of heavenly treasure is universal as well. These *"are meant for everyone*, because they bring out the full meaning of the commandment of love of neighbor, just as the invitation which follows, 'Come, follow me,' is the new, specific form of the commandment of love of God."[216] The commandments and the invitation "stand at the service of a single and indivisible charity, which spontaneously tends towards that perfection whose measure is God alone: 'You therefore, must be perfect, as your heavenly Father is perfect' (Mt 5:48). In the Gospel of Luke, Jesus makes even clearer the meaning of this perfection: 'Be merciful, even as your Father is merciful' (Lk 6:36)."[217]

The Pope's answer to the rich young man's question about lack helps further develop a critical-theological understanding of the AAEC. It grounds Jesus' answer to the initial question about eternal life in human liberty. God's call in the commandments is a call to true freedom. Obedience to that call opens the AAEC to Jesus' invitation to perfection, to that maturing self-giving love "to which human freedom is called." It frees the AAEC, in other words, to choose the path of perfection expressed in liquidation, donation and discipleship on the foundation of the "first step" of keeping the "negative" commands given to protect the neighbor's good and goods.

While it may come as a surprise to Evangelicals, this comports with their view that children should be nurtured in "the discipline and instruction of the Lord" (Eph 6:4). As we saw with Richards in chapter 3, Deuteronomy 6:6–9 is the most common text used by Evangelicals as the impetus for nurturing evangelical faith in their children. Like the Pope, Evangelicals love the Ten Commandments and the Beatitudes, seeing them as profound demonstrations of God's beauty, moral nature and love. But as I pointed out, Evangelicals have failed to read through to Deuteronomy 6:10–12 and as a result have missed the dangers affluence poses to such nurture.[218] It is possible to raise children in the Lord's discipline and instruction with no critical awareness of how affluence subverts rather than sustains evangelical nurture of the Ten Commandments and Beatitudes in the AAEC. Evangelical parents and children would ben-

---

216. John Paul II, *Veritatis Splendor*, para. 18, p. 31 (emphasis in original).

217. Ibid., para. 18, pp. 30–31.

218. Cf. Dt 8:10–20.

efit from a careful, reflective reading of the Pope's meditation on the rich young man. They should applaud the Pope for taking a courageous stand upon the commandments and pointing moral theologians back to them. The claim that they embody moral imperatives for all times is a claim evangelicals heartily endorse. The manner in which the Pope sensitively interprets the story as it bears upon the positive and negative aspects of neighbor love can assist Evangelicals in their nurture of gospel faith in their children.

The Pope's interpretation of the story also helps get to the heart of what is lacking in the AAEC formed in Evangelical affluence in the United States. With Barth and Bonhoeffer, the Pope is correct to point out that the essential lack in the story of the rich young man is the absence of relationship with Christ. The result is a spiritual and ethical lack in relation to God in Christ, others and the world of things. This is the problem of the AAEC. The ethical dimension of such lack is a "moral vacuum where individual experimentation becomes the order of the day and personal desires become harnessed to the powerful interests of the market economy."[219] The positive focus maintained by the Pope upon the *invitation* (as opposed to command) to pursue perfection is a refreshing reminder of the goodness, grace, patience and love of the God who calls the AAEC to the liberty of mature self-giving expressed in self-denial (Mk 8:34), dispossession, donation and discipleship. This kind of morality provides a hopeful contemporary theological framework within which to harmonize individual and social dimensions of human self-interest that subsist in the problem of affluence in late modernity.[220] At the same time, Bonhoeffer's and Barth's emphases on evangelical obedience to Jesus when he calls to detach from the relational commitments of affluence through liquidation and donation preserves the biblical emphasis on the necessity of God's grace at work through faith expressing itself in love for the good of the neighbor in true freedom.[221]

I read the Pope as urging moral theologians to assess with evangelical-critical eyes all neoliberal claims that individual self-interest *ipso facto* serves social interests. The anthropology that sustains such claims must be subjected to critical-theological scrutiny "in every sphere of personal,

219. Barton, "Family Life," 43.

220. Cf. Meyers, *Soul of Modern Economic Man*, 5, 127–31; Goetz, "Theological anthropology, self-interest, and economic justice," 209–31.

221. Eph 2:8–10, Gal 5:6, 13–14.

family, social and political life," the Pope argues, such that a morality "founded upon truth and open in truth to authentic freedom" can render its "primordial, indispensable and immensely valuable service not only for the individual person and his growth in the good, but also for society and its genuine development."[222] The AAEC needs to be nurtured with critical awareness of the metaphysical and anthropological grounding of affluence in the United States, which leads to a deeper understanding of the moral vacuum it can create. Evangelical parents and churches need to realize how affluence endangers the "family values" they hold dear. As has been shown, both the pursuit and possession of affluence in late modernity assume a conception of human liberty divorced from the truth of the gospel that the story of the rich young man illumines. Affluence can circumvent commitment to Christ and the pursuit of mature self-giving that transforms one's pursuits and possessions.

The story of the rich young man teaches us that questions such as those framed by the Pope, "*What must I do? How do I distinguish good from evil?*", are personal questions about what is lacking in late modern life. They span all dimensions of human existence and confront the inquirer with searching questions that must be addressed continually to Christ in whom alone the answers can be found. The habit of asking such questions, of seeking to find and remedy what is lacking, will not be formed in the AAEC if Evangelical parents and churches seek to cultivate instead capitalist habits of acquisition and enjoyment. The pursuit and possession of affluence can blind its possessor to the presence of Christ and the neighbor. At its most fundamental level, affluence can shunt cultivation of the capacity for self-denial necessary to follow Christ in the way of the cross for the benefit of others.[223]

As Stephen Barton has argued, nurture of self-denial begins in the home with little steps of self-giving, putting the interests of others first, giving "ourselves on behalf of those intimate strangers we call 'family.'"[224] Evangelicals must wisely nurture the good news in the AAEC that life does not consist in an abundance of possessions or the good life pursuing one's own happiness and that pursuing such a vision of life can present spiritually and morally perilous obstacles to finding answers to life's

222. John Paul II, *Veritatis Splendor*, para. 101, p. 123.

223. Ibid., paras. 17 and 90–94, pp. 30, 112–16.

224. Barton, 'Family Life', 43.

deepest questions. Failing to nurture the habit of asking those questions, Evangelicals run the risk of forming a spiritual-ethical vacuum in their children that will be filled by the ubiquitous presence and iniquitous claims of late modern capitalist culture. The individualistic desires of the AAEC will be yoked with the interests of affluence, which in turn leads to the subversion of social, familial and ecclesial interests grounded in and energized by the gospel.

Quoting from *Centesimus Annus*, the Pope reminds his readers that various forms of modern totalitarianism arise from the denial of objective, transcendent truth summarized in love for God and neighbor. True human freedom and identity are achieved in obedience to this truth. If no such truth exists then there is no possibility for just human relations at the personal, social or national levels. Self-interest inevitably sets individuals, groups and nations in opposition to one another, and the result is that "the force of power takes over."[225] The critics of American capitalism are keenly aware of how the "force of power takes over" in the market.[226] So are all those outside the economic-political partnership in the market, that is, the poor, marginalized and oppressed, and even the terrorist.[227]

Although the Pope does not make a specific link between American capitalism and totalitarianism, it is not difficult to discern implications for neoliberal democratic capitalism.[228] At the root of totalitarian regimes and systems lies a "denial of the transcendent dignity of the human person who, as the visible image of God, is therefore by his very nature the subject of rights which no one may violate—no individual, group, class, nation or state. Not even the majority of a social body may violate these rights, by going against the minority, by isolating, oppressing, or exploiting it, or by attempting to annihilate it."[229] All parties to the current theological debate over capitalism affirm the dignity of the human, at least in principle if not in practice. Disagreements arise over interpretation of the history, effects and prospects of capitalism.

225. John Paul II, *Veritatis Splendor*, para. 99, p. 121, quoting *Centesimus Annus*, para. 44.

226. Cf. Bell, *Liberation Theology*, 19.

227. See, e.g., Northcott, *Angel Directs the Storm*, 155–56.

228. See, e.g., the helpful, critical interaction with the Pope's reflections on totalitarianism in R. Song, "Political Life," 57–68.

229. John Paul II, *Veritatis Splendor*, para. 99, p. 121, quoting *Centesimus Annus*, para. 44 (end note 91 omitted).

Pope John Paul II addresses the economic issues lying at the center of such disagreements. Evangelicals and the AAEC could benefit from studying the manner in which the Pope reasons from the seventh commandment as exposited in the *Catechism of the Catholic Church*, which he claims sets out a "complete and systematic exposition of Christian moral teaching."[230] The *Catechism* teaches that "the seventh commandment prohibits actions or enterprises which for any reason—selfish or ideological, commercial or totalitarian—lead to the *enslavement of human beings*, disregard for their personal dignity, buying or selling or exchanging them like merchandise. Reducing persons by violence to use-value or a source of profit is a sin against their dignity as persons and their fundamental rights."[231] Thus, in matters relating to the economic dimension of life, respect for human dignity calls for developing habits through virtuous practices of "*temperance . . . justice . . .* [and] *solidarity*" in neighbor relations.[232] Temperance disciplines desire to moderate our attachments to the world of things. The practice of justice disciplines desire such that we respect and preserve the rights of our neighbors and seek to assure that they receive what is due to them. Practicing the virtue of solidarity disciplines human self-interest by binding us to the Golden Rule in Christ-like generosity with our neighbors.

The Pope shows that these virtues are implicated in the story of the rich young man. Instead of cultivating capitalist habits of acquisition and consumption in their children, Evangelicals should intentionally strive to form disciplines of temperance, justice and solidarity in themselves and in their children. This is consistent with Paul's admonition that Christian parents should nurture "discipline and instruction of the Lord" in their children, and if consistently applied it could lead to the kind of self-denial and self-giving that following Jesus in the way of the cross requires in late modernity.

230. John Paul II, *Veritatis Splendor*, para. 5, p. 14.

231. Ibid., para. 100, p. 122 (emphasis in original).

232. Ibid., para. 100, pp. 121–22.

THE AAEC IN CONTEMPORARY THEOLOGICAL PERSPECTIVE

This section examines three contemporary theologies relevant to affluence and provides the final lens for assessing the neoliberal anthropology of freedom upon which Schneider rests his theology of affluence. It presents the final component of an evangelical theology of the AAEC grounded upon a biblical conception of human freedom consistent with the perspectives of Bonhoeffer, Barth and John Paul II. This can help point Evangelicals in the right direction for a theological ethics of nurture confronted by the problem of affluence in late modernity.

Feminist Theology: Marion Grau on male hysteria (lack)

Marion Grau is one of a handful of theologians in the United States who has "worked with an explicit focus on the relationship between contemporary economics and theology."[233] She distinguishes her theological economics as a rereading of "ancient theological texts that deal with economic matters to recover neglected economic images of salvation using a reconstructed typological hermeneutics."[234] The other theologians, she claims, generally "have used the ancient theological texts to perform a theological reading or critique of modern economics."[235]

Grau's goal is to challenge errors arising from theological abstractions about capitalism so that she can "think beyond the danger of [critical] paralysis [in theological economics] to transformative faith in action."[236] She wants to create a "third space" beyond the binaries and polarities of the "increasingly stale reiterations of neoliberal capitalist economics and their neo-Marxist critiques."[237] This is "a space of divine-human action" in which "conceptions of divine and human power are reconceived in the

---

233. On her reckoning, the others are Meeks, *God the Economist*; Long, *Divine Economy*; Cobb, *Common Good*; Taylor, *About Religion*; and McFague, *Life Abundant*. Grau, *Of Divine Economy*, 9; 10 n. 27.

234. Ibid., 10.

235. Grau, *Of Divine Economy*, 10.

236. Ibid., 2. These errors are "fallacies of misplaced concreteness" as defined by Whitehead, *Science and the Modern World*, 51, and used "as a tool to challenge seemingly rational scientific abstractions that erase important distinctions while making great truth claims." Ibid., 2 n. 3.

237. Ibid., 4.

encounter with the sciences of chaos and complexity."[238] Grau does not intend to construct a theology of divine economy that presents "purist idealizations of what a Christian economics should look like."[239] Instead, she wants to inhabit the "messiness of Christian tradition, the untamable power of its jarring images and visions" that enable us to live truthfully within our own complexities in late modernity.[240] This will allow us to see more clearly that standing behind modern usage of the term "economy" is the ancient concept of God's economy which signifies God's agency in the cosmos, particularly redemptive agency, throughout human history.

The central figure in her "reconstructed typological hermeneutics" is the ambivalent figure of "the sacred trickster as one of the shapes an 'economist of God's mysteries' can take on . . ."[241] She claims that it is a figure sufficiently complex to assist her in mapping "spaces for theological thinking and practical agency in a culture that appears strikingly effective at commodifying dissent, where protest and resistance are being branded, packaged, and sold back to us as products."[242] Following Martha Althaus-Reid, Grau uses it to discover Christian attitudes toward wealth in biblical and patristic texts that "formulate embodied 'economic desires' as they 'walk hand in hand with erotic desires and theological needs' . . . [and disclose] structures enforcing power over women and slaves [that] are economic models that express relationships 'based on erotic considerations concerning the economy of bodies, society, their intimacy and distance and the patterns of accepted and unaccepted needs in the market.'"[243] The sacred trickster is "a denizen of the ambivalent borderlands of religion and culture, [who] shows one particular form of agency that can break through, interrupt, even shift the terms of the status quo."[244] Grau uses three specific figures in this hermeneutical strategy—"rich young

238. Ibid., 5.

239. Ibid.

240. Ibid.

241. Ibid., 3. Grau explains the reasons for her choice of such a hermeneutical strategy at pages 10–12.

242. Grau, *Of Divine Economy*, 2 (footnote 4 omitted). Echoes of Miller, "The Commodification of Culture," in *Consuming Religion*, 32–72, can be heard here.

243. Grau, *Of Divine Economy*, 10 (footnote 28 omitted), quoting Althaus-Reid, *Indecent Theology*, 166.

244. Grau, *Of Divine Economy*, 2.

man, poor widow and divine slave—as the narrative concretion of such agency."[245]

My interest is in her interpretation of Matthew's story of the rich young man. In particular, I am interested in her feminist theological exploration of the rich young man's lack of spiritual abundance despite his material affluence. She claims that the "textually embodied" figure of the rich young man is an "iteration of an ancient image of redemptive divine economy" and is a feminist figure in the sense that "feminist figures of humanity . . . cannot be man or woman . . . cannot be the human as historical narrative has staged that generic universal . . . cannot . . . have a name . . . [cannot] be native. Feminist humanity must somehow both resist representation, resist literal figuration, and still erupt in powerful new tropes, new figures of speech, new turns of historical possibility."[246] As such, the typology of the rich young man blurs "the boundaries between man and woman, master and slave . . . [and] the binary opposition of lack and abundance, capitalism and Marxism, divine and earthly economies."[247]

Central to this figural function of the rich young man is "hysteria," which in Matthew is the Greek word translated as "lack." Grau shows that ancient conceptions of the male body's physical and reproductive capacities were associated with ideas of plenitude, whereas the physical and reproductive aspects of the female's body were associated with lack. In fact, both hysteria and uterus come from the same Greek word.[248] Thus, traditionally, women have been perceived as hysterics because of their physical lack which was viewed as giving rise to their emotional hysterics. The uterus is a vacuum that seeks to be filled. The ancients believed that the woman's emotional hysteria was caused by the uterus. At the same time, however, the woman's lack (i.e., her womb) signifies the place from which future male abundance (i.e., descendents and therefore wealth) will arise. But the story of the rich young man discloses something profoundly subversive of this ancient economy. The male is the hysteric, he is lacking despite his abundance. On the other hand, the poor widow who serves as Grau's second "trickster" figure demonstrates that she possesses a spiritual abundance as she gives out of her economic lack (i.e., poverty).

245. Ibid., 3.

246. Ibid., 15, quoting Haraway, "Ecce Homo," 86.

247. Grau, Of Divine Economy, 15.

248. "Hysteria is a cognate of hustera, a term that signifies a woman's womb." Ibid., 48; see her brief history of hysteria at pages 48–51.

What emerges in the story of the rich young man, then, are economic strategies of redemption found in almsgiving and asceticism. These "emerge as two modes of divine and earthly resource management for the wealthy males who interpreted Matthew's text. . . . a smart investment in the heavenly economy."[249] This is where "constructions of human and divine economy stand in close but tenuous relationship to each other."[250] Consequently, the figure of the rich young man inhabits "the borderlands of heaven and earth, wealth and poverty, sincerity and deception."[251] Grau presents the contemporary descendant of the rich young man as a "Holy Fool of divine madness, a countereconomic trickster" whose text unfolds as a "midrash-like" piece which bridges "the millennia of salvation history."[252] It discloses a "genealogy of lingering masculine hysteria still visible in contemporary constructions of economics, redemption, and masculinity."[253] This genealogy leads to "the *homo economicus* of capitalist modernity."[254] Thus, Grau traces the link between the rich young man's hysteria (lack) and that of late modernity's rich young man confronted by scarcity in the midst of affluence.

What precisely do these economic males have in common? Grau locates the link in "the axiomatic quality of 'scarcity' in neoclassical economics [which] seems to invert ancient notions of the persistence of human lack in perfection or essence, transferring them into the modern science of economics, where we find the fundamental concept of the scarcity of goods."[255] This is seen in the gendered nature of economics in the public, academic and private household spheres of modernity. She notes that in the United States men dominate the economic disciplines. Economics is seen as a male domain inhabited by public, energetic and rational masculinity in pursuit of growth and the accumulation of wealth, whereas femininity inhabits the private, flaccid and emotional. Her thesis of a theological gendering of economics in the United States resonates in the theologies of affluence developed by Bushnell and Schneider.

249. Ibid., 17–18.
250. Ibid., 19.
251. Ibid.
252. Ibid., 44, 19.
253. Ibid., 40.
254. Ibid., 50.
255. Ibid., 83 (footnote 151 omitted).

Relying upon an essay by Susan Feiner,[256] Grau identifies several aspects of the *homo economicus* of late modernity in whom traces of Matthew's affluent young man can be found. Like the rich young man, *homo economicus* is "the rhetorical embodiment of an androcentric economic culture' who is burdened with 'the cultural and philosophical baggage of his time."[257] Both exhibit an

> eternal desire, which aims to fill a hysterical lack, appears to be stretching toward . . . perfect markets and mothers that 'meet all of our desires immediately, with no frustration and no anxiety.' The vicissitudes of the market feel similar to the 'vicissitudes of our mothers,' as they 'vacillate between generosity, availability, and affirmation' and 'withholding, scarcity, and punishment,' invoking our earliest horrors and fears of total abandonment.[258]

Thus, both the rich man and *homo economicus* imagine a nurturing and secure maternal divine economy that will satisfy their lack (hysteria). Nevertheless, when confronted with the reality of what investment in the divine economy entails, that is, renunciation of the power and privilege male ownership affords, they realize that the cost is too great. As Grau puts it, "the power/knowledge formations in the young man's mind are too seamlessly constructed to accommodate a different understanding of wealth."[259] Trust in the attachments of affluence proves insurmountable, and the potential of losing control over the affluence and attendant personal and social benefits those attachments afford proves to be too great. Investment in the divine economy is simply too much scarcity to risk.

By making this choice, Grau contends, both the rich young man and the modern *homo economicus* succumb to a notion of God's economy that is subservient to imperial structures of power and domination that perpetuate gendered as well as other forms of oppression. Grau argues that Irenaeus of Lyon was the first of several Church Fathers to provide such a gendered interpretation of the rich young man, the last of which was Augustine.[260] She concludes that the "notion of the *oikonomia theou*, first systematically developed by the Lyonnese presbyter in an 'age of martyrs,'

---

256. Feiner, "Portrait of the *Homo Economicus* as a Young Man," 193–209.

257. Grau, *Of Divine Economy*, 85, 84, citing Feiner, "Portrait," 206.

258. Grau, *Of Divine Economy*, 85, citing Feiner, "Portrait," 195, 197.

259. Grau, *Of Divine Economy*, 85.

260. Ibid., 55–79.

theologically transformed in 'an age of Christian rulers,' later becomes a colonizing narrative of the *tempora christiana* that occasioned the 'legal repression of paganism' as the empire and its phallic swelling appears to be its instrument and incarnation."[261]

Grau's feminist theological reading of the Church Fathers on the affluent young man leads her to discover the "economies of power in their texts" by which they sought to manage not only the lack and "fears of loss" their audiences experienced but their own as well.[262] She claims that their "hysterical fears manifest themselves in the subtexts of their economic tractates and strangely resemble the underlying fears of the notion of scarcity in neoclassical economics. Though their texts manage power, they also economize their fears of lack."[263] Grau contends that late modern interpretations of the text similarly manage fears of lack and power. Thus, in the "modern notion of the *homo economicus*, we have discovered a distant relative of the hysterical male, centered around the basic assumption of the scarcity of goods, always longing for an ever elusive abundance of them."[264]

Certainly, Grau's premises, argument and conclusions are not beyond question. One wonders at how Grau arrives at her interesting insights into what appears to be a universal male psyche lying in plain view of her theological scrutiny. Nevertheless, Grau's interpretation and conclusions can be seen as providing further support for the findings of chapters 2, 3 and 4. Chapter 2 demonstrated the nineteenth-century merger between the ultimate commitments to growth/progress shared by American Evangelicalism and industrialism, and chapter 3 showed the formative consequences of that merger for the child nurtured in Evangelical affluence during the twentieth century. By the end of the 1920s when Herbert Hoover completed his work at the Department of Commerce, American Evangelicals (Fundamentalists) and their children were embedded in a society that had accommodated itself to the dominant economic presuppositions of consumer culture.[265] Within fifty years, as chapter 4 shows, their grandchildren and children would be incorporated within the ma-

261. Grau, *Of Divine Economy*, 57, citing Markus, *Saeculum*, 35.

262. Grau, *Of Divine Economy*, 87.

263. Ibid., 88–89.

264. Ibid.

265. Cf. Mason, *Economics of Conspicuous Consumption*.

trices of mass affluence made possible by technological consumer capital-ism. In this socio-cultural context, the concern for satisfying economic lack is a predominant motive that drives personal, social and political action.

In Grau's view, that context masks the underlying lack (hysteria) in the males formed by that culture and who constitute the institutions of late modern affluent society. (And I would add that females are now in-corporated as well.) Schneider's theology is one example of the masking effect affluence can have. Because he affirms the economics and culture of capitalism, Schneider necessarily embraces a notion of God's economy in which *homo economicus* is bound inexorably to remain in the hysterical lack attendant to capitalist economics. Grau's reading of economic man suggests that Schneider's theology of affluence entails hysteria, or lack, precisely because it assumes a neoliberal conception of human nature that presumes scarcity as a ground motive for human self-interest and sociality. It is, therefore, a gendered theology lacking critical awareness of the "economies of power" by which it seeks to manage male fears of economic lack and the consequent loss of power such lack brings.

Grau's genealogy of the rich young man culminating in the *homo economicus* of late modernity can thus be seen as encompassing the AAEC and as providing a critical perspective of Schneider's theology and ethics of affluence. Nurtured in Evangelical affluence, "the power/knowledge formations" of lack in the AAEC's mind are difficult to overcome when confronted with the call to follow Jesus in the paradoxical path of abun-dant scarcity. The risks and rewards of heavenly investment are simply outweighed by those of neoclassical economics.

But does this mean that the AAEC is hopelessly confined to a sub-category of *homo economicus*? Grau suggests that pursuing "holy wisdom" as a "holy fool" is a path of ascetic renunciation in late modernity open to every human being. It is a path to following Jesus out of affluence when he calls. Grau sees this path as a subversively transformative option in a capitalist culture that equates human worth with the enlargement of net worth and the dominion it affords. The "holy fool" is an option for the AAEC, then, to overcome the "frenzied, hectic life in consumer capital-ism [that] covers up a void of emptiness that claims rationality, the cool calculations, the pretense of precision, predictability, and security. . . . the dense phallic masculinity claimed for scientific economics falls apart, un-folds the void, the lack of rationality as hysteria, that most stereotypically feminine of all disorders."[266] The AAEC can thumb his nose at affluence and become a "trickster that unravels the gendered, rationalist pretenses of deified Western capitalism regarding the world of objects and needs. . . mimicking, if not mocking, the supposed masculine rationality of scarcity by unveiling it, if involuntarily, as irrational and as queerly gendered, psychological economy."[267]

What is the wisdom of the holy fool advocated by Grau and how does she arrive at it? Harvey Cox, Peter Phan, Franz Hinkelammert and Derek Krueger provide Grau with the theology, whereas Billy Talen, Kalle Lasn, Guillermo Gómez-Peña and Michael Moore provide examples of its praxis.[268] Fundamentally, the wisdom of the holy fool is the wisdom found in the foolishness of the cross applied particularly as outrageous, practical critique of consumer culture. Ultimately, Jesus is the "model for holy foolishness" and therefore the true disciple is a holy fool who follows him in culturally subversive teachings and actions.[269] It is surprising, then, to find Grau commending Lasn (owner and editor of *Adbusters* magazine), Gómez-Peña (Mexican-born performance artist), Moore (satirist and social critic) and Talen (culturally critical theatrical actor) as examples of such holy fools. Novel but hardly compelling for an evangelical theology of the AAEC.

It is difficult to see how any of these examples instantiate the foolishness of the cross Grau seeks to locate in the holy fool's wisdom. Talen, Lasn, Gómez-Peña and Moore might be "dangerous because they threaten the

266. Grau, *Of Divine Economy*, 51.

267. Ibid.

268. See Grau's interaction with these modern theologians and holy fools, as well as the development of her constructive "Holy Wisdom, Holy Fools" proposal for ascetic resistance to and subversion of consumer capitalist culture and society. Ibid., 193–200.

269. Ibid., 196. Tracing lines from Cox to Krueger, Grau reaches Jesus as the model of the holy fool. Cox's 1969 *The Feast of Fools* provides the initial insight that "foolery represents a way of connecting, of linking paradoxical and conflicting knowledge . . . needed in times of transition . . . where modernity has been severely questioned." Ibid., 193. Phan provides Grau with an understanding of holy fool wisdom "as a way of 'un/knowing that remains as an alternative path to wisdom in . . . a postmodernity which has so deeply questioned traditional ways of knowing, such as *logos* and *mythos.*" Ibid., 194. Hinkelammert sees divine folly and wisdom as countering the "rational" and as consisting in "the election of what is weak." Ibid., 194 n. 74. Krueger's development of "Symeon the Holy Fool" from Leontius gives Grau the final theological handles she needs to find a "countereconomic third space" for "reconstructing the figure of the ascetic hysterical male . . . as he inhabits the ambivalence between earthly and divine economy." Ibid., 194, 195.

silences and denials of the status quo," but do they accomplish what Grau hopes for her "countereconomic third space"? It is highly doubtful that they do. If the foolishness of the cross is the power of God for salvation to everyone who believes, and if through that foolishness God destroys "the wisdom of the wise" and thwarts "the discernment of the discerning" (1 Cor 1:19), then it seems that a truly subversive countereconomic third space in late modern affluence must in some manner entail the proclamation of the cross. This is particularly true of an evangelical theology of affluence or theological economics of the AAEC. Grau misses the gospel in her theology and praxis of the holy fool. Not only has she missed the bulls eye, but she has failed entirely to hit the target.

Although Grau shows how ancient structures of gendered domination are taken up in consumer capitalism and thus in any contemporary theology that warmly embraces its culture and society, she has overlooked the good news that God has provided for the ultimate subversion of those structures. Failing to keep in mind the genetic link between the gospel and feminist theology, i.e., a biblical, Christ-centered notion of liberty, she has overlooked how centrally important the foolishness of the cross is to her project. Her theology may help the AAEC unmask the lack inherent in Evangelical affluence and might even help form in the AAEC a "post-Weberian reassessment of ascetic practices."[270]

But in the end her theology is found lacking, at least for the AAEC. It is hollow, or hysterical, to use her terms, because it fails to grasp how the good news of the death and resurrection of Jesus Christ must be the essential component of a liberating countereconomic third space in late modernity. An evangelical theology of the AAEC cannot ignore the gospel because in doing so it misses the remedy God has provided for the one thing that still lacks.

The AAEC and Divine Economy

This leads to the second theological resource utilized for constructing an evangelical theology of the AAEC: Long's critique of Novak's theology of economics.

---

270. Grau, *Of Divine Economy*, 19. Grau's endorsement of "simplified living" is somewhat naïve and would have benefited from a more detailed engagement of Twitchell's critique of voluntary simplicity in *Lead Us Into Temptation*, 6–10. Grau was aware of this work but may not have read it closely. Grau, *Of Divine Economy*, 189 n. 51.

The analysis proceeds as follows. I first begin with Grau's criticisms of *Divine Economy*. These provide a helpful cautionary framework for understanding Long's critique of Novak, as well as correlating Grau and Long in relation to the evangelical theology of the AAEC constructed here. Although Grau's case may not convince all, her contention with Long on these points help illumine our perspective of the child nurtured in American-Evangelical affluence.

Next I will briefly summarize how Schneider's doctrines of creation and humanity function in his theology of affluence. Schneider relies heavily upon Novak for his theological framework, and therefore Long's penetrating theological critique of Novak applies equally to Schneider. Finally, Long's critique is presented in the three steps he takes to demonstrate (1) the Weberian fact-value strategy of relating economics to theology Novak employs, (2) the "theology as *analogia libertatis*" found in Novak, and (3) the resultant subordination of Christology and ecclesiology to the doctrine of creation in Novak's theology. These in turn are applied to Schneider's theology of affluence with the AAEC in view.

Grau's critique of *Divine Economy*

Grau applauds Long's efforts at "constructing a radical orthodoxy, [which] aims to inhabit a space beyond the binaries of procapitalist and anticapitalist theologies."[271] But she faults him for what she perceives to be his ultimate failure to escape the binaries inherent in the "metaphysics of scarcity that defines modernity."[272] In other words, Long's affirmation of God as "an original plenitude" and his denial of the modern economic "narrative of scarcity" locks him on the horns of the dilemma Grau claims to have exposed because Long is simply repeating "what became orthodoxy"—that is, what became the orthodox interpretation of theological economics she has exposed as deficiently gendered.[273]

This is a fatal move, in Grau's view, because early Christian orthodoxy and late modern capitalism share essentially the same theological economics. Hence, a radical orthodoxy that seeks to recover a premodern

---

271. Grau, *Of Divine Economy*, 10.

272. Ibid., 86, quoting Long, *Divine Economy*, 85, 148.

273. Grau, *Of Divine Economy*, 86, quoting Long, *Divine Economy*, 146.

orthodoxy is bound to fail.[274] It simply seeks to replace "one grand narrative of omnipotence with another, a theological for an economic dominology."[275] Grau sees Long's claim "to have unrestricted and unpolluted access to an oddly transcendental set of neo-Thomist virtues" free from the modern tendency to subordinate theology to the "metaphysics of being" as contradictory because she doubts whether Aquinas succeeded in giving us a version of Aristotelian virtues in which theology escaped subordination to metaphysics.[276] She seems to read Long as arguing that "metaphysics was a modern invention and not largely derived from the writings of Aristotle himself."[277] This is not what Long argues, however. Consistent with Radical Orthodoxy fundamentals, his claim is that in modernity (i.e., after Aquinas at least) theology became subordinated to a metaphysics of being and was dethroned as "queen of the sciences."[278] Thus, it needs to be liberated from such metaphysics and put back in its rightful place.[279]

Nevertheless, Grau makes a valid point by identifying in Long (and in Radical Orthodoxy in general) "a strong nostalgia for a premodern, prehumanistic universe, refusing to acknowledge, or appropriate positively, their own dependence on either modernity or metaphysics."[280] She argues that Long's reliance upon Aquinas (and therefore Aristotle) only leads him to affirm that which he has vowed to reject: economic scarcity, metaphysics of being and liberalism. Long denies scarcity because God is seen as original plenitude and hence as absolute omnipotence (something

274. Long finds his premodern orthodoxy in Thomas Aquinas, who appears regularly in Radical Orthodoxy's attempts to counter modern theological heterodoxy and heresy. Cf. Raschke, *Next Reformation*, 95: "Radical Orthodoxy thinkers have a reputation for trundling out some antiquated or forgotten figure in Western tradition in order to provide a more historical perspective on a topic in which postmodernists revel."

275. Grau, *Of Divine Economy*, 37.

276. Ibid., 31.

277. Ibid.

278. Long, *Divine Economy*, 270.

279. Along the way, Grau claims, Long makes a futile attempt to reconcile Barth with Aquinas on the issue of natural theology. Grau notes that Long never acknowledges Aquinas as "the father of natural theology" which, she implies, entails the subordination of theology to the metaphysics of being. Grau, *Of Divine Economy*, 31 n. 38.

280. Ibid., 31, 32. One wonders how Grau has managed to escape the same traps of modernity and metaphysics in her feminist theological readings of Scripture and the Church Fathers.

feminists are keen to discern). At the same time scarcity is affirmed in the argument (in reliance upon Milbank) for "the abolition of capitalism and the production of a socialist market" that will overcome scarcity and lead finally to the plenitude that is God.[281] As Grau notes, "Long gets tripped up in the attempt both to locate his theology historically and at the same time to declare null and void the past five hundred years of modernity."[282] These are helpful points and apply equally as well, in my view, to the entire Radical Orthodoxy project.

Grau finds further fault with Long's decision to identify "modernity as the singular culprit for the dominance of economics" because in her view the culprit's genealogy reaches back to the tradition of the rich young man, particularly as first interpreted by Irenaeus.[283] Thus, she seeks instead to appropriate and reconfigure "the gains of modern thought—such as freedom, rationality, human rights, and subjectivity—to meet new circumstances . . . through theological analyses situated in the contested fields of postmodernity."[284] In Grau's opinion, although "the recovery of religious socialism as a third economic space is an important contribution to a countereconomic theology," the manner in which Long develops it "seems primarily polemic and utopian while based on a unilateral and in the end unsatisfying rejection of modernity *in toto*."[285] In other words, Long too easily dismisses the gains of modernity and consequently throws the baby out with the bathwater in his Radical Orthodoxy theological economics.

Grau's criticisms notwithstanding, an evangelical theology of the AAEC can benefit significantly from the Radical Orthodoxy critique of modernity Long brings to bear upon the dominant tradition of theological economics. It can help cultivate a critical-evangelical consciousness of the theological and philosophical origins of capitalist consumer culture

281. Grau, *Of Divine Economy*, 32, guoting Long, *Divine Economy*, 260.

282. Ibid., 31 n. 36. For Grau's critique of Irenaeus' interpretation of the rich young man, see 56–60, 87.

283. Ibid., 31 n. 36.

284. Ibid., 40.

285. Ibid., 32. Though helpful, it must be noted that Grau's representation of Radical Orthodoxy's stance regarding modernity is not entirely accurate. As Milbank puts it, Radical Orthodoxy is neither an "outright refusal, nor outright acceptance [of modernity]. More like an attempt at redirection of what we find." Milbank, *Being Reconciled*, 196.

in the United States. This leads to deeper insights into the role theology plays in the AAEC's interpretation and reproduction of the socio-cultural matrices of Evangelicalism and affluence in the United States. In addition, Long's theological economics is crucial for developing a perspective of the theological problems Schneider's theology of affluence poses for the AAEC in late modernity.

Schneider's doctrine of creation: the "cosmic good" of affluence

Schneider claims that "after all the requisite qualifications have been made" the mandate in Genesis to be fruitful and multiply, fill and subdue the earth "is essentially what human life is all about."[286] Schneider makes this claim with its echoes of realized eschatology as he concludes his interpretation of Luke's Parable of the Pounds. As will be shown, Schneider's doctrine of creation dominates his theology of affluence. Schneider situates it within the Gospel of Luke in order to test and establish his thesis of the cosmic good of affluence, because it provides a litmus test as the most wealth-negative and poverty-affirmative Gospel.

Schneider forces his doctrine of creation into his argument from the Parable of the Pounds and imposes a predetermined theological agenda into the narrative structure of Luke. Thus, in the parable we see "the last act" in Luke's narration of the "creative drama. . . ., in a sense, . . . [of] the death and resurrection of material affluence as a cosmic good. . . . It takes us back, through Christ . . . to the very foundations of . . . the creation itself, and the existence of dominion and delight that God envisioned for human beings."[287] This is a remarkable claim for a Reformed-evangelical to make because it subordinates not only the doctrines of Christ and the church but also the doctrine of salvation to a cosmology of the good of late modern affluence. Schneider neither retracts nor retreats from this claim. The pursuit of a "creative, productive economic life . . . is absolutely true to our humanity and to the identity of God."[288] Furthermore, Schneider leaves parents desiring to form evangelical habits in their children wondering what nurture of this kind of life entails. Schneider believes the "new" culture of capitalism presents the possibility for the first time in human

286. Schneider, *Good of Affluence*, 191.
287. Ibid., 189.
288. Schneider, *Good of Affluence*, 191.

history to realize the cosmic good of affluence God intends for all humans in Genesis 1 and 2. But he is unconcerned about the consequences that may arise from nurturing habits of joyful acquisition under capitalism's late modern flourishing. Furthermore, his reading of the creation account as human enjoyment of affluence rather than the blessings derived from sharing in the goodness of creation is highly suspect. It seems to confuse the fruit from the tree of life with the tree of life itself.

It is no shock, then, to find that Schneider found the cosmic good of creation in the Parable of the Pounds and virtually in every biblical text he examined. That his theological economics ended there is not surprising in light of where it began. His reading of Genesis as presenting a cosmic vision of delight for humanity, the royal image of God, forecasts the terminus of his theology of affluence in liberal democracy rather than in Christ and the church. Schneider sees the "precious doctrine" of humanity as God's image leading inevitably to an anthropology grounded in "the value, dignity, and rights" of every human being.[289] This anthropology is essential for "understanding godly forms of being affluent" and also for providing a framework to build "a spiritual and moral view of affluence as it should be."[290] Not surprisingly, Schneider sees this anthropology as a "pre-democratic idea [that] follows from reverence for the royal dignity of every individual."[291] Schneider's dependence on Novak becomes clear at this point, and it sounds a note dangerously close to liberal theology's unbiblical overemphasis on human freedom, reason and autonomy.[292]

Schneider's liberty of royal servant-dominion and delight

A close reading of *Godly Materialism* and *The Good of Affluence* discloses the influence Novak's thought has had upon Schneider's understanding of the doctrines of creation, humanity and sin in the context of the culture of democratic capitalism.[293] Schneider believes with Novak that

---

289. Ibid., 52.

290. Ibid., 52–53.

291. Ibid., 53 (foonote 18 omitted).

292. For a helpful discussion of essential differences between evangelical and liberal theology, see Bloesch, "Evangelicalism and Liberalism," in *Essentials of Evangelical Theology*, 13–17. Bloesch lists Novak as a contemporary representative of liberal theology. Ibid., 13.

293. Schneider, *Godly Materialism*, 193, n. 53, and 208, n. 14; *Good of Affluence*,

affluence is liberating people from poverty and is leading and will continue to lead millions of people to God in late modernity in profound ways.[294] Democratic capitalism has proven itself to be the most effective (albeit imperfect, fallen and, at times, sinful) means of lifting people out of poverty. Novak established this line of argumentation in 1982 in *The Spirit of Democratic Capitalism*, and it recurs in neoliberal, procapitalist literature often.[295] The argument is an empirical one. It proceeds from the evidence of mass affluence to theological claims about the institutions and economics that sustain it in late modernity.

The anthropology underlying this faith in affluence is grounded in Novak's doctrine of the *imago Dei*. As Long's critique shows, Novak essentially equates human freedom with the image of God. Following Novak, Schneider argues that this doctrine has strengthened individual liberty and the right to own property beyond "anything that Locke, Jefferson, or Adam Smith advocated" and, thus, has been central to the evolution and emergence of the new culture of capitalism made possible by liberal democracy.[296] The point no doubt contains a healthy kernel of truth that must be taken into consideration in doing theological economics, something neo-Marxists and the Radical Orthodoxy theologians alike fail adequately to address.

It is quite another thing, however, to grant the point too much weight, as Schneider seems to do in *The Good of Affluence*. Schneider's

---

1–23, 39, 211–18.

294. Novak's logic is that rich people will be leading a religious revival in the United States because they are "finding that wealth by itself does not bring meaning and fulfillment, and they are starting to search for answers. In the past people came to God because they were suffering, because they were broken. But increasingly, in the West, it is going to be affluence that leads people to God" because although the "Bible tells us that man cannot live by bread alone. . . . you have to have bread to realize that." D'Souza, *Virtue of Prosperity*, 144, quoting Novak; accord Schneider, *Good of Affluence*, 4.

295. Novak, "The Historical Achievements of Democratic Capitalism," in *Spirit*, 16–18. Cf. Schneider, "The 'New' Culture of Capitalism," in *Good of Affluence*, 13–40; Sherman, *Preferential Option*, 8, 205–9; D'Souza, *Virtue of Prosperity*, 142–44. If anticapitalist, feminist and other critics of capitalism have an Achilles heel, it is here. Not because the evidence is incontrovertible but because they simply refuse to acknowledge the evidence pointing to its positive, liberating aspects (i.e., that it has enabled and continues to enable millions to live better lives free from grinding poverty, premature death and various forms of political oppression). Latin America today is, arguably, a strong case in point.

296. Schneider, *Good of Affluence*, 87.

fundamental conclusion from reading Genesis 1 and 2 is that all humans are created in God's image to be royal servants of God's mandate of dominion and delight in superabundance, and the essence of that image is seen in human freedom and its productive (capitalist) fruits. He sees the new culture of late twentieth century technological consumer capitalism as a foreshadowing of the promised restoration of Edenic affluence and a source of genuine hope that the original dominion-delight intended by God for every human will be restored on earth as it is in heaven.

Evangelicals should pay close attention here. If Schneider is correct, then it follows that the most important steps evangelicals can take in late modernity are to evangelize for capitalism simultaneous with promoting the gospel. Proclamation of the foolishness of the cross, it seems, appears either to be secondary or at least unhealthily conjoined to cultivating a productive capitalist ethos. Capitalist expansion is primary and is what makes preaching the gospel possible, meaningful and fulfilling. It provides the bread that makes believing the gospel possible.

Certainly, it is intellectually incredulous to deny that capitalism has played a role in producing facts like the decline of poverty in China from 28% in 1978 to 9% in 1998 or in India from 51% to 26% from 1977–78 to 1999–2000.[297] And it is disingenuous to ignore the role technological consumer capitalism has played in bringing about the escape from hunger and extension of life expectancy over the past 300 years in the West.[298]

At the same time, however, Schneider and other neoliberal theologians press the evidence much too far theologically, in my view, and they seem to place entirely too much faith in the liberating power of capitalism and those who administer it in the public-private partnership of commerce in the United States formed by presidents Roosevelt, Wilson and Hoover in the early 1900s. Not only are the facts of capitalism subject to legitimate contest by those on the underside of humanity, but as I have argued from the story of the rich young man the affluence capitalism brings poses a serious danger of forming a spiritual and moral lack in the affluent rather than a disposition for self-denial, cross-bearing and following Jesus in a manner focused on losing life for him and the good news of his death, burial and resurrection.

297. Bhagwati, *Defense of Globalization*, 65.
298. Fogel, *Escape from Hunger*.

This exposes the deficiency lying at the heart of neoliberal theological anthropology and the kernel of truth in Milbank's dictum, "Pure liberty is pure power—whose other name is evil." The peril of an impoverishing theological amnesia lurks in the neoliberal conception of liberty. Affluence tempts believers to disregard the God who redeems from every aspect of slavery, poverty and oppression and to forget the purpose for which God liberates: to serve the Lord God "joyfully and with gladness of heart for the abundance of everything" (Dt 28:47) and follow Jesus in the path of true freedom. This is the way of the cross and the path of discipleship. Thus, affluence can have a deadening effect on evangelical memory, for it tempts the believer to follow other gods, to walk in prideful unbelief that one's life consists in an abundance of possessions. The fact that both Matthew and Luke have Jesus quoting Deuteronomy 8:3 in battling the devil should cause evangelicals to ponder the implications this encounter has for a theology of affluence, particularly the kind of aggressive, competitive battling in the free market for which Schneider advocates.

If global affluence is coming, as Novak and Schneider argue it is, then the temptation accounts in Matthew and Luke should provide serious cautions against celebrating human formation in the context of affluence. In both, the quest for material affluence (plausibly signified in the temptation to create bread from stones) seems to have been qualified radically by Jesus with the words of Deuteronomy 8:3, "One does not live by bread alone" (Lk 4:4), "but by every word that comes from the mouth of God" (Mt 4:4). As the evangelical believes and the temptation accounts demonstrate,[299] the whole world "lies under the power of the evil one" (1 Jn 5:19), and therefore the temptation to reduce theology to the idolatrous pursuit of eating, drinking and rising up to play seems to lurk beneath the good of affluence at every turn (cf. 1 Cor 10:6–7). Thus, aware that the whole world lies under the devil's power, the children of God are exhorted to keep themselves truly free to love and serve God and neighbor and, hence, to "flee from the worship of idols" (1 Jn 5:21; cf. 1 Cor 10:14).

This aspect of the theological anthropology of affluence is left undeveloped by Schneider. The resistance and renunciation of affluence made by the new Israel in the second, final wilderness says much about the kind

299. The devil showed Jesus "all the kingdoms of the world and their splendor" (Mt 4:8), saying that its "glory and all its authority . . . has been given over to me; and I give it to anyone I please" (Luke 4:6). Jesus was tempted with the "glory," "splendor" and "authority" of global affluence in exchange for a simple act of worship.

of Christian anthropology needed in the context of mass affluence. Jesus may have been the Christ of radical compassion and delight, as Schneider argues forcefully and compellingly, but the manner in which he counseled the rich young man and commended Zacchaeus is contrary to what Schneider advocates. Rather than enacting a neoliberal democratic anthropology grounded in the value, dignity and rights of individual freedom and property ownership, Jesus fasted forty days and nights in the wilderness and then came serving the Lord God joyfully from a heart full of gratitude for "the abundance of everything" as he journeyed to Jerusalem. He fulfilled the Law and the Prophets and the Psalms, as Luke tells us in the glorious conclusion to his Gospel. There, at Jerusalem, Jesus died between two criminals and witnessed the final disposition of his remaining possessions in a soldier's roll of the dice. He successfully resisted the temptations to follow the myriad gods of affluence in the boastful pride of life, and he renounced perfectly the temptation to believe that one's life consists in an abundance of possessions. His final donation was the gift of his body and spirit for the life of the world and for true life in this world, in which he fulfilled and redeemed true human freedom, including the freedom to possess not only a body but also things outside and consumed by the body.

Without an evangelical anthropology centered upon that kind of Christ, Schneider's good of affluence easily transforms into the one thing that is lacking. After twenty years of nurturing modern economic habits of affluence, it should not surprise evangelicals to find the AAEC wondering what is lacking in relation to God and neighbor and why the path of discipleship fails to open before them with delight. After all, why should it? If Schneider's moral theology of affluence is to be believed, the other Jesus is the one to follow. He is the one who is the Lord of delight, the one who came eating and drinking and reveling in the twin capitalist habits of acquisition and enjoyment.

Neoliberal "theology as *analogia libertatis*": Long on Novak

Lying at the heart of the problem of Schneider's theology of affluence and ethic of cultivating capitalist habits is the conception of human freedom. Is it biblical or American? We can gain a perspective on this problem by looking at Long's critique of Novak, upon whom Schneider so heavily relies.

Long argues that Novak's theology of economics is determined by its understanding of human freedom as constrained by original sin. This is what "theology as *analogia libertatis*" means—theological knowledge is made relevant to modern economics by an analogy from human freedom to divine freedom, with the understanding that the analogy breaks down because of sin. As a result, an anthropology of liberty is "the decisive theological theme" in Novak's theological economics.[300] That theme arises from the Weberian fact-value distinction appropriated by the dominant tradition of theological economics as its "strategy of relating theology to ethics."[301] This tradition views economics as giving us facts of human existence, whereas theology gives us values. The two realms are separate except to the extent theological and economic interests come together in human liberty. Thus, theology's role in relation to economics is to uphold human liberty by interpreting ethical issues in terms consistent with the supreme human-divine value of liberty. Theologians in the dominant tradition, therefore, implicitly accept Weber's consignment of theology to the task of addressing the "irrational remainders" that science, math and rationality cannot explain.[302] For Long and other Radical Orthodoxy theologians, this is unacceptable.

In order to gain a fuller understanding of how Long relates Weber to Novak's anthropology of liberty, a brief excursus into John Milbank's seminal *Theology and Social Theory* is needed. This will show the broader critical framework of Radical Orthodoxy within which Long's thought operates in relation to modernity and, hence, in relation to intellectuals like Weber and Novak. Every theologian of Radical Orthodoxy has read Milbank and been influenced by his profound, dense thought. Furthermore, it must be presumed that publication of a "Radical Orthodoxy" volume carries with it a Milbankian imprimatur. Reading the volumes confirms that this is the case. It stands to reason, then, that understanding Long's *Divine Economy* can only be enriched by an evangelical excursion into *Theology and Social Theory*.

---

300. Long, *Divine Economy*, 35.

301. Ibid.

302. Long, *Divine Economy*, 35 (footnote 5 omitted), citing Gerth and Mills (eds.), *From Max Weber*, 281.

Excursus: Milbank's critique of secular reason

For Long and the theologians of Radical Orthodoxy, relegating theology to a minimalist role is heretical. As an evangelical swimming in various twenty-first century Reformed theological streams, I concur wholeheartedly with this assessment. I suggest that evangelicals of all stripes should concur as well.

Long's critical assessment of Weber and Novak reflects a clear dependence upon Milbank's penetrating critique of modern social theory. In his seminal *Theology and Social Theory*, Milbank presents a plausible case that cultures of consumer capitalism, particularly in the United States, are sustained by institutional structures established upon social scientific bases, particularly the psychological, sociological and economic. These are either heretical formations when considered "in relation to orthodox Christianity, or else [are] a rejection of Christianity that is more 'neo-pagan' than simply anti-religious."[303] They are "theologies or anti-theologies in disguise"[304] which, by implication, theologians like Schneider and Novak have failed to recognize to the extent they theologically embrace technological consumer capitalism.

Read carefully, Milbank's critique of secular reason should force evangelicals to reconsider their theology and practice in relation to technological consumer capitalism. If indeed modern political theology and the "new science of politics" Milbank critiques created a "secular" space that once was not, because all there was before in the West was Christendom,[305] then it follows that the United States with its evangelical constituency is one of the galaxies in that space. And if the new science of modern politics, as one of the progenitors of this space, discovered a providential "process of prudent conservation" grounded in the regular, humanly unplanned and unintended operations of the so-called "free market" that provides a means of "non-ethical regulation" of human passions and desires,[306] then it would appear that Evangelical affluence in the United States is a product, or at least a by-product, of that discovery. If this is true, even in part, then evangelicals across the spectrum of faith should be troubled by the fact that the United States is the most ardent

303. Milbank, *Theology and Social Theory*, 3.
304. Ibid.
305. Ibid., 9–26.
306. Ibid., 27.

exporter and powerful advocate of the global extension of this secular space through its empire-like technological-military-political-commercial complex.[307] It would indeed be heretical for evangelicals to claim that expansion of this kind of liberty and democracy around the world equates to, or is some how consistent with, the spread of the kingdom of God on earth as it is in heaven.

If the evangelical literature on affluence is any indication, few evangelicals recognize what Milbank has sought to expose through his dense critique of social theory and secular reason.[308] The virulent technological consumer capitalism of the United States, from which millions of American evangelicals routinely benefit, was made possible in late modernity by the development of secular "political economy" and "speculative history" in the eighteenth century and by economics, sociology and anthropology in the nineteenth.[309] These were the means whereby the secular society most Americans take for granted was ultimately grounded in "the demiurgic wills of human individuals."[310] In other words, they are the secular sources of American individualism, evangelicalism and affluence. Many evangelicals in the United States, however, read the secular history described by Milbank as a sacred history founded upon the faith of its founding fathers and the free market they supposedly endorsed.

Milbank's critique sheds new light on the historical and sociological analyses of chapters 2 through 4. If Milbank is correct, even in part, evangelicals who unequivocally affirm the new culture of capitalism fail to recognize from whence they came and where they are going. They lack a critical consciousness of their problematic embeddedness in a culture of affluence that has arisen from heretical theological and pagan philosophical appropriations.

On Milbank's reckoning, the new culture of capitalism that American Evangelicalism helped generate and also helps sustain involves a "heretical redefinition of Christian virtue and a heretical endorsement of the manipulation of means by ends."[311] Justifications of affluence are joined

---

307. See Bacevich, *New American Militarism* and *American Empire*.

308. Fortunately, one Reformed-evangelical scholar has made a successful attempt to read, understand and interpret Milbank and Radical Orthodoxy. See Milbank's forward to Smith, *Introducing Radical Orthodoxy*, 11–20. Cf. Raschke, *Next Reformation*, 95–98.

309. Milbank, *Theology and Social Theory*, 27.

310. Ibid.

311. Milbank, *Theology and Social Theory*, 45.

with theological defenses of individualist virtue and pragmatism within American Evangelicalism. As Milbank puts it, "Economic theodicy is conjoined with an evangelicalism focused on a narrow, individualist practical reason which excludes the generous theoretical contemplation of God and the world (this is thinned down to a simple acceptance of positive revealed data which ensures salvation)."[312] This is the point at which Long's dependence on Milbank is perhaps most clear. Long develops Milbank's critique of the important role Weber played in the development of social theory in the West, particularly the fact-value relationship of economics to theology.

Milbank and Radical Orthodoxy are not without their critics, however, and properly so.[313] To the extent Milbank is reflected in Long's critique of modern economics Grau's criticisms of Long apply to Milbank and should be kept in mind. Milbank, along with Radical Orthodoxy in general, is particularly vulnerable with respect to his constructive proposal of a Christian socialism by grace. Milbank (followed by Long and others) argues for a reconstituted Christian social order as the solution to renovating and transforming capitalism. Paul Lakeland discerns within this proposal a "Christian social theory" in which lurks a "kind of ecclesial absolutism" in favor of Anglo-Catholic sacramentalism.[314] Carl Raschke argues that an ecclesial solution such as this is strangely exclusive and seems to close doors to evangelicals for whom the power of personal conversion and holiness are essential components of Christian life and worship. He also expresses concern that the "social Christology" upon which Milbank constructs his vision of a "'sacred' totality of the social order . . . is a perilous prospect" because it harkens back to a "metapolitics . . . [of] the fusion of an indeterminable sense of the mysterious with a reverence for social solidarity . . . [which] is the main historical ingredient in fascism and other historical experiments in totalitarianism."[315] In other words, Milbank's theology and philosophy teeter simultaneously on the dangerous precipices of fascism and communism. Raschke's aspersion

312. Ibid.

313. In addition to the critiques of Radical Orthodoxy in Grau, Smith and Raschke, see, e.g., Lakeland, *Postmodernity*; Hyman, *Predicament of Postmodern Theology*; Roberts, "Postmodern quasi-fundamentalism (John Milbank)," 203–5; Hedley, "Should Divinity Overcome Metaphysics?", 271–98.

314. Lakeland, *Postmodernity*, 72.

315. Raschke, *Next Reformation*, 97, citing Viereck, *Metapolitics*.

certainly goes too far, as do critiques from the theological left that suggest the United States (with its conservative Evangelical constituency) shares a family resemblance with the fascism of Nazi Germany.[316]

However, both caricatures make important points. On one hand, any Christian proposal for social and political reconstruction of capitalism is fraught with practical dangers of totalitarianism. The history of Christianity in Western Europe attests to this fact. On the other hand, the economics and politics of capitalism present serious perils not only because of the problems posed by affluence but also because of the "new" American militarism they require.[317] Consequently, millions of American Evangelicals and other citizens of the United States are susceptible to seduction both by affluence and war as they uncritically sanction the use of American military power to protect democratic capitalism at home and to establish it abroad.[318] And, again, this is where in my view Milbank and the Radical Orthodoxy theologians are most helpful. The critique of capitalism begun by Milbank in *Theology and Social Theory* and that continues in the project of Radical Orthodoxy can help evangelicals of all stripes see themselves more clearly in relation to these perils of affluence.

Despite these and other concerns with Radical Orthodoxy, Milbank's critique of secular reason is one with which evangelicals should be familiar. The project of Radical Orthodoxy is an essential source for contemporary theological anthropology and should be consulted for developing a robust critical-evangelical understanding of modern history, sociology, politics and economics.[319] In my view, failure to consider and appreciate it leaves any contemporary theology lacking.

Returning now to Long's critique of Novak in *Divine Economy*, it should be noted that Long brings Milbank's analysis of modern social theory to a sharp focus upon neoclassical economics as theologically appropriated by Novak.

---

316. See, e.g., Hinkelammert and Duchrow, *Property for People, Not Profit*, 208–18; Northcott, *Angel Directs the Storm*, 80, and, less directly, Gorringe, *Capital and the Kingdom*, 155.

317. Bacevich, *New American Militarism*.

318. Bacevich concludes that "were it not for the support offered by several tens of millions of evangelicals, militarism in this deeply and genuinely religious country becomes inconceivable." Ibid., 146.

319. A good starting point would be Smith, *Introducing Radical Orthodoxy*.

Long begins by marshalling evidence demonstrating Novak's intellectual dependence on classic liberal conceptions of human nature. He engages in an extensive, careful review of Novak's writings to adduce this evidence. He argues from the evidence that Novak's "theology is a consistent and passionate defense of liberalism and modernity undertaken by drawing upon the doctrine of creation."[320] This places Novak and, consequently, Schneider squarely in the cross hairs of Radical Orthodoxy critique. Nevertheless, Schneider developed his theology of affluence without critical awareness of how Radical Orthodoxy bears upon his project.

Long discerns three themes that have remained constant throughout Novak's theological journey: (1) Christology is too particular to serve pluralistic economic and political ends, can be harmonized with a universal principle of liberty and "can be transformed into secular language without altering its content"; (2) the universal hunger for liberty expressed in modern revolutionary movements was dormant in the church prior to modernity and must be accommodated and nurtured by the church; and (3) the "doctrine of creation, and the recognition of the human person as a co-creator with God through producing wealth, are at the heart of a Catholic social ethic, rightly understood."[321] Each of these themes runs throughout Schneider's theology of affluence as well. Thus, like Novak, Schneider "consistently argues for a liberal-pluralist democratic society for individuals to have the freedom to create themselves, or at least be co-creators of their own destiny."[322] Christology is strangely muted in Schneider's doctrine of creation as it is harmonized with his conception of human freedom and responsibility to enlarge God's dominion through courageous capitalist trading of the "pounds" Jesus has entrusted to his disciples.

However, Long misses something present in Novak's theological economics that is absent in Schneider's: the role of *caritas* ("compassion, sacrificial love"), or what Long calls "charity."[323] Long certainly overstates his case when he claims that Novak has stretched his argument for human liberty "beyond its breaking point" when he turns to Aquinas for

320. Long, *Divine Economy*, 36.

321. Ibid.

322. Ibid., 37.

323. Novak, *Spirit*, 353; Long, *Divine Economy*, 38, 77.

support.[324] He distinguishes Novak from Aquinas by arguing that Novak grounds human co-creativity in anthropology whereas Aquinas grounds it in theology: "For Thomas, only our participation in God's over-abundant goodness allowed for this co-creative power; his is a theological claim."[325] Human participation in God results in substantive principles of natural law that direct human actions toward moral ends. God is the ground of substantive principles of natural law that lead humans to the virtues. According to Long, this is our heritage from Aquinas. Long argues that, "Novak neglects, or explicitly rejects . . . substantive principles" derived from our participation in God, such as the prohibition against usury, the just wage requirement and the universality of property that delimits private property ownership.[326] He argues further that Novak "seldom develops," as Aquinas did, "the virtues of justice and prudence, *but even more importantly the theological virtue of charity.*"[327]

Long cites no evidence to substantiate these claims, and when he returns to the issue of charity in the conclusion to his argument against the theologians of the dominant tradition he fails to mention Novak.[328] His claim about Novak's failure to develop the virtue of charity is particularly surprising. This is because Novak develops the virtue of charity in his theology of economics *extensively* from Aquinas.[329] Thus, following Aquinas, Novak can claim that love (*caritas*, charity) "is the inner form of all the virtues."[330] Novak quotes Aquinas at length: "To love . . . is to will the good of the other as other"; "Charity is the form, the mover, and the root of the virtues"; "Since to love is to wish the good of someone, that which is said to be loved has a two-fold consideration: it is considered either as one for whom we wish the good; or as the good which we wish for someone."[331] In short, Novak follows classical Catholic ethical teaching: loves infuses all ethics, capitalist ethics included. Long's attempt to

324. Long, *Divine Economy*, 38.

325. Ibid.

326. Ibid.

327. Ibid. (emphasis added).

328. Ibid., 77.

329. Novak, *Spirit*, 353–58, 412 nn. 11–13.

330. Ibid., 354 (endnote 12 omitted).

331. Novak, *Spirit*, 353 (endnote 11 omitted); 412 n. 12; 412 n. 11. Novak cites Aquinas in *On Charity* and *Summa Theologica* here.

claim that Novak fails to ground his anthropology of love theologically, therefore, is a tenuous one.

There are several ways to look at Long's misrepresentation of Novak's relationship to Aquinas on the issue of charity. He may have failed to read Novak's theology of economics closely, but this is unlikely in light of his comprehensive critical interaction with Novak's writings. Or he may have failed to recall reading Novak's section on *caritas* in "A Theology of Economics," which would be a reasonable conclusion in light of the sheer literary breadth of *Divine Economy*. A third option might be that Long purposefully decided not to expose the soft underbelly of his theological critique of Novak at such an early juncture in his argument. Contrary to Long's claim that Novak "seldom develops" the virtue of charity from Aquinas, it is clear that Novak developed it explicitly in reliance upon Aquinas. Thus, the issue between Long and Novak, it would appear, is an issue of the *proper interpretation and application* of Aquinas on the virtue of charity in relation to capitalism, rather than a simple failure to develop Aquinas on that point. This may expose some of the pre-understandings Long brings to his reading of Aquinas, his theological economics and his critique of Novak.

Long, it seems, simply cannot believe that Novak could utilize Aquinas properly on any point of theological economics. Doing so might render a death blow to his constructive proposal for a Milbankian "social-ism by grace . . . [by which] we reform capitalism from within the cor-poration by insuring that all transactions bear witness to justice."[332] This claim is supported by the fact that a form of that proposal immediately precedes the point at which Long accuses Novak of failing to develop the virtue of charity from Aquinas: "That this co-creation was a participa-tion in God meant abiding by certain substantive principles of the natural law that would direct our actions toward virtuous ends, principles such as the usury proscription, the just wage and the universal destination of all our goods which placed limitations upon private ownership."[333] This paragraph, which appears early in *Divine Economy*, can be read as Long's programmatic statement in favor of the "residual tradition" of theological

332. Long, *Divine Economy*, 268.
333. Ibid.

economics which, in my view, culminates in an ill-defined and ultimately incomprehensible proposal to transform capitalism.[334]

Despite this shortcoming, Long's critique of Novak's theology of economics remains useful to the theological anthropology of the AAEC presented here. It helps illumine how Novak views human liberty as constrained only by an original sin inherent in an imperfect creation. The problem, as Long sees it, is that Novak does not allow human liberty to be constrained, governed or interpreted by Christology or ecclesiology. What is important theologically for Novak, Long contends, is that we seek to establish "those social formations that allow . . . freedom to create and produce" because these approximate most closely "how God works. In our liberty to produce we discover God."[335] In other words, Long reads Novak as claiming that God created an imperfect world to give us an opportunity to improve it through imperfect processes of creation, production and consumption as a means of discovering God. This provides the best context for the realistic cultivation of true virtues, and history has proven that capitalism is the best of the imperfect systems available to humanity to attain these ends. Thus, Novak's theology of economics unequivocally embraces the Industrial-Evangelical preunderstandings of progress and growth and reinscribes classical economic theory of human self-interest upon contemporary theological economics.

Schneider echoes this anthropology of liberty constrained solely by original sin. Like Novak, he sees the conditions that make affluence possible "necessarily [as] a state of considerable freedom" and therefore as conditions that make sin a very real possibility.[336] The choice to disobey God in the garden resulted in the first humans coming to know good and evil. This was a divine judgment on Adam and Eve for desiring "to be their own gods, little Yahwehs, autonomous rulers of their own universe."[337] Schneider sidesteps a full theological development of the doctrine of original sin, but offers a view of sinful affluence "as false dominion," and thus the story of the fall from original grace is "a warning to the whole

---

334. This can be seen in both the substance and the structure of his argument. See part III, "The residual tradition: virtues and the true, the good, and the beautiful." Ibid., 38, 175–270.

335. Long, *Divine Economy*, 39.

336. Schneider, *Good of Affluence*, 62.

337. Ibid.

human race, . . . especially to those who are given the freedom that comes with affluence."[338]

But why "especially" the affluent? Schneider fails to make this clear. Following a line on sin and creation similar to Novak, Schneider sees the desire for god-like autonomy and self-rule as lying at the root of every human heart. This fallen human disposition alienates humanity from God, others and creation. It is the source of the "unintended consequences" of capitalism that Novak affirms from Adam Smith and is the reason why we must give attention to such consequences in economics "rather than to virtuous motivations."[339] The sinful desire to be God permeates the entire cosmos with a kind of "serpent-dominion" that sets itself against the "servant-dominion" established by God.[340] Although the "mind of the serpent now gives shape and direction to human power" in the world, it cannot overcome the cosmic good of affluence which erupts even from within evil places like the sinful city of Cain in the form of "arts, technology, and animal husbandry—all good things."[341]

Schneider does not stop to consider whether or how the "new" culture of capitalism he commends may be the product of the "mind of the serpent [which] now gives shape and direction to human power" in the world. He feels no compulsion to subject that culture to critical analysis because he, like Novak, has grounded his theology upon a neoliberal anthropology of liberty. It all boils down to a choice of the right mind. This assumes, of course, it is possible to have a right mind with which to make such a choice. Schneider gives little attention to what goes into forming the mind in capitalism. Nevertheless, he maintains that even the wrong choice cannot overcome the right mind in which the cosmic good of affluence resides. Sin can neither overcome nor contain the integrity of the good forces of God's cosmos. Thus, Schneider can say with sincerity, "Greater is he who is in us, we may paraphrase, than he who is in the world."[342] Even in the evil city of Cain (i.e., the bad aspects of capitalism) the human mind that produces the "good things" of human ingenuity and

338. Ibid.

339. Novak, *Spirit*, 326.

340. Schneider, *Good of Affluence*, 63.

341. Ibid.

342. Ibid.; cf. 1 Jn 4:4.

innovation is the power "in us" that is greater than the power that is in the world through the mind of the serpent.

In Schneider's view, then, the cosmic good of affluence is "in us" (i.e., all humanity) just as it was in the city of Cain. It cannot stop from erupting forth from the fallen cosmos with transformational power. What in the New Testament is "Christ in us," the mysterious "riches of . . . the hope of glory" in the redeemed (Col 1:27), now becomes in Schneider's theology the cosmic good of affluence embedded in the human mind, or spirit, and manifested in capitalist economic sociality.[343] It is realized through the flourishing of capitalism and cultivated through twin habits of acquisition and enjoyment, rather than self-denial, cross-bearing and following Jesus (Mk 8:34). Schneider argues that the goodness of this cosmology is confirmed in God's grace toward Noah, from whom the Genesis narrative graciously reminds us we all descend. Although Genesis 8:21 tells us that from youth the human heart is the font of evil inclinations, God affirms humans as royal image bearers of servant-dominion and delight. It is a good thing, even though the world is still filled with serpent dominion. It discloses God "as resolved as he can be to have a world in which human beings do not merely survive, but flourish in true *shalom* and, therefore, in material delight."[344] The Genesis narratives are not only "narratives of divine rescue, but of cosmic redemption, and material affluence is a part of redemption."[345]

In this manner, Schneider establishes the cosmic good of affluence in Genesis and carries it forward through the rest of Scripture. This, he believes, "is the best explanation we have for the central role the narratives *ever after* give to wealth as the incarnation of God's promise and blessing."[346] It is clear that "ever after" means all biblical narratives, including the Gospels and the rest of the New Testament. The challenge is gaining a true understanding of "what this truth" about the good of affluence means in the Gospels "and what affluence . . . means for the Christian faith."[347] Sin is certainly real and thus the dangers of affluence are real because the mind of the serpent pervades the cosmos. But the

343. Cf. Novak, *Spirit*, 103: "The cause of wealth lies more in the human spirit than in matter."

344. Schneider, *Good of Affluence*, 64.

345. Ibid.

346. Ibid. (emphasis added).

347. Ibid.

cosmic good of affluence cannot be restrained, erupting from sinful socio-cultural contexts in the form of technological consumer capitalism to transform and liberate because the God of creation has made it so. The "cosmic good of affluence" is Schneider's hermeneutical strategy throughout *The Good of Affluence*. Cosmology dominates all other doctrines in its moral theology of affluence.

Although Jesus stepped into the world and redeemed it,[348] instantiating the original Edenic intention of the cosmic good of affluence, he leaves it up to those who trade their pounds to realize that good for humanity. Jesus calls the affluent and poor alike to go about the work of affluence "with royal pride and dignity," and he calls the affluent to be liberators of the poor within their sphere of "moral proximity."[349] It is the *quality* of this kind of servant-dominion and delight not the *quantity* that constitutes the "essence of life" Jesus will one day reward.[350] What must be preserved, though, is the freedom to choose. The important choice that must be made is to obey the call to invest and multiply capital "pounds" for the purpose of advancing the kingdom of God on earth as it is in heaven. The call to discipleship in Schneider therefore becomes a call to multiply capital and enjoy affluence. Lost, it seems, are the sinful dimensions and consequences of affluence in a fallen world that longs for its redemption when the creation will realize its "eager longing for the revealing of the children of God" (Rom 8:19–23). It appears that Schneider believes the labor pains of sin can be overcome by capitalism.

According to Long, the problem that occurs in this neoliberal theological conception of freedom "is that other more substantive theological themes such as Christology and ecclesiology are subordinated to this overarching *analogia libertatis*."[351] Novak, followed by Schneider, locates "Christ in a secular universal morality . . . best exemplified in the American Revolution."[352] Thus, according to Long, "We discover Novak's Christological center in his explication of the revolutionary lessons taught

---

348. Schneider ignores the fact that Jesus became poor (spiritually and materially) through self-dispossession and death.

349. Schneider, *Good of Affluence*, 192.

350. Ibid.

351. Long, *Divine Economy*, 44.

352. Ibid.

by Jesus and embodied in America."[353] The bottom line, Long contends, is that Jesus is not the center of Novak's theological economics.

It is precisely at this point of Long's critique where evangelicals should stop and take notice. Evangelicals claim that Jesus and the gospel are the center of their theology and practice, the sun in the solar system of life. In common evangelicalese, Jesus is Lord over all or not Lord at all. But if they follow a theological economics like Novak's and Schneider's, with its warm embrace of capitalism, then they are effectively carving out a space in life outside his lordship. The economic realm escapes Jesus as Lord of all, since he simply came as the Lord of delight in the cosmic good of affluence which we now see after twenty centuries of enlightenment as best instantiated by technological consumer capitalism.

Long shows that Novak subordinates the doctrine of Christ "to a doctrine of creation, in which creation is identified as rightly ordered without any Christological knowledge. . . . creation is prior to Christology."[354] Jesus is breathtakingly absent from Novak's theology of economics and, by implication, Schneider's theology of affluence as well, notwithstanding the fact that Jesus is presented consistently as the "Lord of delight" in *The Good of Affluence*. Long, in my view, criticizes Novak in a very evangelical manner: "Jesus does not bring the Kingdom: it is already here in every culture through creation and mediated by an *analogia libertatis*. We do not learn anything from Jesus about economics that cannot be learned from nature and found in a number of diverse cultures. . . . Jesus does not bring a new creation. He reveals only the structures within which we must work, a structure marred by tragic irony as well as by creation's latent possibilities."[355]

In other words, Jesus has redeemed simply the possibility of original co-creation that God intended from the beginning. Those who enlarge God's dominion through wealth creation prove they have been redeemed.[356] This opens the door to a new understanding of ecclesiology

353. Ibid., 45.

354. Ibid., 47.

355. Ibid. Long certainly overstates his case here. Novak has made it clear that, "Capitalism does not even come close to being the Kingdom of God." Novak, *Catholic Ethic*, 227. Nevertheless, he makes a good point. Novak's theological economics opens the door to a dominant anthropology of liberty that is contrary to the Bible and evangelical faith.

356. Echoes of Weber's seminal sociological critique of Calvinism in *Protestant*

that encompasses not just the church but also the institutions of democratic capitalism. These institutions, including the church, are composed most importantly of individuals who are truly free. Embracing an anthropology of liberty, the historical and visible church reduces simply to one of the institutions of democratic capitalism. Long makes the salient point that Novak "does not find troubling the American claim on the ecclesiological statement of *e pluribus unum*."[357] He shows from Novak's writings how he utilizes the anthropology of liberty to subvert ecclesiological orthodoxy into a heretical "nonhistorical orthodoxy" which fails to make theology relevant to the historical realities of modernity.[358]

Novak argued that the Roman Catholic Church moved much too slowly in recognizing the central importance of the anthropology of liberty and in fact resisted it at various times in its history. In time, as Novak sees things, the Roman Catholic Church came around. However, it seems that American Evangelicalism embraced the centrality of the neoliberal doctrine of freedom without really knowing either that it has or why it has. Much less are American Evangelicals critically aware of the implications and consequences of such an embrace. Thus, American Evangelicals like Schneider can wholeheartedly affirm Novak when he writes in his *Confessions of a Catholic*[359] that "each of us discovering our uniqueness, we are also called to improvise and to invent, to use our liberty to its fullest to find unexpected resources in ourselves, not to hide insecurities and to bury our talents safely, but to be a new voice, in this way imitating the Creator."[360] As we have seen, Schneider's interpretation of Luke's Parable of the Pounds clearly echoes this fundamental tenet of Novak's theological economics. Schneider is thus responsible for importing Novak's anthropology of liberty, with its subordination of Christology

---

Ethic can be heard here. For an assessment of Weber's critical place in the history of economic sociology, see Trigilia, "Capitalism and the Western Civilization: Max Weber," in *Economic Sociology*, 54–75.

357. Long, *Divine Economy*, 49.

358. Ibid. Long is referring to Novak's 1962 work titled *The Open Church: Vatican II, Act II, A Brilliant Report of the Struggle to Open the Church to the Modern World*.

359. As odd as this may sound to evangelical ears, it is nevertheless true that substantial agreement exists between the theological economics of American Evangelicals and Catholics. Long has made this clear in his critique of the "dominant tradition" of Christian economics.

360. Long, *Divine Economy*, 49, quoting from Novak, *Confessions*, 55.

and ecclesiology, into the heart of American-Evangelical theology in *The Good of Affluence.*

According to Novak, it is heretical for the church to embrace a theology of economics that fails to uphold a neoliberal conception of liberty. The anthropology of liberty is determinative of what is orthodox and what is heretical. "Orthodoxy and heresy" in Novak, Long notes, "now function as modalities related to the need for human beings to express a creative liberty within the limitations of the political orders in which they express this liberty."[361] They no longer have any vital relation to Christ. Whether a belief or practice is orthodox or heretical depends upon whether it transgresses the neoliberal doctrine of human freedom with its analogy to divine freedom. The result is that the church is subordinated to "the market and . . . a formal liberty as the decisive site of God's action in the world, independent of any ecclesial presence."[362]

Novak claims that the United States serves as the best example of the political order in which the ideal of liberty has been realized. America is a paradigm of new creation and serves to illustrate the doctrine of creation through which he interprets the doctrines of Christ and the church. Compared to communism this claim is no doubt true. Those persecuted Polish Christians who read and were sustained by Novak's *Spirit of Democratic Capitalism* certainly would agree. As Long correctly recognizes, however, Novak fails to "develop the central ecclesiological insight that Jesus' gathering of the twelve and the institution of the church is the restoration of Israel and the establishment of a new creation that is primarily signified and embodied in the historical church."[363] In Novak's theology of economics, democratic capitalism best preserves the unity and universality of Jesus' teachings, not the church.

Like Novak, Schneider holds to a doctrine of creation to which other key theological doctrines are subordinated. Both Novak's theology of economics and Schneider's theology of affluence fit "comfortably with the dominance of global capitalism and the culture that makes it possible and is produced by it."[364] Schneider follows Novak: democratic capitalism is

---

361. Long, *Divine Economy*, 49.

362. Ibid.

363. Ibid., 49 (endnote 29 omitted). Long cites Lohfink, *Jesus and Community*; Hays, *Moral Vision*, 20–27; and Wright, *New Testament and People of God.*

364. Long, *Divine Economy*, 10.

the system that comes closest to satisfying the biblical ideal of liberty and human flourishing.

Schneider fails to appreciate, however, the manner in which that system enmeshes twenty-first century evangelicals seeking to live faithfully to Jesus and the gospel (Mk 8:35) in a web of contradictions. The three interrelated and interdependent cultural aspects of democratic capitalism guarantee it: "a predominantly market economy; a polity respectful of the rights of the individual to life, liberty and the pursuit of happiness; and a system of cultural institutions moved by ideals of liberty and justice for all. In short, three dynamic and converging systems functioning as one: a democratic polity, and economy based on markets and incentives, and a moral-cultural system which is pluralistic and, in the largest sense, liberal."[365]

This is not "just a system but a way of life. Its *ethos* includes a special evolution of pluralism; respect for contingency and unintended consequences; a sense of sin; and a new and distinctive conception of community, the individual, and the family."[366] Evangelicals must critically contest theological claims that this "way of life" equates to the truth, way and life of Jesus Christ. Novak sees a univocal relationship between the liberty of democratic capitalism and Christian theology. In other words, he views the doctrine of creation of humanity as *imago Dei* as disclosing the anthropology of liberty upon which democratic capitalism rests. This anthropological conception grounds the moral-cultural ethos found both in the Bible and in the systems of democratic capitalism. Schneider likewise embraces these anthropological-theological presuppositions.

The question that arises is whether these presuppositions are adequate for a contemporary theological anthropology of the AAEC. Nurtured in Schneider's theological ethics of affluence, the AAEC interpretively reproduces the social and cultural artifacts of technological consumer capitalism and its institutions with no critical awareness of the one thing still lacking. As a result, a false freedom can be formed in the AAEC. The freedom to choose is the ultimate good, not the freedom to obey Jesus when he calls, which may require renunciation of the attachments of affluence and repentance that proves the reality of such renunciation. Upon

---

365. Novak, *Spirit*, 14. Novak's belief in the neoliberal gospel of liberty embodied in democratic capitalism has remained strong, as evidenced by his recent *Universal Hunger for Liberty*.

366. Novak, *Spirit*, 29 (emphasis in original).

maturation, the AAEC soon realizes that there is a tension between this conception of freedom and that set out by Jesus in the Gospels.

Consequently, the AAEC is free to create and consume affluence and also free to interpret and reproduce peer cultures of Evangelical affluence in the United States. But the AAEC may not be truly free to follow Christ because one thing is still lacking. Schneider's theology of affluence provides, in my view, evangelicals with ill-advised moral-theological grounds upon which to base evangelical nurture. With all due respect for Schneider the evangelical-Reformed theologian and the many good things Schneider says in *The Good of Affluence*, it seems to me that the moral theology of affluence presented there risks (mal)formation of spiritual-moral lack in children raised by American-Evangelical parents and churches. Following Novak, Schneider establishes his theology on a neoliberal anthropology of liberty that privileges the doctrine of creation over Christology, ecclesiology and soteriology. But Schneider goes even further than Novak. He equates the gospel with the cosmic good of affluence in humanity rather than with the good news that in Christ and the church God has brought about a new creation in which all who believe and obey participate irrespective of affluence.

Schneider arrives at this quite un-evangelical end in his theology of affluence because he fails to assess critically the culture of capitalism in which he and millions of other evangelicals are formed. On Schneider's account, the "new" culture of capitalism ultimately is good for evangelicals and, hence, for the AAEC. His interpretation of that culture in chapter 1 of *The Good of Affluence* is, however, highly suspect. This will be demonstrated in the final section of this chapter below, where the Radical Orthodoxy critique of capitalism developed by Daniel M. Bell, Jr., will be utilized to expose fatal deficiencies in Schneider's assessment of capitalism.

The AAEC in the "infinite undulations of the snake"[367]

According to J. K. A. Smith, Bell's "brilliant analysis" of late modern capitalism's relationship to human desire warrants serious attention.[368] A close reading of Bell's *Liberation Theology After the End of History* con-

367. Bell, "The infinite undulations of the snake: capitalism, desire, and the state-form," in *Liberation Theology*, 9–41.

368. Smith, *Introducing Radical Orthodoxy*, 247.

firms Smith's opinion and highlights further deficiencies in Schneider's theology of affluence, which overlooks Bell's work.[369]

Bell provocatively describes capitalism as a sinful socio-cultural formation with serpentine qualities that undulate infinitely in late modernity, taking human desire and sociality captive to its ends: "It is a form of sin, a way of life that captures and distorts human desire in accord with the golden rule of production for the market."[370] Bell's conception of capitalism as "a way of life" is thus diametrically opposed to that of Novak and Schneider. Furthermore, whereas Schneider sees the "mind of the serpent" only shaping and directing capitalist power in the world today within a providential cosmic good of affluence, Bell views the serpent as in total control.

Smith notes two significant contributions Bell makes to Radical Orthodoxy's overall project. The first is to its critical recovery of "the Augustinian vision of the creature as a desiring agent."[371] The second is to its relentless critiques of capitalism. Both contributions are helpful to the task of constructing an evangelical theology of the AAEC. The focus Bell places on desire as it is formed in a virulent capitalist context like the United States highlights an important dimension of theological anthropology that evangelical theologians and educators like Schneider tend to overlook.

Smith points out that Bell refines the Yoderian-Hauerwasian line of critique that sees the state as "the looming idol . . . the church is most tempted to worship."[372] Bell argues that free market capitalism is the new empire that contests Christ and the church, "a global transnational phenomenon—an empire of which states are only colonies."[373] The economic dimension of human being in the world is absolutized in this new empire, such that "every mode of life becomes construed in terms of the

---

369. Schneider may not have had access to Bell's *Liberation Theology* (2001) prior to submitting the manuscript for *Good of Affluence* (2002). However, it is difficult to understand Schneider's failure to engage Bell's journal articles pertinent to his theology of affluence. See, e.g., Bell, Jr., "After the End of History" and "Men of Stone."

370. Bell, *Liberation Theology*, 2 (endnotes 5 and 6 omitted).

371. Smith, *Introducing Radical Orthodoxy*, 243.

372. Bell, *Liberation Theology*, 248.

373. Ibid.

economic."[374] The church is incorporated into the empire simply as one of its constituent institutions.

Bell argues that late modern capitalism is a complex of cultural, social, political and economic formations infected with sin. He is in essential agreement with Novak at this point. Unlike Novak, however, Bell describes "capitalism as a form of madness" and agrees with Franz Hinkelammert that it is "wild" and "savage."[375] Furthermore, he goes on to argue that it is a totalizing formation that claims authority over every person, thing and religion, Christianity included. It does this through its "successful capture and discipline of the constitutive human power, desire."[376] Capitalism has achieved its victory not just in the economic and cultural realms but, more importantly, in the ontological. Penetrating deeper than economics, capitalism has triumphed not through capturing "modes of production, the efficient manipulation of labor, and the creation of wealth" but by capturing human desire.[377] Thus, the real competition and war in late modernity is for the human heart. This is the essence of the late modern contest between Capitalism versus Christianity. Neoliberal democratic capitalism and Christianity are in a Fukuyaman war to see which one will satisfy "humanity's most basic human longings."[378]

Bell sees economics as the discipline that drives the capitalist machine and forces every institution of late modernity into its framework. He argues that

> Neoliberal government aggressively encourages and advocates the extension of economic reason into every fiber and cell of human life. Economic or market rationale controls all conduct. Capitalism has enveloped society, absorbing all the conditions of production and reproduction. It is as if the walls of the factory had come crumbling down and the logics that previously functioned in that enclosure had been generalized across the entire space-time continuum.[379]

374. Ibid., 249.
375. Ibid., 3, 10.
376. Ibid., 13.
377. Ibid., 12–13.
378. Ibid., 1, quoting Fukuyama, "Reflections on The End of History," 241.
379. Ibid., 31.

Bell's thesis is that "the conflict between capitalism and Christianity is nothing less than a clash of opposing technologies of desire."[380] He relies upon the "history of desire and capitalism" of Gilles Deleuze to discover that capitalism is a "discipline of desire and that . . . the state is not an emancipatory agent but a repressive instrument of the capitalist order."[381] He supplements Deleuze with the "work on governmentality" developed by Michael Foucault in order to establish that the "state-form" of capitalism administers a host of "technologies of the self" by which it governs "capitalist dominion."[382] There are "four technologies of power" the state utilizes to this end which are particularly insidious in their operation upon human desire.[383] Bell's goal is to present a Radical Orthodoxy version of Christianity as an alternative to these technologies that is sufficient to liberate human desire from the economic discipline of capitalism. He aims to present a "strange" kind of Christian "therapy" for human desire, one "that resists capitalist incorporation, breaks the cycle of violence, and wards off the temptation to acquire."[384]

Conflating Michel Foucault's theory of "governmentality" based on technologies of the self and power with Deleuze's ontology of desire,[385] Bell conceives of capitalism as "an ensemble of technologies of desire that exercises dominion over humanity and disciplines desire through" the state-form of technologically advanced governments.[386] The "small-state, strong-state" matrix of savage capitalist governmentality has emerged as the servant of the global capitalist empire, the head of which is the United States.[387] Relying upon Foucault, Bell analyzes the "pastoral" power of capitalism's governmentality.[388] He traces the genealogy of Foucault's account of governmentality from the Hebrew concept of a king or deity shepherding the people he owns to the Christian appropriation of the

---

380. Ibid., 2.

381. Ibid., 12, 19.

382. Ibid., 19. Bell uses "technologies of the self" interchangeably with "technologies of desire." Ibid., 3, 7, 19, 21. This is consistent with the conception of the human being as constituted by desire or as a desiring self.

383. Ibid., 21.

384. Ibid., 130.

385. Ibid., 9–41; 40, n. 98.

386. Ibid., 144.

387. Ibid., 11, 19, 35 n. 6.

388. Ibid., 21–32.

concept, which incorporated Greco-Roman ideas of self-examination and confession ("care of the self") and intensified the process through the practices of confession and penance.[389] These developed over time into obedience and the concomitant renunciation and sacrifice of the self on behalf of one's sovereign master. With the advent of the modern state in the fifteenth and sixteenth centuries, the "reason of state" and "science of police" doctrines arose as the "individualizing pastoral power" of Christianity and the "totalizing power of the state" coalesced.[390]

The sustaining rationale for the "reason of state" doctrine was the fact that the state exists and, presumably, should continue to exist. The controlling concern of any state is how to strengthen and perpetuate its function and service, which the ministers of state learned was inextricably tied to the strength and prosperity (whether real or perceived) of its subjects. Consequently, the doctrine and practice of police science developed in seventeenth century Europe in order to serve the state. As Bell puts it,

> In essence, police science included everything—all persons and things—that provided the state with resilience and splendor. . . . The science of police was about . . . forming the social body, shaping the newly conceived "population" into an efficient and productive body. The extent of the regulation they proposed to accomplish this feat went far beyond anything that had previously been enacted. . . . In sum, police science underwrites political governance by the extension of an individualizing, pastoral power.[391]

Bell adds that the "police science of reason of state" that emerged during this period and has developed since entails "the convergence of technologies of domination (the disciplines) with technologies of the self (sciences of population), with the result that the modern art of government, governmentality, was born."[392]

Thus, the advanced governmentality of late modern capitalism has its roots in the early modern period. The seeds giving rise to these roots are spawned from human desire. Governmentality can be viewed as a development within Christendom that, until the twentieth century, received very little critical assessment. Bell's analysis illumines how the stage was

389. Ibid., 21–22.

390. Ibid., 23.

391. Ibid., 25.

392. Ibid., 26 (chapter endnote 69 omitted). Echoes of Milbank's critique of secular reason and modern social theory are evident here in Bell's artful prose.

set for capitalism's eventual triumph and dominance in the second half of the twentieth century.

In addition to governmentality, other varieties of capitalist rhetoric emerged to recodify American behavior under capitalism. One example is advertising, which may be seen as the poetic expression of economic discipline in late modernity. Cultural historian Jackson Lears traces the genealogy of advertising in "Anglo-American Protestant culture" over the past two hundred years, concluding that "as rhetorical constructions, advertisements did more than stir up desire; they also sought to manage it—to stabilize the sorcery of the marketplace by containing dreams of personal transformation within a broader rhetoric of control."[393] For instance, in a 1926 speech to the American Association of Advertising Agencies, then President Calvin Coolidge exhorted his listeners by arguing that advertising "*ministers* to the spiritual side of trade. It is a great power that has been entrusted to your keeping which charges you with the high responsibility of inspiring and ennobling the commercial world. It is all part of *the greater work* of the regeneration and redemption of mankind."[394] Advertising thus helps to shepherd human desire in the emerging capitalist empire. It paints pictures of paths into peace and plenty, making disingenuous promises to restore the soul.

This points to a dimension of human being in the world that is deeper than economics. Bell utilizes Deleuze to argue that "the victory of savage capitalism is not simply economic; it is, more insidiously, ontological."[395] He shows how Deleuze relied upon Duns Scotus for "an ontology of difference anchored in the univocity of being. . . . God is deemed 'to be' in the same univocal manner as creatures."[396] Because humans are desiring beings, it follows that God is a desiring being. The difference lies in the objects and the degrees of intensity of human desire. For Deleuze, desire is productive—giving, working, creating. It is not negation, lack, privation or deficiency. Nor is it absence, acquiring or grasping. Desire is productive, "a positive force, an aleatory movement that neither destroys nor consumes but endlessly creates new connections with others, embraces differences, and fosters a proliferation of relations between fluxes

393. Lears, *Fables of Abundance*, 10.

394. Twitchell, "The Language of Things: Advertising and the Rhetoric of Salvation," in *Lead Us Into Temptation*, 50 (emphasis added).

395. Bell, *Liberation Theology*, 9.

396. Ibid., 13 (chapter endnotes 23 and 24 omitted).

of desire."[397] Human desire, then, is malleable, changing, always in flux. It resists restraint and management, always seeking new ways to exploit the various social, economic and cultural formations that confront it. This is why, according to Bell, Foucault's theory of governmentality is essential. Human desire must be disciplined. Or to put it in classical economic terms, human self-interest must be stimulated and regulated for the common good. Governmentality evolved with advances in human knowledge as the framework for disciplining human desire and managing societal best interests.

According to Bell, Deleuze views the history of capitalism and desire as the historical evolution and mutation of three different state-forms: ancient regal states practicing overcoding or enslavement of "lineal-territorialized" human desire; diverse states practicing increasingly deterritorialized regulation, coordination and integration of desire; and diverse states overwhelmed by capital flows associated with progressive deterritorializion of desire.[398] Such is the nature of savage capitalism. It amplifies, leverages and distorts human desire to the extent that it overwhelms the state and converts it into its servant. This is the final mutation of the state-form in human history, which corresponds to Fukuyama's point about the prospect of history's end being realized in liberal democratic capitalism. For Bell, that such an end would come through capitalism is anathema: "The capitalist machine deterritorializes desire: it overruns all previous social formations and releases the flows of desire that these formations had organized and regulated. The capitalist machine also reterritorializes desire: it subjects desire to the axiomatic of production for the market. In this process capitalism relies on the state-form to prepare desire for participation."[399]

Bell argues from Deleuze that humanity is a complex mass of ever-expanding and producing desire that seeks continually to break out of any restraints. Capitalism is the field in which desire is cultivated, harvested and replanted on the fecund landscape of human self-interest and sociality. In advanced capitalism, the "economy escapes the state. Not only does it escape the state, but it returns to capture its former master. Now the state finds itself immersed in a field that it had previously sought to contain and

---

397. Ibid., 14.
398. Ibid., 15–17.
399. Ibid., 19.

control."[400] Following Deleuze, Bell argues that all "states serve capitalism. The capitalist axiomatic is like a megapolis of which all the nations constitute neighborhoods. And these neighborhoods need not look alike. As an international ecumenical organization, capitalism neither proceeds from an imperial center that imposes itself on and homogenizes an exterior nor is it reducible to a relation between similar formations."[401]

Bell develops a Christian therapy for healing and liberating desire from capitalist captivity through interaction with Bernard of Clairvaux and the Cistercian monks. Bernard's teachings and practices represent a "counter-ensemble" of Christian technologies of desire. It is a brilliant retrieval of Bernard, one from which the AAEC can no doubt benefit. Bell makes the bold claim that in his retrieval of Bernard and the Cistercians, "Christianity is reclaimed as a therapy of desire that may be capable of both liberating desire from its capitalist captivity and enabling it once again to flow freely as it was created to do."[402] This is possible because, "Christianity is, no less than capitalism, an ensemble of technologies that shapes and forms desire. As an ensemble of knowledges [sic], systems of judgment, persons, institutions, and practices, Christianity governs desire; through a host of technologies such as liturgy, catechesis, orders, and discipleship, Christianity exerts an ontological influence on humanity."[403] Consistent with the agenda and totalizing tendency of Radical Orthodoxy, Bell posits Christianity as "a fully social, political, economic reality" that can defeat capitalism at its own game.[404] The imprint and echoes of Milbank's and Long's visions of a "socialism by grace" can be discerned clearly here.

But did Bernard and the Cistercians themselves manage to free desire from all economic encroachments, as Bell seems to claim? Can we discern perhaps a bit of naïve nostalgia in the reading of Bernard and the Cistercians proffered by Bell? The otherwise brilliant retrieval of Bernard and the Cistercians Bell presents is marred by at least two defects. First, Bell fails to acknowledge that the Cistercians have been shown to be premodern capitalists who created, innovated and litigated to protect

400. Ibid., 27.

401. Ibid., 17–18 (endnote 44 omitted).

402. Ibid., 4. Bell develops these claims at 88–96 and anticipates objections at 96–99.

403. Ibid., 4.

404. Ibid., 87.

their inventions. They engaged in some of the capitalist technologies and entrepreneurial activities Bell and other Radical Orthodoxy theologians vehemently disdain.[405] Thus, rather than the virtuous premodern anti-capitalists Bell seeks to portray, at least some of the Cistercians appear to have been more like the aggressive, competitive, war-like capitalists of late modernity that Schneider affirms and Radical Orthodoxy theologians condemn.

Bell apparently missed some literary evidence that bears negatively on his idyllic view of the Cistercians. William Baumol has recently noted:

> The Cistercians were fierce in their rivalrous behavior and drive for expansion, in the process not sparing other religious bodies—not even other Cistercian houses. There is a record of "pastoral expansionism and monopolies over access established by the wealthiest Cistercian houses . . . at the expense of smaller abbeys and convents . . . effectively pushing out all other religious houses as competitors."[406]

Bell might be tempted to respond that this behavior of some Cistercians is evidence of what he seeks to prove: capitalism "is a form of sin." Yet Baumol's evidence shows quite clearly that capitalist habits existed even among the Cistercians, while Bell's argument seems to be that the Cistercians were free from this form of sin and therefore offer a kind of pristine premodern counter-technology for the therapy of Christian desire taken captive within late modern capitalism. Bell's neglect of literary evidence contrary to his representations of Bernard and the Cistercians weakens his constructive proposal for contesting the hegemony of late modern capitalism.

The second defect in Bell's critique is that he fails to address evidence that weighs against his thesis that capitalism reduces to nothing more than a form of sin. Bell is unequivocal on this point:

---

405. Landes, *Wealth and Poverty of Nations*, 58; Baumol, *Free-Market...Growth Miracle*, x, 259–61. Baumol discloses literary evidence of the premodern capitalistic and entrepreneurial activities of the Cistercians. Ibid., 260. Radical Orthodoxy scholars have not, to my knowledge, evidenced any critical awareness of this literature.

406. "Historians tell us that they have no ready explanation for the entrepreneurial propensities of this monastic order." Baumol, *Free-Market . . . Growth Miracle*, 260, citing Berman, *Medieval Agriculture . . . and the Early Cistercians*, 112.

> Capitalism is sin because it fractures the friendship of humanity with God. It disrupts the original, peaceable flow of desire that is charity; it ruptures the sociality of desire, which by nature seeks out new relations in joyous conviviality that is love. Capitalism is sin because it harnesses the productive power of desire in its original mode, which is donation or giving to the market. In so doing it corrupts it, rendering it proprietary.[407]

It is true that late modern technological consumer capitalism poses serious threats in each of these areas. In addition, Bell is certainly correct to warn of the spiritual and moral dangers posed by capitalism. But capitalism is not all sin, neither in its ontology nor its economics. Many good things and good deeds flow from both capitalism and capitalists. Billions of dollars of charity flow from capitalists and the capitalist system each year. Hunger has been eliminated and life expectancy has increased dramatically in the West over the past 300 years because of capitalism and the capitalists who have helped bring it about. Staggering scientific and technological advances have been made possible by capitalism, just as capitalism has been made possible by scientific and technological advances. Even scholarship such as Bell's, it could be argued, is made possible by capitalism. Many other positive aspects of capitalism could be named as well.

While Bell was researching and writing his doctoral thesis at Duke under the supervision of Stanley Hauerwas, the body of literary evidence identified by Baumol was extant and thus pointed to such liberating, non-sinful aspects of capitalism. Not only this, Bell also ignores readily available evidence indicating that global capitalism has at least some correlation to the reduction in world poverty rates (e.g., from 1980 to 2000, there was a 41% decrease in world poverty due primarily to the advances of free market capitalist economies in China and India). The tendency to ignore such evidence and to dismiss relevant literature on capitalism without critically engaging it is a glaring scholarly shortcoming exhibited by Bell, other Radical Orthodoxy theologians, and resurgent neo-Marxist theologians.

These criticisms notwithstanding, Bell's critique of capitalism and desire is an invaluable resource in constructing a critical-theological anthropology of the AAEC. Not only does it demonstrate the glaring deficiency in Schneider's approbation of capitalist culture in his theology

---

407. Bell, *Liberation Theology*, 151.

of affluence, it also illumines the formative-cultural processes at work in bringing about the one thing that is lacking in the AAEC. Nurtured in the matrices of late modern Evangelical affluence in the United States, the AAEC's desires and sociality are captured and formed for capitalist culture, harnessed to the ends of the market.

Thus, Bell's analysis helps further illumine how nurture in the socio-cultural matrices of such affluence impedes spiritual and moral formation of the AAEC for discipleship in the way of the cross. It illumines how nurture in such a context risks disciplinary formation of the AAEC for capitalist culture and can cultivate the delusional belief that life consists in an abundance of possessions. Bell demonstrates how two decades of formation in capitalist culture can hinder the practice of evangelical liberation of the poor on humanity's underside. Formed by and formative of affluence, the AAEC walks away from Jesus lacking spiritually in relation to God and morally in relation to neighbors, particularly those who are poor, oppressed, destitute and without hope.

CONCLUSION

Evangelicals seeking God in a culture of wealth pursuant to a theology like Schneider's have little reasonable hope of escaping the cultural realities of capitalism that Bell exposes. Formed by the beliefs and practices of that theology, evangelicals will lack critical faculties to discern their socio-cultural context, to see themselves in historical context and thus to see where they are going in late modernity. Because they are led to affirm capitalist culture uncritically by that theology, they think they are doing God's good and pleasing will in serving the ends of the market. They are led to believe that the ends of the market ultimately serve the ends of the gospel.

But evangelicals do not realize that such thinking and practice conforms them to the world rather than transforms them in the renewing of their minds. At the heart of this problem lies a faulty conception of liberty. It is an idolatrous conception that leads evangelicals to believe the freedom Christ accomplished through the gospel is simply a freedom of choice rather than a freedom to obey the call to discipleship. Long's critique of Novak makes this abundantly clear. Christ does not set believers free for freedom's sake but for his sake and the sake of following him in self-denial and cross-bearing (Mark 8:34–35, 10:29).

This is what the story of rich young man shows us. Evangelical freedom is the freedom to obey, not the freedom to choose. The rich young man was not truly free because he could not obey. He could not obey because of his attachments to affluence. His relational network of affluence was his undoing because he could not detach from it. Whether relations to family or friends, to power or prestige, or simply to the many goods affluence affords, the call to follow Jesus is a call to sever all attachments that impede obedience to discipleship in the way of the cross. Unable to hear the call of Jesus and thus unable to see or enter the kingdom that has come, the affluent walk away because their affluence cements their lack and secures their fears. Detached from life-giving, truly free relations to God and others in the way of the cross, the affluent remain attached to their affluence lacking that one thing that really matters: a right spiritual relationship with God in Christ which expresses itself in right moral relationships with others. Evangelical formation of the AAEC must counter the neoliberal conception of freedom that lies at the heart of this spiritual-moral lack. If the AAEC is going to find an answer to what is lacking in affluence, evangelical parents and churches must identify and destroy the idol of liberty that the neoliberal conception of freedom commends for worship in late modernity.

6

Conclusion: Whither the AAEC?

The preceding chapters give rise to the question of what path the AAEC will take in the twenty-first century. The global hegemony of technological consumer capitalism and resultant expansion of affluence should give American Evangelicals, and all evangelical believers, cause for concern and force them to wonder about the future prospects of the AAEC.

This conclusion explores the vulnerable situation of the AAEC in two parts. First, the findings of the preceding chapters will be summarized and drawn together as a whole. Second, areas of further research will be presented with a view to mapping potentially promising programs of future study.

SUMMARY AND SYNTHESIS

The introduction surveyed the theological literature on American Evangelicalism and affluence with a view to situating the child within those contexts. Noting the relatively sparse and recent attention paid to the child in theological and social scientific literature, focus turned specifically to locating the child in relation to the problem of Evangelical affluence in the United States. The conclusion reached was that within American Evangelicalism critical-theological reflection of this kind either does not exist or is extremely rare. As a result, I proposed the neologism of the AAEC as a subject for study in the construction of a theological anthropology of the child in late modern Evangelical affluence in the United States.

Late modern American-Evangelical affluence indicates several contours of the historical, cultural, social and economic perspectives presented in this work. First, it signals the fact that the goal here has not been to present a "postmodern" theological anthropology of the AAEC through engagement with "postmodern theory" of some philosophical or cultural sort. Instead, "late modernity" points particularly to the social changes that began to take place in the United States after World War II as a result of technological consumer capitalism's growth and eventual, so-called "triumph" in 1989.[1] Thus, late modernity is essentially equivalent to "postmodernity" insofar as the latter term signals a focus on the social changes arising from the exhaustion of modernity or, perhaps better, modernity's accelerated technological evolution in the past several decades. Thus the focus has been on the AAEC embedded in the new kind of capitalist society that has emerged in the United States over the past fifty years.

Late modernity also signals the particular relationship this work has to the modern period covered in the thesis, which ranges from Jonathan Edwards in the eighteenth century through Horace Bushnell in the nineteenth to Lawrence Richards in the twentieth (chapters 2 and 3). The goal has been to discern and critique formative theological anthropologies of the child found in the writings of these representative American-Evangelical theologians. Those theologies were then set in relation to the emergence of industrial capitalism in the nineteenth century and its transformation into technological consumer capitalism from the 1920s through the end of the century, during which time the AAEC began to emerge in the 1950s as mass affluence began to be realized for the first time in American history. As was shown, Evangelicals and their institutions played a major role in bringing the nineteenth century dream of mass affluence to reality in the twentieth. It was shown further that they, with the children nurtured by them, continue to play a crucial role in sustaining the culture of Evangelical affluence (chapter 4).

Finally, late modernity has more to do with the synchronic aspects of the culture and society of affluence in which the AAEC is nurtured over the first two decades of life and in which the AAEC becomes embedded once fully formed. These concerns were addressed in chapters 4 and 5. Chapter 4 demonstrated that the AAEC is formed with little, if any, critical awareness of the history or sociology of the context of affluence in the United States. The "interpretive reproduction" model of childhood sociology developed by William Corsaro served to show that the AAEC is

---

1. Fukuyama, "The End of History?"

an active interpreter-reproducer of the relational matrices of American-Evangelical affluence.

Chapters 2 through 4 thus presented a picture of how the AAEC evolved and emerged in late modernity. The conditions of complex differentiation instantiated by the dominance of economics in late modernity determine the trajectory of the AAEC's formation by and for the institutions of liberal democratic capitalism. Thus, the various spheres of the AAEC's social life are coordinated in terms of efficient rationality to ends of effective, rational and productive action. By the age of twenty, the AAEC is a full-fledged member of the consumer society and culture of affluence. This leads, in terms coined by Jürgen Habermas, to the "uncoupling" of the systems of late modernity (i.e., the institutions of neoliberal democratic capitalism) from the AAEC's "lifeworld."[2] The media that coordinate these radically differentiated social systems—money capital[3] and administrative power—are potent tools of capitalist discipline that form the AAEC for the market.

Daniel Bell's Radical Orthodoxy critique of capitalism and desire, analyzed in chapter 5, corroborated these claims. The AAEC is embedded in a context in which these tools of late modern institutions (e.g., economic, political and legal systems) enact themselves in the "way of life" described by Novak as the "spirit" of democratic capitalism. Chapter 5 demonstrated that this way of life can lead to the formation of a spiritual and moral "lack" in the AAEC's relationship to God and others. Like the rich young man in Matthew 19, the AAEC is found lacking when confronted by Jesus in the way of the cross. Evangelical parents and churches are complicit in the formation of this lack by failing to form the capacity for self-denial and cross-bearing that following Jesus requires in the context of affluence (Mark 8:34–35; 10:21–30).

Money capital and administrative power now coordinate individual and social life so efficiently in the United States that the systems of democratic capitalism have begun to operate autonomously. Americans now define themselves in terms of the reified systems of late modern capitalism. The lifeworlds of evangelicals are colonized by these systems such that "privatised hopes for self-actualisation and self-determination are

---

2. Habermas, *Communicative Action II*.

3. In this sense, capital is "money available for investment" which has evolved as the primary form of capital in late modernity. Bernstein, *Birth of Plenty*, 16, 125–60.

primarily located . . . in the roles of consumer and client."[4] This is the practical outworking of both individual and group relationships within the economic, political and legal systems by which capitalist society is administered. These systems effectively dislodge and transform the language and cultural routines of individuals and groups into an interpretive-reproductive framework of language, values, understandings and norms based on the systems. Thus, cultural reproduction, social integration and socialization become saturated with a discourse of roles, futures and functionality, reshaping individual and collective self-understandings, relationships, and practices to the ends of the market.

Such are the cultural and social realities of the "mystery of capital" which Fernando de Soto has empirically discovered, Schneider wholeheartedly affirms, and Bell and others vehemently decry. Chapter 5 explored this "mystery" in critical interaction with Novak and Schneider in light of Stephen Long's *Divine Economy*. Long shows that lying at the heart of the mystery of capital in the United States is a particular construal of the correlation between human freedom and the pursuit of happiness. An anthropology of liberty conceived as the pursuit of happiness grounds democratic capitalism and at the same time subordinates the doctrines of Christ, the church, salvation and the future to a doctrine of creation dominated by a conception of humanity as the *imago Dei* liberated to create and exercise dominion like God. Individual self-interest (pursuit of happiness) is believed to facilitate societal best interests (group pursuit of happiness) when grounded in the liberty of democratic capitalism. The freedom of the human is the freedom of God enacted in human history. In Long's terms, this is "a theology as *analogia libertatis*" in the service of neoliberal democratic capitalism. It is an idolatrous theology.

From the standpoint of theological anthropology, the mystery at work in the intersection of human freedom and the pursuit of happiness is the mystery of sin/lawlessness. But in the neoliberal theology of Novak and Schneider, sin is simply an "unintended consequence" of human-divine freedom that must be overcome by the power of creation enacted in capitalism. Of course Schneider adds that Christ has redeemed all sin, or in other words has accomplished complete and final liberation from sin, but the redemption serves human freedom to co-create with God through the liberating power present in the "new" culture of capitalism.

---

4. Habermas, *Communicative Action II*, 356.

264 THE CHILD IN AMERICAN EVANGELICALISM

Lost on Schneider are insights into deeper dimensions of the mystery of sin in capitalism, the lack inherent in affluence that theologians such as Bonhoeffer, Barth, John Paul II and Grau helped chapter 5 illumine in its interaction with their interpretations of the rich young man.

Unfortunately for the AAEC, theologies like Novak's and Schneider's provide *theological* traction for the mystery of capital to co-opt the mystery of God in Christ and the gospel. They lead the AAEC theologically into a faith and practice that effectively, though unconsciously, attempts to accomplish the simultaneous worship of God and Mammon in the service of capitalism. The mysteries at work in the kingdom of God, Christ and the gospel are effectively shut off from the eyes and ears of faith that gospel-motivated parents and churches hope to nurture in their children. As a result, an impoverishing spiritual-moral vacuum is formed in the AAEC. The path to discovering the presence of God's kingdom in the way of the cross, and thus to experiencing eternal life in the kingdom that has arrived in Jesus, is foreclosed because of the lack affluence brings. In this sense the AAEC is not truly free. Thus, the freedom liberal democratic capitalism offers the AAEC is a false freedom.

The interpretations of John Paul II, Bonhoeffer, and Barth helped the theological anthropology of the AAEC presented here establish that the human liberty Jesus offers is a freedom in truth, a freedom for obedience, a freedom to keep God's commands for good of the neighbor and for the glory of God. An anthropology of liberty that leaves the AAEC in the lack of affluence, unfree to obey, is not an evangelical anthropology of liberty. The essence of a so-called "scandal of the evangelical conscience" in late modernity reveals itself clearly at this point.[5] Evangelicals uncritically accept a neoliberal conception of freedom without realizing its unbiblical nature. Such a conception is contrary to the freedom about which Jesus speaks in the story of the rich young man. Until evangelicals overcome this deficiency in their theological anthropology, an evangelical conscience capable of overcoming the lack affluence brings cannot be cultivated and thus evangelicals will continue living "just like the rest of the world."[6]

It is no surprise, then, that American Evangelicalism produces the AAEC. Since the 1950s the current generation of American-Evangelical

5. Sider, *Scandal of Evangelical Conscience*.
6. Subtitle to Sider, *Scandal of Evangelical Conscience*.

grandparents, parents, children and churches have been formed within the social and cultural matrices of affluence afforded by the systems of neoliberal democratic capitalism. Some, to be sure, such as Mark Noll, Ron Sider and Randy Alcorn,[7] have cultivated evangelical minds and consciences critical of the culture of capitalism in the United States. Some evangelicals might even come to Jesus like the rich young man wondering what they still lack. But the answer Jesus gives compounds incomprehension in affluent Evangelicals, as it did both for the rich young man and for the disciples (Matt 19:22, 25). As my evangelical appropriation of Bell in chapter 5 has shown, capitalism is a form of sin at least to the extent that it captures, disciplines and forms human desire for the ends of the market rather than the ends of evangelical discipleship. Evangelicals, particularly conservatives, find it difficult to see Bell's point. They affirm the systems of democratic capitalism (though tainted with sin) as the best option short of the actual kingdom of God on earth as it is in heaven (which occurs when Jesus returns and does away with sin) because they have been formed within them and enjoy the "blessings" they provide. And even if evangelicals can see into anticapitalist critiques like Bell's or Long's, they are at a loss over what to do. Thus, the recent evangelical debates over capitalism and the good of affluence continue apace with nurture of a spiritual-moral lack (poverty) in the AAEC.

What remedies does a theological anthropology of the AAEC offer? Ultimately, it exposes late modern capitalism not only as a social and cultural phenomenon but also as a pseudo-religion in competition with the God of Israel and Jesus. As Novak consistently argues and Schneider affirms, democratic capitalism is "not just a system but *a way of life.*"[8] A way of life calls for ultimate commitments to be formed in the individuals who make up the society that expresses and sustains them. It harmonizes personal, social and ultimate (i.e., religious and spiritual) concerns. These are all things democratic capitalism seeks to do. It is totalizing, and in the twenty-first century United States it is taking on an increasingly global imperial tense.[9]

Although evangelicals claim that the true "way of life" is found in Jesus and the gospel, the majority of them also agree with Novak and Schneider

---

7. See Noll, *Scandal of Evangelical Mind*; Sider, *Rich Christians*; Alcorn, *Money*.

8. Novak, *Spirit*, 29 (emphasis added).

9. See, e.g., Bacevich, ed., *Imperial Tense*; cf. Hardt and Negri, *Empire*.

that democratic capitalism is a way of life worthy of personal, social and (at least to some extent) ultimate commitments as well. As chapters 2 and 3 demonstrated, this groundwork was laid in American Evangelicalism on the eve of the Civil War in 1861, the same year Bushnell's final edition of *Christian Nurture* was published. Furthermore, as the election in 2004 proved, the vast majority of Evangelicals apparently agree that the democratic-capitalist way of life warrants expansion around the world through the sacrifice of American young people, including their own. They believe with their e/Evangelical president, George W. Bush, "*In the face of grave threats, American power will ensure the ultimate triumph of freedom.*"[10] Long has exposed the political anthropology of liberty at work in this statement as one that subordinates all theological interests to a doctrine of creation in which humanity is free for the sake of freedom itself, not for the sake of Jesus and the gospel. For the AAEC in this vision of life, the choice to serve Jesus and the gospel is just one of several. What matters ultimately in a theology as *analogia libertatis* is that the AAEC is free to choose. Freedom for freedom's sake is the one thing that is truly good. But as the interpretations of the rich young man by Bonhoeffer, Barth and Pope John Paul II help us see, this is not true freedom because it does not truly liberate one to the freedom of discipleship, the freedom for obedience that makes evangelical faith, self-denial and sacrifice possible.[11] To the extent that the neoliberal democratic anthropology of liberty calls for faith and sacrifice, it is a call to believe and die for something other than Jesus and the gospel.

How did American Evangelicals fall into such a trap? How can they hold simultaneously to faith in neoliberal democratic capitalism and Jesus Christ? Once again Bell's critique of the cultural and ontological dimensions of capitalism is helpful. By capturing and distorting human desire to the ends of the market, capitalism subverts Christianity as a rival religion. Capitalism becomes a functional God in competition with the God of Israel and Jesus. It won by capturing the human heart and converting it to a new religion. Without knowing it, the font of evangelical affections (i.e., the heart) has been taken captive in the matrices of affluence produced by technological consumer capitalism. Like other idols, capitalism does

10. Bush, "America's Responsibility," in Bacevich, ed., *Imperial Tense*, 5 (emphasis in original).

11. Mark 8:35 and 10:29 give the formula "for my sake and for the sake of the gospel" as a summary statement for this evangelical motivation.

not mind sharing those affections with the God of Israel and Jesus. The converse is not, and cannot, be true however. "I am the Lord, that is my name; my glory I give to no other, nor my praise to idols" (Isa 42:8), and "You cannot serve God and wealth" (Matt 6:24).

Evangelicals earnestly affirm these words of Scripture. But they fail to recognize how an uncritical affirmation of democratic capitalism contradicts and unconsciously subverts them. The first step toward resolving the contradictions and cultivating a consciousness of the problem is to examine the desires expressed in the beliefs and practices of democratic capitalism. The aim must be to identify evidence of whether evangelicals have accepted "the meta-myth of our culture . . . the sacred narrative of success and affluence, gained through a proper relationship with the economy, and revealed in the ever-expanding material prosperity of society through the ever-increasing acquisition and consumption of products by individuals."[12] The foregoing chapters provide strong evidence that American Evangelicalism holds to this meta-myth and thus engages in a form of *cosmological* faith that locates its ultimate religious and cultural concerns, the essence of life or ground of being, in the material (i.e., economic) dimension of American life. They do so while holding simultaneously to a *transcendental* faith in Jesus and the gospel with ultimate religious and cultural concerns in the supernatural realm. It is an attempt at faith simultaneously in a rival god and the true God arising out of a radical dualism of matter and spirit. This cosmological aspect of American-Evangelical religion is, I contend, principally an unconscious one formed in the AAEC during the first two decades of life around the meta-myth of success and affluence. Religion in this sense is understood as the dimension of human consciousness, culture and society where ultimate concerns are held and fleshed out in the course of life, and the process is not always a conscious one. But affluence is where the ultimate cosmological concerns of American-Evangelical faith can be found. It is not surprising, then, to find that Novak's and Schneider's theological economics are dominated by a doctrine of creation dominated by a view of individual humans as God's image free to co-create within the constraints of original sin.

Furthermore, since religious expression always brings issues of power to the surface, it is not surprising to find power at the heart of American-

---

12. DeChant, *Sacred Santa*, 53.

Evangelical expressions of faith. The previous quote from President Bush is a case in point. In addition, Schneider's theology of affluence is grounded in capitalist power. He uses warfare terminology to describe Jesus and those contemporary disciples given royal pounds to trade for profit in aggressive competition so the king's dominion can be enlarged. This requires cultivation and practice of the twin habits of capitalism: acquisition and enjoyment. Thus, if religion is the aspect of cultural and societal consciousness where one encounters ultimate concerns, then a moral theology like Schneider's is a contemporary expression of ultimate concern over happiness realized through production and consumption. This is the religious dimension of democratic capitalism's ultimate concern, which chapter 3 showed culminated in Hoover's 1920s work in the U.S. Department of Commerce and his singular term as President.

Thus, the affluence of technological consumer capitalism is a register of the beliefs and behaviors of what functions as religion for American Evangelicals. It mediates their relationships with the ultimate or sacred sources of power in their lives.[13] From womb to tomb, it suggests and cultivates (and in times of crisis commands) the beliefs necessary to sustain these relationships in society. It forms the relationships necessary to maintain the personal and communal commitments such beliefs require. The special spiritual narratives, or myths, that convey these beliefs and rituals are endued with personages and stories that convey the sacred meanings of success and affluence.[14] These cosmological aspects of religion give American Evangelicals a certain degree of security to the extent that they provide power over material conditions of late modern life. At the same time they find answers to ultimate issues in the transcendental dimension of their faith. The grand narrative of Jesus and the gospel may provide American Evangelicals with answers to eternal life (the transcendent or spiritual), while the fundamental myth of ever-expanding prosperity provides answers to temporal life (the cosmological or material). The economic dimension of contemporary Evangelical life in the United States is thoroughly infused with concerns for material comfort, happiness and security that have all the trappings of cosmological religious ex-

13. See Northcott, *Angel Directs the Storm*, for a penetrating perspective on how power and apocalypticism lie at the heart of the cosmological, material aspect of evangelical faith.

14. Cf. Fox, *Jesus in America*; Dark, *Gospel according to America*; Apel, *American Myths*; Shelley, *Gospel and American Dream*.

pression. Practically, the material can dominate the spiritual dimension of American-Evangelical faith and practice, resulting in the formation of a spiritual-moral lack in the AAEC.

Evidence for this can be observed in the producing-consuming rituals that mark the American calendar, particularly the Thanksgiving through New Year holidays. Christmas is the high holy day of American temporal religion, and Evangelicals in the United States practice it with great zeal. Measurements of expenditures during this period are staggering and provide perhaps the most telling evidence that American Evangelicals simultaneously practice a material and spiritual religion.[15] A radical material-spiritual dualism is evident in all this, and it lies at the heart of why Evangelicals in the United States live like the rest of the world in both consuming and in donating to charity.[16] In this religious-cultural context, the material subverts the spiritual. This is displayed in the emergence of the AAEC since 1950.

Chapters 2 and 3 demonstrated the evolution of the AAEC in the United States from the eighteenth through twentieth centuries by critically interacting with the anthropologies of the child found in Jonathan Edwards, Horace Bushnell and Lawrence Richards. As was shown, the AAEC has been formed in an American Evangelicalism with no tradition of cultivating a theological-critical awareness of affluence. In child-rearing texts, both popular and academic, Evangelicals simply overlook affluence as a formative factor in cultivating the "discipline and instruction of the Lord."

Chapter 2 uncovered conversionist and developmentalist theological anthropologies of the child in the writings of Edwards and Bushnell. Edwards and the nineteenth century evangelical revivalists who followed him held an ambivalent theological anthropology regarding children, what I have identified as a kind of "cognitive idolatry" in relation to the child that diminishes the humanity and potential of the child until such time as conversion can take place on the basis of sufficient understanding of the gospel. Bushnell termed this manner of relating to children as cruel "ostrich nurture," turning the phrase back on Edwards and the nineteenth century revivalists who held Edwards's theological anthropology of the child. This was a significant advance for the child in American

15. See, e.g., deChant, "Christmas by the Numbers," in *Sacred Santa*, 155–71.

16. See, e.g., Sider, "The Depth of the Scandal," in *Scandal of Evangelical Conscience*, 17–29.

Evangelicalism because it focused attention on the critical importance of the early years of spiritual and moral formation in children. Bushnell's prescience is confirmed by social scientific research over the last century. Children thrive spiritually and morally in nurturing, loving relations during the first decades of life. They need someone to love them well and someone stable enough for them to love. Contemporary evangelicals recognize this as well in their consistent claims that most people who come to faith in Christ do so during the first twenty years of life. Although they do not emphasize the Bushnellian aspects of nurture as much as they do the Edwardsian, they nevertheless acknowledge the critical importance of the early years for evangelical faith formation.

But in originating a new and important perspective on child nurture Bushnell set a trap for the child, parent and church nurtured in affluence in the United States. He put them on a path of pursuing affluence while at the same time pursuing the way of the cross. He developed a theology of prosperity not entirely unlike the theology of affluence Schneider developed over a century later. As was shown, Bushnell argued for a muscular Christianity of men expanding the kingdom of God on earth through entrepreneurship. It was their primary Christian duty, just as it was the primary duty of women to nurture children and maintain the hearth and home for the succor of men upon their return from war-like competition in the marketplace. This was the means whereby the "money power" would be sanctified to God and the last revival would come.

Chapters 2 and 3 demonstrated the link between Bushnell's theologies of nurture and prosperity, showing the common ground they shared in the presupposition of the good of gendered progress and growth with nineteenth century industrialism and republican individualism. The works of Robert Wauzzinski, William Leach, and Mark Edwards proved particularly useful in establishing these claims and connecting them to the evangelical theology of nurture developed by Lawrence Richards in the twentieth century. As was shown in chapter 3, Richards was nurtured in the womb of America's transformation into a great consumer paradise characterized by the diffusion of production into consumption and the explicit incorporation of children into its social, cultural, political and economic matrices. Nurtured in such a context, it is not surprising to find that Richards demonstrates no critical awareness of affluence in the familial-ecclesial socialization model he developed for his theology of nurture. The result was that Richards and other American Evangelicals nurtured the AAEC in affluence unaware of the perils it poses to faith formation. Affluence simply was taken for granted in American-Evangelical nurture and education.

Moving from the diachronic perspective of the AAEC provided in Part I (chapters 2 and 3), an evangelical sociology of the AAEC was developed in chapter 4 as the first part of a synchronic look at the contemporary social conditions in which the AAEC is nurtured and embedded. Since 1950 the AAEC has emerged with his American peers as a creative interpreter-reproducer of American society and culture. Compared with children at the turn of the nineteenth century into the twentieth, Hoover's dreams for children in middle class single-family home ownership and the diffusion of production into consumption have become reality for the vast majority of children in the United States. The AAEC is embedded in a land of desire, interpreting and reproducing it with peers and adults alike. William Corsaro's model of interpretive reproduction in childhood proved to be a useful sociological tool for understanding the language and cultural routines of the AAEC and the reproductive nature of the AAEC's evolving membership in the subculture of Evangelical affluence in the United States. The AAEC is both formed by and formative of that subculture, learning the language and cultural routines of individualistic American Evangelicalism. The AAEC reproduces, modifies, expands and adapts these linguistic-cultural habits to their interests within their own peer cultures, reflecting those of the adult world.

As was shown, the AAEC is socially formed by the time of adolescence in the problematic tensions of affluence with little critical self-understanding within that context. Few, if any, evangelical resources are available to the AAEC to resist the encroachments of consumer culture. Affluence remains immune to penetrating, transformational critique within American Evangelicalism. Thus, the evangelical sociology of the AAEC in chapter 4 serves to shed further light upon formation of the AAEC in affluence. It links the AAEC's historical and sociological contexts, filling a gap in American-Evangelical self-understanding of the correlation between affluence and nurture of the AAEC. The interpretive reproductions of the AAEC in affluence also illumine the affluentizing processes at work in the AAEC's first decades of life. This facilitates a fuller critical understanding of the modified Bushnellian socialization theory that Richards incorporated into his theology of Christian nurture and a deeper awareness of affluence as a significant factor in the AAEC's formation. Critical awareness of the formative effects of affluence is needed during the first decades of life if evangelical parents and churches hope to cultivate in the AAEC counter-disciplines of resistance to consumer culture and society. Such awareness is needed much earlier in the AAEC's discipline and instruction of the Lord, and it must first be developed in the parents and churches.

The evangelical sociology of the AAEC in chapter 4 provided a bridge to chapter 5's evangelical theology of the AAEC, the second synchronic lens for the theological anthropology of the AAEC and the heart of the work. The centerpiece of critique was John Schneider's theology of affluence. It was shown there, that if embraced by evangelicals, this theology may help perpetuate the AAEC's developmental enmeshment within the matrices of Evangelical affluence in the United States. In other words, the AAEC will continue to be found lacking in relation to God and others, a lack that may lead to risking the AAEC's departure from the path leading to the kingdom of God and eternal life.

This claim was established in three steps. First, Schneider's interpretations of Luke's rich ruler, story of Zacchaeus and Parable of the Pounds were set out. As we saw, Schneider resolved the "harsh" moral theology of the rich ruler through a narrative reading of Luke's Gospel that places the stories of the rich ruler and Zacchaeus in tension to show that "selling all" cannot be a universal norm. But as was shown, Schneider's interpretation of both stories misses the important theological-anthropological issue of lack. Jesus raises that issue explicitly with the rich ruler, and it is implied with Zacchaeus. Schneider made a mistake in focusing on the ethical practices implied in the passages rather than the theological anthropology upon which those practices are based. In other words, it was a mistake to look for a narrative or other manner of reconciling what he perceived to be conflicting ethical norms in the two stories. He did not need to juxtapose the "radical Jesus" seen in the story of the rich ruler with the "Lord of delight" seen in the encounter with Zacchaeus and then seek to resolve them in a "radical Jesus as Lord of delight."

Instead, Schneider should have focused on the *theological and anthropological* significance of the respective responses of the rich ruler and Zacchaeus. The responses of both men point to how the lack of affluence was resolved in their lives. In the rich ruler the lack remained. He went away grieving, outside the kingdom of God and far from eternal life. In the story of Zacchaeus, however, the lack was removed through repentance, faith and restitution. Salvation "happened" in the house of this "son of Abraham" (Luke 19:9) because he produced fruit worthy of repentance for the forgiveness of sins (Luke 3:3, 8). The fruit of his repentance was dispossession and donation to the poor plus restitution to those he defrauded (Luke 19:8; cf. 3:12). The response of Zacchaeus demonstrated the presence of that essential love of God, which is proven by love of neighbor, through repentance proven by deeds of a changed life. Schneider failed to develop repentance, faith and restitution as part of his moral theology of affluence, a major oversight for a work purporting to give advice to wealthy Christians seeking God in a culture of wealth. Without repentance and faith proven by appropriate deeds, a theology of affluence cannot be evangelical.

This conclusion was supported by the contemporary interpretations of the story of the rich young man by Bonhoeffer, Barth, Pope John Paul II, and Grau. Those interpretations, when read with the AAEC in view, help confirm that the AAEC's sociality is profoundly shaped by nurture in affluence, and from a theological-anthropological standpoint this has serious implications for the call to discipleship. According to John Paul II, the first order of business for the AAEC in light of the story of the rich young man is to keep the commands. Bonhoeffer and Barth emphasize obedient trust in the person and work of Jesus in the context of affluence, including a disposition to dispossess, donate and follow Jesus. These steps toward freedom in affluence open the AAEC to the invitation (John Paul II) to pursue perfection and also to obey (Bonhoeffer and Barth) Christ's call to follow in the way of the cross. Ultimately they lead to the formation of a capacity for self-denial that cross-bearing in the world requires. According to John Paul II, it ultimately opens the AAEC to a capacity for martyrdom for the sake of Jesus and the gospel, which is the ultimate dispossession and gift one can give and expresses in the most profound way the perfection of which Jesus speaks to the AAEC through the story of the rich young man. The way of the cross is always the only way to loving God and neighbor. It is the path to perfection that may require sacrifice. As Bonhoeffer famously said, ultimately the call of Jesus, "follow me," is a call to come and die.

The Pope's positive emphasis on obedience to the commands is a powerful reminder of the moral theology that lies at the heart of the story of the rich young man. As the Pope notes, Christ says first, "keep the commands," and only then does he say "follow me." Implicit in this is the fact that the grace of God precedes obligation because God gives what he commands and commands what he gives (Augustine). Following Christ comes from a heart that is truly free to obey. But an evangelical freedom to obey flows from a heart that has been set free in God's grace and mercy and love, free to detach from all impediments to following Christ. Affluence is a secondary issue at best, as are its dispossession and donation. The primary issue is the obedience of true freedom that begins with keeping the commands once, as Bonhoeffer put it, the grace of freedom and the power to be obedient has been granted and obeyed. The story of the rich young man in Matthew thus provides a window into the contemporary theological context of the AAEC. It shows that affluence may be a symptom of a deeper spiritual and moral problem. Affluence raises the question of what might be lacking in the AAEC's relationships with God and others.

The final step of chapter 5 was to explore more deeply the issue of freedom through a critical examination of the anthropology of liberty that lies at the heart of Schneider's theology of affluence. Marion Grau's feminist interpretation of the rich young man as "hysterical" (i.e., "lacking") in the economy of redemption set the stage for Long's critique of Novak and Bell's critique of capitalism. Beginning with Irenaeus, Grau illumined the gendered nature of the economics of redemption in the history of interpretation of the rich young man and helped sharpen the focus on the theological nature of the lack identified in his life. This highlighted once again the issue of freedom, or the anthropology of liberty, that lies at the heart of the problem of affluence. Grau's criticisms of Long's *Divine Economy* served as a helpful introduction to Long's critique of Novak, setting the tone for a cautionary approach to Long's argument. But as I showed, Long's critique of Novak is immensely helpful to my critique of Schneider. This is because Schneider depends heavily upon Novak for his theological economics. In exposing the deficiencies in Novak's doctrine of creation as it operates in his theology of economics, Long also exposed the unstable foundation of the cosmic good of affluence in Schneider's theology. His doctrine of creation with its overemphasis on human freedom as the *imago Dei* ends up subordinating Christology, ecclesiology and soteriology to an anthropology of freedom in the service of democratic capitalism. This anthropology lies at the heart of the AAEC's lack in the problem of affluence. It is insufficient to sustain a theological anthropology that can overcome the one thing that is lacking—a relationship with Christ truly free for love of God and neighbor, as Bonhoeffer and Barth help us understand. The one thing that matters and thus fulfills and satisfies all that is lacking is a relationship with Christ in the way of self-denying, cross-bearing discipleship for the sake of Jesus and the gospel (Mark 8:34–35; 10:21, 29).

Finally, the appropriation of Bell's penetrating critique of capitalism exposed the battle for desire lying at the heart of the AAEC's formation in affluence. Lack in the AAEC is formed by the disciplinary function of the technologies of the self that capitalism employs in the war for human desire, the war for the human heart by which one believes and trusts in God and, hence, is saved (Rom 10:9–10). Evangelicals like Schneider who warmly affirm the culture of capitalism are unaware of the economic and ontological victory capitalism in late modernity has won over human desire. What is needed is a therapy of desire only Christianity can provide through the "ensemble" of formative spiritual and moral "technologies" available in the community of Christian faith and practice. These technologies help those embedded in affluence resist the "infinite undulations of the snake" of capitalism and at the same time aid those suffering on the underside of savage capitalism to "refuse to cease suffering" through a therapy of Christ-like forgiveness.

Thus, by way of summary, the AAEC can overcome the problem of affluence (i.e., spiritual-moral "lack" or poverty cultivated in affluence) through three steps. First, by developing a critical-historical awareness of how the theological anthropology of the child in American Evangelicalism evolved and emerged during the eighteenth through twentieth centuries. The second step is to develop a critical-sociological understanding of the processes of interpretive reproduction of the culture of affluence at work in American Evangelicalism from womb to tomb. Third, a critical-theological anthropology that rejects the "theology as *libertatis analogia*" of democratic capitalism should help evangelical parents and churches nurture in the AAEC an evangelical freedom from attachments to affluence.

Employing these steps, American-Evangelical parents and churches can cultivate an evangelical-critical consciousness of the (mal)formative effects of the culture produced by technological consumer capitalism and overcome the spiritual-moral lack that nurture in affluence can form. Seen in terms of Paul's conception of formation-transformation-conformation, these are late modern steps of faith and practice that evangelicals can take toward Christ being formed in them (Gal 4:19), being transformed by the renewing of their minds (Rom 12:2) as they are being transformed from one degree of glory to the next (2 Cor 3:18), and thus being conformed to the image of God in Jesus Christ (Rom 8:29). It can enable them to resist being conformed to the culture of affluence (Rom 12:2) and follow the path of offering their bodies as living sacrifices that are holy and acceptable to God (Rom 12:1).

The evangelical theology of the AAEC developed in chapter 5 focuses attention on the spiritual and moral lack that can arise from nurture in affluence. In so doing, it points a way forward for evangelical parents and churches seeking to form a passion for Jesus and the gospel in their children. That way must address the issue of affluence in spiritual and moral formation, and thus it must proceed with critical awareness of historical, sociological and theological dimensions of the problem of affluence in an American Evangelicalism both formed by and formative of technological consumer capitalism in the United States. These conclusions point to promising areas of further research with the AAEC in view.

AREAS OF FURTHER RESEARCH

The preceding investigation has, of necessity, had a limited focus. Nevertheless, it paves the way for a number of promising areas of further research. Broadly speaking, one of the desired outcomes of this work is to encourage interdisciplinary evangelical research focused on the child in relation to the problem of affluence. For instance, chapters 4 and 5 point to the need for further sociological and theological study of the child embedded in late modern technological consumer capitalism.

In the following subsections, I want to focus particular attention on two areas of future research. The first concerns ecclesiology, and the second is in relation to psychology and pedagogy. What I want to suggest is the need for interdisciplinary evangelical, theological-critical engagement of these disciplines with the child nurtured in American-Evangelical affluence in mind.

An Evangelical Ecclesiology of the AAEC

The tendency within American Evangelicalism to embrace a low ecclesiology in favor of a high theology of the family is indicated in the theological anthropologies of the child found in Edwards, Bushnell and Richards (chapters 2 and 3). Research might fruitfully explore the manner in which family and church mediate Christian and cultural values, particularly economic ones, in the relational processes and matrices associated with nurturing evangelical faith and discipline in the child embedded in affluence.

Four potentially fruitful paths for an ecclesiology of the AAEC may be suggested here. The first is Radical Orthodoxy. Both Long and Bell explore ecclesiological issues in promising ways in light of their respective critical interactions with capitalism. Like all Radical Orthodoxy theologians, Long argues that the Eucharist must be central to ecclesiology because it is "the definitive social practice wherein the divine-human drama occurs . . . [and] provides the script within which all exchanges should take place."[17] This is consistent with Radical Orthodoxy's insistence on reclaiming the material and economic culture in a distinctly Christian way. For Bell, "only a more substantive ecclesiology . . . that begins by collapsing the distinction between the theological and the social, between religion and politics, stands a chance of resisting capitalist discipline . . . [it] must reclaim the theological as material, that is, as a fully social, political, economic reality."[18] This kind of ecclesiology is needed because resistance to capitalism must entail a manner of living that counters capitalist captivity and distortion of desire precisely "by liberating and healing desire."[19] To resist savage capitalism the church must meet the civil society of capitalism on its own terms as an "uncivil society," as a public and politic in its own standing.[20]

According to Radical Orthodoxy as originally articulated by Milbank in *Theology and Social Theory*, because there once was a time when the secular was not (i.e., before modernity) we must reclaim the church as an alternative body politic that rejects the sacred-secular dualisms of modernity which map onto private-public dualisms such as those found in American Evangelicalism. Failure to do so is essentially to capitulate to false worship. As James K. A. Smith puts it, "We will end up spending our workweek making cakes for the queen of heaven and spending our weekends [or perhaps just part of Sundays] with Yahweh (Jer 7:16–19)—with-

---

17. Long, *Divine Economy*, 268.

18. Bell, *Liberation Theology*, 72.

19. Ibid.

20. Ibid., 72–73; cf. Clapp, *Border Crossings*.

out seeing the way in which our service to the queen of heaven is forming us into queen-of-heaven kinds of people."[21]

A second avenue for developing an ecclesiology of the AAEC might be found in Miroslav Volf's ecclesiology. Volf critiques Bell's doctrine of the church on two grounds, one political and the other pneumatological. On the political point, Bell argues that because transnational capitalism has made the state and civil society its servants, the only viable option for resisting capitalism's deterritorializing effects is a transnational, un-civil (i.e., subversive) church.[22] Volf understands Bell to argue that the church should be "an alternative to the state" and therefore is wary about Bell's ecclesiology.[23] Bell is not saying that the church should become the state, however, which of course would be problematic in light of Western Europe's history of church-state relations. Instead, Bell is arguing that the church should contest the state's idolatrous servitude to the capitalist order. It must be subversive of this order in a peaceful but prophetic manner.

Volf's second criticism of Bell is more substantial and warrants close attention. He argues that the Holy Spirit is either absent or insufficiently present "in Bell's technology of desire. In other words, the church with its practices has absorbed the Holy Spirit."[24] Volf is concerned that Bell's ecclesiology eliminates the need for "subjective appropriation" of the gospel.[25] In light of Bonhoeffer's and Barth's interpretations of the rich young man, Volf makes an important point that tends to be overlooked in Radical Orthodoxy. In its zeal to counter modernist tendencies toward idolatrous individualism such as those existing in American Evangelicalism's faith practices, Radical Orthodoxy leans toward totalizing the church. In so doing it takes on the totalizing tendency of modernity it seeks to supplant. Volf's point is clear: God sovereignly regenerates with "no strict correlation between external means of grace ([i.e., Bell's] "technologies") and their internal effect."[26] The Spirit regenerates the heart (transforms desire), puts to death the flesh, makes the new creation alive, indwells

---

21. Smith, *Introducing Radical Orthodoxy*, 253.

22. For Bell's rejoinder to Volf's criticisms see Bell, "What Gift is Given?" 271–80.

23. Volf, "Exchange," 263.

24. Ibid., 265.

25. Ibid., 266.

26. Volf, "Pretentious Church," 283.

the believer's soul, "all the self-binding of God to the means of grace notwithstanding."[27]

In light of Volf's criticisms, it seems that one particularly promising way forward in developing an ecclesiology of the AAEC would be to engage the ecclesiology of Radical Orthodoxy and Volf together. For evangelicals in particular this seems like a good option because Volf remains appropriately sensitive to aspects of the Protestant Reformed tradition's focus on personal responsibility for faith and obedience within an overarching framework of redemptive history, although he is careful to counter tendencies in Protestant ecclesiology to exalt pietistic individualism. He develops his ecclesiology through critical interaction with Roman Catholic theologian Joseph Cardinal Ratzinger and Eastern Orthodox theologian John Zizioulas in the process of developing a penetrating ecclesiology of persons and communities as an image of the Trinity.[28]

A third fruitful avenue of investigation into an ecclesiology for the AAEC may be in the extensive and radical ecclesiological reflections of Stanley Hauerwas.[29] Hauerwas in particular would be helpful in assisting American Evangelicalism to develop a critical-ecclesiological perspective on its relation to the United States. Hauerwas has been persistent in his prophetic critique of the church's failure to witness against the violent and idolatrous aspects of the political and economic structures of the United States.[30] He has carried the torch first lit by John Howard Yoder and started fires of a critical ecclesiology around which evangelicals may beneficially gather for warmth and light.[31] As John B. Thompson has recently shown, the ecclesiology developed by Hauerwas "offers a political understanding of Christian freedom which seeks to transcend the limitations of liberal thought and theology."[32] At the same time, Thompson provides several suggestions for improving Hauerwas's project as an adequate ecclesiology

---

27. Ibid. Smith implies that Volf departs from Calvin on the "correlation of the means of grace with the advent of grace." Smith, *Introducing Radical Orthodoxy*, 254 n. 72. I doubt Volf is as far from Calvin as Smith suggests.

28. Volf, *After Our Likeness*.

29. See, e.g., Hauerwas, *Better Hope*; and *With the Grain*.

30. See, e.g., Hauerwas and Willimon, *Resident Aliens*; Hauerwas, *Better Hope*, 44, 171, 274–75 n. 28; and *With the Grain*, 221–24.

31. Yoder, *Royal Priesthood*; Carter, *Politics of the Cross*.

32. Thompson, *Ecclesiology of Hauerwas*, 203.

of deliverance from the liberal hangovers of modernity, including helpful critical insights into deficiencies in the Constantinian thesis.[33]

A fourth resource for constructing an ecclesiology for the AAEC might be The Ekklesia Project, one of the fires of critical ecclesiology Hauerwas has helped to light. Hauerwas dedicates *A Better Hope* to The Ekklesia Project and appends its Declaration to the end of that book.[34] The Project is a non-profit member-based organization that produces pamphlets for popular education, hosts a website (www.ekklesiaproject. org) and meetings for congregational formation and outreach, and engages in book publishing through its network of members.

The Project's website declares the organization's intent "to remind the church of its true calling as the real-world community whose primary loyalty is to the Body of Christ, the priorities and practices of Jesus, and the inbreaking Kingdom of God"; this is necessary because today the central questions of ecclesiology are "stark and straightforward: to whom or what do we belong? To what body do we pledge our allegiance? What commitments do we recognize as those to which all others must bend or bow?"; and these questions give rise to the observations that issues of

> ultimate loyalty and allegiance were kept at bay by most Christian churches. The Church as the Body of Christ—the material, living community that crosses all borders and human divisions—has been too easily and often compromised and fragmented by unwise accommodations with states, ethnic and racial imperatives, and the naturalized imperatives of class, gender, and ideology. By minimizing or denying the distinctiveness of the life of discipleship—a set of affections, dispositions and practices learned within churches faithful to the Gospel of Jesus Christ—too many churches have turned the clear and unambiguous call of Jesus and the Holy Spirit into a confused and contradictory mix of caution and self-interest.[35]

33. Ibid., 203–18.

34. Hauerwas, *Better Hope*, 7: "I would not want anyone to assume that The Ekklesia Project and what I am about are one and the same . . . Yet as the Declaration makes clear, we are united in our commitment to reclaiming the church as an alternative people for the good of the world."

35. Ekklesia Project, "About Us." For a contemporary critique of evangelical ecclesiology and potentially helpful starting point for developing an evangelical ecclesiology of the AAEC, see Stackhouse, *Evangelical Ecclesiology: Reality or Illusion?*

These four resources—Radical Orthodoxy, Miroslav Volf, Hauerwas, and The Ekklesia Project—could help evangelicals develop an ecclesiology of the AAEC with strands capable of resisting the disciplines of capitalist culture. A subversive evangelical church must seek to nurture the capacity for self-denial and cross-bearing in the AAEC. It must be historically, socially and theologically aware of the problem of affluence in late modernity, and it must be aware of the role Evangelicalism has played in bringing about the culture of affluence in the United States and the role it plays in sustaining that culture.

A critical understanding of the present context in which American Evangelicalism is embedded must be an essential aspect of an evangelical ecclesiology of the AAEC. It must grasp that the problem of affluence is formed in the first decades of life as a spiritual and moral lack. Ecclesial awareness of that problem should lead evangelical churches to reject the neoliberal idol of liberty that privileges individual and family interests in favor of the market over the corporate interests of Christ and the church. An ecclesiology of the AAEC should seek to subvert the formative effects of affluence while at the same time encouraging evangelical families and churches to join forces in nurturing faith in their children along lines such as those proposed by Lawrence Richards. In so doing, however, it must avoid the mistake that Richards made and proceed with critical awareness of the problem of affluence in late modernity.

One final point about my suggestion of an evangelical ecclesiology of the AAEC requires attention before turning to consider the need for an evangelical psychology and pedagogy of the child in American Evangelicalism. Evangelicals may wonder why I have suggested four non-Evangelical ecclesial resources for my proposal. In addition to the reasons inherent in the foregoing discussion, I would simply point to the volume edited by John G. Stackhouse, Jr., *Evangelical Theology: Reality or Illusion?* and an article by John Webster, "On Evangelical Ecclesiology." Webster properly recognizes that American Evangelicalism (he labels it "Evangelical Christianity") has an "instinctive ecclesiological indifference or minimalism . . ."[36] In other words, the doctrine of the church is not one of American Evangelicalism's strong suits. Evangelical ecclesiology, as Stackhouse's volume demonstrates, is largely a theological hodge-podge

36. Webster, "On Evangelical Ecclesiology," 34.

or plethora of variant, relatively incoherent traditions. Stanley Grenz puts it this way on the back cover of the book:

> Like most things 'evangelical,' evangelical ecclesiology is up for grabs today. Even evangelical theologians, in their attempts to discern what the church is called to be, find themselves looking in a plethora of directions for constructive models, from the free church tradition to Eastern Orthodoxy and the Celtic church. The essays in *Evangelical Ecclesiology* display not only the tensions within contemporary evangelical thought about the variety of ways in which evangelical thinkers seek to assist the people of God in the task of being the church in the contemporary world but also the vitality of the current discussion.

The points made by Grenz and the essays found in *Evangelical Ecclesiology: Reality or Illusion?* lend credence to my suggestions of resources for an evangelical ecclesiology of the AAEC. Evangelical theologians, pastors and believers in the United States find themselves "looking in a plethora of directions" among a "variety of ways" in their attempts to ground their doctrines of the church in late modernity. They are drawing from, and learning through critical-evangelical interaction with, other traditions. I think this is a good thing and can only benefit the AAEC and strengthen faith seeking understanding (among other things) of the psychology and pedagogy at play in a culture of mass affluence.

An Evangelical Psychology and Pedagogy of the AAEC

To speak of ecclesial and parental formation necessarily implicates issues of psychology and pedagogy. Thus, the need for an evangelical psychology and pedagogy of the AAEC is indicated. This was seen in chapter 4's evangelical sociology of the AAEC, where it was noted that the sociology of children and childhood engages and in many respects depends heavily upon developmental psychology in its theory and methods in studying the sociality of children. This is a second promising area of future research that might arise from the present work.

The evangelical sociology of the AAEC developed in chapter 4 provides a theoretical lens through which empirical sociological studies of the AAEC could be conducted. The application of William Corsaro's theory of interpretive reproductions to the AAEC in the problem of affluence can promote further synchronic understanding of how children develop in the context of mass affluence. Evangelical educators sensitive to cultural and sociological issues in nurture and pedagogy should, I contend, consciously begin factoring affluence into their theories and methods of spiritual, faith and moral formation in children.

Psychology and its correlate discipline of pedagogy are important aspects of theological anthropology,[37] as demonstrated in chapter 4's interaction with Juliet Schor's *Born to Buy* and Susan Linn's *Consuming Kids*. An evangelical psychology of the AAEC could explore beneficially the theological-anthropological issue of lack in light of psychological theory and practice. As I have argued regarding Matthew 19, the affluent young man's lack points to a spiritual-moral vacuum in the AAEC that correlates in some way to nurture in affluence. Within Evangelical theology and pedagogy, however, the issue of affluence has been overlooked as a factor in Christian nurture, spiritual formation, faith development and Christian education.

The need for an evangelical psychology of the AAEC is manifested by Schneider's unabashed theological advocacy of cultivating "twin habits of capitalism" and Bell's exposure of the "infinite undulations" inherent in the systems that have arisen from those habits in modernity.[38] A substantial body of psychological literature offers many resources for interdisciplinary development of a critical evangelical psychology of the AAEC.[39] The American Dream is a dream of happiness and the freedom to pursue it as one chooses. But although freedom is essential to well-being and the successful functioning of democracy, psychological and sociological data are proving that the affluence freedom brings does not translate directly into happiness.[40] Like the young man seeking eternal life in the midst of first-century abundance, the AAEC needs help finding the way to true happiness in twenty-first century affluence.[41] The AAEC, it seems, is put

37. Cf. Shults's reflections on developmental psychology and pedagogical practice in *Reforming Theological Anthropology*, 39–76.

38. Cf. Bellah, et al., *Habits of the Heart*.

39. See Luthar and Latendresse, "Children of the Affluent," 49–53; Luthar and Sexton, "High Price of Affluence," 126–62; Luthar, "Culture of Affluence," 1581–93; Frankfort, "Affluence: The impact of family money on daughters."

40. See, e.g., Myers, *American Paradox*; Buss, "Evolution of Happiness," 15–23; and Csikszentmihalyi, "If We Are So Rich," 821–27.

41. For the most recent data correlating wealth and growth with various political, economic and social measurements of well-being compiled by sociologists, political scientists and economists for more than one hundred nations, see Bernstein, *Birth of*

on a "hedonic treadmill" of affluence from birth that threatens to keep him off the path of discipleship, which according to Jesus is the answer to his lack and thus to his pursuit of happiness in late modernity.[42]

One promising avenue for developing an evangelical psychology of the AAEC sensitive to the lack of affluence might be found in James Loder's theological anthropology of the child in *The Logic of the Spirit* (1998). This was his book length rejoinder to Fowler's ground-breaking *Stages of Faith* (1981), coming seventeen years after the two squared off in debate over their respective theories of human development.[43] Although Loder commended Fowler for developing a better clinical interview process and for his creative use of a fictional dialogue between Piaget, Kohlberg and Erikson, he was not persuaded by Fowler's definition of faith or his attempt at describing normative staging of faith in human development. Loder argued that a more accurate title to Fowler's seminal *Stages of Faith: The Psychology of Human Development and the Quest for Meaning* would be *"The Psychology of Human Development and the Quest for Meaning: Stages of an Aspect of Faith."*[44]

Loder viewed Fowler's work as "a sensitive, insightful study of the ego's competence in structuring meaning"; however, "it is only potentially but not necessarily related to faith in a biblical or theological sense."[45] In short, Loder believed that Fowler's stages assist in psychological understanding of the anthropological dimension of faith but ultimately fail to contribute to a theological understanding of faith. Loder also found fault with Fowler's attempt to describe faith development normatively, describing his position as insufficiently "self-conscious or self-critical."[46] Loder argues that stage 6 universalizing faith as the normative goal of human faith development contains "the seeds of its own falsification" because if one were to reach stage 5 the previous four stages would become ambigu-

---

Plenty, 297–334.

42. Bernstein concludes: "Modern man is on a sort of 'hedonic treadmill.' As nations grow wealthier, they must produce an ever-increasing amount of goods and services to maintain the same degree of satisfaction among citizens, but the correlations to increased happiness are not direct due to the 'neighbor effect' and other factors." Bernstein, "God, Culture, Mammon, and the Hedonic Treadmill," in *Birth of Plenty*, 333, 332.

43. See Loder and Fowler, "Conversations," 133–48, reflecting the debate between Loder and Fowler at Michigan State University in 1981.

44. Loder, *Logic of the Spirit*, 256.

45. Ibid.

46. Ibid., 258.

ous and at stage 6 they become either redundant or inconsequential; that is, "they would appear to be of minor interest and not definitive of anything. Indeed, insofar as they were thought to be definitive, they would be representative of an error with respect to the stage 6 normative way of constructing meaning and being."[47] In other words, Loder is arguing that if one were to reach beyond stage 4 of individuative-reflexive human faith into stages 5 or 6, then the previous four stages would be seen as erroneous and therefore as meaningless. The prior four stages would be viewed as sub-faith, either as incoherent or specious. If the normative goal is the universalization of stage 6, then Fowler's entire model fails upon its realization. The previous stages are not really stages of faith because faith in the biblical sense, as Loder sees it, is essentially the same as Fowler's universalizing stage 6 faith.

For Loder, the usefulness of Fowler's stages ends at stage 4 (arising around the time of adolescence) because that is the point at which the human subject becomes interested in such a thing as faith development and is able to comprehend differentiation in stages of the human aspect of faith. Loder describes Fowler's stages in terms of his logic of human spirit-to-divine Spirit as "the creative achievement of the human spirit as it strives for universality phase by phase, moving out of egocentrism toward a universal comprehension of all things."[48] The human spirit strives toward this because of its mysterious grounding in the divine Spirit. The reality of the union of the divine and human in Jesus Christ discloses the telos of human spirit-divine Spirit logic. Fowler's stages help describe the human spirit's developmental side of that logic.

Loder interprets the Fowlerian stages as exhibiting what the human spirit consistently exhibits in ego development. But they miss an essential dimension of human experience because they ignore the "dark side of human development" (i.e., sin); as a result, Loder contends, "much that is important to developing persons gets deleted in the name of faith."[49] In other words, Fowler fails to account in faith development for the negative, traumatic and painful aspects of human development, "the pervasive negation of life that relentlessly haunts the human spirit and the unfolding

47. Ibid.
48. Ibid.
49. Ibid., 258–59.

of life through time."[50] Loder is talking about the sin and death that pervade every dimension of creation and beget the labor pains of redemption for which both creation and the human body long. Fowler's stages fail to account for "the deeper order of transformation" of the divine Spirit that makes possible the human spirit's lifelong endeavors "to construct a stadial order that appears rational, coherent, and comprehensive" in light of the reality of the sin and death that pervades human experience.[51] Thus, Fowler's "unclarity lies partly in the fact that since these are stages of ego development, the negation that underlies the ego is repressed, and the concern for the dark side of human development plays no part in the developmental process until middle adulthood."[52] During the first two decades of life, that is, Fowler's stages of faith are unhelpful because they fail to account for the reality of sin and fear of death (i.e., the nihilism) underlying ego development.

Loder admits that Fowler's stages do in fact illumine what appears to be a normative description of the young adult's cognitive domain and thus confirm what Piaget has helped us see. The young adult is in the individuative-reflexive stage of faith (stage 4, around adolescence), constructing an ideological view of the world and associating with others sharing similar views "compatible with the explicit system of beliefs and practices she is constructing for herself."[53] She is demythologizing her world, interpreting its symbols and images in a search for a world that makes sense and has meaning.

The relevance of this for the AAEC is readily apparent. By the age of twenty the AAEC has been formed within a religious subculture of Evangelical affluence in the United States. Beginning in adolescence and perhaps much earlier, the symbols and images of American Evangelicalism and American-Evangelical affluence are those the AAEC is seeking to demythologize in the pursuit of a purposeful, meaningful and coherent life. That is, the AAEC is seeking an answer to what is lacking in late modern life. What are the positive and negative aspects of human development in theological perspective during the first two decades of life in such a context? What are the distinctive characteristics of the AAEC's

50. Ibid., 340.
51. Ibid., 258.
52. Ibid., 259.
53. Ibid.

spirit as it strives to construct the self in affluence? What contradictions, negations and incoherence accompany development within American Evangelicalism and affluence? How can the AAEC and Evangelical parents and churches benefit from a deeper understanding of the psychological aspects of development in affluence, and how can Loder's theological anthropology assist them in developing that understanding? These are questions an evangelical psychology of the AAEC would seek to answer, which in turn would inform an evangelical pedagogy of the AAEC that leads to transformational learning in the context of affluence.

These two areas of future research would enhance the theological anthropology of the AAEC developed here. A theological anthropology concerned with the problem of affluence in late modernity inevitably implicates ecclesiology, psychology and pedagogy. The church plays an important role in nurturing children embedded in the social and cultural matrices of that problem. The interpretation of the story of the rich young man in Matthew 19 offered in chapter 5 can help evangelical theologians, pastors and educators begin the journey of developing a critical ecclesiology, psychology and pedagogy of the AAEC.

As supplements to the theological anthropology of the AAEC, such evangelical theologies might help the child in American Evangelicalism find an answer to the question, "What do I still lack?" For evangelicals in the United States, however, the question remains: "Whither the AAEC in the twenty-first century?"

Bibliography

Abercrombie, N., and S. Hill et al. *Sovereign Individuals of Capitalism*. London: Allen & Unwin, 1986.

Abrams, D. C. *Selling the Old-Time Religion: American Fundamentalists and Mass Culture, 1920–1940*. Athens: University of Georgia Press, 2001.

Acuff, D. S., with R. H. Reiher. *What Kids Buy and Why: The Psychology of Marketing to Kids*. New York: Free Press, 1997.

Adler, P., and P. Adler, editors. *Sociological Studies of Child Development*. Vol. 1. Greenwich, CT: JAI, 1986.

Agnew, J. C. "Coming Up for Air: Consumer Culture in Historical Perspective." In *Consumption and the World of Goods*, edited by John Brewer and Roy Porter, 19–39. New York: Routledge, 1993.

Aird, E. G., "Lamentations of a Rachel in the Digital Age." *Theology Today* 56 (2000) 555–65.

Alcorn, R. *Money, Possessions, and Eternity*. Rev. ed. Wheaton, IL: Tyndale, 2003.

Alfino, M., J. Caputo, et al., editors. *McDonaldization Revisited: Critical Essays on Consumer Culture*. London: Praeger, 1998.

Althaus-Reid, M. *Indecent Theology: Theological Perversions in Sex, Gender, and Politics*. London: Routledge, 2001.

Ambert, A. "Sociology of Sociology: The Place of Children in North American Sociology." in *Sociological Studies of Child Development*, edited by P. Adler and P. Adler, 1:11–31. Greenwich, CT: JAI, 1986.

Anan, K. "Remember This Girl." *UN Chronicle* 39.1 (2002) 4–6.

Anderson, H., and S. B. W. Johnson. *Regarding Children: A New Respect for Childhood and Families*. Louisville: Westminster John Knox, 1994.

Anderson, J. E., and G. Langelett. "Economics and the Evangelical Mind." *Faith and Economics* 28 (1996) 5–24.

Anderson, R. S. *On Being Human: Essays in Theological Anthropology*. Pasadena, CA: Fuller Seminary Press, 1982.

Anderton, C. H. "Conflict Economics in Christian Perspective." *Faith and Economics* 37 (2001) 1–9.

Apel, Pat. *Nine Great American Myths: Ways We Confuse the American Dream with the Christian Faith*. Brentwood, TN: Wolgemuth & Hyatt, 1991.

Ariès, Phillipe. *Centuries of Childhood: A Social History of Family Life*. Translated by Robert Baldick. New York: Vintage, 1962.

Asad, Talal. "Anthropological Conceptions of Religion: Reflections on Geertz." *Man* 18 (1983) 237–59.

Ashbrook, J. B., and C. R. Albright. *The Humanizing Brain: Where Religion and Neuroscience Meet*. Cleveland: Pilgrim, 1997.

Astley, J. "Formative Education and Critical Education." In *The Philosophy of Christian Religious Education*, 78–107. Birmingham, AL: Religious Education Press, 1994.

————, editor. *How Faith Grows: Faith Development and Christian Education*. London: National Society/Church House Publishing, 1991.

————, and L. Francis, editors. *Christian Perspectives on Faith Development*. Grand Rapids: Eerdmans, 1992.

Astley, J., L. J. Francis, and C. Crowder, editors. *Theological Perspectives on Christian Formation: A Reader on Theology and Christian Education*. Grand Rapids: Eerdmans, 1996.

Atherton, J. *Christianity and the Market: Christian Social Thought for Our Times*. London: SPCK, 1992.

Bacevich, A. J. *American Empire: The Realities and Consequences of U. S. Diplomacy*. Cambridge: Harvard University Press, 2003.

————. *The Imperial Tense: Prospects and Problems of American Empire*. Chicago: Ivan R. Dee, 2003.

————. *The New American Militarism: How Americans Are Seduced by War*. New York: Oxford University Press, 2005.

Baird, R. D. "Religion is Life: An Inquiry into the Dominating Motif in the Theology of Horace Bushnell." PhD dissertation, University of Iowa, 1964.

Balmer, R. *Mine Eyes Have Seen the Glory: A Journey Into the Evangelical Subculture in America*. 3rd ed. New York: Oxford University Press, 2000.

Barth, K., *Church Dogmatics*. 4 vols. Translated by Geoffrey W. Bromiley and T. F. Torrance. Edinburgh: T. & T. Clark, 1936–69.

————. "Parents and Children." In *Church Dogmatics*, III.4:240–85 (§54.2).

Bartholomew, C. "Consuming God's Word: Biblical Interpretation and Consumerism." In *Christ and Consumerism: Critical Reflections on the Spirit of Our Age*, edited by C. Bartholomew and T. Moritz, 81–99. Carlisle, UK: Paternoster, 2000.

Bartholomew, C., and T. Moritz, editors. *Christ and Consumerism: A Critical Analysis of the Spirit of the Age*. Carlisle, Carlisle, UK: Paternoster, 2000.

Barton, S. C. "Child, Children." In *Dictionary of Jesus and the Gospels*, edited by Joel B. Green and Scot McKnight, 100–104. Downer's Grove, IL: InterVarsity, 1992.

————. *Discipleship and Family Ties in Mark and Matthew*. Cambridge: Cambridge University Press, 1994.

————, editor. *The Family in Theological Perspective*. Edinburgh: T. & T. Clark, 1996.

————. "Family Life." In *Veritatis Splendor—A Response*, edited by C. Yeats, 37–45. Norwich: The Canterbury Press, 1994.

————. "Jesus—Friend of Little Children?" In *The Contours of Christian Education*, edited by Jeff Astley and David Day, 30–40. Great Wakering, UK: McCrimmons, 1992.

————. "Living as Families in the Light of the New Testament." *Interpretation* 52 (1998) 130–44.

————. "Living as Families in Light of the New Testament." In *Life Together: Family, Sexuality and Community in the New Testament and Today*, 37–56. Edinburgh: T. & T. Clark, 2001.

————. "New Testament Interpretation As Performance." In *Life Together: Family, Sexuality and Community in the New Testament and Today*, 223–50. Edinburgh: T. & T. Clark, 2001.

————. "The Relativisation of Family Ties in the Jewish and Graeco-Roman Traditions." In *Constructing Early Christian Families: Family as Social Reality and Metaphor*, edited by Halvor Moxnes, 81–100. London: Routledge, 1997.

————. *The Spirituality of the Gospels*. Peabody, MA: Hendrickson, 1992.

Bauman, Z. *Postmodernity and its Discontents*. Cambridge: Polity, 1997.

Baumol, W. J. *The Free-Market Innovation Machine: Analyzing the Growth Miracle of Capitalism*. Princeton, NJ: Princeton University Press, 2002.

Beard, C. A. *The Economic Interpretation of the Constitution of the United States*. New York: Macmillan, 1913.

Beck, J. R., and B. Demarest. *The Human Person in Theology and Psychology: A Biblical Anthropology for the Twenty-First Century*. Grand Rapids: Kregel, 2005.

Belk, R., and M. Wallendorf. "The Sacred Meaning of Money." *Journal of Economic Psychology* 11 (1990) 35–67.

Bell, D. *The Cultural Contradictions of Capitalism*. Twentieth Anniversary ed. New York: Basic Books, 1996.

Bell, D. M., Jr. "After the End of History: Latin American Liberation Theology in the Wake of Capitalism's Triumph." *Journal of Religion & Society*. 2000. No pages. Online: http://www.creighton.edu/JRS.

———. *Liberation Theology after the End of History*. New York: Routledge, 2001.

———. "'Men of Stone and Children of Struggle': Latin American Liberationists at the End of History." *Modern Theology* 14 (1998) 113–41.

———. "What Gift is Given? A Response to Volf." *Modern Theology* 19 (2003) 271–80.

Bellah, R. N., et al. *Habits of the Heart: Individualism and Commitment in American Life*. Berkeley: University of California Press, 1985.

Bellah, R. N., et al, editors. *The Good Society*. New York: Knopf, 1991.

Bello, Walden. *Dilemmas of Domination: The Unmaking of the American Empire*. New York: Holt, 2004.

Bendroth, M. "Horace Bushnell's *Christian Nurture*," in Marcia J. Bunge, ed. *The Child in Christian Thought*, edited by Marcia J. Bunge, 350–64. Grand Rapids: Eerdmans, 2001.

Benson, W. "Evangelical Philosophies of Religious Education." in M. J. Taylor, ed. *Changing Patterns of Religious Education*, edited by M. J. Taylor, 52–72. Birmingham, AL: Religious Education Press, 1984.

Berdyaev, N. *The Fate of Man in the Modern World*. Ann Arbor: University of Michigan Press, 1935.

Berman, C. H. *Medieval Agriculture, the Southern French Countryside, and the Early Cistercians*. Philadelphia: American Philosophical Society, 1986.

Bernstein, W. J. *The Birth of Plenty: How the Prosperity of the Modern World Was Created*. New York: McGraw-Hill, 2004.

Best, E. *Following Jesus: Discipleship in the Gospel of Mark*. Sheffield: JSOT Press, 1981.

Bhagwati, J. *In Defense of Globalization*. New York: Oxford University Press, 2004.

Bloesch, D. G. *Essentials of Evangelical Theology: Volume One: God, Authority, and Salvation*. Peabody, MA: Prince, 2001.

Blomberg, C. L. "Is Affluence Good?" *Faith & Economics* 40 (2002) 11–14.

———. *Neither Poverty Nor Riches: A Biblical Theology of Possessions*. Downers Grove, IL: InterVarsity, 1999.

Boettner, L. *The Reformed Doctrine of Predestination*. Phillipsburg, NJ: Presbyterian & Reformed, 1963.

Bonhoeffer, D. *The Cost of Discipleship*. Rev. ed. New York: Macmillan, 1963.

Boorman, J. A. "A Comparative Study of the Theory of Human Nature as Expressed by Jonathan Edwards, Horace Bushnell and William Adams Brown, Representative

American Protestant Thinkers of the Past Three Centuries." PhD dissertation, Columbia University, 1954.

Boorstin, D. *The Image: A Guide to Pseudo-Events in America*. New York: Harper & Row, 1961.

Bourdieu, P. *Acts of Resistance: Against the Tyranny of the Market*. New York: New Press, 1998.

Brekus, C. "Children of Wrath, Children of Grace: Jonathan Edwards and the Puritan Culture of Child Rearing." in M. Bunge, ed. *The Child in Christian Thought*, edited by Marcia J. Bunge, 300–38. Grand Rapids: Eerdmans, 2000.

Brown, W. *States of Injury: Power and Freedom in Late Modernity*. Princeton: Princeton University Press, 1995.

Browning, D. S., et al. *From Culture Wars to Common Ground: Religion and the Family Debate*. 2nd ed. Louisville: Westminster John Knox, 2000.

Brusselmans, C., et al. *Toward Moral and Religious Maturity*. Morristown, NJ: Silver Burdett Company, 1986.

Bunge, M., ed. *The Child in Christian Thought*. Grand Rapids: Eerdmans, 2000.

Burner, D. *Herbert Hoover: A Public Life*. New York: Knopf, 1979.

Burns, J. P. *Theological Anthropology*. Translated and edited by J. P. Burns. Sources of Early Christian Thought. Philadelphia: Fortress, 1981.

Burns, T., editor. *After History? Francis Fukuyama and His Critics*. Lanham, MD: Rowman & Littlefield, 1994.

Bush, G. W. "America's Responsibility, America's Mission." In *The Imperial Tense: Prospects and Problems of American Empire*, edited by A. J. Bacevich, 3–5. Chicago: Ivan R. Dee, 2003.

Bushnell, H. *Building Eras in Religion*. New York: Scribner, 1881.

———. *Christian Nurture*. 5th reprint. New Haven: Yale University Press, 1967.

———. *God in Christ: Three Discourses*. New York: AMS, 1972.

———. *Nature and the Supernatural as Together Constituting One System of God*. New York: Scribner, 1858.

———. *The Spirit in Man: Sermons and Selections*. New York: Scribner, 1907.

Buss, D. M. "The Evolution of Happiness." *American Psychologist* 55 (2000) 15–23.

Butler, J., and J. Scott, editors. *Feminists Theorize the Political*. New York: Routledge, 1992.

Calvin, J. *Institutes of the Christian Religion*. Edited by J. T. McNeill. Translated by F. L. Battles. Philadelphia: Westminster, 1960.

Cambell, C. "Consuming Goods and the Good of Consuming." *Critical Review* 8 (1994) 503–20.

———. "Consumption: The New Wave of Research in the Humanities and Social Sciences." *Journal of Social Behaviour and Personality*. Special Issue 6.6 (1991) 57–84.

Campanini, G. "Change in the Family and the Challenges of Contemporary Culture." In *The Family*, edited by L. S. Cahill and D. Mieth, 37–42. Maryknoll, NY: Orbis, 1995.

Canada, M. "History and Culture: Postbellum America, 1866–1914." No pages. Online: http://www.uncp.edu/home/ canada/work/allam/18661913.

Cannell, L., and S. May. "Kids' Community: Children's Ministry for Today's Child." *Christian Education Journal* 4.1 (2000) 41–55.

Capps, Donald. *The Child's Song: The Religious Abuse of Children*. Louisville: Westminster John Knox, 1995.

———. "'Curing Anxious Adolescents Through Fatherlike Performance.'" *Interpretation* 55 (2001) 135–47.

Carroll, J. T. "Children in the Bible." *Interpretation* 55 (2001) 121–34.

Carter, C. *The Politics of the Cross: The Theology and Social Ethics of John Howard Yoder.* Grand Rapids: Brazos, 2001.

Cavaletti, S. *The Religious Potential of the Child 6 to 12 Years Old.* Chicago: Liturgy Training Publications, 2002.

———. *The Religious Potential of the Child: Experiencing Scripture and Liturgy with Young Children.* Chicago: Liturgy Training Publications, 1992.

Cavalletti, Sofia, et al. *The Good Shepherd & the Child: A Joyful Journey.* Chicago, IL: Archdiocese of Chicago, Liturgy Training Publications, 1996.

Cavanaugh, William T. *Torture and Eucharist: Theology, Politics, and the Body of Christ.* Malden, MA: Blackwell, 1998.

Charry, Ellen T. "Who's Minding the Children?" *Theology Today* 56 (2000) 451–55.

Childs, B. H., and D. W. Waanders, editors. *The Treasure of Earthen Vessels: Explorations in Theological Anthropology.* Louisville: Westminster John Knox, 1994.

Chouliaraki, L., and N. Fairclough. *Discourse in Late Modernity: Rethinking Critical Discourse Analysis.* Edinburgh: Edinburgh University Press, 2000.

Clapp, R. *Border Crossings: Christian Trespasses on Popular Culture and Public Affairs.* Grand Rapids: Brazos, 2000.

———. editor. *The Consuming Passion: Christianity & the Consumer Culture.* Downers Grove, IL: InterVarsity, 1998.

———. *Families at the Crossroads: Beyond Traditional & Modern Options.* Downers Grove, IL: InterVarsity, 1993.

———. *A Peculiar People: The Church as a Culture in a Post-Christian Society.* Downers Grove, IL: InterVarsity, 1996.

Clark, E. *Reading Renunciation: Asceticism and Scripture in Early Christianity.* Princeton, NJ: Princeton University Press, 1999.

Cobb, J. B., Jr. *The Earthist Challenge to Economism: A Theological Critique of the World Bank.* New York: Macmillan, 1999.

———. *Postmodernism and Public Policy: Reframing Religion, Culture, Education, Sexuality, Class, Race, and the Economy.* Albany, NY: SUNY Press, 2002.

Coe, G. A. *A Social Theory of Religious Education.* New York: Arno, 1967.

———. *What is Christian Education?* New York: Scribners, 1929.

Cohen, L. *A Consumers' Republic: The Politics of Mass Consumption in Postwar America.* New York: Knopf, 2003.

Colatosti, C. "Children in the Global City." *The Witness Magazine.* A Globe of Witnesses (January 25, 2002). No pages. Online: http://thewitness.org/agw/colatosti.012502. html.

Coles, R. *Children of Crisis.* 1st ed. New York: Little, Brown, 2003.

———. "Entitlement." In *Children of Crisis,* 666–87.

———. *The Political Life of Children.* Boston: Atlantic Monthly Press, 1986.

———. "Privileged Ones." In *Children of Crisis,* 593–693.

———. *The Spiritual Life of Children.* New York: Houghton Mifflin, 1990.

Collier, Paul. *The Bottom Billion: Why the Poorest Countries Are Failing and What Can Be Done About It.* New York: Oxford University Press, 2007.

Colón, A. R., with P. A. Colón. *A History of Children: A Socio-Cultural Survey across Millennia.* Westport, CT: Greenwood, 2001.

Cherry, C. *The Theology of Jonathan Edwards: A Reappraisal.* Bloomington: Indiana University Press, 1966.

Child, S. *Poverty and Affluence: An Introduction to the International Relations of Rich and Poor Economies.* New York: Schocken, 1970.

Conforti, J. A. *Jonathan Edwards, Religious Tradition, and American Culture.* Chapel Hill: University of North Carolina Press, 1995.

Conwell, R. H. *Acres of Diamonds.* New York: Harper, 1915.

Corsaro, W. *The Sociology of Childhood.* Thousand Oaks, CA: Pine Forge, 1997.

———. *The Sociology of Childhood.* 2nd ed. Thousand Oaks, CA: Pine Forge, 2005.

Countryman, L. W. *The Rich Christian in the Church of the Early Empire: Contradictions and Accommodations.* New York: Mellen, 1980.

Couture, P. "A Practical Theology of Children and Poverty." *Seeing Children, Seeing God: A Practical Theology of Children and Poverty,* 91–125. Nashville: Abingdon, 2000.

———. *Seeing Children, Seeing God: A Practical Theology of Children and Poverty.* Nashville: Abingdon, 2000.

Cox, H. "Mammon and the Culture of the Market: A Socio-Theological Critique." in *Meaning and Modernity: Religion, Polity and Self,* edited by G. Madsen, W. M. Sullivan, A. Swidler, and S. M. Tipton, 124–35. Berkeley: University of California Press, 2002.

Cross, B. *Horace Bushnell: Minister to a Changing America.* Chicago: University of Chicago Press, 1958.

Csikszentmihalyi, M. "If We Are So Rich, Why Aren't We Happy?" *American Psychologist* 54 (1999) 821–27.

Cunningham, H. *Children and Childhood in Western Society Since 1500.* New York: Longman, 1995.

———. "Histories of Childhood." *American Historical Review* 103 (1998) 1195–1207.

Daly, H., and J. B. Cobb Jr. *For the Common Good: Redirecting the Economy toward Community, the Environment, and a Sustainable Future.* 2nd ed. Boston: Beacon, 1994.

Damasio, A. *The Feeling of What Happens: Body and Emotion in the Making of Consciousness.* New York: Harcourt & Brace, 1999.

Dark, D. *The Gospel According to America: A Meditation on a God-blessed, Christ-haunted Idea.* Louisville: Westminster John Knox, 2005.

Davies, J. "A Preferential Option for the Family." In *The Family in Theological Perspective,* edited by S. C. Barton, 219–36. Edinburgh: T. & T. Clark, 1996.

Davies, W. D., and D. C. Allison, Jr. *A Critical and Exegetical Commentary on the Gospel according to Matthew.* Vol. 3. New York: T. & T. Clark, 1997.

Dawn, M. J. "The Concept of 'the Principalities and Powers' in the Works of Jacques Ellul." PhD dissertation, University of Notre Dame, 1992.

Dawn, M. J. *Is It a Lost Cause? Having the Heart of God for the Church's Children.* Grand Rapids: Eerdmans, 1997.

DeChant, D. *The Sacred Santa: Religious Dimensions of Consumer Culture.* Cleveland: Pilgrim, 2002.

The Declaration of Independence and the Constitution of the United States of America. Washington, DC: Cato Institute, 1998.

Deddo, G. W. *Karl Barth's Theology of Relations: Trinitarian, Christological, and Human: Towards an Ethic of the Family.* New York: Lang, 1999.

De Graaf, J., D. Wann, and T. H. Naylor. *Affluenza: The All-Consuming Epidemic.* San Francisco: Berret-Koehler, 2001.

De la Sierra, Adolfo García. "A New Agenda for Economic Theory." In B. Goudzwaard, *Globalization and the Kingdom of God*, edited by J. W. Skillen, 83–90. Grand Rapids: Baker, 2001.

DeLong, B. "Neoliberalism." No pages. Online: http://en.wikipedia.org/wiki/Neoliberalism.

DeMause, L., editor. *The History of Childhood.* London: Souvenir, 1974.

De Soto, F. *The Mystery of Capital: Why Capitalism Triumphs in the West and Fails Everywhere Else.* New York: Basic Books, 2000.

———. *The Other Path: The Economic Answer to Terrorism.* New York: Basic Books, 1989.

DeVries, D. "'Be Converted and Become as Little Children': Friedrich Schleiermacher on the Religious Significance of Childhood." in M. Bunge, ed. *The Child in Christian Thought*, edited by Marcia J. Bunge, 329–49. Grand Rapids: Eerdmans, 2000.

Dommen, E. *How Just is the Market Economy?* Geneva: WCC Publications, 2003.

Dorr, D. *Option for the Poor: A Hundred Years of Vatican Social Teaching.* Maryknoll, NY: Orbis, 1983.

Dorrien, G. J. "Imagination Wording Forth: Horace Bushnell and the Metaphors of Inspiration." In *The Making of American Liberal Theology: Imagining Progressive Religion, 1805–1900*, 111–78.

———. *The Making of American Liberal Theology: Idealism, Realism, and Modernity, 1900–1950.* Louisville: Westminster John Knox, 2001.

———. *The Making of American Liberal Theology: Imagining Progressive Religion, 1805–1900.* Louisville: Westminster John Knox, 2001.

———. "The Victorian Gospel: Religion and Modernity in Progress." In *The Making of American Liberal Theology: Imagining Progressive Religion, 1805–1900*, 393–411.

Downs, P. G. "Christian Nurture: A Comparative Analysis of the Theories of Horace Bushnell and Lawrence O. Richards." PhD dissertation, New York University, 1982.

D'Souza, D. *The Virtue of Prosperity: Finding Values in an Age of Techno-Affluence.* New York: Free Press, 2000.

Duchrow, U. *Alternatives to Global Capitalism: Drawn from Biblical History, Designed for Political Action.* Utrecht, Netherlands: International Books, 1995.

Duchrow, U., and F. Hinkelammert. *Property for People, Not Profit: Alternatives to the Global Tyranny of Capital.* Translated by E. Griffiths, W. T. Davie, M. Marten, and P. Réamonn. New York: Zed, 2004.

Duffy, S. J. *The Dynamics of Grace: Perspectives in Theological Anthropology.* Collegeville, MN: Liturgical, 1993.

Dunnavant, A. L., editor. *Poverty and Ecclesiology: 19th-Century Evangelicals in Light of Liberation Theology.* Collegeville, MN: Liturgical, 1992.

Durkheim, E. *The Division of Labor in Society.* New York: Macmillian, 1933.

Dworkin, Ronald W. *Artificial Happiness: The Dark Side of the New Happy Class.* New York: Carroll & Graf, 2006.

Edwards, J. *A Faithful Narrative of the Surprising Work of God.* Rev. and corr. by E. Hickman. Vol. 1. 4th reprinting. Carlisle, PA: The Banner of Truth Trust, 1987.

———. *Freedom of the Will.* In P. Ramsey, editor, *The Works of Jonathan Edwards.* Vol. 1. New Haven: Yale University Press, 1957.

———. *Original Sin.* In C. A. Holbrook, editor, *The Works of Jonathan Edwards.* Vol. 3. New Haven: Yale University Press, 1970.

———. *Personal Narrative.* In C. H. Faust and T. N. Johnson, editors, *Jonathan Edwards: Representative Selections.* New York: Hill & Wang, 1962.

———. *Religious Affections.* In J. E. Smith, editor, *The Works of Jonathan Edwards.* Vol. 2. New Haven: Yale University Press, 1959.

———. *Some Thoughts Concerning the Present Revival of Religion in New England, and the Way in which it Ought to be Acknowledged and Promoted, Humbly Offered to the Public, in a Treatise on that Subject.* In *The Works of Jonathan Edwards.* Revised and corrected by E. Hickman. Vol. 1. 4th reprinting. Carlisle, PA: The Banner of Truth Trust, 1987.

Edwards, M. "'My God and My Good Mother': The Irony of Horace Bushnell's Gendered Republic." *Religion and American Culture: A Journal of Interpretation* 13 (2003) 111–37.

Edwards, R. L. *Of Singular Genius, of Singular Grace: A Biography of Horace Bushnell.* Cleveland: Pilgrim, 1992.

Edwards, T. *Contradictions of Consumption: Concepts, Practices and Politics in Consumer Society.* Buckingham: Open University Press, 2000.

Ehrlich, P. R. *The End of Affluence: A Blueprint for Your Future.* New York: Ballantine, 1974.

The Ekklesia Project. "About Us." No pages. http://www.ekklesiaproject.org/about.

Ellul, J. *Sources and Trajectories: Eight Early Articles by Jacques Ellul That Set the Stage.* Translated by M. J. Dawn. Grand Rapids: Eerdmans, 1997.

Elzinga, K. E. "Markets Without Guilt." *Faith & Economics* 40 (2002) 1–3.

Emerson, M. O., and C. Smith. *Divided by Faith: Evangelical Religion and the Problem of Race in America.* New York: Oxford University Press, 2000.

Erickson, M. J., P. K. Helseth, and J. Taylor, editors. *Reclaiming the Center: Confronting Evangelical Accommodation in Postmodern Times.* Wheaton, IL: Crossway, 2004.

Erikson, E. *Childhood and Society.* New York: Norton, 1994.

Eskridge, L., and M. A. Noll, editors. *More Money, More Ministry: Money and Evangelicals in Recent North American History.* Grand Rapids: Eerdmans, 2000.

Fangmeier, J. *Theologische Anthropologie des Kindes.* Zurich: EVZ, 1964.

Feiner, S. F. "A Portrait of the *Homo Economicus* as a Young Man." In *The New Economic Criticism*, edited by M. Woodmansee and M. Osteen, 193–209. New York: Routledge, 1999.

Ferber, M. and J. A. Nelson, editors. *Beyond Economic Man: Feminist Theory and Economics.* Chicago: University of Chicago Press, 1993.

Fikkert, B. "The Entire World Needs to be Awakened." In B. Goudzwaard, *Globalization and the Kingdom of God*, edited by J. W. Skillen, 45–60. Grand Rapids: Baker, 2001.

Fishburn, J. *Confronting the Idolatry of Family.* Minneapolis: Fortress, 1997.

Fogel, R. W. *The Escape from Hunger and Premature Death, 1700–2000: Europe, America, and the World.* New York: Cambridge University Press, 2004.

Foley, L., J. Weigel, and P. Normile. *To Live as Francis Lived: A Guide for Secular Franciscans.* Cincinnati, OH: St. Anthony Messenger Press, 2000.

Fowler, J. W., *Stages of Faith: The Psychology of Human Development and the Quest for Meaning.* New York: HarperCollins, 1981.

Fox, R. W. *Jesus in America: Personal Savior, Cultural Hero, National Obsession.* New York: HarperCollins, 2005.

Fox, R. W., and T. J .J. Lears, editors. *The Culture of Consumption: Critical Essays in American History 1880–1980.* New York: Pantheon, 1983.

Frank, T. *One Market Under God: Extreme Capitalism, Market Populism, and the End of Economic Democracy.* New York: Anchor, 2000.

Frankfort, L. A. "Affluence: The Impact of Family Money on Daughters." PhD dissertation, California Institute of Integral Studies, 2002.

Freire, P. *Education for Critical Consciousness.* New York: Continuum, 1973.

———. *Education: The Practice of Freedom.* London: Writers and Readers, 1976.

———. *Pedagogy of Hope: Reliving Pedagogy of the Oppressed.* New York: Continuum, 1994.

———. *Pedagogy of the Oppressed.* trans. M. B. Ramos. New York: Herder & Herder, 1970.

Friedman, B. J. *The Moral Consequences of Economic Growth.* New York: Alfred A. Knopf, 2005.

Fukuyama, F. "Culture and Economic Development." In *International Encyclopedia of the Social and Behavioral Sciences,* edited by N. J. Smelser and P. B. Baltes, 3130⊠34. Oxford: Pergamon, 2001.

———. "The End of History?" *National Interest* 16 (Summer 1989) 3–18.

———. *The End of History and the Last Man.* New York: Free Press, 1992.

———. *The Great Disruption: Human Nature and the Reconstitution of Social Order.* New York: The Free Press, 1999.

———. *Our Posthuman Future: Consequences of the Biotechnology Revolution.* New York: Farrar, Straus and Giroux, 2002.

———. "Reflections on The End of History, Five Years Later." in T. Burns, ed. *After History? Francis Fukuyama and His Critics.* Lanham, MD: Rowman & Littlefield, 1994. 239–58.

———. "Second Thoughts: The Last Man in a Bottle." *National Interest* 56 (1999) 16–33.

———. *Trust: The Social Virtues and the Creation of Prosperity.* New York: Simon & Schuster, 1995.

Gangel, K. O., and J. C. Wilhoit. editors. *The Christian Educator's Handbook on Spiritual Formation.* Wheaton, IL: Victor, 1994.

Garland, Diana R. *Family Ministry: A Comprehensive Guide.* Downers Grove, IL: InterVarsity, 1999.

———. *Precious in His Sight: A Guide to Child Advocacy.* Birmingham, AL: New Hope, 1993.

Garrido, A. M. "The Gift of the Child: Implications of the Catechesis of the Good Shepherd for the Discipline of Preaching." DMin project, Aquinas Institute of Theology, St. Louis, Missouri, 2003.

Garrison, J. *Dewey and Eros: Wisdom and Desire in the Art of Teaching.* New York: Teachers College Press, 1997.

Gascho, Victoria. "Parker Palmer and Christian Nurture." *Christian Education Journal* 2.1 (1998) 91–113.

Gaudoin-Parker, M. *Hymn of Freedom: Celebrating and Living the Eucharist.* Edinburgh: T. & T. Clark, 1997.

Gay, C. M. *The Way of the. Modern World: Or, Why It's Tempting to Live as if God Doesn't Exist.* Grand Rapids: Eerdmans, 1998.

———. *With Liberty and Justice for Whom? The Recent Evangelical Debate over Capitalism.* Grand Rapids: Eerdmans, 1991.

Geertz, C. *Local Knowledge: Further Essays in Interpretive Anthropology.* 3rd ed. New York: Basic Books, 2000.

———. "Thick Description: Toward an Interpretive Theory of Culture." In *The Interpretation of Cultures: Selected Essays,* 3–30. New York: Basic Books, 1973.

Gerstner, John H. *The Rational Biblical Theology of Jonathan Edwards.* Vol. 1. Powhatan, VA: Berea, 1991.

———. *The Rational Biblical Theology of Jonathan Edwards.* Vol. 2. Powhatan, VA: Berea, 1992.

Gerth, H. H., and C. W. Mills, editors. *From Max Weber: Essays in Sociology.* New York: Oxford University Press, 1964.

Gill, R., editor. *Theology and Sociology: A Reader.* London: Chapman, 1987.

Glendon, M. A., editor. *Intergenerational Solidarity, Welfare and Human Ecology.* Vatican City: Pontifical Academy of the Social Sciences, 2005.

———. *Rights Talk: The Impoverishment of Political Discourse.* New York: The Free Press, 1991.

Goetz, R. F. "Theological Anthropology, Self-Interest, and Economic Justice in Contemporary Protestant Critiques of Capitalism." PhD dissertation, Marquette University, 1998.

Gordon, B. *The Economic Problem in Biblical and Patristic Thought.* Leiden: Brill, 1989.

Gorringe, T. *Capital and the Kingdom: Theological Ethics and Economic Order.* Maryknoll, NY: Orbis, 1994.

———. *The Education of Desire: Towards a Theology of the Senses.* Harrisburg, PA: Trinity Press International, 2002.

Goudzwaard, B. *Capitalism and Progress: A Diagnosis of Western Society.* Translated by J. V. N. Zylstra. Grand Rapids: Eerdmans, 1979.

———. *Globalization and the Kingdom of God.* Edited by J. W. Skillen. Grand Rapids: Baker, 2001.

———. *Idols of Our Time.* trans. M. V. Vennen. Downers Grove, IL: Inter-Varsity, 1981.

Goudzwaard, B., and H. de Lange. *Beyond Poverty and Affluence: Towards a Canadian Economy of Care.* Toronto: University of Toronto Press, 1994.

Grau, M. *Of Divine Economy: Refinancing Redemption.* New York: T. & T. Clark, 2004.

Graustein, K., with M. Jacobsen. *Growing Up Christian.* Phillipsburg, NJ: Presbyterian & Reformed, 2005.

Green, J. *God's Fool: The Life and Times of Francis of Assisi.* Translated by P. Heinegg. San Francisco: Harper & Row, 1985.

Green, J., J. Guth, C. Smidt, and L. Kellstedt, editors. *Religion and the Culture Wars: Dispatches from the Front.* Lanham, MD: Rowman & Littlefield, 1996.

Greenberg, A., and J. Berktold. "American Evangelicals." *Religion and Ethics NewsWeekly.* Washington, DC: Greenberg Quinlin Rosner Research, Inc., 2004. 3–23. Online: http://www.Greenbergresearch.com /campaigns_us/publications.php.

Greene, C. "Consumerism and the Spirit of the Age." In *Christ and Consumerism: Critical Reflections on the Spirit of Our Age,* edited by C. Bartholomew and T. Moritz, 13–33. Carlisle: Paternoster, 2000.

Gregersen, N. H., W. B. Drees, and U. Görman, editors. *The Human Person in Science and Theology.* Grand Rapids: Eerdmans, 2000.

Grenz, S. J. *The Social God and the Relational Self: A Trinitarian Theology of the Imago Dei.* Louisville: Westminister John Knox, 2001.

Gries, J., and J. Ford, editors. *Housing Objectives and Programs*, vol. 11, in *The President's Conference on Home Building and Home Ownership*. Washington, DC: Government Printing Office, 1932.

Guelzo, A. C. *Edwards on the Will: A Century of American Theological Debate*. Middletown, CT: Weslyean University Press, 1989.

Gugino, J. G. "Abstract." in "Television's Impact on Children's Faith Development and Religious Experience: A Theological Inquiry into the Challenges of Technology, Using the Work of Philosopher Gabriel Marcel and Psychologist Lev Vygotsky." PhD dissertation, Harvard University, 1997.

Gundry-Volf, J. "The Least and the Greatest: Children in the New Testament." In *The Child in Christian Thought*, edited by Marcia J. Bunge, 29–60. Grand Rapids: Eerdmans, 2000.

———. "To Such as These Belongs the Reign of God." *Theology Today* 56 (2000) 469–80.

Gunter, B., and A. Furnham. *Children as Consumers: A Psychological Analysis of the Young People's Market*. New York: Routledge, 1998.

Gunton, C. E., and C. Schwöbel, editors. *Persons, Divine and Human: King's College Essays in Theological Anthropology*. Edinburgh: T. & T. Clark, 1991.

Gura, P. F. *Jonathan Edwards: America's Evangelical*. New York: Hill & Wang, 2005.

Gutiérrez, G. *A Theology of Liberation: History, Politics, and Salvation*. Translated and edited by C. Inda and J. Eagleson. 15th anniversary ed. Maryknoll, NY: Orbis, 1988.

Habermas, J. *Philosophical Discourse of Modernity: Twelve Lectures*. Translated by F. G. Lawrence. Cambridge, MA: MIT Press, 1987.

———. *Theory of Communicative Action, Vol. 1: Reason and the Rationalisation of Society*. Translated by T. McCarthy. Boston: Beacon, 1984.

———. *Theory of Communicative Action: Vol. 2, Lifeworld and System: A Critique of Functionalist Reason*. Translated by T. McCarthy. Boston: Beacon, 1987.

Hamilton, M. S. "Financing of American Evangelicalism Since 1945." In *More Money, More Ministry: Money and Evangelicals in Recent North American History*, edited by L. Eskridge and M. A. Noll, 81–103. Grand Rapids: Eerdmans, 2000.

Hanby, M. "Desire." In *Radical Orthodoxy*, edited by J. Milbank, K. Pickstock, and G. Ward, 109–26. London: Routledge, 1999.

Handy, R. *The Protestant Quest for a Christian America, 1830–1930*. Philadelphia: Fortress, 1977.

Haraway, D. J. "Ecce Homo, Ar'n't I a Woman, and Inappropriate/d Others: The Human in a Post-Humanist Landscape." In *Feminists Theorize the Political*, edited by J. Butler and J. Scott, 82–97. New York: Routledge, 1992.

Harding, L. S., Jr. "Christian Nurture Revisited: A Theological and Psychological Exposition and Development of Horace Bushnell's Work on the Foundations of Christian Child-Rearing." PhD dissertation, Boston College, 1989.

Hardt, M. "The Withering of Civil Society." *Social Text* 45 (Winter 1995) 27–44.

Hardt, M., and A. Negri. *Empire*. Cambridge: Harvard University Press, 2000.

———. *Multitude: War and Democracy in the Age of Empire*. New York: Penguin, 2004.

Harrington, D. J. *The Gospel of Matthew*, Sacra Pagina 1. Collegeville, MN: Liturgical, 1991.

Harris, C. C. *Kinship*. Buckingham: Open University Press, 1990.

———. "Kinship and Economic Life." In *Kinship*, 84–97.

Harris, H. A. *Fundamentalism and Evangelicals*. Oxford: Clarendon, 1998.

Harrison, N. V. "Raising Them Right: Early Christian Approaches to Child Rearing." *Theology Today* 56 (2000) 481–94.

Harrisville, R. A. "In Search of the Meaning of 'The Reign of God.'" *Interpretation* 47 (1993) 140–51.

———. "Jesus and the Family." *Interpretation* 23 (1969) 425–38.

Hart, D. G. *Deconstructing Evangelicalism: Conservative Protestantism in the Age of Billy Graham*. Grand Rapids: Baker Academic, 2004.

———. *The Lost Soul of American Protestantism*. Lanham, MD: Rowman & Littlefield, 2002.

———. *That Old-Time Religion in Modern America: Evangelical Protestantism in the Twentieth Century*. Chicago: Ivan R. Dee, 2002.

Hart, S. *What Does the Lord Require? How American Christians Think About Economic Justice*. New York: Oxford University Press, 1992.

Hartropp, A. "Affirmation of Affluence, or Awkward Ambivalence?" *Faith & Economics* 40 (2002) 3–6.

Haskell, T. L., and R. F. Teichgraeber, editors. *The Culture of the Market: Historical Essays*. Cambridge: Cambridge University Press, 1996.

Hatch, N. O. *The Democratization of American Christianity*. New Haven: Yale University Press, 1989.

Hatch, N. O., and Harry S. Stout, editors. *Jonathan Edwards and the American Experience*. New York: Oxford University Press, 1988.

Hauerwas, S. *A Better Hope: Resources for a Church Confronting Capitalism, Democracy, and Postmodernity*. Grand Rapids: Brazos, 2000.

———. *With the Grain of the Universe: The Church's Witness and Natural Theology*. Grand Rapids: Brazos, 2001.

Hauerwas, S., and W. H. Willimon. *Resident Aliens: Life in the Christian Colony*. Nashville: Abingdon, 1989.

Hauerwas, S., and F. Lentrichhia, editors. *Dissent from the Homeland: Essays after September 11*. Durham: Duke University Press, 2002.

Hauerwas, S., C. Huebner, H. Huebner, and M. T. Nation, editors, *The Wisdom of the Cross: Essays in Honor of John Howard Yoder*. Grand Rapids: Eerdmans, 1999.

Hay, D. *Economics Today: A Christian Critique*. Grand Rapids: Eerdmans, 1989.

———, with R. Nye. *The Spirit of the Child*. London: Fount/HarperCollins, 1998.

Hay, David, R. Nye, and R. Murphy. "Thinking About Childhood Spirituality: Review of Research and Current Directions." In *Research in Religious Education*, edited by L. J. Francis, W. K. Kay, and W. S. Campbell, 47–72. Leominster, UK: Gracewing, 1996.

Hays, R. B. *The Moral Vision of the New Testament*. New York: HarperCollins, 1996.

———. "Scripture-Shaped Community: The Problem of Method in New Testament Ethics." *Interpretation* 44 (1990) 42–55.

Hays, S. P. *The Response to Industrialism: 1885–1914*. Chicago: University of Chicago Press, 1957.

Hawes, J. M. *The Children's Rights Movement: A History of Advocacy and Protection*. Boston: Twayne, 1991.

Hedley, D. *Coleridge, Philosophy and Religion: Aids to Reflection and the Mirror of the Spirit*. Cambridge: Cambridge University Press, 2000.

———. "Should Divinity Overcome Metaphysics? Reflections on John Milbank's Theology Beyond Secular Reason and Confessions of a Cambridge Platonist." *Journal of Religion* 80 (2000) 271–98.

Heller, D. *The Children's God*. Chicago: University of Chicago Press, 1986.

Heller, S. "The Meaning of Children Becomes a Focal Point for Scholars." *The Chronicle of Higher Education* (August 7, 1998) A14–16.

Helpman, E. *The Mystery of Economic Growth*. Cambridge: Harvard University Press, 2004.

Henderlite, R. "The Theological Basis of Horace Bushnell's Christian Nurture." PhD dissertation, Yale University, 1947.

Hennion, A., and C. Méadel. "The Artisans of Desire: the Mediation of Advertising Between Product and Consumer." *Sociological Theory* 7 (1989) 191–209.

Hetherington, E. M., M. Cox, and R. Cox. *Mother-Child, Father-Child Relations*. Washington, DC: National Association for the Education of Young Children Press, 1978.

Hewitt, G. A. *Regeneration and Morality: A Study of Charles Finney, Charles Hodge, John W. Nevin, and Horace Bushnell*. Brooklyn: Carlson, 1991.

Heywood, C. *A History of Childhood*. Malden, MA: Blackwell, 2001.

Hilton, B. *The Age of Atonement: The Influence of Evangelicalism on Social and Economic Thought, 1795–1865*. Oxford: Clarendon, 1988.

Himmelfarb, G. *Poverty and Compassion: The Moral Imagination of the Late Victorians*. New York: Knopf, 1991.

Hine, T. *I Want That! How We All Became Shoppers*. New York: HarperCollins, 2002.

Hirst, I. R. C., and W. D. Reekie, editors. *The Consumer Society*. London: Tavistock, 1977.

Hobson, J. A. *God and Mammon: The Relations of Religion and Economics*. London: Watts, 1931.

———. *Problems of Poverty: An Inquiry Into the Industrial Condition of the Poor*. New York: Kelley, 1971.

Hobson, J. A. *Wealth and Life: A Study in Values*. London: Macmillan, 1929.

Hochschild, A. *The Managed Heart: Commercialization of Human Feeling*. Berkeley: University of California Press, 1983.

Hoksbergen, R. "A Reformed Approach to Economics: The Kuyperian Tradition." *Faith and Economics* 20 (1992) 7–27.

———. "Is There a Christian Economics? Some Thoughts in Light of the Rise of Postmodernism." *Christian Scholar's Review* 24 (1994) 26–42.

———. "That the Work of God Might Be Displayed: Debt Forgiveness and Development." *Faith and Economics* 35 (2000) 16–19.

———. "The Morality of Economic Growth." *Reformed Journal* (December 1982) 10–13.

Holbrook, C. A., "Editor's Introduction." In J. Edwards, *Original Sin*, edited by C. A. Holbrook, 8–39. *The Works of Jonathan Edwards*. Vol. 3. New Haven: Yale University Press, 1970.

Holbrook, C. A. *Jonathan Edwards, the Valley and Nature: an Interpretive Essay*. Crandbury, NJ: Associated University Presses, 1987.

Holbrook, M. B., and E. C. Hirschman. *The Semiotics of Consumption: Interpreting Symbolic Consumer Behavior in Popular Culture and Works of Art*. New York: de Gruyter, 1993.

Hollander, J. M. *The Real Environmental Crisis: Why Poverty, Not Affluence, is the Environment's Number One Enemy*. Berkeley: University of California Press, 2003.

Hollinger, D. *Individualism and Social Ethics: An Evangelical Syncretism*. Lanham, MD: University Press of America, 1983.

Holt, J. *Escape from Childhood: The Needs and Rights of Children.* New York: Ballantine, 1974.

Hooper, J., and D. Teresi. *The Three Pound Universe: The Brain, from Chemistry of the Mind to New Frontiers of the Soul.* New York: Dell, 1986.

Hoopes, J., "Jonathan Edwards's Religious Psychology." *Journal of American History* 69 (1983) 849–65.

Hoover, H. *American Individualism.* New York: Doubleday, 1922.

———. *Herbert Hoover: Public Papers of the Presidents of the United States.* Washington, DC: Government Printing Office, 1974.

———. *The Memoirs of Herbert Hoover: The Cabinet and the Presidency, 1920–1933.* vol. 2. New York: Macmillan, 1952.

———. No pages. Online: http://www.geocities.com/americanpresidencynet/31st.htm. [AQ: what is this page—it is no longer available]

Hoppe, L. J. *There Shall Be No Poor among You: Poverty in the Bible.* Nashville: Abingdon, 2004.

Horgan, J. *The Undiscovered Mind: How the Human Brain Defies Replication, Medication, and Explanation.* New York: Free Press, 1999.

Horowitz, D. *The Anxieties of Affluence: Critiques of American Consumer Culture, 1939–1979.* Amherst: University of Massachusetts Press, 2004.

———. *The Morality of Spending: Attitudes Toward the Consumer Society in America, 1875–1940.* Baltimore: Johns Hopkins University Press, 1985.

Horowitz, R., and A. Mohun, editors. *His and Hers: Gender, Consumption, and Technology.* Charlottesville: University Press of Virginia, 1998.

Hovland, R., and G. B. Wilcox, editors. *Advertising in Society: Classic and Contemporary Readings on Advertising's Role in Society.* Lincolnwood, IL: NTC Business Books, 1990.

Howe, D. W. *The Political Culture of the American Whigs.* Chicago: University of Chicago Press, 1979.

Howell, J. E. "A Study of the Theological Method of Horace Bushnell and Its Application to His Cardinal Doctrines." PhD dissertation, Duke University, 1963.

Howes, D., ed. *Cross-Cultural Consumption: Global Markets, Local Realities.* London: Routledge, 1996.

Hull, J. M. "Christian Education in a Capitalist Society: Money and God." In *Essentials of Christian Community, Essays in Honour of Daniel W. Hardy*, edited by D. Ford and D. L. Stamps, 241–52. Edinburgh: T. & T. Clark, 1995.

———. "Money and God: Christian Education in a Capitalist Society." *PACT South West* 5 (January/February 1996) 1–8.

———. "Money, Modernity, and Morality: Some Issues in the Christian Education of Adults." *Religious Education* 95.1 (2000) 4–22.

———. "Spiritual Education, Religion and the Money Culture." In *Catholic Education: Inside-Out/Outside-In*, edited by J. C. Conroy, 285–301. Dublin: Veritas, 1999.

———. *When You Receive a Child: Reflections on Luke 9:46–48.* St. Meinrad, IN: Abbey, 1980.

Hunter, James Davison. *American Evangelicalism: Conservative Religion in the Quandary of Modernity.* New Brunswick, NJ: Rutgers University Press, 1987.

———. *Culture Wars: The Struggle to Define America.* New York: Basic Books, 1991.

———. *Evangelicalism: The Coming Generation.* Chicago: Chicago University Press, 1987.

Hutchinson, M., and O. Kalu, editors. *A Gobal Faith: Essays on Evangelicalism and Globalization*. Sydney: Centre for the Study of Australian Christianity, 1998.

Hyde, K. *Religion in Childhood and Adolescence: A Comprehensive Review of the Research*. Birmingham, AL: Religious Education Press, 1992.

Hyman, G. *The Predicament of Postmodern Theology: Radical Orthodoxy or Nihilist Textualism?* Louisville: Westminster John Knox, 2001.

Hymowitz, K. S. *Liberation's Children: Parents and Children in a Postmodern Age*. Chicago: Ivan R. Dee, 2004.

Institute for the Study of American Evangelicals. No Pages. Online: http://www.wheaton. edu /isae/definingevangelicalism.html.

"Interviewing the Brain." No pages. Online: http://www.olsonzaltman.com/oza/zmet. html.

James, A., C. Jenks and A. Prout. *Theorizing Childhood*. New York: Teachers College Press, 1998.

Jameson, F. *Postmodernism, or the Cultural Logic of Late Capitalism*. Durham: Duke University Press, 1991.

Jelen, T. G. *To Serve God and Mammon: Church-State Relations in American Politics*. Boulder, CO: Westview, 2000.

Jenkins, P. *The Next Christendom: The Coming of Global Christianity*. New York: Oxford University Press, 2002.

Jenson, R. W. *America's Theologian: A Recommendation of Jonathan Edwards*. New York: Oxford University Press, 1988.

———. "The Kingdom of America's God." *Essays in Theology of Culture*, 50–66. Grand Rapids: Eerdmans, 1995.

Joas, H. "Social Theory and the Sacred: A Response to John Milbank." *Ethical Perspectives* 7 (2000) 233–43.

Pope John Paul II. *Centesimus Annus*. No pages. Online: http://www.vatican.va/ holy _ father/john_ aul_ii/encyclicals/ documents/hf_jp-ii_enc_01051991_centesimus-annus_en.html.

———. *The Splendor of Truth, Veritatis Splendor*. Boston: Pauline Books and Media, 1993.

Johnson, C. *The Sorrows of Empire: Militarism, Secrecy, and the End of the Republic*. New York: Holt, 2004.

Johnson, L. T. *The Gospel of Luke*. Sacra Pagina 3. Collegeville, MN: Liturgical, 1991.

———. *The Literary Function of Possessions in Luke-Acts*. Society of Biblical Literature Dissertation Series 39. Missoula, MT: Scholars, 1977.

———. *Sharing Possessions: Mandate and Symbol of Faith*. Overtures to Biblical Theology. Philadelphia: Fortress, 1981.

Johnson, S. "Remembering the Poor: Transforming Christian Practice." In *Redemptive Transformation in Practical Theology*, edited by D. R. Wright and J. D. Kuentzel, 189–215. Grand Rapids: Eerdmans, 2004.

Johnson, W. A. *Nature and the Supernatural in the Theology of Horace Bushnell*. Studia theologica Lundensia 25. Lund: Gleerup, 1963.

Johnston, C. *The Wealth or Health of Nations: Transforming Capitalism from Within*. Cleveland: Pilgrim, 1998.

Jones, D. A. "The Social and Political Thought of Horace Bushnell: An Interpretation of the Mid-Nineteenth Century Mind." PhD dissertation, Northwestern University, 1973.

Jones, L. G. "A Thirst for God or Consumer Spirituality? Cultivating Disciplined Practices of Being Engaged by God." *Modern Theology* 13 (1997) 3–28.

Jones, L. G., and J. J. Buckley, editors. *Spirituality and Social Embodiment.* Oxford: Blackwell, 1997.

Jones, T. *Nurturing a Child's Soul.* Nashville: Word, 2000.

Joseph, R., et al. *NeuroTheology: Brain, Science, Spirituality, Religious Experience.* 2nd ed. New York: University Press, 2003.

Junker-Kenny, M., and N. Mette, editors. *Little Children Suffer.* Maryknoll, NY: Orbis, 1996.

Kail, R. V., editor. *Advances in Child Development.* Vol. 32. San Diego: Academic Press, 2004.

Kamitsuka, D. G. *Theology and Contemporary Culture: Liberation, Postliberal and Revisionary Perspectives.* New York: Cambridge University Press, 2000.

Kavanaugh, J. F. *Following Christ in a Consumer Culture: The Spirituality of Cultural Resistance.* Rev. ed. Maryknoll, NY: Orbis, 1991.

———. *Who Count as Persons? Human Identity and the Ethics of Killing.* Washington, DC: Georgetown University Press, 2001.

Kay, J. *Culture and Prosperity: The Truth about Markets—Why Some Nations Are Rich but Most Remain Poor.* New York: HarperCollins, 2004.

Keener, C. S. *A Commentary on the Gospel of Matthew.* Grand Rapids: Eerdmans, 1999.

Keller, T. *Ministries of Mercy: The Call of the Jericho Road.* 2nd ed. Phillisburg, PA: Presbyterian & Reformed, 1997.

Kemp, K. W. *God's Capitalist: Asa Candler of Coca-Cola.* Macon: Mercer University Press, 2002.

Kidd, R. *Wealth and Beneficence in the Pastoral Epistles: A "Bourgeois" Form of Early Christianity?* Society of Biblical Literature Series 122. Atlanta: Scholars, 1990.

Kielburger, C., with K. Major. *Free the Children.* Toronto: McClelland & Stewart, 1998.

Klay, R. "Godly Delight, Christian Vocation, and Moral Obligation: A Much Needed Perspective on Capitalism." *Faith & Economics* 40 (2002) 6–10.

Klein, N. *No Logo: Taking Aim at the Brand Bullies.* New York: Picador, 1999.

Kline, S. *Out of the Garden: Toys, TV and Children's Culture in the Age of Marketing.* London: Verso, 1993.

———. "The Play of the Market: on the Internationalization of Children's Culture." *Theory, Culture and Society* 12 (1995) 103–29.

Kodel, J. "Luke and the Children." *Catholic Biblical Quarterly* 49 (1987) 415–30.

Kotulak, R. *Inside the Brain.* Kansas City: Andres & McMeel, 1996.

Kowinski, W. *The Malling of America: An Insider Look at the Great Consumer Paradise.* New York: Morrow, 1985.

Kozol, J. *Amazing Grace: The Lives of Children and the Conscience of a Nation.* New York: Crown, 1995.

———. *Ordinary Resurrections: Children in the Years of Hope.* New York: Crown, 2000.

Krahn, J. H. "Nurture vs. Revival: Horace Bushnell on Religious Education." *Religious Education* 70 (1975) 370–90.

Krugman, P. *Peddling Prosperity: Economic Sense and Nonsense in the Age of Diminished Expectations.* New York: Norton, 1994.

Kuhl, R. G. "The Reign of God: Implications for Christian Education." *Christian Education Journal* 1 (2002) 73–88.

Lagercrantz, H. "The Child's Brain—On Neurogenetic Determinism and Free Will." In *The Human Person in Science and Theology*, edited by N. H. Gregersen, W. B. Drees, and U. Görman, 65–72. Edinburgh: T. & T. Clark, 2000.

Lakeland, P. *Postmodernity: Christian Identity in a Fragmented Age*. Minneapolis: Fortress, 1997.

Landes, D. S. *The Wealth and Poverty of Nations: Why Some Are So Rich and Some So Poor*. New York: Norton, 1998.

Lasn, K. *Culture Jam: How to Reverse America's Suicidal Consumer Binge—and Why We Must*. New York: Quill, 2000.

Latham, R. *Consuming Youth: Vampires, Cyborgs, and the Culture of Consumption*. Chicago: University of Chicago Press, 2002.

Lasch, C. *The Culture of Narcissism: American Life in an Age of Diminishing Expectations*. New York: Norton, 1978.

Lash, N. "Beyond the End of History?" In *The Beginning and the End of "Religion,"* 252–64. Cambridge: Cambridge University Press, 1996.

———. *A Matter of Hope*. Notre Dame, IN: University of Notre Dame Press, 1981.

———. "Performing the Scriptures." In *Theology on the Way to Emmaus*, 37–46. London: SCM, 1986.

———. "What Might Martyrdom Mean?" In *Theology on the Way to Emmaus*, 75–92. London: SCM, 1986.

Lea, Stephen E. G., Paul Webley, and Brian M. Young, editors. *New Directions in Economic Psychology: Theory, Experiment and Application*. Brookfield, VT: Elgar, 1992.

Leach, William. *Land of Desire: Merchants, Power, and the Rise of a New American Culture*. New York: Vintage, 1994.

Lears, T. J. J. *Fables of Abundance: A Cultural History of Advertising in America*. New York: Basic Books, 1994.

———. *No Place of Grace: Anti-Modernism and the Transformation of American Culture, 1880–1920*. New York: Pantheon, 1981.

———. "From Salvation to Self-Realization." In *The Culture of Consumption: Critical Essays in American History 1880–1980*, edited by R. W. Fox and T. J. J. Lears, 1–38. New York: Pantheon, 1983.

Lebergott, S. *Pursuing Happiness: American Consumers in the Twentieth Century*. Princeton: Princeton University Press, 1993.

Lebergott, S. *The Americans: An Economic Record*. New York: Norton, 1984.

LeDoux, J. *Synaptic Self: How Our Brains Become Who We Are*. New York: Viking, 2002.

Lee, J. M., editor. *Forging a Better Religious Education in the Third Millennium*. Birmingham, AL: Religious Education Press, 2000.

Lee, N. *Childhood and Society: Growing Up in an Age of Uncertainty*. Philadelphia: Open University Press, 2001.

Lee, S. H. *The Philosophical Theology of Jonathan Edwards*. Princeton, NJ: Princeton University Press, 1988.

Légasse, S., et al. *Gospel Poverty: Essays in Biblical Theology*. Translated by M. D. Guinan. Rev. ed. New York: Paulist, 1981.

———. *Jésus et L'Enfant: 'Enfant', 'Petits' et 'Simples' dans la Tradition Synoptique*. Paris: Lecoffre, 1969.

———. "The Call of the Rich Man." In *Gospel Poverty*, 53–80.

Lenski, R. C. H. *The Interpretation of St. Mark's Gospel*. Minneapolis: Augsburg, 1961, 1946.

Leuchtenburg, W. E., and D. J. Boorstin. *The Perils of Prosperity 1914–1932*. 2nd ed. Chicago: University of Chicago Press, 1993.

Levison, D. "Children as Economic Agents." *Feminist Economics* 6 (2000) 125–34.

Lewis, D. M., ed. *Christianity Reborn: The Global Expansion of Evangelicalism in the Twentieth Century*. Grand Rapids: Eerdmans, 2004.

Libby, Larry. *The Cry of the Poor*. Bothell, WA: Actional International Ministries, 1986.

Linn, S. *Consuming Kids: The Hostile Takeover of Childhood*. New York: New Press, 2004.

Loder, J. E. *The Logic of the Spirit: Human Development in Theological Perspective*. San Francisco: Jossey-Bass, 1998.

———. "The Place of Science in Practical Theology: The Human Factor." *International Journal of Practical Theology* 4 (2000) 22–41.

———. *The Transforming Moment*. 2nd ed. Colorado Springs: Helmers & Howard, 1989.

Loder, J. E., and W. J. Neidhardt. *The Knight's Move: The Relational Logic of the Spirit in Theology and Science*. Colorado Springs: Helmers & Howard, 1992.

Loder, J. E., and J. W. Fowler. "Conversations on Fowler's *Stages of Faith* and Loder's *The Transforming Moment*." *Religious Education* 77 (1982) 133–48.

Lohfink, G. *Jesus and Community: The Social Dimension of Christian Faith*. Translated by John P. Galvin. Philadelphia: Fortress, 1982.

Long, K. T. *The Revival of 1857–58: Interpreting an American Religious Awakening*. New York: Oxford University Press, 1998.

Long, S. *Divine Economy: Theology and the Market*. London: Routledge, 2000.

Luthar, S. S. "The Culture of Affluence: Psychological Costs of Material Wealth." *Child Development* 74.6 (2003) 1581–93.

Luthar, S. S., and S. J. Latendresse. "Children of the Affluent: Challenges to Well-Being." *Current Directions in Psychological Science* 14 (2005) 49–53.

Luthar, S. S., and C. Sexton. "The High Price of Affluence." In *Advances in Child Development*, vol. 32, edited by R. V. Kail, 126–62. San Diego, CA: Academic Press, 2004.

Lyon, D. *Jesus in Disneyland: Religion in Postmodern Times*. Cambridge: Polity, 2000.

———. *Postmodernity*. Minneapolis: University of Minnesota Press, 1994.

———. *The Steeples' Shadow: On the Myths and Realities of Secularization*. Grand Rapids: Eerdmans, 1985.

Maas, R. "Christ as the Logos of Childhood: Reflections on the Meaning and Mission of the Child." *Theology Today* 56 (2000) 456–68.

Madrick, J. *The End of Affluence: The Causes and Consequences of America's Economic Dilemma*. New York: Random House, 1995.

Madsen, G., W. M. Sullivan, A. Swidler, and S. M. Tipton, editors. *Meaning and Modernity: Religion, Polity and Self*. Berkeley: University of California Press, 2002.

Maitra, P. *The Globalization of Capitalism in Third World Countries*. Westport, CT: Praeger, 1996.

Makowski, L. J. "Horace Bushnell: A study of his sermons from the perspective of his Christian anthropology." PhD dissertation, Catholic University of America, 1992.

Marsden, G. *Fundamentalism and American Culture: The Shaping of Twentieth-Century Evangelicalism 1870–1925*. New York: Oxford University Press, 1980.

Markus, R. A. *Saeculum: History and Society in the Theology of St. Augustine*. Cambridge: Cambridge University Press, 1970.

Marsden, George M., ed. *Evangelicalism and Modern America*. Grand Rapids: Eerdmans, 1984.

———. *Reforming Fundamentalism: Fuller Seminary and the New Evangelicalism.* Grand Rapids: Eerdmans, 1987.

———. *Understanding Fundamentalism and Evangelicalism.* Grand Rapids: Eerdmans, 1991.

Marshall, K., and P. Parvis. *Honouring Children: The Human Rights of the Child in Christian Perspective.* Edinburgh: St. Adrian, 2004.

Martinson, T. *American Dreamscape: The Pursuit of Happiness in Postwar Suburbia.* New York: Carroll & Graf, 2000.

Marty, M. *Righteous Empire: The Protestant Experience in America.* New York: Dial, 1970.

Matthew, M. T. "Toward a Holistic Theological Anthropology: Jonathan Edwards and Friedrich Schleiermacher on Religious Affection." PhD dissertation, Emory University, 2000.

Mason, R. S. *The Economics of Conspicuous Consumption: Theory and Thought since 1700.* Cheltenham, UK: Elgar, 1998.

May, H. F. *Protestant Churches and Industrial America.* New York: Harper, 1967.

Mayhew, A. "Review of Karl Polanyi, *The Great Transformation: The Political and Economic Origins of Our Time.*" *Economic History Services.* Online: http://www.eh.net/bookreviews/library/polanyi.shtml.

McDannell, C. *The Christian Home in Victorian America, 1840–1900.* Bloomington: Indiana University Press, 1986.

McDonald, F. *We the People: The Economic Origins of the Constitution.* 1958. Reprinted, New Brunswick, NJ: Transaction Publishers, 1994.

McFague, S. *Life Abundant: Rethinking Theology and Economy for a Planet in Peril.* Minneapolis: Fortress, 2000.

McGrath, A. *A Passion for Truth: The Intellectual Coherence of Evangelicalism.* Downers Grove, IL: InterVarsity, 1996.

———. *Evangelicalism and The Future of Christianity.* Downers Grove, IL: InterVarsity, 1995.

———. *The Future of Christianity.* Malden, MA: Blackwell, 2002.

McGuire, R. A. *To Form a More Perfect Union: A New Economic Interpretation of the U.S. Constitution.* New York: Oxford University Press, 2003.

McKee, A. *Economics and the Christian Mind.* New York: Vantage, 1987.

Meeks, M. D. *God the Economist: The Doctrine of God and Political Economy.* Minneapolis: Fortress, 1989.

Mette, N. "Not a 'Century of the Child': the Situation of Children in the World in the 1990s." In *Little Children Suffer,* edited by M. Junker-Kenny and N. Mette, 3–8. Maryknoll, NY: Orbis, 1996.

Meyers, M. L. *The Soul of Modern Economic Man: Ideas of Self-Interest, Thomas Hobbes to Adam Smith.* Chicago: University of Chicago Press, 1983.

Milbank, J. *Being Reconciled: Ontology and Pardon.* London: Routledge, 2003.

———. "Sovereignty, Empire, Capital, and Terror." In *The Imperial Tense: Prospects and Problems of American Empire,* edited by A. J. Bacevich, 159–71. Chicago: Ivan R. Dee, 2003.

———. *Theology and Social Theory: Beyond Secular Reason.* Oxford: Blackwell, 1990.

Milbank, J., C. Pickstock, and G. Ward, editors. *Radical Orthodoxy.* London: Routledge, 1999.

Miles, M. R. *Desire and Delight: A New Reading of Augustine's Confessions.* New York: Crossroad, 1992.

Miles, S. *Consumerism as a Way of Life.* London: Sage, 1998.

Miller, D., editor. *Acknowledging Consumption: A Review of New Studies.* London: Routledge, 1995.

———. *Material Culture and Mass Consumption.* Oxford: Blackwell, 1987.

———. *Worlds Apart: Modernity through the Prism of the Local.* London: Routledge, 1995.

Miller-Adams, M. *Owning Up: Poverty, Assets, and the American Dream.* Washington, D.C.: Brookings Institution Press, 2002.

Miller, V. "Desire and the Kingdom of God." *Consuming Religion: Christian Faith and Practice in a Consumer Culture.* New York: Continuum, 2004. 107–45.

Miller-McLemore, B. *Let the Children Come: Reimagining Childhood from a Christian Perspective.* San Francisco: Jossey-Bass, 2003.

Miller, P. *Jonathan Edwards.* Amherst: University of Massachusetts Press, 1981.

———. "Jonathan Edwards on the Sense of the Heart." *Harvard Theological Review* 41 (1948) 123–45.

———. *The New England Mind: The Seventeenth Century.* Cambridge: Harvard University Press, 1954.

Miller, R. C. *Christian Nurture and the Church.* New York: Scribners, 1956.

———. editor. *Theologies of Religious Education.* Birmingham, AL: Religious Education Press, 1995.

Miller, E., and M. Porter. *In the Shadow of the Baby Boom.* Brooklyn: EPM Communications, 1994.

Minkema, K. P., compiler. "A Jonathan Edwards Chronology." 2003. No pages. Online: http://www.yale.edu/wje/html/chronology.html.

Mitchell, N. "The Once and Future Child: Towards a Theology of Childhood." *Living Light* 12 (1975) 423–37.

Moberly, W. "The Use of Scripture." In *Veritatis Splendor — A Response,* edited by C. Yeats, 8–24. Norwich: The Canterbury, 1994.

Moessner, D. P. *Lord of the Banquet: The Literary and Theological Significance of the Lukan Travel Narrative.* Minneapolis: Fortress, 1989.

Moltmann, J. "Child and Childhood as Metaphors of Hope." Translated by Marion Grau. *Theology Today* 56 (2000) 592–603.

Montessori, M. *The Absorbent Mind.* Translated by C. A. Claremont. 1958. New York: Holt, 1995.

———. *The Discovery of the Child.* Translated by M. J. Costelloe. New York: Ballantine, 1967.

———. *The Secret of Childhood.* Translated by M. J. Costelloe. New York: Ballantine, 1966.

Mooney, C. G. *Theories of Childhood: An Introduction to Dewey, Montessori, Erikson, Piaget and Vygotsky.* St. Paul, MN: Redleaf, 2000.

Moore, A. J., editor. *Religious Education as Social Transformation.* Birmingham, AL: Religious Education Press, 1989.

Moore, R. L. *Selling God: American Religion in the Marketplace of Culture.* New York: Oxford University Press, 1994.

Moreland, J. P. "A Defense of a Substance Dualist View of the Soul." In *Christian Perspectives on Being Human,* edited by J. P. Moreland and David M. Ciocchi, 55–79. Grand Rapids: Baker, 1993.

———. "Spiritual Formation and the Nature of the Soul." *Christian Education Journal* 4 (2000) 25–43.

Morgenthaler, S. K., editor. *Exploring Children's Spiritual Formation.* River Forest, IL: Pillars, 1999.

———. "Research Possibilities and Interests." In *Exploring Children's Spiritual Formation,* edited by S. K. Morgenthaler, 265–76. River Forest, IL: Pillars, 1999.

Moritz, T. "New Testament Voices for an Addicted Society." In *Christ and Consumerism: Critical Reflections on the Spirit of our Age,* edited by C. Bartholomew and T. Moritz, 54–80. Carlisle, UK: Paternoster, 2000.

Moxnes, H., editor. *Constructing Early Christian Families: Family as Social Reality and Metaphor.* New York: Routledge, 1997.

———. *The Economy of the Kingdom: Social Conflict and Economic Relations in Luke's Gospel.* Overtures to Biblical Theology. Minneapolis: Fortress, 1988.

Muers, R. "Idolatry and Future Generations: The Persistence of Molech." *Modern Theology* 19 (2003) 547–61.

Muller, J. Z. *The Mind and the Market: Capitalism in Modern European Thought.* New York: Knopf, 2002.

Mullin, R. B. *The Puritan as Yankee: A Life of Horace Bushnell.* Grand Rapids: Eerdmans, 2002.

———. "The Bushnell Controversy." In *The Puritan as Yankee: A Life of Horace Bushnell,* 151–79. Grand Rapids: Eerdmans, 2002.

Munger, T. T. *Horace Bushnell, Preacher and Theologian.* New York: Houghton, Mifflin, 1899.

Munro, Harry C. *Protestant Nurture.* Englewood Cliffs, NJ: Prentice-Hall, 1956.

Murray, I. H. *Evangelicalism Divided: A Record of Crucial Change in the Years 1950 to 2000.* Edinburgh: Banner of Truth, 2000.

———. *Revival and Revivalism: The Making and Marring of American Evangelicalism 1750–1858.* Edinburgh: Banner of Truth, 1994.

Murray, J. *Redemption Accomplished and Applied.* Grand Rapids: Eerdmans, 1955.

Myers, C. *Binding the Strong Man: A Political Reading of Mark's Story of Jesus.* Maryknoll, NY: Orbis, 1988.

Myers, D. G. *The American Paradox: Spiritual Hunger in an Age of Plenty.* New Haven: Yale University Press, 2000.

Narotzky, S. *New Directions in Economic Anthropology.* Chicago: Pluto, 1997.

Nash, G. H. *The Life of Herbert Hoover: The Engineer, 1874–1914.* New York: Norton, 1983.

———. *The Life Herbert Hoover: The Humanitarian, 1914–1917.* New York: Norton, 1988.

Nash, R. H. *Freedom, Justice and the State.* Lanham, MD: University Press of America, 1980.

———. ed. *Liberation Theology.* Milford, MI: Mott Media, 1984.

———. *Poverty and Wealth: The Christian Debate Over Capitalism.* Westchester, IL: Crossway, 1986.

———. *Social Justice and the Christian Church.* Lanham, MD: University Press of America, 1992.

Nicholls, D. *Deity and Domination: Images of God and the State in the Nineteenth and Twentieth Centuries.* New York: Routledge, 1989.

Nee, V., and R. Swedberg, editors. *The Economic Sociology of Capitalism.* Princeton: Princeton University Press, 2005.

Nelson, R. H. *Reaching for Heaven on Earth: The Theological Meaning of Economics.* Savage, MD: Rowman & Littlefield, 1991.

Niebuhr, H. R. *Christ and Culture.* New York: Harper, 1951.

Noell, E. S. "Delight, Danger, and Duty: *The Good of Affluence* and Current Research on Wealth in the Gospels." *Faith & Economics* 40 (2002) 14–21.

———. "A Reformed Approach to Economics: Christian Reconstructionism." *Faith & Economics* 21 (1993) 6–20.

Noll, M. A. *American Evangelical Christianity: An Introduction.* Malden, MA: Blackwell, 2001.

———. *America's God: From Jonathan Edwards to Abraham Lincoln.* Oxford: Oxford University Press, 2002.

———. ed. *God and Mammon: Protestants, Money, and the Market, 1790–1860.* New York: Oxford University Press, 2002.

———. *The Rise of Evangelicalism: The Age of Edwards, Whitefield and the Wesleys.* Downers Grove, IL: InterVarsity, 2003.

———. *The Scandal of the Evangelical Mind.* Grand Rapids: Eerdmans, 1994.

Northcott, M. *An Angel Directs the Storm: Apocalyptic Religion and American Empire.* New York: Taurus, 2004.

Novak, M. *The Catholic Ethic and the Spirit of Capitalism.* New York: Free Press, 1993.

———. *Confessions of a Catholic.* San Francisco: Harper & Row, 1983.

———. *The Spirit of Democratic Capitalism.* New York: Simon & Schuster, 1982.

———. "A Theology of Economics." In *The Spirit of Democratic Capitalism,* 237–360. Lanham, MD: Madison, 1991.

———. *The Universal Hunger for Liberty: Why the Clash of Civilizations is Not Inevitable.* New York: Basic Books, 2004.

O'Donovan, O. *The Desire of the Nations: Rediscovering the Roots of Political Theology.* Cambridge: Cambridge University Press, 1996.

O'Neill, J. H. *The Golden Ghetto: The Psychology of Affluence.* Milwaukee: Affluenza Project, 1997.

Ochs, E. *Culture and Language Development.* New York: Cambridge University Press, 1988.

Olasky, M. *Compassionate Conservatism.* New York: Free Press, 2000.

———. *Renewing American Compassion.* New York: Free Press, 1996.

———. *The Tragedy of American Compassion.* Washington, DC: Regnery, 1992.

Oslington, P. "A Theological Economics." *International Journal of Social Economics* 27 (2000) 32–44.

———. Review of *Divine Economy: Theology and the Market* by D. Stephen Long in *Markets & Morality* 4 (2001) 1–5. Online: http://www.acton.org /publicat/m and_ m/2001_ spring/onsington.html.

Osmer, R. R. "The Christian Education of Children in Protestant Tradition." *Theology Today* 56 (2000) 506–23.

Osmer, R. R., and F. W. Schweitzer, editors. *Religious Education Between Modernization and Globalization: New Perspectives from the United States and Germany.* Grand Rapids: Eerdmans, 2003.

Packer, J. I., and T. C. Oden. *One Faith: The Evangelical Consensus.* Downers Grove, IL: InterVarsity, 2004.

Pais, J. *Suffer the Children: A Theology of Liberation by a Victim of Child Abuse.* New York: Paulist, 1991.

Pannenberg, W. *Anthropology in Theological Perspective.* Translated by M. J. O'Connell. Philadelphia: Westminster, 1985.

Parsons, T. "Social Science and Theology." In *America and the Future of Theology*, edited by W. A. Beardslee, 136–57. Philadelphia: Westminster, 1967.

Pazmiño, R. W. *Latin American Journey: Insights for Christian Education in North America.* Cleveland: United Church Press, 1994.

Perelman, M. *The Invention of Capitalism: Classical Political Economy and the Secret History of Primitive Accumulation.* Durham: Duke University Press, 2000.

Perkins, J., *Confessions of an Economic Hit Man: How the U.S. Uses Globalization to Cheat Poor Countries Out of Trillions.* San Francisco: Berrett-Koehler, 2004.

Penning, J. M., and S. E. Smidt. *Evangelicalism: The Next Generation.* Grand Rapids: Baker Academic, 2002.

Peters, T. "Designer Children: The Market World of Reproductive Choice." *Christian Century* 111 (1994) 1193–96.

———. "The Dignity of the Child." *Dialog* 37 (1998) 190–94.

———. *For the Love of Children: Genetic Technology and the Future of the Family.* Louisville: Westminster John Knox, 1997.

Phillips, Kevin. *American Theocracy: The Peril and Politics of Radical Religion, Oil and Borrowed Money in the 21st Century.* New York: Penguin, 2006.

Pilgrim, W. *Good News to the Poor: Wealth and Poverty in Luke-Acts.* Overtures to Biblical Theology. Minneapolis: Augsburg, 1981.

Polanyi, K. *The Great Transformation: The Political and Economic Origins of Our Time.* 1944. Reprinted, Boston: Beacon, 1957.

Polanyi, M. *Personal Knowledge: Towards a Post-Critical Philosophy.* New York: Harper & Row, 1964.

Post, S. G., editor. *The Fountain of Youth: Ethical, Religious, and Existential Perspectives on a Biomedical Goal.* New York: Oxford University Press, 2003.

Postman, N., *The Disappearance of Childhood.* 1982. Reprinted, New York: Vintage, 1994.

Pottebaum, G. A. *To Walk with a Child: Homiletics for Children.* Loveland, OH: Treehaus Communications, 1993.

Preston, R. H. *Religion and the Ambiguities of Capitalism: Have Christians Sufficient Understanding of Modern Economic Realities?* London: SCM, 1991.

Princen, T., M. Maniates and K. Conca, editors. *Confronting Consumption.* Cambridge, MA: MIT Press, 2002.

Prigogine, I., I. Stengers. *Order Out of Chaos: Man's New Dialogue with Nature.* New York: Bantam, 1984.

Purdy, J. "Universal Nation." In *The Imperial Tense: Prospects and Problems of American Empire*, edited by A. J. Bacevich, 102–10. Chicago: Ivan R. Dee, 2003.

Quart, A. *Branded: The Buying and Selling of Teenagers.* New York: Basic Books, 2004.

Rahner, K. "Ideas for a Theology of Childhood." *Theological Investigations*, 8:33–50. Translated by D. Bourke. London: Darton, Longman & Todd, 1971.

Rainer, T. S. *The Bridger Generation.* Nashville: Broadman & Holman, 1997.

Rashcke, C. *The Bursting of New Wineskins: Religion and Culture at the End of Affluence.* Pittsburgh Theological Monograph Series 24. Pittsburgh: Pickwick, 1978.

————. *The Next Reformation: Why Evangelicals Must Embrace Postmodernity.* Grand Rapids: Baker Academic, 2004.

Ratcliff, D. *Children's Spirituality: Christian Perspectives, Research and Applications.* Eugene, OR: Cascade Books, 2004.

Rece, Jr., E. H. "Theology in the Thought of Horace Bushnell." PhD dissertation, Emory University, 1971.

Reed, L. "A Ten-Trillion-Dollar Stewardship." In B. Goudzwaard, *Globalization and the Kingdom of God,* edited by J. W. Skillen, 61–81. Grand Rapids: Baker, 2001.

Reeves, E. *This Man Hoover.* New York: Burt, 1928.

Reimer, S., *Evangelicals and the Continental Divide: The evangelical subculture in Canada and the United States.* Montreal: McGill-Queen's University Press, 2003.

Reimer, S., and J. Park. "Revisiting the Social Sources of American Christianity 1972–1998." *Journal for the Scientific Study of Religion* 41 (2002) 735–48.

Reimer, S., D. Hoover, M. Martinez, and K. Wald. "Evangelical Protestantism Meets the Continental Divide: Moral and Economic Conservatism in the United States and Canada." *Political Research Quarterly* 55 (2002) 351–74.

Richards, L. O. *Children's Ministry: Nurturing Faith Within the Family of God.* Grand Rapids: Zondervan, 1983.

————. *Creative Bible Teaching.* Chicago: Moody, 1970.

————. *A New Face for the Church.* Grand Rapids: Zondervan, 1970.

————. "Pre-Evaluative Research on a Church/Home Christian Education Program." PhD dissertation, Garrett-Evangelical Theological Seminary/Northwestern University, 1972.

————. *A Theology of Children's Ministry.* Grand Rapids: Zondervan, 1983.

————. *A Theology of Christian Education.* Grand Rapids: Zondervan, 1975.

————. "Why Sunday School Plus?" *Direction* 6.1 (1977) 21–24.

————. *Youth Ministry: Its Renewal in the Local Church.* Grand Rapids: Zondervan, 1972.

Roberts, P. *Education, Literacy and Humanization: Exploring the Work of Paulo Freire.* Westport, CT: Bergin & Garvey, 2000.

Richard, P., et al. *The Idols of Death and the God of Life: A Theology.* Translated by B. E. Campbell and B. Shepard. Maryknoll, NY: Orbis, 1983.

Roberts, R. H. "The Closed Circle: Marxism, Christianity and the 'End of History.'" In *Religion, Theology and the Human Sciences,* 15–35. Cambridge: Cambridge University Press, 2002.

Roberts, R. H. "Postmodern Quasi-fundamentalism. John Milbank." In *Religion, Theology and the Human Sciences,* 203–5. New York: Cambridge University Press, 2002.

Robertson, R. "Glocalization: Time-Space and Homogeneity-Heterogeneity." In *Global Modernities,* edited by M. Featherstone et al., 25–44. London: Sage, 1995.

————. "The Sociological Significance of Culture: Some General Considerations." *Theory, Culture and Society* 5 (1988) 3–23.

Robinson, E. *The Original Vision: A Study of the Religious Experience of Childhood.* London: Seabury, 1977, 1983.

Rodger, L. "The Infancy Stories of Matthew and Luke: An Examination of the Child as a Theological Metaphor." *Horizons in Biblical Theology* 19 (1997) 58–81.

Rogoff, B., *The Cultural Nature of Human Development.* New York: Oxford, 2003.

Ronsvalle, J. L. and S. Ronsvalle. *The State of Church Giving through 2001.* Champaign, IL: Empty Tomb, 2003.

Ruether, R. R., *Liberation Theology: Human Hope Confronts Christian History and American Power*. New York: Paulist, 1972.

———. "The Making of the Victorian Family: 1780–1890." In *Christianity and the Making of the Modern Family*, 83–106. Boston: Beacon, 2000.

———. *Radical Kingdom: The Western Experience of Messianic Hope*. New York: Harper & Row, 1970.

———. *Sexism and God-Talk: Toward a Feminist Theology, with a New Introduction*. Boston: Beacon, 1993.

———. *Women and Redemption: A Theological History*. Minneapolis: Fortress, 1998.

Russell, R. J., N. Murphy, T. C. Meyering, and M. A. Arbib, editors. *Neuroscience and the Person: Scientific Perspectives on Divine Action*. Berkeley: Center for Theology and the Natural Sciences, 1999.

Ryan, M. A., and T. D. Whitmore, editors. *The Challenge of Global Stewardship: Roman Catholic Responses*. Notre Dame: University of Notre Dame, 1997.

Sachs, J. D. *The End of Poverty: Economic Possibilities for Our Time*. New York: Penguin, 2005.

Salamone, F. A., and W. R. Adams, editors. *Anthropology and Theology: God, Icons, and God-Talk*. Landham, MD: University Press of America, 1999.

Sánchez-Eppler, K. "Raising Empires Like Children: Race, Nation, and Religious Education." *American Literary History* 8 (1996) 399–425.

Sardar, Z. *Postmodernism and the Other: The New Imperialism of Western Culture*. London: Pluto, 1998.

Sartre, J. P. *Being and Nothingness*. Translated by H. E. Barnes. New York: Philosophical Library, 1956.

Schieffelin, B. *The Give and Take of Everyday Life*. New York: Cambridge University Press, 1990.

Schipani, D. S. *Conscientization and Creativity: Paulo Freire and Christian Education*. Lanham, MD: University Press of America, 1984.

———, editor. *Freedom and Discipleship: Liberation Theology in an Anabaptist Perspective*. Maryknoll, NY: Orbis, 1989.

———. *Religious Education Encounters Liberation Theology*. Birmingham, AL: Religious Education Press, 1988.

Schneider, J. R. *Godly Materialism: Rethinking Money and Possessions*. Downers Grove, IL: Intervarsity, 1994.

———. *The Good of Affluence: Seeking God in a Culture of Wealth*. Grand Rapids: Eerdmans, 2002.

———. "In Defense of Delight." *Faith & Economics* 40 (2002) 21–25.

———. *Philip Melanchthon's Rhetorical Construal of Biblical Authority: Oratio Sacra*. Texts and Studies in Religion 51. Lewiston, NY: Mellon, 1990.

Schor, J. "Inside the Child Brain." In *Born to Buy: The Commercialized Child and the New Consumer Culture*, 109–12. New York: Scribner, 2004.

———. *The Overspent American: Upscaling, Downshifting, and the New Consumer*. New York: Basic Books, 1998.

Schumpeter, *Capitalism, Socialism and Democracy* = Schumpeter, J., *Capitalism, Socialism and Democracy*. 3rd ed. New York: Harper & Row, 1950.

Schwartzman, H. B. "Children and Anthropology: A Century of Studies." In *Children and Anthropology*, edited by H. B. Schwartzman, 15–37. Westport, CT: Bergin & Garvey, 2001.

———. *Children and Anthropology*. Westport, CT: Bergin & Garvey, 2001.

Schweiker, W., and C. Mathewes, editors. *Having: Property and Possession in Religious and Social Life*. Grand Rapids: Eerdmans, 2004.

Scitovsky, T. *Human Desire and Economic Satisfaction: Essays on the Frontiers of Economics*. New York: New York University Press, 1989.

———. *The Joyless Economy: The Psychology of Human Satisfaction*. New York: Oxford University Press, 1992.

Scott, B. B. "The Rules of the Game: A Response to Daniel Patte." *Semeia* 29 (1983) 117–24.

Scudder, H. E. *Childhood in Literature and Art: With Some Observations on Literature for Children*. Boston: Houghton, Mifflin 1894.

Segdwick, P. H. *The Market Economy and Social Ethics*. New York: Cambridge University Press, 1999.

Seidel, D.F. "Schleiermacher on Marriage and Family." PhD dissertation, Toronto School of Theology, 1987.

Seiter, E. *Sold Separately: Children and Parents in Consumer Culture*. New Brunswick, NJ: Rutgers University Press, 1993.

Segundo, J. L. *Signs of the Times: Theological Reflections*. Edited by A. T. Hennelly. Translated by R. R. Barr. Maryknoll, NY: Orbis, 1993.

———. *The Liberation of Theology*. Translated by J. Drury. 1976. Reprinted, Eugene, OR: Wipf & Stock, 2002.

———. *Theology and the Church: A Response to Cardinal Ratzinger and a Warning to the Whole Church*. Translated by J. W. Diercksmeier. Minneapolis: Winston, 1985.

Selvanayagam, I. "Children Laugh and Cry: Authentic Resources for Christian Theology." *Asia Journal of Theology* 9 (1995) 352–66.

Sen, A. "Poor, Relatively Speaking." *Oxford Economic Papers* 35 (1983) 153–69.

———. *Commodities and Capabilities*. Amsterdam: Elsevier, 1985.

———. *Development as Freedom*. New York: Anchor, 1999.

———. *Resources, Values and Development*. Cambridge: Harvard University Press, 1984.

———. *The Standard of Living: The Tanner Lectures*. Cambridge: Cambridge University Press, 1987.

Shank, H., and W. Reed. "A Challenge to Suburban Evangelical Churches: Theological Perspectives on Poverty in America." *Journal of Interdisciplinary Studies* 7 (1995) 119–34.

Shelley, B. L. *The Gospel and the American Dream*. Sisters, OR: Multnomah, 1989.

Sherman, A. L. *Preferential Option: A Christian and Neoliberal Strategy for Latin America's Poor*. Grand Rapids: Eerdmans, 1992.

———. *The Soul of Development: Biblical Christianity and Economic Transformation in Guatemala*. New York: Oxford University Press, 1997.

Shults, F. L. *The Postfoundationalist Task of Theology: Wolfhart Pannenberg and the New Theological Relationality*. Grand Rapids: Eerdmans, 1999.

———. *Reforming Theological Anthropology: After the Philosophical Turn to Relationality*. Grand Rapids: Eerdmans, 2003.

Sider, R. J. "Evangelism, Salvation and Social Justice." *Evangelical Review of Theology* 2.1 (1978) 70–88.

———. *Good News and Good Works: A Theology for the Whole Gospel*. Grand Rapids: Baker, 1993.

———. *Just Generosity: A New Vision for Overcoming Poverty in America.* Grand Rapids: Baker, 1999.

———. *Rich Christians in an Age of Hunger: Moving from Affluence to Generosity.* 20th anniversary ed. Dallas: Word, 1997.

———. *The Scandal of the Evangelical Conscience: Why Are Christians Living Just Like the Rest of the World?* Grand Rapids: Baker, 2005.

Sisemore, T. A. *A Theology of Children.* Unpublished, 1998, cited by Don Ratcliff at "Books on Children's Religion and Spirituality Research." No pages. Online: http:// childspirituality.org/ database/books.htm.

———. *Of Such Is the Kingdom: Nurturing Children in the Light of Scripture.* Fearn, UK: Christian Focus, 2000.

Slater, D. *Consumer Culture and Modernity.* Cambridge: Polity, 1997.

Slater, D., and F. Tonkiss. *Market Societies and Modern Social Thought.* Cambridge: Polity, 2000.

Slater, G. *Children in the New England Mind.* Hamden, CT: Archon, 1977.

Slater, P. *Wealth Addiction: America's Most Powerful Drug—How It Weakens Us, How We Can Free Ourselves.* New York: Dutton, 1980.

Smith, C. *American Evangelicalism: Embattled and Thriving.* Chicago: The University of Chicago Press, 1998.

———. *Christian America? What Evangelicals Really Want.* Berkeley: University of California Press, 2000.

Smith, D. L. *Symbolism and Growth: The Religious Thought of Horace Bushnell.* American Academy of Religion Dissertation Series 36. Missoula, MT: Scholars, 1981.

Smith, D. W. *Transforming the World? The Social Impact of British Evangelicalism.* Carlisle, UK: Paternoster, 1998.

Smith, H. S., *Changing Conceptions of Original Sin: A Study in American Theology Since 1750.* New York: Scribner, 1955.

———. *Faith and Nurture.* New York: Scribners, 1941.

———. *Horace Bushnell.* New York: Oxford University Press, 1965.

Smith, L. D. "An Awakening Conscience: The Changing Response of American Evangelicals Toward World Poverty." PhD dissertation, The American University, 1986.

Smith, J. K. A. *Introducing Radical Orthodoxy: Mapping a Post-Secular Theology.* Grand Rapids: Baker Academic, 2004.

———, and J. H. Olthius, editors. *Radical Orthodoxy and the Reformed Tradition: Creation, Covenant, and Participation.* Grand Rapids: Baker Academic, 2005.

Smith, T. L. *Revivalism and Social Reform: American Protestantism on the Eve of the Civil War.* Baltimore: Johns Hopkins University Press, 1980.

Speidel, T. H., editor. *On Being Human . . . and Christian: Essays in Celebration of Ray S. Anderson.* Eugene, OR: Wipf & Stock, 2002.

Spohrer, J. A. "The Perceived Relationship and Roles of Parents and Evangelical Churches in the Spiritual Nurture of Children." Ed. dissertation, The Southern Baptist Theological Seminary, 2002.

Sobrino, J. "Central Position of the Reign of God in Liberation Theology." In *Systematic Theology: Perspectives from Liberation Theology,* edited by J. Sobrino and I. Ellacuria, 38–74. Maryknoll, NY: Orbis, 1996.

———, and I. Ellacuría, editors. *Systematic Theology: Perspectives from Liberation Theology.* Maryknoll, NY: Orbis, 1996.

Song, R. "Political Life." In *Veritatis Splendor—A Response*, edited by C. Yeats, 57–68. Norwich, UK: Canterbury, 1994.

Spade, P. V. "William of Ockham." *The Stanford Encyclopedia of Philosophy*. Fall 2002 edition. Edited by E. N. Zalta. No pages. Online: http://plato.stanford. edu /archives/ fall2002/entries/ockham.

Spurgeon, C. H. *Come Ye Children: A Book for Parents and Teachers on the Christian Training of Children*. London: Passmore & Alabaster, 1897.

Stackhouse, J. G., Jr. *Evangelical Ecclesiology: Reality or Illusion?* Grand Rapids: Baker Academic, 2003.

Stearns, P. N. *Consumerism in World History: The Global Transformation of Desire*. New York: Routledge, 2001.

Stevens, M. L. *Kingdom of Children: Culture and Controversy in the Homeschooling Movement*. Princeton: Princeton University Press, 2001.

Stonehouse, C. *Joining Children on the Spiritual Journey: Nurturing a Life of Faith*. Grand Rapids: Baker, 1998.

Storkey, A. *Foundational Epistemologies in Consumption Theory*. Amsterdam: Free University Press, 1993.

———. *Jesus and Politics: Confronting the Powers*. Grand Rapids: Baker Academic, 2005.

Storkey, A. "Postmodernism is Consumption." In *Christ and Consumerism: Critical Reflections on the Spirit of Our Age*, edited by C. Bartholomew and T. Moritz, 100–117. Carlisle, UK: Paternoster, 2000.

Stout, H. S. "'Baptism in Blood": The Civil War and the Creation of an American Civil Religion." *Books and Culture* 9 (July/August, 2003) 16–17, 33–35.

Strommen, M. P., and R. Hardel. *Passing on the Faith: A Radical New Model for Youth and Family Ministry*. Winona, MN: St. Mary's, 2000.

Sturm, D. "On the Suffering and Rights of Children: Toward a Theology of Childhood Liberation." *Cross Currents* 42.1 (1992) 149–73.

Sullivan, E. V. "The Scandalized Child: Children, Media, and Commodity Culture." In *Toward Moral and Religious Maturity*, edited by C. Brusselmans et al., 550–73. Morristown, NJ: Silver Burdett Company, 1983.

Summey, W. J., Jr. "Do Not Hinder Them: A Practical Theological Evaluation of a Popular Evangelical Approach to Child Rearing. Gary Ezzo, Anne Marie Ezzo." PhD dissertation Vanderbilt University, 2004.

Tanner, K. *Economy of Grace*. Minneapolis: Fortress, 2005.

———. *Theories of Culture: A New Agenda for Theology*. Guides to Theological Inquiry. Minneapolis: Fortress, 1997.

Tawney, R. H. *Religion and the Rise of Capitalism*. 1926. Reprinted, Harmondsworth, UK: Pengiun, 1938.

Taylor, C. *Sources of the Self: The Making of the Modern Identity*. Cambridge: Cambridge University Press, 1989.

Taylor, M. *Poverty and Christianity: Reflections at the Interface between Faith and Experience*. London: SCM, 2000.

Taylor, M. C. *About Religion: Economies of Faith in Virtual Culture*. Chicago: University of Chicago Press, 1999.

Taylor, M. J., editor. *Changing Patterns of Religious Education*. Birmingham, AL: Religious Education Press, 1984.

Taylor, M. K. "What Has Anthropology to Do with Theology?" *Theology Today* 41 (1985) 379.

———. *Beyond Explanation: Religious Dimensions in Cultural Anthropology.* Macon, GA: Mercer University Press, 1986.

Taylor, V. *The Gospel according to St. Mark.* 2nd ed. London: Macmillan, 1966.

Thatcher, A. "A Theology of Liberation for Children." In *Marriage after Modernity: Christian Marriage in Postmodern Times,* 132–70. New York: New York University Press, 1999.

Thomas, G. M. *Revivalism and Cultural Change: Christianity, Nation Building, and the Market in the Nineteenth-Century United States.* Chicago: University of Chicago Press, 1989.

Thompson, J. B. *The Ecclesiology of Stanley Hauerwas: A Christian Theology of Liberation.* Burlington, VT: Ashgate, 2003.

Todd, Emmanuel. *After the Empire: The Breakdown of the American Order.* Translated by C. Jon Delogu. New York: Columbia University Press, 2003.

Tönnies, F. *Community and Association.* Translated by C. Loomis. London: Routledge & Kegan Paul, 1955.

———. *Community and Society.* Translated and edited by C. Loomis. East Lansing: Michigan State University, 1957.

Torrance, T. F. *The Ground and Grammar of Theology.* Charlottesville: University Press of Virginia, 1980.

———. *Theological Science.* Oxford: Oxford University Press, 1978.

Trachtenberg, A. *The Incorporation of America: Culture and Society in the Gilded Age.* New York: Hill & Wang, 1982.

Tracy, G. E. *Transforming the Poverty of Affluence, Preparing the Affluent Poor for Leadership in the Renewal of the World.* Petersham, MA: St. Bede's, 1999.

Trigilia, C. *Economic Sociology: State, Market, and Society in Modern Capitalism.* Malden, MA: Blackwell, 2000.

Turpin, K. M. "Consumer Capitalism and Adolescent Vocational Imagination: An Exploration of the Pedagogical Dynamics of Ongoing Conversion." PhD dissertation, Emory University, 2004.

Twitchell, J. *Adcult USA: The Triumph of Advertising in American Culture.* New York: Columbia University Press, 1996.

———. *Lead Us into Temptation: The Triumph of American Materialism.* New York: Columbia University Press, 1999.

UNICEF. "The State of the World's Children 2005: 'Childhood Under Threat.'" No pages. Online: http://www.unicef.org/ sowc05/ english/fullreport.html.

Valantasis, R., and V. L. Wimbush. *Asceticism.* Oxford: Oxford University Press, 1995.

Veblen, T., *The Theory of the Leisure Class: An Economic Study of Institutions.* 1899. Reprinted, Somerset, NJ: Transaction Publishers, 1991.

Via, D. O., Jr. *The Ethics of Mark's Gospel: In the Middle of Time.* 1985. Reprinted, Eugene, OR: Wipf & Stock, 2005.

Viereck, P., *Metapolitics: The Roots of the Nazi Mind.* Rev. ed. New York: Capricorn, 1965.

Volf, M. *After Our Likeness: The Church as the Image of the Trinity.* Grand Rapids: Eerdmans, 1998.

———. "Against a Pretentious Church: A Rejoinder to Bell's Response." *Modern Theology* 19 (2003) 281–85.

———. "Liberation Theology after the End of History: An Exchange." *Modern Theology* 19 (2003) 263.

Balthasar, H. U. *Unless You Become Like This Child.* Translated by E. Leiva-Merikakis. Ft. Collins, CO: Ignatius, 1991.

Wachtel, P. *The Poverty of Affluence: A Psychological Portrait of the American Way of Life.* Philadelphia: New Society, 1989.

Walker, J. D. "The Psycho-Epistemology of Religious Maturity: Heuristic Faith as a Matrix for Growth." East Texas Baptist University. April 1, 2003. No pages. Online: http://www. etbu.edu/nr/etbu/temp_files/word _JoshWalker.pdf.

Wall, J. "Let the Children Come: Child Rearing as Challenge to Contemporary Christian Ethics." *Horizons* 31.1 (2004) 64–87.

Wallerstein, Immanuel. *The Decline of American Power: The U.S. in a Chaotic World.* New York: New Press, 2003.

Walton, B. *Jonathan Edwards, Religious Affections and the Puritan Analysis of True Piety, Spiritual Sensation and Heart Religion.* Studies in American Religion 74. Lewiston, NY: Mellon, 2002.

Ward, G. "Cities of Endless Desire." In *Cities of God,* 52–77.

———. *Cities of God.* Radical Orthodoxy. New York: Routledge, 2000.

———. "Communities of Desire." In *Cities of God,* 117–51.

———. "A Theology of Desire." In *Cities of God,* 187–89.

———. "In the Economy of the Divine: A Response to James K. A. Smith." *Pneuma: Journal of the Society for Pentecostal Studies* 25 (2003) 118–19.

Ward, P. *God at the Mall: Youth Ministry That Meets Kids Where They're At.* Peabody, MA: Hendrickson, 2001.

———. *Growing Up Evangelical: Youthwork and the Making of a Subculture.* London: SPCK, 1996.

Watts, S. *The Republic Reborn: War and the Making of Liberal America, 1790–1820.* Baltimore: Johns Hopkins University Press, 1987.

Wauzzinski, R. A. *Between God and Gold: Evangelicalism and the Industrial Revolution, 1820–1914.* Cranbury, NJ: Associated University Presses, 1993.

Wayland, F. *The Elements of Political Economy.* Boston: Gould & Lincoln, 1872.

Weber, H. R. "A Child in the Midst of Them." In *Jesus and the Children,* 34–51.

———. *Jesus and the Children: Biblical Resources for Study and Preaching.* Geneva: World Council of Churches, 1979.

Weber, M. *The Protestant Ethic and the Spirit of Capitalism.* Translated by T. Parsons. 1930. Reprinted, New York: Routledge, 2004.

Webster, J. "On Evangelical Ecclesiology." *Ecclesiology* 1.1 (2004) 9–35.

Weigle, L. A. "Introduction." In H. Bushnell, *Christian Nurture,* xxxi–xl. 5th reprint. New Haven: Yale University Press, 1967.

Wells, D. F. *Above All Earthly Pow'rs: Christ in a Postmodern World.* Grand Rapids: Eerdmans, 2005.

———. *God in the Wasteland: The Reality of Truth in a World of Fading Dreams.* Grand Rapids: Eerdmans, 1994.

———. *Losing Our Virtue: Why the Church Must Recover Its Moral Vision.* Grand Rapids: Eerdmans, 1998.

———. *No Place for Truth: Or Whatever Happened to Evangelical Theology?* Grand Rapids: Eerdmans, 1993.

———. *The Courage to Be Protestant: Truth-lovers, Marketers, and Emergents in the Postmodern World.* Grand Rapids: Eerdmans, 2008.

Werpehowski, W. "Reading Karl Barth on Children." In *The Child in Christian Thought*, edited by M. J. Bunge, 386–405. Grand Rapids: Eerdmans, 2000.

Wheatley, M. J. *Leadership and the New Science*. San Francisco: Berrett-Koehler, 1994.

Wheeler, S. E. *Wealth as Peril and Obligation: The New Testament on Possessions*. Grand Rapids: Eerdmans, 1995.

Whitehead, A. N. *Essays in Science and Philosophy*. New York: Philosophical Library, 1947.

———. *Modes of Thought*. New York: Macmillan, 1938.

———. *Process and Reality*. New York: Macmillan, 1929.

———. *Science and the Modern World*. New York: Free Press, 1925.

Whitmore, T. D., with T. Winright. "Children: An Undeveloped Theme in Catholic Teaching." In *The Challenge of Global Stewardship: Roman Catholic Responses*, edited by M. A. Ryan and T. D. Whitmore, 161–85. Notre Dame: University of Notre Dame, 1997.

Wilhoit, J. C., and John M. Dettoni, editors. *Nurture That Is Christian: Developmental Perspectives of Christian Education*. Wheaton, IL: Victor, 1995.

Wilk, R. R. *Economies and Cultures: Foundations for Economic Anthropology*. Boulder, CO: Westview, 1996.

Williams, R. *Marxism and Literature*. New York: Oxford University Press, 1988.

Williams, T. "John Duns Scotus." In *The Stanford Encyclopedia of Philosophy*. Fall 2004 Edition. E. N. Zalta, ed. No pages. Online: http://plato.stanford. edu/archives/ fall2004/entries/duns-scotus.

Willmer, H. "Towards a Theology of the State." In *Essays in Evangelical Social Ethics*, edited by D. F. Wright, 85–104. Exeter: Paternoster, 1978.

Winter, G. *The Suburban Captivity of the Churches*. New York: Doubleday, 1961.

Wishy, B. *The Child and the Republic: The Dawn of Modern American Child Nurture*. Philadelphia: University of Pennsylvania Press, 1968.

Wolterstorff, N. *Until Justice and Peace Embrace*. Grand Rapids: Eerdmans, 1993.

Wood, Diana, editor. *The Church and Childhood*. Oxford: Blackwell, 1994.

Wood, Ellen Meiksins. *Empire of Capital*. New York: Verso, 2005.

Woodhead, L. "Faith, Feminism and the Family." In *The Family*, edited by Lisa Sowle Cahill and Dietmar Mieth, 43–52. Maryknoll, NY: Orbis, 1995.

Woodmansee, M., and M. Osteen, editors. *The New Economic Criticism: Studies at the Intersection of Literature and Economics*. New York: Routledge, 1999.

Work, T. "Veggie Ethics: What 'America's Favorite Vegetables' Say about Evangelicalism." *Theology Today* 57 (2001) 473–83.

Wortley, G. F. "The Status of the Child in New England Congregationalism from Jonathan Edwards to Horace Bushnell." PhD dissertation, Hartford Seminary, 1927.

Wright, D. F. *Essays in Evangelical Social Ethics*. Exeter: Paternoster, 1978.

Wright, D. R. "James Edwin Loder, Jr." In *The Christian Educators of the 20th Century Project*. No pages. http://www.talbot.edu/ceacademic/loder.cfm.

Wright, D. R., and J. D. Kuentzel, editors. *Redemptive Transformation in Practical Theology*. Grand Rapids: Eerdmans, 2004.

Wright, N. T. *The New Testament and the People of God*. Christian Origins and the Question of God 1. Minneapolis: Fortress, 1992.

Wuthnow, R., editor. *After Heaven: Spirituality in America since the 1950s*. Berkeley: University of California Press, 1998.

———. *God and Mammon in America*. New York: Free Press, 1994.

———. *Growing Up Religious: Christians and Jews and Their Journeys of Faith.* Boston: Beacon, 1999.

———. *Loose Connections: Joining Together in America's Fragmented Communities.* Cambridge: Harvard University Press, 1998.

———. "The Political Rebirth of American Evangelicals." In *The New Christian Right: Mobilization and Legitimation*, edited by R. Liebman and R. Wuthnow, 168–85. New York: Aldine, 1983.

———. *The Restructuring of American Religion: Society and Faith since World War II.* Princeton: Princeton University Press, 1988.

———, editor. *Rethinking Materialism: Perspectives on the Spiritual Dimension of Economic Behavior.* Grand Rapids: Eerdmans, 1995.

———. *Sharing the Journey: Support Groups and America's New Quest for Community.* New York: Free Press, 1994.

Wyckoff, D. C. *The Gospel and Christian Education: A Theory of Christian Education for Our Times.* Philadelphia: Westminster, 1959.

Yarbrough, S. R., and J. C. Adams. *Delightful Conviction: Jonathan Edwards and the Rhetoric of Conversion.* Westport, CT: Greenwood, 1993.

Yeats, C., editor. *Veritatis Splendor—A Response.* Norwich: Canterbury, 1994.

Yoder, J. H. *The Politics of Jesus: Vicit Agnus Noster.* 2nd ed. Christian Family Library 35. 1972. Reprinted, Grand Rapids: Family Christian Press, 2001.

———. *The Royal Priesthood: Essays Ecclesiological and Ecumenical.* Edited with an Introduction by M. Cartwright. Grand Rapids: Eerdmans, 1994.

Yuengert, A. M. "Free Markets and Character." *Faith and Economics* 27 (1996) 4–12.

Yust, K. M. *Real Kids, Real Faith: Practices for Nurturing Children's Spiritual Lives.* San Francisco: Jossey-Bass, 2004.

Zagano, P. "Communicating Belief: A Historical Look at Christian Catechesis—and Catechisms." *Christian Education Journal* 12.2 (1992) 48–56.

Zelizer, V. A. *Pricing the Priceless Child: The Changing Value of Children.* New York: Basic Books, 1985.

Zinbarg, E. D. *Faith, Morals, and Money: What the World's Religions Tell Us about Ethics in the Marketplace.* New York: Continuum, 2001.

Zizioulas, J. D. *Being as Communion: Studies in Personhood and the Church.* New York: St Vladimir's Seminary Press, 1985.

———. "Human Capacity and Human Incapacity: A Theological Exploration of Personhood." *Scottish Journal of Theology* 28 (1975) 401–48.

Zukin, L. A. *Landscapes of Power: From Detroit to Disney World.* Berkeley: University of California Press, 1991.

Zuck, Roy B. *Precious in His Sight: Childhood and Children in the Bible.* Grand Rapids: Baker, 1996.

Index of Subjects

abundance: ix–xii, 4, 11, 25, 65, 65n98, 79, 79n153, 81, 98, 102, 132–33, 167, 202, 211, 216, 219, 229–31, 253n393, 258, 283

acquisition and enjoyment: x, 9, 123, 154, 170, 173, 171, 176, 196, 198, 211, 231, 242, 268

affluence: x–xi, 25, 34, 85, 133–56, 174, 223, 260, 262, 276, 286; cosmic good of, 163n24, 165, 174, 181–83, 226–27, 241–44, 248–49, 274; idolatry of, 65; late modern, 11, 24, 69, 115, 156, 173, 177, 222, 226; late modern evangelical, 30, 258, 260; mass, 2, 11, 12, 79, 90, 95, 132, 155, 160, 189, 220, 228, 231, 261, 282–83; matrices of evangelical, 5, 11, 156, 272; problem of, 1, 4, 11, 25, 29, 98, 105, 107, 113, 135, 154, 161, 169, 171, 199, 204, 210, 214, 274–76, 281–82, 287. *See also* affluent Christians

Affluent American Evangelical Child (AAEC): x, 24, 38, 75, 107, 122; and *Divine Economy*, 222–59; and the rich young man, 175–213; as a complex metaphorical system, 160; evangelical ecclesiology of, 11, 64, 276–82; evangelical psychology and pedagogy of, 282–87; evangelical sociology of, 127–56; evangelical theology of, 157–259; Herbert Hoover and the evolution of

the, 87–102; in contemporary theological perspective, 214–58; in the "infinite undulations of the snake", 248–58, 275; Lawrence Richards and the, 85–87, 103–121; problem of the, x, 2–6, 11, 29–30, 114, 170, 204, 210; theological[1] economics of the, 19

affluent Christians: 161, 170–73, 17–78, 190

American Dream: 38, 121, 268n14, 283

American Evangelicalism: 16 (defined). *See also* Evangelicalism

American Evangelicals, x–xi, 15–16, 25, 34, 85, 133–56, 137, 142, 169, 174, 187, 219, 223, 236, 245, 260, 262, 266, 268–70, 276, 286

analogia libertatis: 164, 223, 231–32, 243–44, 263, 266

anthropology: of liberty, 11, 18–19, 30, 70, 82, 88, 113–15, 120, 159, 164, 169, 182, 193, 206, 232, 240–48, 263–66, 274; of modern economic man, 158; conversionist theological anthropology of the child, 38–58; neoliberal anthropology of freedom, 192, 214; neoliberal anthropology of liberty, 169, 193, 241, 248; revivalist, 83; theological anthropology of the child, 58–82, 157; theological anthropology of the child, 58–82, 157

Index of Names

Index of Scripture References